# RESEARCH IN INTERNATIONAL BUSINESS AND FINANCE

*Volume 1* • 1979

THE ECONOMIC EFFECTS
OF MULTINATIONAL
CORPORATIONS

# RESEARCH IN INTERNATIONAL BUSINESS AND FINANCE

*An Annual Compilation of Research*

## THE ECONOMIC EFFECTS OF MULTINATIONAL CORPORATIONS

*Editor:* **ROBERT G. HAWKINS**
*Graduate School of Business Administration*
*New York University*

---

**VOLUME 1 • 1979**

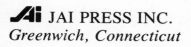 **JAI PRESS INC.**
*Greenwich, Connecticut*

# CONTENTS

v

# PREFACE

Controversies surrounding multinational corporations (MNCs)—their motives, their operations, their economic effects, their political and social results—have been many, varied, and intense. But most of the controversies stem from different perceptions, different estimates, or different assumptions about the economic impacts of MNC operations. Perceived negative economic impacts turn rapidly into political or social issues.

In the 1970s, there has been a virtual explosion of interest in MNCs, and this has resulted in a vast amount of research, writing, and publications pertaining to multinational corporations. It has become so vast that interested scholars cannot fully follow all of the literature even in one narrow aspect of foreign direct investment and MNCs. Since 1971, the New York University Graduate School of Business Administration has conducted a research project on "The Multinational Firm in the U.S. and World Economy," which has focused its activities mainly on economic impacts of MNCs. This project has made a modest contribution to that explosion of research and writing on the economic aspects of the topic.

By 1976, it was decided that the more accessible literature on MNCs needed a guide, and that it needed to be critically assessed as to relevance, methodology, and findings. Given the economic-impact focus of the NYU research project, and the fact that most of the controversies can be ultimately reduced to a debate over economic effects, a conference was organized around important areas of economic controversy with respect to MNCs. That conference was held in December 1976 and this volume is its final result. The intent of the conference was to have major survey papers, with appropriate new or additional research or interpretation by the authors, serve as the focus of the conference. Eight areas of significant controversy over economic impacts were identified. These eight papers were commissioned to authors who were not already widely published or whose views on a particular issue were not pre-set, so that a 'fresh look' at the literature could be accomplished. Each review paper was then subjected to critical appraisal by a major academic contributor to the MNC literature and to a "practitioner"—MNC executive, labor leader, or government official—at the conference. Both the papers and the comments of the discussants are included here.

The timeliness of the topic, the conference, and the inauguration of the JAI Press series on Research in International Business and Economics coincided to provide an appropriate vehicle for the publication of this guide through the critical appraisal of the literature on the economic effects of MNCs.

The conference and this volume are a part of the NYU research program on MNCs. The conference was financially supported by the NYU Project, which gratefully acknowledges the past or current support of the Alcoa Foundation, American Express Foundation, CPC International, Continental Oil Company, the Exxon Foundation, the Ford Foundation, the General Electric Foundation, the General Motors Corporation, the U.S. Department of Labor, Pfizer Incorporated, the Rockefeller Foundation, the Scaife Family Trust, and the United Nations Conference on Trade and Development.

Appreciation for their assistance in planning and administering the conference goes to Ms. Kathy Alamo. Elizabeth Webbink assisted with the editing of the papers, and she and V.S. Somanath are responsible for developing and checking the comprehensive bibliography. Marion Epps has been tolerantly helpful in all aspects of the project, and she and Donna Wolensky typed and retyped the manuscript. All of these people have my sincere thanks.

Robert G. Hawkins
New York City

# INTRODUCTION

Robert G. Hawkins

---

This volume is concerned with the *economic* impacts of multinational corporations (MNCs). More specifically, its focus is on particular issues about which there continues to be—and may always be—controversy and debate about how to analyze the impacts and interpret the results of those analyses.

The past decade has seen an extensive literature developed on foreign direct investment and MNCs. Much of that work, and perhaps the most successful, has involved the conceptualization of MNC behavior and the application of micro-economic analysis to it. Thus, much progress has been made in understanding the process and motivations of companies becoming multinational, as the references in the papers which follow to the works of Penrose, Aharoni, and others suggest. And there is by now a "conventional wisdom" on the sources of competitive strength of MNCs, stemming from the works of Harry G. Johnson, Richard Caves, Raymond Vernon, John Dunning, and many others. Also, considerable agreement has been reached in hypothesizing about and testing the factors which influence where MNCs locate their foreign activities and which processes are placed in which locations, advanced by the research of Horst, Parry, Stobaugh, and many others. Finally, there has developed a reasonably coherent literature on the characteristics of industries dominated by MNCs and of MNCs themselves, with major impetus coming from the Harvard Project on Multinational Enterprise, John Dunning, and others.

This vast amount of literature, and evolving body of 'received doctrine' provides the backdrop for this volume, as the repeated references to that literature will testify. But further contributions to this literature is not the intent of this volume. Although there remains room for more research on specific topics, and for rounding out and filling in gaps on motivations, location, sources of strength and growth of MNCs, the main areas of controversy are on the *economic impact* of MNCs. Whose welfare is affected and in which direction? And what is the time pattern of those effects?

The continuing controversies over the economic impacts of MNCs stem from several sources. One is that there is lack of agreement on the appropriate methodology for assessing the various economic impacts. In order to estimate an impact, one must know what would have occurred either without the MNC, or with a (marginally) different degree of MNC involvement. Yet this is almost impossible to establish by econometric techniques—at least to everyone's satisfaction—and must frequently be done inferentially on the basis of inadequate evidence, or by assumption. Second, the controversies are whetted by the fact that MNC activities involve conflicts of interest. Some groups gain, and some groups are likely to lose. This colors both the methodology (and issues) used in the analyses of MNC activities so that the outcome is preordained. Third, controversy continues in the interpretation of the data about MNCs and what it means. This extends to the interpretation of the results of some of the academic studies of MNC impacts.

Yet the study and correct interpretation of MNC impacts on economies and groups within economies is of paramount importance. The economic impacts of MNCs determine the relationship between the benefits of and costs of such MNC activities to home economies, to host economies, or to specific interest groups within each. And governments do, and will continue to, apply policies and regulate MNC activities in ways which are perceived to affect favorably the benefit-cost trade-off. Sensible policies require sound analysis of the impacts and their magnitudes. To date, too much policy has been made on inadequate (or misleading) evidence and/or inappropriate analysis.

The papers and their comments deal with eight types of economic effects of MNC activities. The broad topic headings were chosen with three criteria in mind: they are effects which are controversial and a source of continuing and frequently intensifying debate; they are economic in nature and have seen at least some amount of economic research and estimates about their magnitudes; and they are issues which have resulted in actual changes, proposed changes, or agitation for changes in government policies toward foreign direct investment.

The issues fall conveniently into three broad groups—issues relating to the economic impact of foreign direct investment on *home* or base countries of MNCs; issues relating to effects which transcend both home and host countries; and issues arising from impacts largely in *host* countries from MNC operations.

The first two chapters deal with the major issues in the home countries. Chapter I is concerned with the impact of MNC foreign operations on the demand for labor in the home country, i.e., the "jobs" issue. A related impact is the effect of MNC international operations on the relative bargaining strength of management and organized labor. This issue is examined in Chapter II. The issues of employment, jobs, and union bargaining strength were singled out for treatment here because they represent the principle major economic controversies and policy issues in the home countries. These also represent areas of substantial completed research and of intensely held policy positions.

The issues involving effects which are felt in both host and home countries are also matters of major and growing controversy. One is the cause, effects, and extent of MNCs avoidance of taxes and restrictive financial regulations through their capacity to set transfer prices and use alternative sources of funds transfers across national frontiers. These issues are the subject of Chapter IV. The other issue involves the role of MNCs in the creation and transfer of technology, which is presented in Chapter V.

The other four chapters are concerned with issues arising from MNC impacts in *host* countries. Although all of these are of importance to developing host countries, Chapters VI-VIII are concerned with issues which are almost exclusively in the province of LDCs. These issues are also all matters of policy debate in many host countries. They include the impact of MNC operations on the degree of competition (or monopoly) in host markets (Chapter III); the cost, types, and appropriateness of MNC technology transferred to LDCs (Chapter IV); the impact of MNC activities on indigenous investment and entrepreneurship in host countries (Chapter VII); and the impact of MNCs in the depletable resource industries in LDCs (Chapter VIII).

This list of issues does not pretend to be exhaustive, but hopefully does include the most controversial issues about which a fresh look, a synthesis of existing research, or some new analysis can lead to better understanding and better policy. The papers constituting the bulk of the chapters review and critically appraise the vast amount of writing on the various topics. In most instances, new insights and alternative interpretations of results are provided. And in several papers, new analyses were carried out which pushed ahead the frontier of understanding. The role of the commentators was to "appraise the appraisals," and in some cases to provide the reader with an alternative interpretation of the same literature. In combination, the result is a hopefully useful guide through the economic literature, policy positions, and empirical evidence for professionals who seek to fit together its many pieces.

It will be obvious to the reader, and should be expected, that the papers and discussion of this volume do not eliminate the controversies on any of the points. That was, of course, not the intent. But the papers do, in many instances, narrow the range of disagreement, sharpen the reasons—i.e., the conflicts of economic interest—for that disagreement, and appraise the potential usefulness of several past and proposed policy alternatives. All the same, there are few generalizations from this volume which can be neatly summarized.

One point can be made—but even on this there would be reservations by some contributors to this volume. This is that MNC activity represents a "positive sum game" in almost all instances, and not a zero sum game as sometimes implied. Most of the issues thus are about the distribution of the net benefits of MNC foreign activities which obviously affect the benefit-cost ratio for any single country—host or home—or any interested group within a country. Thus, in developing policies toward MNC activities, home and host countries should not—and normally do not—seek to extinguish all of or even most MNC operations. Rather, they seek to influence the benefit-cost ratio within the constraints implicitly set by the MNCs and other governments. It is hoped that this volume will narrow further the gaps in our understanding and set the stage for further fruitful research to widen our understanding and achieve peaceful coexistance with appropriately regulated MNCs.

# TABLES

# FIGURES

# 1. JOBS AND THE MULTINATIONAL CORPORATION: THE HOME-COUNTRY PERSPECTIVE*

Stephen P. Magee, UNIVERSITY OF TEXAS – AUSTIN

This paper is an outsider's critical review of the literature on home-country jobs, multinational corporations, and U.S. foreign direct investment. The activities of U.S. MNCs are imperfectly correlated with U.S. foreign direct investment; the multinationals are doing much more than moving physical capital internationally. The microeconomics of U.S. MNC activity are explored in the first section. The hypothesis is advanced that an important portion of the apparent windfalls earned by MNCs may be amortization of past R & D investments, and not pure rents. To the extent that this is true, taxation of MNC profits is not a costless transfer to U.S. labor (throughout, by "labor" we refer to un-

Research in International Business and Finance, Vol. 1, pp. 1–23.
ISBN 0-89232-031-1

skilled labor), but comes at the expense of the supply of future innovation and technology as well as future skilled-labor income.

In the second section it is suggested that the question of jobs and the MNCs can be most fruitfully viewed as a normative domestic political squabble over distributive shares of income in the U.S. and can be analyzed using the tools employed in the economics of pork-barrel politics. It suggests that some of the paradoxes in this literature are just logical conundrums hatched from the sloppy language employed in redistributive arguments. The third section is directed to the results of the studies in this area, their strengths and weaknesses, and the final section suggests a technique by which organized labor could raise its real income worldwide.


# MULTINATIONAL CORPORATION BEHAVIOR

Before exploring the relationship between labor and the multinational corporations, we must understand the forces driving the multinationals. One widely accepted theory is that the multinationals are principally engaged in international trade in technology. The work of Hymer (1960), Vernon (1966), Caves (1971a), and others, plus the empirical evidence, suggests that this is the case. The best summary of the technology view is outlined in Vernon's (1966) product cycle.

Vernon's cycle assumes that the life of each product can be broken into three distinct stages: the new product, the maturing product, and the standardized product stages. Vernon suggested that the locus of production would move from a DC (a developed country such as the U.S.) in the first stage through the other developed countries in the second stage and finally to LDCs (less developed countries) in the third stage. He cited three reasons production would occur first in the DC for new products. On the demand side, high unit labor costs generate demand for labor-saving investment goods such as machines to replace unskilled labor while high incomes in the DCs stimulate demand for sophisticated and differentiated new consumer products. On the supply side, the research intensity of new products is high and the relatively large endowments of skilled labor in the DCs (scientists, engineers, etc.) dictate that these countries have a comparative advantage in producing new products. Third, demand and supply factors interact: Rapid changes in new products dictate that there be swift and relatively costless communication between producers and consumers. All of these considerations suggest that the initial production of new products occur in a DC.

In the second stage, production moves from the originating DC to secondary DCs as markets and incomes grow in the latter, as secondary country import barriers rise, and as transport costs become a larger proportion of the final product price which falls throughout the cycle. In the third stage, production shifts to the LDCs as the products become standardized: Little interaction is needed between producers and consumers; small inputs of R & D are required; and the production technologies become routinized so that unskilled labor can be utilized more in the production process. The products are exported back to the DCs. Many products in this stage compete directly with unskilled-labor-intensive products in the United States and other DCs. This leads to the political activity of DC labor against the importing of these goods.

An extension of the industrial organization approach to the multinationals and international trade in technology has been attempted by the present author (Magee, 1977a,b). This work offers empirical evidence in support of a theory of the MNC based explicitly on the "appropriability problem" posed by private market creation of new information.[1] *Appropriability* is the ability of private originators of new information to obtain their social return. Information is a durable good in that present resources such as scientists and engineers must be devoted to its creation and its existence results in a stream of future benefits (patent-protected monopoly profits). It is also a public good in that, once it is created, its use by second parties does not preclude its continued use by the party that discovered it. However, the ownership claims remain a private good. In the case of privately created information, use by second parties reduces the private return on the technology accruing to the first party. This is the appropriability problem (see Arrow, 1962). As Johnson (1970) pointed out in his article on the MNC, private firms will undercreate new technology unless the private returns to these investments are protected by some social mechanism.

In the case of the MNC, the protection is provided either by patents or trade secrets, but neither provides complete protection. Simple technologies are usually harder to protect from interlopers and emulators than more complicated ones. For this reason, private firms and multinational corporations produce sophisticated technologies, since the appropriability per dollar invested in scientists and engineers is higher for sophisticated technologies than for simple ones.

Furthermore, the multinationals generate four distinct types of information. The first is for *product development:* applied research, preparation of product specifications, prototype production, pilot plant construction, and the tooling up of manufacturing facilities. Second, the multinational must "create" the *production function*. Economists usually assume that production functions are provided by beneficent engineers. However, production functions themselves are like any other economic good and require large investments in information to create them. Creation of production functions is one of the roles that multinationals play in the product life cycle. Third, MNCs gather information on *potential markets* for new products. This too is a costly and time-consuming process.

Finally, multinationals invest information resources to secure the *appropriability* of the technology itself. Expenditures on legal staffs and R & D are made to reduce the loss of information and technology created by the firm. The rational MNC seeks to maximize the present value of the private return on each investment in new technology, and the expected success of preventing emulators from stealing the returns during the life of a patent is an important consideration in this calculation.

Appropriability provides an explanation for the positive correlation between concentrated industry structures and high industry R & D. Highly competitive industry structures do not encourage the creation of new information, since the likelihood of loss of returns on new ideas is greater the greater are the potential emulators. Conversely, concentrated industry structures (a few large firms) may encourage R & D because the returns are more appropriable with fewer potential emulators. At the same time, a firm possessing a valuable new technology is more likely to expand to capture more fully the private return on the new technology (i.e., to expand so as to internalize an externality). There may thus be bidirectional causality between R & D intensity and industrial concentration. The patent system confers monopoly rights to the returns on new technologies for a specified time period. But monopoly rights do not guarantee large firms; other factors are required.

Five reasons may contribute to the positive correlation between firm size and the creation of new information for product innovation. First, there is a tendency for new products to be "experience goods" and for standardized products to be "search goods." (See Nelson [1970] for this distinction.) Experience goods are those for which it is impossible to determine from physical examination whether or not their services will actually live up to those advertised (*e.g.,* high technology goods and Vernon Stage I goods). A search good is one for which the qualities advertised can be tested before purchase by visual inspection (*e.g.,* the appearance of an article of clothing). Many standardized goods (Vernon Stage III) are search goods. There is a tendency for optimum firm size to be larger for retailers of experience goods than for retailers of search goods. The reason is that brand names confer market information about the quality of the types of goods being sold (for example, there is a clear distinction by consumers between the quality of products sold by Sears, Saks Fifth Avenue, and J. C. Penney's).

There is a similar tendency in international trade in information, since information and new products purchased from a multinational give the purchaser some assurance of the quality level of the items purchased. The argument, then, is that MNCs are conferred monopoly privileges to exploit technology worldwide; that new technology is an experience good for which the reputation (brand name) of the seller is an important determination in the decision to buy; that the MNC can develop his brand name (reputation for high-quality work) more efficiently intrafirm (through subsidiaries) than through the market (through licensing or sale); hence, international sellers of technology are large MNCs rather than small licensing or consulting firms.

Second, sales in many high-technology products are accompanied by sales of service information. The firm's optimum size is larger because service subsidiaries are required in the sale of information. IBM's servicing of its computers is a case in point. Third, the average number of products produced by multinationals is large because of complementarities in the use of new information across products. For example, mistakes made in the creation of one product can be avoided in the creation of others. Fourth, complementarities also exist among the four types of information: Information from the development stage helps in formulating the production function, which in turn helps in developing schemes to increase the private appropriability of the returns. Furthermore, most of these forms of information are transmitted more effectively intrafirm than extrafirm. Fifth, as products become older and new information becomes common knowledge, the spread narrows between buyer and seller evaluations of the products embodying the information. Since less search is required, the cost of market transactions is reduced relative to intrafirm transactions. Thus, smaller firms will be the rule in industries that are selling older products. Evidence that this is the case is presented in Magee (1976a).

All of the aforementioned bears upon the legitimacy of the criticism that MNCs are "too large." To the extent that they are large because past investments act as barriers to entry and explicit collusion to exercise market power occurs, this criticism is justified. However, to the extent that the large size reflects the normal exercise of monopoly power conferred by society through the patent system, or the appropriation of returns to R & D, the issue is more complicated. The benefits of more competition among more firms exercising less market power may be achieved only at the cost of less privately created information in the future. An important and unexplored empirical question is the elasticity of supply of future technology with respect to present firm size.

There is a failure to understand, both by the public generally and by organized labor, that there are virtues in MNCs being large. It is not well understood that firms may have to be large to help protect the returns on their information, nor is it seen that monopoly behavior is society's way of rewarding innovators for creating a public good (*i.e.*, new information).

Furthermore, the monopoly profits earned by technology creating firms are, to a significant extent, simply an amortization of past investments in scientists and engineers hired to create the new technology; and, in fact, the MNC will invest in scientists and engineers until the *ex ante* rate of return equals the return on the best risk-equivalent alternative investment.

Another interpretation is that organized labor *does* understand that the patent system creates relatively more jobs for scientists and engineers than for unskilled labor, and by limiting high R & D industries through policy actions, hope to increase their return through the Stolper-Samuelson effect. Regardless of the motivation, the point of the above discussion is that the "countervailing power" view that monopoly profits can be redistributed with no social cost by political market competition is incorrect to the extent that these profits are returns on information creation.

Labor unions and others have sought to increase production at home by supporting measures, such as the Burke-Hartke bill, designed to prevent MNCs from setting up subsidiary production facilities abroad. However, the options of multinational corporations are not restricted solely to increasing production at home. Thus, the intent of these measures could be thwarted. One alternative is to license or sell the new technology to foreign producers for fees or royalties. This is more likely for sales of disembodied technologies than for embodied ones. The more embodied the technology, the greater the likelihood that the product will be exported rather than its production licensed to a foreign firm.

Another term frequently used in the discussion of multinational corporate behavior is that they move abroad, in Stage II of Vernon's product cycle, as a "defensive" measure. This term is used to justify to American labor that U.S. MNCs keep production facilities in the United States as long as possible. (See Stobaugh, 1973). If the American MNC goes abroad reluctantly and only at the last possible moment, then it has delayed the "exporting" of American jobs as long as possible.

"Defensive investment" is frequently cited as evidence that MNCs are irrational and do not maximize profits. If MNCs are, in fact, irrational, what are the policy implications? Should the government subsidize the MNCs to shake them out of their lethargy and get them to increase output above monopoly levels? Or should it tax the MNCs to reduce monopoly profits but further push their output below the already restricted collusive levels?

But defensive investment does make sense within the framework of the appropriability theory. According to this view, the firm discovering a new product or process must decide constantly whether or not to begin production abroad and obtain worldwide profits immediately, thus contributing positively to the firm's present value. But at the same time foreign production would increase the likelihood that foreign emmulators would copy the idea and successfully undercut the firm's sales abroad sooner, thus reducing the expected present value of the firm because of a shorter period of appropriated economic rent. The multinational faces a trade-off between these two considerations, and the fact that many multinationals begin production abroad so late in the product cycle suggests that appropriability may be an important consideration.

In contrast to a struggle over market shares, American MNC's mergers with foreign firms in the production of a new technology might be interpreted as a less costly way of preventing the erosion of a new product's appropriability. MNCs have comparative advantages in developing new information, but host country firms are better able to decide whether a new item will sell in their market. It may be rational for the MNC to wait until host firms move in, since the loss in sales before entry may be more than made up by the savings of a world market search. Thus, market information has some of the same aspects of public goods as do invention and innovation.

## A DISTRIBUTIVE SHARES VIEW OF THE ORGANIZED LABOR–MNC CONFLICT OVER JOBS

The hypothesis advanced in this section is that the issue between labor and the multinationals over jobs can be explained best as simply a political struggle between the two groups over the distributive shares of income. The economic debate to date has been largely cast in political terms. Economists have discussed the economic issues using the normative terminology of the political redistribution struggle rather than positive economic terms. For example, the debate has been over jobs rather than income; over defensive investment rather than maximizing the present value of firms; and in terms of runaway industries rather than the optimum location of world production.

If the conflict may be simply over the distribution of income, a few principles are needed to focus the discussion. Economic markets are guided largely by efficiency considerations: maximization of welfare, maximization of profits, etc. Political markets adjudicate conflicts among groups through policy variables such as taxes, subsidies, tariffs, and other instruments that adjust distributive shares. A key focus in political markets is redistributive equity. In both economic and political markets, rents can be generated for actors in the other market. For example, politicians pass laws favoring certain groups (the economic results of which have been examined in, among other, the Stolper-Samuelson theorem), and economic groups can contribute campaign funds and labor time in favor of certain politicians.

There are two principles of economic interaction of specific interest to this discussion. The first is the "equity rule": It is easier to generate public voter sentiment for transferring wealth from large and visible entities (*e.g.,* MNCs) to small ones (*e.g.,* taxpayers, workers, and other disadvantaged groups) than vice versa. The second principle relates to the technology of political organizations: The organization costs of large numbers of small economic units are higher than the costs for small numbers of large entities. The fixed costs of organization are higher for the first group and, as Olson (1971) has pointed out, the free-rider problem particularly plagues political organization involving large numbers of small units.

Since votes generated by the equity principle and money (contributions) generated from small numbers of large entities by the principle of the technology of political organization both contribute positively to the election of politicians, the latter will propose redistributive schemes (which deviate from the existing shares) in response to changes in the underlying forces up to the point where the marginal effect on the probability of their election of the last dollar contributed from the well-organized group is just equal to the negative marginal effect on election probability from the larger mass of redistributees. This approach explains why labor makes a more public pitch for its side, and pushes the equity principle to redistribute income in its direction (jobs), while MNCs quietly contribute money to political campaigns to obtain their perceived ends (efficiency).

A third principle of economic interaction is that obfuscation is important for success in redistribution. If the struggle is purely over income distribution, the most efficient method to effect a change (following Bhagwati's principle of policy efficiency) is through a subsidy to the most powerful group. However, the taxpayers and voters react quickly and negatively when the redistributive intent is clear. Voters object much less to transfers if the redistributee is a disadvantaged party (*e.g.,* American labor harmed by the loss of jobs) losing at the hands of a politically identifiable culprit (*e.g.,* the MNC) who can be punished and to whom the burden of the taxpayer can be shifted. In short, it is necessary to obfuscate the redistributive process if it is to be accepted by the average voter. Furthermore, justification of the proposed policies must be couched in terms of a long-overdue equity payment.

Economists, however, have tools of analysis that show the fallacy of accomplishing a permanent redistribution in the shares of national income. The problem is comparable to that posed by nation-states competing over the international distribution of income and using the optimum tariff as a policy tool. Any one group, such as labor, can increase its welfare at the expense of another group by levying an implicit tax on the latter. If all groups in society simultaneously attempt to transfer income to themselves through legislation, then they may all be made worse off. In my view, economists should clearly state the jobs issues in redistributive terms and encourage both parties to cease the struggle to increase their respective shares of the national income.

Parry's study (1973, pp. 1204–1205) illustrated the political and redistributive terms used in the ongoing conflict between labor and MNCs and the way in which these terms have permeated economic discussions.

More recently, home-country relations with the multinational enterprise have been brought into focus by United States labor unions concerned with the exported employment by "runaway industries" . . .

The conflict is essentially one of "national interest" versus various extranational considerations. An example of this might be the ability of the international firm to distort prices involving inter-affiliate transfers, discussed below. Possible tax revenue losses by national governments are one result of the distortions, however "rational" they are for an international firm in the pursuit of its objectives, or the result of the conflict arising from the shift in the locus of decision making. A more serious issue along the same lines, especially with the possibility of controls, such as those imposed in the Burke-Hartke legistlation, concerns the location of new (and, indeed, existing) employment generated by multinational-firm activities.

This quotation describes well the circular reasoning used in political arguments over the issues at stake. The reasoning could be reshaped in redistributive terms. First, corporate taxes would be high in countries where the labor movement is stronger. Second, multinational corporate affiliates would locate production facilities outside of countries with high corporate income tax rates in order to avoid tax payments. Third, multinational corporations leaving these countries would then be criticized for exporting employment and becoming runaway industries. Finally, Burke-Hartke type restructions would be placed on such multinationals, removing their tax advantages and increasing their effective tax rates. The final point leads back to the first, illustrating that political arguments frequently run in vicious circles, as Parry realizes. The economist must be careful to avoid the terminology of redistribution, for it often produces logical impossibilities and a normative prejudging of the results.

# MNCs AND LABOR MARKETS

The first section of this paper developed one view of the activities of MNCs; the second hypothesized that the conflict between the MNCs and American labor was simply competition in political arenas over distributive shares of national income. In this section, we examine the empirical evidence on the effects of MNCs and their direct investment activity on labor markets. This review is not exhaustive. We review three areas: jobs, substitutes *vs.* complements, and income and welfare.

## The Number of Jobs

Many studies have attempted to estimate the effect of foreign affiliates of U.S. firms on the number of American jobs. Stobaugh (1973c) estimated that 250,000 U.S. jobs, primarily in production, would be lost if there were no U.S. foreign investment. Vernon (1971b) estimated that another 250,000 jobs exist in the main offices of U.S. multinational corporations. Stobaugh (1973c) then added another 100,000 jobs not included by the Vernon calculations to come up with a "Harvard" estimate of 600,000 jobs created by U.S. foreign direct investment.

The Tell (1976) study estimated that there was a net creation of 260,000 jobs in the United States as a result of U.S. foreign direct investment. The study was based on a market share analysis of production and employment between 1966 and 1970. The U.S. Tariff Commission Study (1973) estimated, on the other hand, that the job effects of U.S. foreign direct investment may range from a gain of 500,000 to a loss of 1,300,000, depending on the assumptions.

Finally, Hawkins (1972) summarized the results of these and other studies:

> . . . the estimates of net job effects of multinational corporate operations may range from significant net creations to fairly sizeable net dislocations. On the basis of reasonable, mid-range assumptions of each, it can be shown that the creations tend to offset any dislocations. At worst, then, the employment effects of multinationals appear to be a "wash" while at best there may be an actual gain.

What is an outsider's view of these results? First, it would seem that this discussion is couched, to varying degrees, in a shifting mixture of microeconomic and macroeconomic considerations. It is a mistake to discuss government policy on MNCs in the same context with monetary and fiscal policy. While MNCs are large and have some observable aggregate effects, a neo-Keynesian approach to MNCs is not pleasing analytically. The aggregative approach has permeated our discipline through the political arena and has led to the use of sloppy redistributive language more characteristic of political arguments. The proof that some of these issues are more political than economic is the relative absence of public discussion about the transfer of new technologies and jobs abroad by smaller firms. The reason for this is both economic and political: For the government, it is more efficient to control a few large firms than many small ones with the same total output. At the same time, large firms are highly visible and politically vulnerable because of the equity principle. In this sense, it is hard to imagine American labor waging a successful campaign against small innovating firms transferring jobs abroad.

Second, if we are concerned about the job effects of MNCs, an argument must be made for giving special treatment to persons who lose their jobs because an MNC moves facilities overseas relative to those who lose their jobs because a domestic firm moves its plant from New York to Tennessee. Both firms are responding to market forces. Unemployment compensation is available to the workers in both cases. Why should workers affected by MNC behavior be favored?

Third, the magnitudes involved must be kept in perspective. The most favorable estimate of the job effects of MNCs (+600,000) is only 0.7 percent of the U.S. labor force (86.0 million) and 12 percent of those unemployed (4.99 million) in 1971; the most unfavorable estimate doubles these numbers.

Fourth, the more sophisticated the study, the more likely the results are to show no net effect of MNCs on U.S. jobs. The quotation from Hawkins (1972) showing that the positive and negative gross employment effects of the MNCs are a "wash" is a case in point. The question, then, borders dangerously close to a tautology: If a person no longer works for a MNC, then he works for (or a job becomes available with) someone else. Thus, the only net effect that a change in government policy towards MNCs could have on the level of employment would have to operate through the labor/leisure choice affecting the supply of labor.

Fifth, this line of reasoning, it is argued, is too long-run a view. In the shortrun, we could use tax policy to shut down U.S. multinational operations abroad and reduce unemployment in the U.S. This raises the serious and, in my view, dangerous policy of using redistributive government microeconomic policy to solve domestic unemployment problems. Economists and many policymakers have wisely backed away from that position since the disastrous beggar-thy-neighbor tariff policies of the Smoot-Hawley period in the 1930s.

Sixth, even if a tax policy were adopted on the basis of, say, the need to restrict U.S. MNC expansion abroad, would it be efficacious? Even if it acted like an optimum tariff for the U.S., this implicit redistribution from the rest-of-the world to the U.S. would eventually encourage foreign retaliation, which would lower U.S. and foreign welfare in the long run.

Seventh, there is the possibility that severe restrictions on U.S. MNC activities abroad would lower U.S. welfare even in the absence of foreign retaliation. To the extent that the monopoly profits of the U.S. multinationals are indirect compensation to the abundant factor in the U.S. (*i.e.*, scientists and engineers creating new technologies), major restrictions on MNC activities reduces the ability of the U.S. to exploit its comparative advantage. My best guess is that major new restrictions on U.S. MNC activity would lower aggregate U.S. welfare even before retaliation is considered. U.S. multinationals may be using subsidiary production rather than licensing to minimize loss of appropriability. Forced licensing would permit foreigners to share in a larger part of the rents from new patent-protected U.S. technologies.

Eighth, would increased taxation and regulation increase U.S. welfare in the long run? The more likely scenario is that substitution would undo the intended effect of taxation *à la* Mundell (1957), who showed that taxation of international trade can be offset by factor movements, and regulation *à la* Stigler (1971), who showed that the regulators are eventually co-opted by regulatees.

Finally, the problem with most of the "jobs" studies is the absence of any consideration of prices and wages. The relevant variable for the economics of redistribution is the *opportunity cost* of the labor involved and not the number of jobs gained or lost. The extent to which organized labor lobbies in favor of compensation for displaced workers depends not upon the number of workers affected but upon the magnitude of the wage adjustment forced upon them as a result of the MNCs's decision to move abroad. It the domestic labor market is able to absorb the affected workers quickly and at a wage close to the former level, then income redistribution effects—and political pressure for compensation—will be minimized. Conversely, the longer the adjustment period and the greater the wage differential, the greater the redistribution effects will be and, hence, the greater the pressure for political retribution.

### Substitutes and Complements

This subsection surveys some of the microfoundations that various authors have used to estimate the domestic output effects of foreign affiliate activities. Lipsey and Weiss (1975) report a positive complementary relationship between U.S. export sales to foreign markets and sales of U.S.-controlled foreign affiliates in these markets for pharmaceuticals and hand tools. Horst (1975c) reports the same result for sixteen industries: both U.S. exports from parents and all U.S. exports are positively related to U.S. foreign affiliate sales. Stobaugh (1973c) found the same result in eight of nine case studies of the job effects.

Hawkins' (1976) summary of Tell's (1976) market share analysis reports that U.S. exports gained more from foreign indigenous producers than form U.S. foreign affiliates sales, suggesting relatively more complementarity between U.S. exports and the latter. On the other hand, U.S. exports captured more sales from U.S. affiliates than from non-U.S. international suppliers, suggesting greater complementarity of U.S. exports with the latter than with U.S. foreign affiliate sales.

The first problem with this line of analysis is that the statistical results may have been dominated by *supply* considerations and may not be related to complementarity in *demand* between U.S. exports and U.S. foreign affiliate sales. If this is the case, then the arguments made in political arenas by the pro-multinational corporation groups (that jobs will be lost if foreign investment is cut back) is weakened. The apparent complementarity may be a result of the supply effects predicted by Vernon's (1966) product cycle theory: Industries creating new technologies simultaneously develop new products for export (Stage I) and transfer production to foreign affiliates for slightly older products (Stage II).

A second problem is that many of these studies used no price data but merely trace movements in the quantities to infer complementarity and substitutibility. Since income effects are more significant than price effects in many statistical studies of international trade, we should be cautious of labeling pairs of quantities as "substitutible" or "complementary" in price on the basis of gross movements.

## Income and Welfare

An approach that is economically superior to study the "jobs" question has been proposed by Musgrave (1975). She correctly emphasizes that both the employment and balance of payments effects of foreign direct investment are transitory. The importnat economic question is the long-run effect of foreign direct investment (through MNC activity) on U.S. income and its distribution, taking international tax differentials and other factors in account. Her hypothetical experiment is to assume that the $80 billion stock of U.S. direct investment abroad in 1968 had instead been made in the U.S.

Assuming an elasticity of substitution of .75 between U.S. capital and labor, this experiment leads to a $2.3 billion increase in U.S. national income, a $9.9 billion increase in labor income after tax, an $8.1 billion decrease in after-tax capital income, and a $.5 billion drop in U.S. tax revenue. There would also be a slight decrease in the U.S. terms of trade; a decrease caused by a lower foreign income, which more than offsets a positive effect because of the reduced competitiveness of foreigners previously able to compete with U.S. exports with the help of U.S. foreign direct investment.

There are difficulties with this approach as well. One is that the results are built on a highly aggregative model, thereby ignoring many important questions such as the microeconomic operation of the MNCs. A second is that no policy change would ever result in the massive transfer of capital hypothesized in the Musgrave experiment. It is then an open question whether these calculations are the appropriate ones to determine the effects of switching foreign taxes from a credit to a deduction for U.S. MNCs. The virtues of this study are many; among others, it is a decent scientific effort that avoids the political-redistribution rhetoric over jobs.

# SOME NEOCLASSICAL CONSIDERATIONS[2]

This section comments on the redistributive issues that I think are at the heart of the conflict between organized labor and the multinationals. Throughout this paper, the term "labor" has referred to the scarce U.S. factor, unskilled and production worker labor largely represented by the trade union movement. Skilled labor, the relatively abundant factor in the U.S., has very different interests.

Labor wishes to increase its real income. Consider a simple two-by-two model with labor and a composite of all other factors (label it "capital" for expositional ease). Import-competing production (industry X) is labor intensive. The U.S. is labor scarce relative to the rest of the world. Several insights follow immediately from even this simplest of frameworks. (Nonbelievers in the neoclassical framework and laymen should substitute the word "jobs" for the words "increase in real wages" in the discussion that follows.)

First, U.S. real wages will increase if import-competing production is expanded. This can be accomplished by a tariff on U.S. imports, raising $P_x/P_y$ from $P$ to $P_{US}$ in Figure 1.1; or by a wage differential introduced by a union in the export industry Y. The negative profits would cause Y to contract, releasing much capital relative to labor and raising $w/r$ from $PA$ to $PB$ in $X$ and $PE$ in $Y$. As an aside, this author finds a positive correlation of .3 between unionization and industry capital intensity in the United States. While there are many other reasons besides Stolper-Samuelson effects that unions would organize in this way, the result is consistent with real wage maximization. (See Magee, 1976.)

Second, a higher U.S. tariff inevitably lowers real wages in the countries supplying U.S. imports. Thus, using this single policy, there is no way that U.S. labor and foreign labor can be simultaneously made better off. If U.S. real wages rise, they must fall abroad. $P$ would rise to $P_{US}$ in the U.S. and fall to $P_f$ abroad, with $w/r$ rising in the U.S. and falling abroad.

Third, if U.S. and foreign unions simultaneously organized and raised

*Figure 1.1* Employment and Production

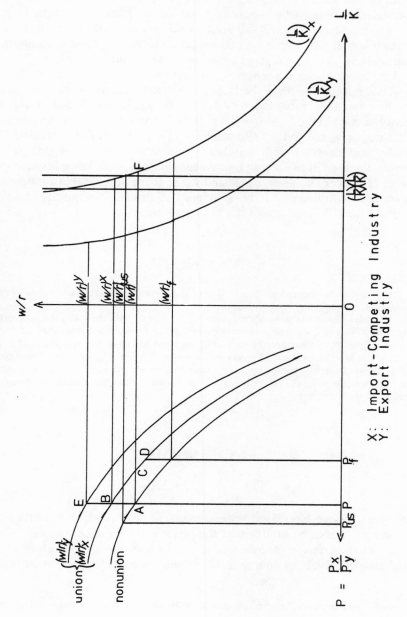

X: Import-Competing Industry
Y: Export Industry

15

wages worldwide in the capital-intensive industry, $Y$, $w/r$ would rise in both countries at existing prices $(P_x/P_y)$. However, these prices cannot persist, since the world supply of $Y$ has fallen. Thus, as the relative price of $Y$ increases, $P_x/P_y$ will fall until world product markets clear. It is not clear whether real wages abroad would be higher in the new equilibrium, particularly since the foreign terms of trade would have fallen.

Finally, consider a scenario in which labor contrived to increase the real wage income both in the U.S. and abroad. Unions would raise wages in the capital-intensive industry both in the U.S. and abroad. Simultaneously, unions in the U.S. would press for lower tariff barriers to guarantee that wages would indeed rise abroad. The alternative of increased U.S. protection coupled with tougher unionization abroad might, in fact, guarantee the fall of foreign real wages, making U.S. labor less competitive. However, if, as is suggested here, increased foreign unionization were to be coupled with a move to free U.S. trade, then the rise of foreign along with U.S. real wages might be guaranteed.

## FOOTNOTES

*The author is indebted to Robert Berry for research assistance and to the National Science Foundation for research support.

1. Richard Caves has privately suggested an offsetting consideration to the appropriability theory. Oligopolistic industries may be less prone to innovate because of the fear by member firms that a commercially successful discovery will upset the collusive equilibrium.

2. While MNCs operate in idustries with notorious product and factor market imperfections, these distortions have been incorporated into neoclassical trade theory with surprisingly minor effects on the basic theorems (see Magee, 1976). The material in this section builds on that literature.

# COMMENT

## THOMAS HORST*

Stephen Magee has raised several major issues on which I would like to comment. First, he argues that the private development of new technology depends on the innovator's ability to appropriate the return on that technology. Such, of course, is the economic basis for the patent system.

*U.S. Department of Treasury, on leave from the Fletcher School of Law and Diplomacy.

Because of various economies of size in developing and applying new technology, innovative firms tend to be large:

> There is a failure to understand, both by the public and by organized labor, that there are virtues in MNCs being large. It is not well understood that firms may have to be large to help protect the returns on their information. Nor is it seen that monopoly behavior is society's way of rewarding innovators for creating a public good (*i.e.,* new information). Furthermore, the monopoly profits earned by technology creating firms are to a significant extent simply an amortization of past investments in scientists and engineers hired to create new technology . . .

While Magee qualifies his argument frequently and acknowledges in a footnote that size may possibly inhibit innovation, the thrust of his argument is homage to Joseph Schumpeter—monopoly is the price of innovation.

This old argument has often been subjected to empirical scrutiny, and an excellent summary of the many studies is in Frederic Scherer (1970, Chapter 15). Scherer's conclusion in a nutshell is that there *do* seem to be economies of size in industrial innovation, but only up to a certain point. As Scherer states:

> What we find from analyzing the available qualitative and quantitative evidence is a kind of threshold effect. A little bit of bigness—up to sales levels of roughly $75 million to $200 million in most industries—is good for invention and innovation. But beyond the threshold further bigness adds little or nothing, and it carries the danger of diminishing effectiveness of inventive and innovative performance (p. 361).

Although $200 million is more than Magee or I will accumulate in our lifetime, as multinational corporations go, it's small potatoes. Most corporations on Fortune's 500 are well above this threshold—General Motors is more than one hundred times as large. The tradeoff between size and innovation may be far less severe than Magee implies.

Magee raises an interesting point when he argues that restrictions on foreign investment would encourage patent licensing and other forms of technological transfer. The ill-fated Burke-Hartke Bill recognized this possibility and sought to restrict international patent licensing as well as foreign direct investment. But that provision of the Burke-Hartke Bill was probably unworkable. A foreign licensee, including a U.S.-owned subsidiary, does not have rights to a U.S. patent; rather, it has the rights to a *foreign* patent assigned to it by the U.S. owner. Many countries require patents to be worked locally if the rights are to be retained. Countries that do not have a local-use requirement would doubtless enact such legislation if the United States were unilaterally to prohibit local use. Restrictions on the outflow of patented technology are wholly infeasible.

In the second section of his paper, Magee argues that "the issue between labor and the MNCs over jobs can be explained best as simply a political struggle between the two groups over the distributive shares of income." While this may well be true, the main provisions of the Burke-Hartke Bill—repealing deferral and replacing the foreign tax credit with a mere deduction for foreign taxes on subsidiaries' income—could be justified as necessary to maximize national income (where national income includes the net return on foreign investment). The usual objection to this policy prescription is that it takes no account of foreign retaliation. While the United States and foreign countries *taken together* would be worse off if a "tax war" were to occur, the United States *taken alone* might well come out ahead. Under the current practice of giving a U.S. tax credit for income and dividend withholding taxes paid to foreign governments, the United States collects virtually no tax on its investors' foreign income. Given this skewed distribution of international tax payments, the United States might benefit from eliminating the foreign tax credit even if foreign countries retaliated. The major argument for retaining the foreign tax credit is that the United States has international obligations that preclude its following nationalistic policies. But if that is the case, then labor's claim for compensation is hard to ignore—they are paying the price of a policy serving broader national interests. Continued domestic support for liberal international trade and investment policies depends in no small part on compensating those who are hurt. Finding effective and efficient ways of doing this is difficult, but in the long run worth the effort.

Let me comment on one final point. Stobaugh and others who argue that foreign investment is "defensive" claim that U.S. companies will not invest abroad as long as domestic production earns a minimal rate of return. "Defensive" behavior derives from investors' inertia—the preference, if you will, for the *status quo*. Corporations, like individuals or other institutions, do not maximize current profits, the discounted present value of future earnings, or the value of any other objective function. They change only when their behavior is threatened and becomes untenable. If all foreign investment were defensive, then public policies restricting foreign investment could not prevent the "export" of jobs. While Magee and I have more faith in the willingness of U.S. multinationals to maximize global income than the Harvard Business School does, the evidence that corporations are not as clever and calculating as we economists often suppose cannot and should not be ingored.

# COMMENT
## ROBERT B. STOBAUGH*

I believe that Professor Magee's major contribution is pointing out that the question of jobs and the multinational enterprise is really a domestic political squabble over who gets what share of U.S. income. Therefore, the tools employed in the economics of pork-barrel politics can be used to analyze the question.

He made a number of other arguments with which I am also in general agreement (Stobaugh, 1976):

1. The "apparent windfalls" earned by multinational corporations may be, to a sizable extent, amortization of past R & D investments rather than "pure rents"; and to the extent that this is true, taxation of the corporations' profits comes at the expense of the supply of future innovation and technology and hence is not a costless transfer to U.S. labor.

2. It would be an unwise policy to use redistributive government macroeconomic policy to solve unemployment problems.

3. The employment and balance-of-payments effects of foreign direct investment are transitory and the important economic question is the long-run effect of such investment on U.S. income and its distribution.

4. The relevant variable for the economics of redistribution is the opportunity cost of labor involved.

And, finally, perhaps his most important policy conclusion:

5. Major new U.S. restrictions on the foreign activities of U.S. multinational enterprises would lower U.S. Gross National Product (GNP).

But I am more likely to make a useful contribution if I highlight those items on which we *disagree,* or on which I believe that major clarifications are required, and therefore I will concentrate on these.

A common omission running through his paper, perhaps because of insufficient space, is the lack of recognition that the view of decision-makers within an organization or group might differ from an economist's view of what is best for that organization or group. Two examples illustrate this weakness.

First, Magee assumes that leaders of labor unions represent the interest of all unskilled and production-worker labor. In fact, labor union leaders represent their own interests, which usually means the interests of their members. Thus, they are much more likely to attempt to increase the income, membership, and political power of their union than to pursue a policy that would create higher-skilled jobs outside the union for union

*Harvard University

members or their sons and daughters. Hence, labor leaders tend to favor policies that help import-competing industries, where unions are heavily represented, rather than export industries, where unions are less well represented.

Second, company executives can have a different risk preference than would be optimum for their stockholders; this difference often causes executives to be reluctant to invest in "risky" investments abroad rather than safer investments at home, even if the risky investment would be better for their stockholders. Thus we often see the so-called "defensive" investment, that is, one which the firm makes abroad in order to serve profitably a given market that cannot be served profitably from the United States. The decision-maker in this case, like the labor leader, is quite rational; and the scholar who does not recognize the decision-maker's motivation has an unduly narrow view of the world. True, Magee recognizes one category of risk—the risk that foreign emulators will copy the U.S. investor's idea—but this explanation suffers from not recognizing that most U.S. multinational enterprises, rather than competing abroad against local firms, in fact, compete against non-U.S. multinationals that have the ability to obtain information from the United States. Furthermore, he fails to recognize that the executive faces a host of other risks.

As I indicated above, Magee is correct when he emphasizes that in analyzing the effects of foreign direct investment, the opportunity cost of labor is a more relevant variable than the number of jobs. I believe, however, that he misses an important point in not recognizing more explicitly that U.S. foreign direct investment increases the level of skills in the United States.

For example, in our nine case studies of the effects of foreign direct investment on the U.S. economy, we found that the skill levels of jobs created at home by U.S. foreign direct investment are higher than those in U.S. manufacturing as a whole.[1] Figure 1.2, which shows the hypothesized effect of U.S. foreign direct investment on U.S. employment in a given U.S. industrial sector over time, helps to explain why this is so. During the early and middle parts of a sector's life, U.S. foreign direct investment helps create U.S. employment in two ways: (1) It generates U.S. exports, which would not otherwise exist, of capital equipment, parts and components, and other products for which foreign sales are made because of the existence of U.S. foreign affiliates (Stobaugh et al., 1973c, pp. 199–204); and (2) it generates U.S. employment in R & D facilities because of the added world market for which the fruits of U.S. R & D may be used.[2]

As a U.S. industrial sector becomes older, it gradually loses its advantage over similar industrial sectors abroad. U.S. foreign direct investment, by aiding the U.S. balance of payments, keeps the U.S. dollar at a

*Figure 1.2*   Hypothesized Effect of U.S. Foreign Direct Investment on Employment in a Given U.S. Industrial Sector over Time

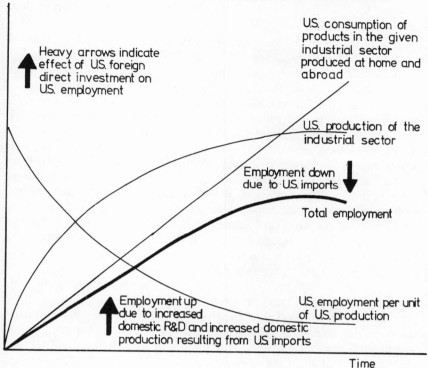

Heavy arrows indicate effect of U.S. foreign direct investment on U.S. employment

U.S. consumption of products in the given industrial sector produced at home and abroad

U.S. production of the industrial sector

Employment down due to U.S. imports

Total employment

Employment up due to increased domestic R&D and increased domestic production resulting from U.S. imports

U.S. employment per unit of U.S. production

Time

higher level vis-à-vis foreign currency than it would otherwise be. Thus, in order for the U.S. dollar to be in equilibrium with the rest of the world, U.S. imports of products for which the United States has lost its advantage over the rest of the world are higher than they would otherwise be—such products, of course, are in industrial sectors that are relatively old.[3] The "lost" U.S. production resulting from increased U.S. imports, of course, causes U.S. employment in such industrial sectors to be lower than it would otherwise be.

Hence, the net U.S. employment effects of U.S. foreign direct investment are to create the higher-skilled jobs found in the early and middle stages of an industrial sector's life cycle at the expense of the lower-skilled jobs found in the late stages of the life cycle. In this process, U.S. foreign direct investment is beneficial to the U.S. economy if the added income from the higher U.S. job skills created by such investment exceeds the added cost of training, and at times relocating, the labor force.

As I have stated elsewhere, we do not have sufficient evidence to state unequivocally that U.S. foreign direct investment results in a net increase in income level in the United States, but my judgment is that it does (Stobaugh et al., 1972).

Figure 1.2 shows one other force that affects total U.S. employment—the increasing efficiency of the U.S. workforce that causes a decline in U.S. employment per unit of U.S. production.[4] This factor causes U.S. employment to rise less, and to fall more, than U.S. production and, as depicted in Figure 1.2, this factor can have a much greater effect on total U.S. employment than changes in U.S. trade patterns (Stobaugh, 1971c).

Furthermore, on the question of jobs, Magee does not give a representative picture of my studies at Harvard. (I accept that the fault might lie with my exposition rather than with Professor Magee.) Although, I did state that 600,000 jobs would be "lost" if there were no U.S. foreign direct investment, I further stated that if these jobs were eliminated, "the workers would not go idle," and added that no one should claim that "this many U.S. workers would be unemployed if there were no U.S. foreign direct investment" (Stobaugh et al., 1972). The reason is obvious. U.S. fiscal and monetary policy has a far greater influence on the number of U.S. jobs than does U.S. foreign direct investment.[5]

Indeed, Professor Magee recognizes that fiscal and monetary policy can be used to create jobs, but in his reference to Peggy Musgrave's (1975) paper, he fails to mention that such policies also can be used to create investment. By inference from Magee's argument No.5, I conclude that he might well agree with me that a reduction in U.S. national income likely would result from the adoption of the policy that Professor Musgrave's study seems to approve—the placing of higher U.S. taxes on U.S. foreign direct investors in manufacturing. Yet I believe that in the end he finds too many virtues in the Musgrave paper. He fails to conclude explicitly that her study is not sufficiently realistic for policy-making purposes. I would like to emphasize the following limitations in the Musgrave work:

1. Because Musgrave's economic model is one in which national income is determined by an equation with two homogeneous variables—labor and capital—she ignores the creation of job skills and their contribution to national income and thereby understates the benefits that the U.S. economy derives from the U.S. multinationals.

2. Her model rests upon a number of unrealistic assumptions that are crucial to her results. She assumes the existence of full employment. She assumes the existence of perfect competition. She further assumes that a dollar invested abroad, even if from retained earnings of foreign subsidiaries, displaces a dollar of investment in the United States. And she

assumes that the flow of portfolio investment to and from the United States would not be affected by a decline in profits of U.S. firms.

The final flaw that I find in Magee's paper is his equating of the public welfare with GNP. Authors have begun to recognize that this single-minded approach avoids recognition of the effect of a person's relative economic position on his happiness (Morgenstern, 1975, and Scitovsky, 1976). Although I agree with Magee that "labor wishes to increase its real income," I believe that their income relative to management's income also is quite important. There are some who believe that "labor" might prefer Policy A, which results in a 20 percent increase in labor's unit income and a zero increase in management's income rather than Policy B, which results in a 30 percent increase in labor's unit income and a 50 percent increase in management's income.

In summary, Professor Magee has provided a useful review and some important ideas concerning the political arena and the labor market, but he was limited by his lack of recognition of some real-world factors that are crucial to our increased understanding of the political and economic issues surrounding MNCs.

# FOOTNOTES

1. Stobaugh, Telesio, and de la Torre (1973). This is consistent with the finding that U.S. labor skills are higher in U.S. export industries than in U.S. industries competing with imports. See various contributions in Kenen and Lawrence (1968).

2. Of course, if foreign direct investment does not occur, then R & D output can be sold to unrelated foreign firms. But I argue elsewhere that the returns from foreign direct investment often are higher than from selling technology to unrelated parties (Stobaugh, 1970a). For an example of the returns that can be made from operating a coordinated group of foreign affiliates rather than a group of uncoordinated entities, as licensees likely would be, see Pomper (1976). For additional reasons that multinational enterprises prefer ownership to licensing abroad, see Telesio (1977).

3. This statement represents an extension of the well-known concept of a product life cycle to the concept of an industry (or industrial sector) life cycle. For a discussion of product life cycle, see Vernon (1966). For a discussion of industry life cycle, see Stobaugh (1972).

4. This increase in production efficiency may be attributed both to static and dynamic scale economies. See Stobaugh and Townsend (1975b), pp. 19–29.

5. The U.S. Tariff Commission study (1973, p. 649) concluded that U.S. fiscal and monetary policies have a much greater influence on U.S. investment than does U.S. foreign direct investment.

# 2. COLLECTIVE BARGAINING AND LABOR RELATIONS IN MULTINATIONAL ENTERPRISE: A U.S. PUBLIC POLICY PERSPECTIVE

Duane Kujawa, FLORIDA INTERNATIONAL UNIVERSITY

The purpose of this paper is to present an overview and synthesis of recent research and positions on major issues evident at the interface between the MNC and organized labor. The intention is to do this in a reasonably crisp fashion with due consideration to the following facts:

1. An enormous amount of research on the subject has been reported in the last six years or so. Only the more significant (in fact or fantasy) will be noted in this report.

2. Positions on major issues, to the extent they are those of the parties directly involved at the interface, i.e., enterprise management or labor representative, are adversary positions. Public expressions of these positions thus frequently seek to create or sustain an advantage, or to diminish

Research in International Business and Finance, Vol. 1, pp. 25–61.

a disadvantage. Actions and statements of either party then must be accepted with caution and, where possible, measured against some objective benchmark.

3. Neither U.S. multinationals nor the U.S. industrial relations environment has a monopoly over MNC-labor problems and interactions. However, these will be emphasized, given the author's personal research experience and reticence to suggest or imply public policy alternatives for any country other than his own.

To give this overview and synthesis substance and relevance, due consideration is also paid to the general theme of this paper: The emergence and very nature of the multinational corporation compromise the efficacy of present U.S. labor law, at best; or demonstrate that present U.S. labor law is itself a source of instability in relations between MNCs and organized labor, at worst. If either conclusion is true, then present law (as it relates to multinationals) is ineffective, no longer serves the public interest, and should be changed.

The U.S. national interest, as enunciated by the U.S. Congress in the National Labor Relations Act is

> . . . to define and protect the rights of employees and employers, to encourage collective bargaining, and to eliminate certain practices on the part of labor and management that are harmful to the general welfare.[1]

Although each objective mentioned in this quotation is important to this paper's focus, the encouragement of collective bargaining is especially so. Indeed, to some extent, labor and management representatives use collective bargaining to attain elements of the other two objectives of defining and protecting the rights of the parties and eliminating certain harmful practices. Encouragement of collective bargaining might thus be judged a superior objective. The core or essence of collective bargaining, in turn, rests in the power relationship between mangement and labor (Chamberlain and Cullen, 1971). The interest of present U.S. labor law is to encourage the practice and procedure of collective bargaining by, *inter alia,* promoting equality in this power relationship.[2]

This paper thus begins with effects of multinationals on the power relationship. It addresses questions such as: Is there anything intrinsic to the substance and operations of MNCs that tips the balance of power to their benefit? What are the perceptions of unions regarding the effects of MNCs on power relationships? Subsequently, the paper reviews responses of labor to the MNC and evaluates these relative to the U.S. national interest. Finally, a specific modification to present labor law is suggested.

# EFFECTS OF MULTINATIONAL OPERATIONS ON BARGAINING POWER

The essence of the power relationship in collective bargaining is the capability and willingness of either management or labor to inflict and sustain economic injury to attain its own objectives. The implementing of injury is constrained, or kept within reasonable limits, by the presence of countervailing power, *i.e.,* given the interdependency of the parties, the exercise of power by either injures both. A gain won by either side is not without its costs. There are many dimensions or facets to the development and exercise of this power that are relevant to the distinctive nature of MNCs. Several of these appear especially important, or at least illustrative, and are herein presented as *working hypotheses* in allegation form:[3]

1. The MNCs reduce employment in the parent country as they establish and expand production in foreign markets. Thus, the size of the bargaining unit is reduced and concerns of unit members shift to employment stability and away from conditions of employment.

2. In the event of a strike in the parent-company country, the union does not totally "shut down" the flow of financial resources to the MNC. Operations in other countries continue to generate profits for the parent. Thus, the "duality of injury" concept intrinsic to the power relationship is compromised—in favor of management.

3. The MNCs that internally dual source on a transnational basis can force a union to bargain down on wages, benefits, and other conditions of employment to approach or equal those at the least-cost production unit. In the familiar jargon, this would be "whipsawing" the union.

4. The MNCs that internally dual source on a transnational basis can offset or diminish the effects of a strike at one facility by expanding production at another facility. Thus, the potency of the strike as the ultimate economic weapon is compromised.

5. The MNCs, with their transnational tiers of management structure, don't delegate authority to local management to make decisions on labor relations issues. This inaccessibility of decision makers diminishes the integrity and value of collective bargaining, while adding to the complexity and instability of the negotiation process.

6. The MNCs, with their transfer-pricing practices and transnational sourcing and marketing patterns, can locate profits at different subsidiaries irrespective of local productivity and similar considerations. Likewise data of interest to labor on operations in other countries are either not available or not provided. Effective, "good faith" collective bargaining requires access by both management and labor to the facts necessary to address and resolve collective bargaining issues. Thus good faith bargaining is impossible given these conditions and practices.

28                                                  DUANE KUJAWA

*Employment Effects*

The job-loss question is exceedingly complex. The most recent debate began with estimates provided by former Secretary of Labor George Schultz in a 1969 statement to the Congressional Joint Economic Committee. His testimony implied that approximately 500,000 U.S. jobs were lost during 1966–1969 because of imbalances in the growth of U.S. external trade.[4] These data, in turn, were extrapolated by the AFL-CIO to an estimate of 900,000 jobs lost between 1966–1971, and, quite importantly, were related not only to external trade changes, but also to the nature and growth of the multinational corporation (Goldfinger, 1973).

Given these developments, and the introduction of the "Burke-Hartke" bill in the Congress, numerous empirical studies were performed on the U.S. domestic employment effects of multinationals and of international trade. The conclusions, methodologies, and assumptions of these studies varied considerably. For example, Dewald (former Director, Office of Foreign Economic Research, International Labor Affairs Bureau, U.S. Department of Labor) (1975, p. 6), using aggregated data for the U.S. economy as a whole reported

. . . a strong positive association between imports, employment and income and a lack of association between the unemployment rate and imports, contrary to the neomercantilist hypothesis that exports gain jobs and imports cost jobs.

His conclusion, which begs a rather broad identification of the issues, is that there are no job losses (or gains) attributable to international trade. However, of interest to this paper's focus, Dewald acknowledge earlier in his report that trade changes required human readjustments in labor markets, and that the adjustment assistance provisions of the Trade Act of 1974 will ". . . provide them [i.e., displaced workers] with the means and incentives to get better jobs than they lost."[5] Does this imply "better" jobs were created while "lesser" jobs were destroyed?

The 1972–1973 U.S. Tariff Commission study (USTC, 1973), requested by the Senate Finance Committee for use in its own deliberations on "Burke-Hartke," concluded that in the most probable of three alternative scenarios hypothesized, MNCs created a net of 488,000 jobs in the United States during 1965–1970, despite a loss of 603,100 "production" jobs. This study presented employment impact data disaggregated at the industry sector level and identified growth in "headquarters employment" as a major component of the total net job loss/gain. This latter point—the shift to headquarters employment away from blue-collar, production employment is of special significance.

Similarly, studies by the U.S. Department of Commerce, National

Foreign Trade Council, and Emergency Committee for American Trade generally concluded that the rise of the U.S. multinational resulted in a concurrent expansion of jobs in the U.S.[6] Building on these reports, de la Torre, Stobaugh, and Telesio (1973) reported empirical support for the contention that foreign investment results in a change in the skill composition of employment at an investing firm (MNC) and that this change is toward a higher share of professional employment within total employment when compared to other firms within the same industry.

On balance, these empirical studies, notwithstanding biases and deficiencies, *imply* that there were both job losses and job gains, and jobs lost were more likely to be bargaining unit jobs, while jobs gained were more likely to be outside the bargaining unit.[7] Thus, the allegation cited above may be supported at least in its latter statement that the growth of U.S. MNCs occasioned reductions in bargaining unit size. Bargaining power is judged to be at least a partial function of unit size (number of members, financial resources generated, etc.) and the solidarity of unit members in pressing demands on management. Declining and unstable employment conditions for unit members undermine this power.

*Financial Flows and Strike Effectiveness*

If an MNC operated on a totally integrated production basis, where the output from operations in one country was a specific component essential for production in another country, it would be no different from a firm producing only intranationally in terms of the potential for a union to eliminate totally the financial inflows to the firm via the strike.[8] In the former case, technology and location of production give the union sufficient leverage. In the latter, direct control over production is exercised by the union, or at least the union has the potential for such.

The necessary question then is whether or not the MNC possesses a fully transnationally integrated production scheme. Anything less than complete transnational interdependence will result in residual financial inflows in spite of a strike, and would usually enable the firm to experience something less than the injury being experienced by the workers on strike, whose income, or financial inflow, is zero. (That workers on strike may develop and/or benefit from sources of income outside the firm, such as "strike funds," unemployment compensation, alternate employment, etc., must be acknowledged. However, one useful distinction here is that the firm with "parallel" production operations, sustains a financial inflow while routinely functioning as it generally had been. Workers, on the other hand, are forced to adjust with less certainty associated with the level and duration of benefit inflows, especially relative to what may be necessary to win a strike.)

There has apparently been no systematic attempt to identify empirically the extent of transnational production in multinational enterprise. Some evidence exists, however, which implies that complete production integration is far from the reality. Musgrave (1975), for example, reports that the ratio of the value of foreign sales by U.S. MNCs to U.S. exports grew from 2.1 in the period 1962–1964 to 2.8 in 1968. This could infer the extent of transnational production integration between the U.S. and foreign countries is even declining. In their study of 100 foreign multinationals operating in the United States, Jedel and Kujawa (1976) found not a single instance of foreign production dependency on U.S. production output. The aforementioned Tariff Commission study (USTC, 1973, p. 291) concluded ". . . most of the MNCs' activity overseas consists of local production for local markets." Kujawa found some evidence of transnational production integration in the United States, based on MNCs in the automotive industry, but it was far from total or even substantial (except in the Ford Motor Company case in Europe), and was negligible relative to a U.S.-foreign country integration pattern, with the exception of Canada, of course.[9] On balance, the evidence must be taken as suggestive that transnational production integration is not presently a distinguishing characteristic of MNC operations.

There is some theoretical support for this conclusion too. The product life-cycle model of foreign trade and investment developed by Vernon and others suggests that initial U.S. foreign investment (in manufacturing) is frequently required to meet local foreign market needs, and is a defensive move to meet increasing, foreign-based competition (Vernon, 1971a). The key is production flexibility to serve different and changing product market conditions. This implies local production autonomy except where the return to the MNC for standardized production and intrafirm exports is greater than the market loss associated with the inability to meet varied market conditions. This is obviously not a ubiquitous circumstance.

### "Whipsawing" the Union

The ability of an MNC to force a settlement condition on a union is best enhanced when accompanied by the threat of the immediate and permanent loss of employment unless the MNC's position prevails. This would appear to be a rare circumstance. It has occurred, however.

In the late 1960s in a situation involving General Motors Corporation's European subsidiaries, unions representing workers at the GM continental plant in Antwerp conceded that the standard workweek on the new afternoon shift for production workers be expanded to 40 hours from the existing 37.5 hour workweek for maintenance personnel on that shift. The GM continental management was convinced the expansion of the workweek from 37.5 to 40 hours as the afternoon production shift came into being was necessary to maintain a competitive stance vis-à-vis Opel's plant in Bochum, West Germany, which shared with the Antwerp plant in the assembly of Opel automobiles for export to the United States. Furthermore, management believed the shift was necessary to respond to the underlying competitive structure of the product market in the United States and the necessity for cost minimization. The GM continental management was able to convince the Belgian unions of this belief (Kujawa, 1971, p. 228).

Moving from a situation where a dual sourcing capability was directly related to a collective bargaining issue, the longer-run threat implied in the MNCs's flexibility on the location of future production facilities could be viewed by unions as "whipsawing." For example, labor problems at Chrysler United Kingdom in 1973 were reportedly

> . . . leading company planners to consider switching substantial production to its French (Simca) plants and/or to a partner operation in Japan (ILO, 1975).

Preceding this, and underscoring the proximity of the implied threat of moving production to the conduct of collective bargaining, the managing director of Chrysler U.K., writing in the company's employee newspaper, warned that

> . . . beyond everything else, we need a year of stable industrial relations and uninterrupted production within our own plants. . . . Another year of disruption of the damaging scale of the past 12 months might well put us out of business (WSJE, 11/30/70).

Another example involved public statements made in London by Henry Ford II that British labor relations were making the U.K. unattractive to new foreign investment, that product quality was declining in the U.K., and that Ford was getting a better return on its German investments (WSJE, 3/16/71). Subsequently, Ford Motor Company located a new facility in the United States for Pinto engine production for the North American market, displacing that which previously came out of the U.K. (ILO, 1975).

Similar cases-in-point, involving other than the U.S. automotive companies, have been reported by union representatives to the International Labor Office during its 1975 study of industrial relations of multinationals in Western Europe. Quite significantly, the study concluded

> One of the most serious charges, which unions make . . . is that [MNCs] . . . use their internationally spread facilities as a threat to counter union demands and power. If the union will not yield, the company can . . . transfer its production to another country, or the company may utilize already existing facilities in another country to penalize the "demanding" union . . . (ILO, 1975, p. 19).

The question may be raised at this point that when a union and workers are confronted with the (alleged) economic facts and competitive circumstances affecting the marketability of their product, it does not necessarily mean the company is seeking to extract some advantage by exploiting its employees. This is certainly a complex and important issue. Management concerns encompass a variety of considerations, of which those involving employee practices and compensation are important, but not exclusive. But, to better understand union behavior and interests, one should acknowledge at least that the ability to compare productivity of workers across national boundaries (and legal jurisdictions), and to present effectively such comparisons within the context of otherwise "nationally-bound" labor negotiations, are uniquely characteristic to MNCs. Purely domestic companies have no such capabilities. Thus, MNCs are viewed by unions and workers as having the ultimate power; that is, control over the "fact" of employment. How they specifically use this power many be a less substantive, but still important, issue to the labor side.

A closing point to be addressed on this issue is that the plant location decision for the MNC may appear at first no different from any "intra-U.S." company that moves operations within the United States, so long as the desire to escape a union is not a determining factor in the decision process. But the MNC case is different. In the instance involving an intra-U.S. move, the union can at least attempt to organize the new plant under protection of U.S. law. In the foreign investment case, this is not an option. (In many foreign countries, especially in continental Europe, where industry-wide bargaining is practiced, intracountry plant relocation is even less an issue from a union viewpoint, whereas an investment outside the country is certainly beyond any direct union jurisdiction.)

### Production Shifts to Offset Strike Losses

Ability to shift production from a struck plant to one not struck affects the power balance in ways other than just "whipsawing." Shifting production also undermines the effectiveness of the strike weapon by allowing the management side to offset the economic consequences of the strike intended by the union. If the dislocation expense to the company of shifting production in the event of a strike is less than the hardships imposed on workers (*e.g.*, the total loss of income), the balance of power shifts in favor of the management side.

Little systematic research has been done on this question, especially as it relates to operations of U.S. MNCs abroad. However, Jedel and Kujawa (1976) found that in only three of the sixty-four companies studied involving foreign MNCs in the United States where there was a formal company-union relationship

> . . . the report of a strike alerted the parent to the anticipated inability of the U.S. subsidiary to meet sales commitments, with the expectation that the parent or some other subsidiary could pick up the production lost in the United States.

These firms cautioned, however, that the desire to serve the U.S. market with production abroad

> . . . had to be considered in terms of the availability of excess capacity outside the United States and the interchangeability in design and function of the U.S.-made and the imported product.[10]

The ILO (1975) study on multinationals' industrial relations in Western Europe reported several instances of production shifts to offset strike losses, including examples from the food products and processing industry.

While convincing empirical evidence has yet to be developed, the indications are that the dual sourcing threat may indeed be perceived by labor as very real. Certainly the concerns expressed by labor of the need to neutralize this threat imply that dual sourcing compromises union power. For example, the International Federation of Chemical and General Workers' Unions (ICF) formed a network of unions outside the United States to assist the (U.S.) United Rubber Workers in its 1973 collective bargaining with the major U.S. tire companies. This assistance from these unions included a ". . . refusal to build up inventories, refusal to increase overtime, [and] refusal to divert production to the United States or to make exceptional transfers of output to world markets" (Hershfield, 1975). Similarly, the President of the United Automobile, Aerospace and Agricultural Implement Workers of America (UAW) expressed concern:[11]

> . . . Ford of Europe has at least two sources—one on the Continent and one in Britain—for most of the components of its common car models. This puts the company in a position to switch suppliers during strikes.

Finally, in its 1975 study on multinational unions, the Conference Board reported 10 percent of the 134 U.S. MNCs participating had experienced contacts by unions at foreign affiliates. These included requests to alter MNC policies to include refusals to work overtime at nonstruck units, or to handle shipments to or from struck foreign operations (Hershfield, 1975). The purpose of these requests was obviously aimed at strengthening the strike weapon.

The inference from this is that some situations may exist where MNCs possess a dual sourcing capability. Clearly though, labor is especially concerned about the effects of dual sourcing on strike effectiveness. In support of the union view, one could argue "good management" is obliged in a strike situation to seek alternate product resource "routes" in satisfying a current market demand. If this involves expanding production at a nonstruck facility to compensate for lost production at a struck facility, so be it. Indeed, where market share is an important strategic, competitive factor, management may feel compelled to switch "struck" production even where cost factors are such that short-run profits are zero or even negative.

## The Locus of Decision Making

Union concern over the inaccessibility of decision makers is perhaps best expressed in a report by the International Labor Office reflecting the concerns of trade union representatives at a special ILO-sponsored meeting on multinationals and social policy (ILO, 1973, p. 91). One concern was

> . . . that, in the case of a multinational's subsidiary, the locus of managerial decision making, particularly as regards matters arising in collective bargaining, is not always where the confrontations between management and trade unions take place. Rather, it is contended, the relevant decisions are made at the headquarters of the multinational, beyond the reach of the trade union concerned. This means that trade union negotiators do not have the opportunity of personally presenting their case to those who ultimately take the decisions.

Thus, the question of with whom a union prefers to negotiate turns ultimately on the authority of that person in committing the firm to a negotiated agreement. A corollary to this is that only the decision maker possesses the factual background adequate to a proper evaluation of the union's interests and proposals. Thus, the integrity of the bargaining process itself is at stake also in this issue. Similarly, long decision-making chains within the management structure give rise to response delays, communications errors, etc. This adds to the complexity of the negotiations and enhances the probability of errors being made on the substance of the issues and positions, and inferences from certain tactics. This may be especially true where the management structure is cross-cultural, as in the case of the MNC.

The management response to this union concern is that decisions on industrial relations questions and collective bargaining issues at the foreign subsidiary are best handled by subsidiary management. This is consistent with the belief that the MNC is a "guest" within the foreign society and should reflect that society's cultural and social norms as effectively as possible. Furthermore, the MNC must respond to local labor market conditions and meet the local competition to produce on a competitive basis. And only local foreign management may possess the detailed knowlegdge of union and other worker representation structures—and their possible internal rivalries—and of economic and other priorities of the work force to deal responsibly and responsively to worker-related interests and issues. Testimony generally consistent with this view has been offered by various management representatives during recent years. These include the Labor Relations Director of General Motors Overseas Operations (Angle, 1975), and the Overseas Liaison Manager, Labor Relations Staff, Ford Motor Company (Copp, 1973). Testimony somewhat contrary to this view has been offered by the vice President of Industrial Relations, Massey-Ferguson, Ltd. (Belford, 1970), who advocates a more expanded, but not total, parent company participation and policy control over the subsidiary's industrial relations.

The 1969–1970 Kujawa study (1971) of the U.S. automotive MNCs concluded that managers at foreign subsidiaries exercised considerable autonomy in the conduct of their industrial relations. Decision-making areas covered in the study included collective bargaining structures, development and presentation of collective bargaining positions, strike positions, the decisions to take a strike and resolution of strike issues, contract administration, grievance handling, and government relations (germane to industrial relations issues). Some exceptions to local autonomy, for example, turned on the nature of the issue (*e.g.,* pensions, where the special expertise and the contingent liability of the parent were factors); and on the competitive strategy of the parent where a restructuring of subsidiary industrial relations was necessitated (*e.g.,* where Chrysler Corporation implemented an interplant production scheme at Rootes Motors, Ltd., which in turn required a complete realignment of the internal industrial relations structure and changes in the payment system).

In their 1975 study of 100 foreign multinationals in the United States, Jedel and Kujawa (1976) found:

> Parent company involvement in subsidiary industrial relations decision-making patterns and policies was minimal. [However,] . . . Japanese-owned subsidiaries were more prone to feel a union presence might complicate employee relations. [Involvement] . . . in collective bargaining was also quite limited, except with Canadian-owned firms . . . or in "turn around" situations where economic issues were especially important.

In the "turn around" situations (two cases out of sixty-four), parent-company management approved the positions developed by the subsidiary management on economic issues only. The subsidiaries were in tight competitive situations and the parents had recently contributed additional capital to sustain the viability of the subsidiaries. Even in these cases, however, the parents did not unilaterally dictate subsidiary positions.

The recent ILO study on multinationals in Europe concluded that if parent companies are prone to intervene, their influence over affiliates' labor relations vary by issue or topic area, by technological or market forces present, and by country to country (ILO, 1975). A major deficiency of this study, though, is that it assumes the parent company motivation to intervene or implies it by innuendo. This is the key point. Also, use of the word "influence" is unfortunate. It is not a precise term, and was subsequently elaborated upon in the ILO report as "wishing" to be kept informed, "leaning on" the overseas subsidiary, and "tending to regard" overseas problems as an extension of home country operations and "imposing" home country "standards."

The 1975 Conference Board study reported in its survey of 134 U.S.-owned MNCs operating abroad and thirty-four foreign-owned MNCs in the United States, that 27 percent of the respondents required subsidiary management to seek specific authority to conclude formal labor agreements on economic issues (Hershfield, 1975). In the remaining 73 percent, the parent involvement was much less direct and ranged from "consultation" to the general requirement that local management just be able to meet financial objectives. On the question of the form of economic benefit, the approval requirement dropped one-third to 18 percent, suggesting that it was the budgetary impact and not what was required to secure an agreement that may have been a predominant consideration in the approval process. Unfortunately, this study failed to differentiate among the responses on the basis of the (country) location of the subsidiary. If the specific approval requirement by the parent was imposed on even one subsidiary, the entire MNC response was recorded as positive relative to that requirement. The fact that many U.S. MNCs have subsidiaries in Canada with close industrial relations management ties to the U.S. parent compromises the usefulness of these data. Kujawa (1971) found, for example, that industrial relations management structures between U.S. and Canadian operations of the U.S. automotive companies were highly integrated, while those between U.S. and Western European operations were considerably less so, if at all.

Notwithstanding that empirical evidence tends to support the contention that subsidiary management does indeed possess sufficient authority to negotiate a labor agreement and to make commitments, the labor side may still be justified in their fears that they are not confronting the locus of "power" within the management structure. Budget decisions are made between parent and subsidiary and these in turn temper the subsidiary's response to union demands. Also, investment decisions are made at the parent level without that level being directly impressed with a union interest. Labor's frustration here must invariably be exacerbated too when subsidiary management uses the dual sourcing threat to counter labor's bargaining demands, and yet labor cannot get to the locus of that dual sourcing decision.

## Inadequacy of Data

The ILO reported that a general conclusion, from the workers' representatives at its 1972 tripartite (*i.e.,* government, management, worker representatives) meeting on MNCs and social policy, was that MNCs' transfer pricing practices affect collective bargaining when rendering a subsidiary "unprofitable," a situation used by subsidiary management to counter union claims for wage and other improvements (ILO, 1973). This is true, of course, only to the extent that a subsidiary actually claims during bargaining that lack of profits does not allow for such improvements. Evidence on this is difficult to obtain or is thin at best since: (1) managements do not like to discuss specific bargaining tactics in a public forum; and (2) in continental Europe, wages and other improvements are frequently negotiated within the context of employer associations or are legislated and thus rendered irrelevant to any management problems regarding the subsidiary's "ability to pay." The Jedel and Kujawa (1976) survey of foreign multinationals in the United States provides some evidence on this question. They found that in virtually every case wages at the U.S. subsidiary "were determined by examining competitive wages in the particular local labor market . . ."

The union concern here, though, should not be dismissed out of hand. In the event of plant closures, cost comparisons among different operations are usually the determining variable. Transfer prices, management and technical fees and royalties do affect profitability comparisons and, thus, the disinvestment decision. That decisions in these areas are made without some union influence, and that these decisions so greatly affect workers' interests, must be unacceptable to labor. Also, U.S. unions have been very much accustomed to bargaining in the United States on, among other things, "ability to pay" (Marshall and Marshall, 1971). The "ability to pay" criterion has obviously become more complicated, and its validity with unions is perhaps suspect, because of the international expansion of U.S. enterprise.

Similarly, other data and information felt by unions to be of value in formulating their demands and strategies vis-à-vis MNCs have become much more cumbersome to accumulate and keep current. The MNCs hesitate to furnish any information on their operations unless clearly required to do so by law or by the power balance at the bargaining table. For example, the International Union of Electrical Workers (IUE), during the 1969 negotiations with the General Electric Company (GE), proposed a contract clause prohibiting GE from relocating U.S. operations to any foreign facility. In support of this proposal, the IUE requested company-provided information on location of foreign plants, identification of work performed therein, and operating data (sales volume, pay rates, etc.) on these plants. The company refused to supply this information and a subsequent unfair labor practice charge filed by the IUE was ultimately denied by the General Council of the National Labor Relations Board (NLRB).[12]

Kassalow (1976) reports unions rank highly their concern over "lack of sufficient information about most multinational companies." To illustrate, he quotes a Dutch trade union leader (Spit, 1973) that unions' "weakness" vis-à-vis the MNCs was "due in particular to our defective knowledge of the structure of these corporations, . . . their decision making centres and . . . procedures, [and], criteria that prevail in management and long term planning."

Attempts to fill this information void have been initiated within the labor side. Indeed, data accumulation is one of the major functions of the International Trade Secretariats (ITS).

# UNION RESPONSES TO THE MNC

The implication of the preceding evidence favors the view that the rise and operations of MNCs indicate a shift in the balance of power away from labor and in favor of the MNC. Of equal significance for understanding the response patterns of labor, the latter clearly *perceives* this erosion of its bargaining power as being caused by characteristics unique to the MNC. Motivated and influenced by these perceptions, labor has defined and is continuing to develop specific responses to redress the power imbalance. These responses have been mainly along two lines: multi-union, transnational action by unions and groups of unions; and actions aimed at adjusting the national environment regulating operations or decision-making structures of the enterprises operating therein.[13]

*The Union Response at the Transnational Level*

Thus far the most distinguishing characteristic of transnational industrial relations has been its misinterpretation by those concerned with understanding it. This had admittedly been caused, at least in part, by the adversary positions necessarily assumed by both management and labor. Also, labor, which has taken on the challenge to construct a transnational structure of operational significance sufficient to meet the challenge of the

MNC, must necessarily be somewhat opportunistic in its approach. It needs to be ready to capitalize on whatever opportunities might come along to develop and promote its institutions, values, or "press." Thus, the adversary nature of the parties and labors' "opportunistic responses" have created complex and allegedly confusing patterns of behavior. To illustrate, Cox (1976) writes ". . . labor today has managed to generate only a confused, partial and lopsided response to the multinational corporation." The remainder of this section suggests that Cox's conclusion is inaccurate.

Studies and published observations on the behavior allegedly evident between labor and the MNCs at the transnational level have perhaps contributed more to the advancement of confusion than they have to clarification. To illustrate, Richard Robinson (1973) presents as examples of "multinational labor negotiations": a situation where the UAW "coached" a local union dealing with Ford Motor in Peru; a "meeting" between Philips' management and some of the unions representing its employees in different European countries; and the "working out" by unions representing Saint-Gobain workers in nine countries of a "common strategy." As for such examples of "multinational labor negotiations," one must wonder what is meant by "coached"; how can the Philips' union meetings be characterized as "negotiations" when Dronkers (1975), the Philips' Industrial Relations Director, has clearly indicated that they could hardly be considered as such; and how can "strategy harmonization" be equated to "negotiations"?

The 1975 Conference Board report, *The Multinational Union Challenges the Multinational Company* (Hershfield, 1975), portrays similar misunderstanding. For example, it empirically profiles companies that had been "targets of multinational union actions" as those that are larger and "more multinationally involved." Certainly a firm with no multinational operations would hardly be the objective of any transnational union action. Likewise, the larger a firm's international operations, the greater the propensity for it to be involved in international trade union problems and approaches. The conclusion, then, relating the extent of international operations to the incidence of trade union "interactions" at the international level is basically tautological! Also, the identification by the Conference Board of these larger, more internationally involved companies as "target companies" implies that transnational trade union actions are more deliberately planned and coordinated than they really are. Deliberate strategy may be evident in a few instances, such as the 1972–1973 Ford Motor Company case involving the International Metalworkers' Federation (Kujawa, 1975a, p. 148), but the more useful model involves trade union reactions in response to specific initiatives taken by MNCs, such as the Enka plant closings in Belgium, Holland, and West Germany

in 1975 (NYT, 11/2/75). The situation is more appropriately concep-
tualized in terms of Dunlop's (1958) "systemic" model where a group of
participants is identified, each with set objectives and certain tools available, and operating within complex and interactive environments while
seeking some optimum posture or position in light of the circumstances.
Thus, the origins of specific labor/MNC interactions may reflect more
fortuitousness than long-range planning or deliberation.

### International Labor Structure

The key international labor groups directly concerned with the MNCs
are the various International Trade Secretariats (ITSs), whose member-
ships consist of national unions from various countries. Most ITSs of
consequence, in turn, are affiliated with the International Confederation
of Free Trade Unions (ICFTU), an organization of national confedera-
tions generally espousing free trade unionism. The ITSs are organized
into departments reflecting different industrial sectors, and several of
these departments, in turn, have recently developed "world company
councils" bringing together delegates from member unions representing
workers at different subsidiaries of the same MNC.[14]

The International Metalworkers Federation has established world company councils for companies in the automotive and electronics industries,
such as Ford, General Motors, Volkswagen, and General Electric. (At its
most recent world congress, it adopted a resolution calling for creation of
world company councils in the other major industrial sectors it represented, such as iron, steel and non-ferrous metals; shipbuilding; and
mechanical engineering). Saint-Gobain and Michelin councils have been
formed by the Federation. Other examples could be cited. The objectives
of the councils are quite similar, and could be typified by those originally
expressed by the world auto councils: recognition of the right to organize,
upward harmonization of wages and social benefits, adequate relief time,
the vacation bonus, suitable pension levels, worker protection against
"technological obsolescence," and reduction of working time (UAW,
1966). These ambitious goals have required a varied set of activities and a
substantial commitment of resources.

### International Labor Activities

Transnational trade union activities, implemented to a considerable degree through the world company councils, can best be categorized in
terms of four discrete objective areas:

1. *Information*—generating and sharing industrial relations data among
different national/local unions.

2, *Intervention*—directly presenting and promoting positions of union interest to MNC officials on worker-related issues or problems in the subsidiaries.

3. *Involvement*—participating in transnational collective bargaining.

4. *Intimidation*—managing (and perhaps even manipulating) external relations, especially those with MNCs, in support of other objectives.

The "information" objective is one of the most important ones to the world company councils and the other units within the ITSs. Implementing it involves the development of both interpersonal ties among the representatives of different national unions, as well as data accumulation via surveys. The councils and ITS departments hold periodic meetings to exchange information on conditions of interest in the various countries; to focus on particular "problems," if necessary, and to develop some form of coordination in terms of national strategies and goals. For example, the first world conference of the auto councils (Detroit, 1966) included "country" reports by union delegates from each country represented, such as the "current situation of the Japanese automobile industry"; working party summaries on specific auto companies, such as General Motors, where topics covered included GM's organization structure, production by country, and specific working conditions by country; and recommendations on the need for some form of survey research on employment practices, leadership training, and development of an organization to provide solidarity support when requested (International Metalworkers Federation, 1966).

Regarding data accumulation and dissemination, examples include the preparation and publication of "regional reports" containing detailed narratives on the "state" of the automobile industry in various parts of the world (International Metalworkers Federation, 1968). A "Survey of Latin American Auto Contracts (1970)" was prepared by the United Auto Workers Federation for use by all affiliates. It covered responses from worker representatives in six Latin American countries and listed contract (or legally required) provisions affecting workers across 132 different topics. Subsequently, the world auto councils conducted and published a "Survey of Collective Bargaining Agreements in the Automobile Industry in North America, Europe and Australasia," covering 175 different topic areas listed in contracts (or required by law) at subsidiaries of twelve different MNCs operating in nineteen different countries.

These data and information are used by unions for both "offensive" and "defensive" reasons. The union can cite useful precedents of a condition or concession at one subsidiary to support its claim for like treatment at another subsidiary, or even at the parent company. For example, the Ford world auto council (UAW, 1966) called for "implementation throughout the world of the vacation bonus principle already conceded by the Big Three in certain countries." Viewed from a slightly different perspective, knowledge of company employment conditions in different countries enables a union to respond more forcefully to company resistance that the firm "in principle" cannot yield on a collective bargaining issue, such as, for example, salary status for production workers.

The "intervention" objective involves a direct contact between a union representative and MNC management over specific employee or labor relations problems or onerous management practices at the subsidiary level. Examples of intervention include a 1975 situation involving General Motors and the closing of a plant in Bienne, Switzerland. Representatives of the International Metalworkers Federation's Automotive Department charged the closure was done without advance notice. A union-related information source reported the UAW intervened with the GM corporate industrial relations staff, which, in return, requested the GM Board Chairman to reconsider the decision and suggested that directors of GM Overseas Operations meet with Swiss union officials (ILO, 1975).

Numerous other examples could be noted here. But there is a problem in finding "clean" examples. Frequently union claims of "success" in intervention are made, but it is often difficult to pin down the causal link between the union action and the resolution of the problem. A case in point involved Coca Cola in Italy and the International Union of Food and Allied Workers' Associations (IUF) in 1971:

> . . . the IUF requested affiliates to support Italian unions . . . protesting against the closing of a Coca Cola plant . . . Affiliates from some 11 countries are reported to have indicated their support by intervening with management at their own Coca Cola plants. The IUF Danish food affiliate sent financial aid to the workers. Food unions affiliated to the French CGT [i.e., Confédération Générale du Travail, a communist union] and the Hungarian union trade centre, neither affiliated to the IUF, are also reported to have indicated their support of the Italian strikers. The IUF adds that after some drawn out negotiations, with the help of intervention by the Italian government, most of the jobs affected were saved. (ILO, 1973)

This situation was presented to the ILO by union representatives, apparently as an example of successfully coordinated action by an ITS, in this case the IUF. Any positive judgment on the cause-effect relationship linking the IUF to a solution of the problem, at least in light of information on the case as it stands above, must certainly be suspect.

Nonetheless, "successes" in interventions seem especially important to international union activities. They represent (alleged) concrete examples of the value of transnational action and solidarity to union members. Thus, they are useful for internal propaganda purposes.

"Involvement" means collective bargaining with an MNC on a transnational scale. Its most distinguishing feature, aside from the case of U.S.-Canada, is that it has yet to occur. There is a problem, though, in getting people to believe this—partly because unions manage well the "intimidation" function, and partly because the "press" likes to present eye-catching headlines. On the latter point, *Business Week* (10/27/75) reported on the 1975 Enka plant closings under a caption "Multinationals: Bargaining on an International Scale," and the *New York Times* (11/2/75) captioned it "A Multinational vs. United Unions." The facts are that Enka refused in the end to meet with union representatives and implemented the plant closings via legally required meetings with the works councils in each country (NYT, 2/1/76).

Levinson (1973, p. 11) at the ICF appears to be at the leading edge in terms of "intimidation," or the management of external relations. He engineered a self-proclaimed breakthrough in dealings with Saint-Gobain in 1969—an event that, he touted, ". . . opened a new era of industrial relations by showing what might be achieved . . . through international labor solidarity." Subsequent research has shown that the "success" Levinson claimed was more the result of nationally related events, fortuitous in terms of timing, with the outcome determined by a set of different, and substantially nationally determined, actions.[15] In a 1974 press release, Woodcock of the UAW called for "multinational collective bargaining," a "new system of industrial relations" based on "the fact that labor relations policies of its subsidiary companies anywhere are set at the multinational corporation's central headquarters" (UAW, 1974). Interestingly, during the same week as the Woodcock statement, the International Metalworkers Federation coordinator of the world auto councils stated that *he* did not know of any specific instances of actual mutlinational collective bargaining (Bendiner, 1974). There apparently have been no instances of it since.

Indeed, recent interviews with other U.S. labor leaders suggest the transnational bargaining objective is moving down on their priority scales, because of the lack of "successes" in this area to take home to (U.S.) union members. As one representative put it to the author: "We've built up the expectations of the 'rank and file' on the potential of transnational bargaining, but never delivered."

However, it is not enough to note that transnational bargaining has never occurred, while some labor leaders are downplaying it and others continue to hold it out as the "key" to future success. The fact is that transnational bargaining ("involvement") is impossible to realize given the nature of the economic, legal and cultural relationships in today's world.[16]

If transnational bargaining were to evolve, it would have to be realized in the form of deterministic labor-management negotiations at the international level on specific subjects, such as wages and overtime premiums. The expectation of such then must turn on the suitability of these subjects to "transnational determination." A rather extensive inquiry (Kujawa, 1975a) on this question, covering such items as direct wages, supplements, job classifications, vacations, holidays, and the like, as to their potential for transnational determination across only three countries (Great Britain, West Germany, and France), concluded that legal, structural and other circumstances peculiar to each country precluded ". . . meaningful transnational bargaining resulting in the determination of substantive issues."'Other variables, germane to the *international* dimension of transnational bargaining, such as productivity differentials among countries and their effects on exchange rates, were also identified as obstacles to the international standardization of wages, benefits, etc. via transnational bargaining.

There appear to be important legal barriers perculiar to U.S. unions and MNCs that preclude transnational bargaining, or substantial actions necessary for the success of such "involvement." Woodcock (1974) observes, for instance, "Some countries, the U.S. among them, have laws prohibiting secondary boycotts, which would include strikes in sympathy with workers abroad." Also, citing the IUE-GE situation as a case in point, Rowan and Northrup (1975) contend

> If . . . the I.U.E., or any other group, would attempt to alter the bargaining structure with General Electric by insisting that G.E. bargain about matters pertaining to plants not included within the I.U.E. bargaining unit. . ., such an attempt would be contrary to the court order which has compelled General Electric to admit outsiders chosen by the I.U.E. to the bargaining sessions. For the law . . . requires that the outsiders maintain the legal fiction that they are I.U.E. representatives and that they bargain only for matters pertaining to the I.U.E. bargaining unit. If, at an I.U.E.-G..E. bargaining session, union representatives persisted in attempting to bargain about, for example, labor conditions in . . . plants in Colombia, the company could not only refuse to bargain about the matter, but would be able to bring a refusal to bargain in good faith charge against the American union involved.

In addition to the above considerations is the question of the legality of U.S. union actions that might result in "trade-offs" in benefits being made between U.S. workers and workers in foreign countries. The U.S. union is characterized in law as the "exclusive bargaining agent" for bargaining unit members. To the extent it bargained for increased benefits for nonunit members at the "expense" of unit members, the union may be in violation of the law for failing to represent the employees it is charged with exclusively representing. At least it may be liable to such a charge, especially if some unit member disapproved of the union action.

The conclusion from all this is that, presently, significant barriers exist to the transnational determination of subjects generally considered *conditions* of employment, especially as it involves U.S. unions and MNCs. But what of the *fact* of employment? Several recent cases of union-company interactions at the international level identify the fact of employment as the ultimate issue. The (1973) Ford (Kujawa, 1975b) and (1967–1975) Philips (Dronkers, 1975) cases seem especially illustrative. In each of these, the topic for discussion eventually devolved to new investment decisions—at which point the MNCs refused further meetings with the international union groups. The recent ILO (1975) report also identifies MNCs' investment decisions as ". . . a great source of concern" of the union representatives queried.

To a certain extent conditions of employment are locally applied and are currently subject, to some degree, to a union jurisdiction and interest. Problems on the labor side over conditions of employment are thus not as compelling as those over the fact of employment. Since neither national nor transnational bargaining has been effective in dealing with foreign investment decisions by MNCs, labor has supported alternative approaches to controlling, or sharing in, decisions of this subject.

*International Labor Activities and the U.S. National Interest*

A judgment as to whether or not international labor activities are beneficial to the U.S. national interest would depend on just which activity was being considered and how one defined the national interest. The question of how collective bargaining and U.S. MNCs affect the national interest has yet to be debated by any U.S. public body. For instance, Congress has neither passed nor considered legislation to codify or express the U.S. national interest relative to international trade union activities. This begs caution and implies conservative decision rules for present purposes. U.S. law clearly recognizes and protects the institution of the trade union. A more debatable issue in national policy is whether net economic or other social benefits should accrue to United States citizens or institutions because of the international actions by U.S. labor.

The "information" and "intervention" functions appear to be supportive of the U.S. national interest. Information is used to strengthen the capability of the union to bargain more intelligently at the domestic level. It also helps, perhaps frequently in only a minor way, to offset the imbalance of bargaining power attributable to the availability of full information on operations for the MNC side, and less information available for the labor side. "Intervention," to the extent it results in the correction of individual grievances based on legal, contractual, or socially unacceptable improprieties, also appears consistent with the national interest. This implies that few or no costs are involved for the U.S. economy or industrial relations as management moves to resolve these grievances.

An evaluation of "intimidation" relative to the national interest must turn on the nature of what the intimidation is intended to support. Intimidation in support of intervention may well be consistent with the national interest, for example.

"Involvement" is the one function difficult to support when measured against the national interest. Transnational bargaining, which definitionally involves trade-offs in terms of the allocation of employment benefits among societies, implies potential sacrifices by American workers to benefit foreign workers, or, depending on the specific trade-offs involved, subsidization of American workers by foreign workers. While such trade-offs may possibly be linked to institutional stability (i.e., of governments, unions, or enterprises), this appears dubious at best. Transnational bargaining, as it results in upward harmonization of real wages and benefits across national boundaries, must either make the product of U.S. workers less competitive in world markets, implying U.S. job losses, or contribute to U.S. inflation. Neither outcome is commonly judged in the national interest. Transnational bargaining on investment decisions may move these decisions quite a distance from the commercial, financial, and technological fundamentals upon which they would otherwise be based. It injects a transnational political component into the location of investment, and reduces the role of economic optimization, cost minimization, and the like. Finally, activities essential to the conduct of transnational bargaining appear contrary to present U.S. law. For example, U.S. strikes in support of benefits for foreign workers are likely illegal as indicated above.

*The Union Response at the National Level*

Very little has been done by U.S. unions at the national level in response to MNC operations. There have been but a few instances of unions seeking to bargain collectively over some international aspect of a U.S. MNC's operations (Kujawa, 1972). The aforementioned situation, where the IUE sought unsuccessfully in its 1970 contract talks to limit GE's right to transfer work from its U.S. plants to foreign plants, is one case in point. Interestingly, the IUE did not bring up this issue again in either its 1973 or 1976 contract talks.

Just prior to the 1970 Ford-UAW contract negotiations, the union raised the issue of the foreign sourcing of Pinto engines and gear boxes and how this practice affected "new employment opportunities" and the "possible loss of employment." Ford denied the validity of the union's contentions.[17] During the 1976 UAW contract negotiations, the union again raised the foreign sourcing issue. Specifically questioned were the

U.S. employment effects of the practice itself, and the issue of control of work traditionally performed by UAW members (Stillman, 1976). At the time of writing, the UAW had apparently not pressed this specific issue further.

Some unions have taken positions on U.S. public policy issues vis-à-vis the MNCs, but this type of effort has been mainly within the purview of the AFL-CIO (1974 and 1976). Actions by the AFL-CIO to propose alternate policies to existing ones, or to policies sought by other groups in the American society, will not, for purposes of this analysis, be judged as supportive of or contrary to the public interest. Instead, these are viewed as part of the process by which society settles upon or determines its national interest.


# A SUGGESTED PUBLIC POLICY ALTERNATIVE TO PRESENT U.S. LABOR LAW

Several conclusions may be restated. Substantial evidence suggests that the rise of the MNC has shifted the balance of power in collective bargaining toward the MNC on certain specific issues involving the international dimensions of MNC operations. Of perhaps even greater significance, unions *perceive* that MNCs have eroded their bargaining power. Based on these perceptions, unions have sought to reestablish the power balance by creating a transnational union structure of sufficient strength to meet the MNC "head on." However, union success in international activities must be limited to areas other than transnational bargaining over the conditions or fact of employment. Transnational bargaining is virtually impossible given the variations in laws, cultures, workers' interests, productivity levels, etc., across the different countries. And transnational bargaining over the fact of employment is improbable, since unions presently have little power to compel MNCs to bargain on investment decisions. The limitations in transnational bargaining lead to an interest and concern over other union approaches to the MNC that can be taken at the national level, presuming that the establishment and maintenance of a balance of power between labor and management is identified within the national interest.

One possible approach involves a significant modification of current U.S. labor law. It might involve an amendment to the National Labor Relations Act (NLRA) mandating that management and union representatives meet and discuss the economic factors involved in an intended management decision (1) to establish a new foreign facility to serve the U.S. market or to serve a foreign market currently being supplied from U.S. plants; or (2) to have an existing overseas subsidiary commence to serve the U.S. market or a third market previously served from U.S. plants. Before discussing the merits of this proposal, it would be best to further explain what it means.

The legal requirement would be to "meet and discuss," not codetermine. Management retains the initiative and the right to invest overseas or to serve the U.S. or other markets with exports from foreign subsidiaries. It would be compelled to present to the union its tentative conclusions on the economic and competitive factors affecting the proposed decision. It would also be compelled to allow the union the opportunity to respond to these conclusions, possibly in such a way that the economic factors favoring the initial conclusion might be altered, thus saving U.S. jobs while alleviating the competitive pressures on the firm. Clearly, the interest of the union would be only in preserving jobs for its unit members. Lack of expansion of unit employment resulting from a management decision on foreign investment would *not* be a mandatory "meet and discuss" issue under this proposal.

The legal requirement to "meet and discuss" implies good faith. Thus, since management is the initiator of the proposed action, it would be required to supply information to the union sufficient for the union to understand the intention and effects of the proposed management action. Only then could the union intelligently respond. The management would have to maintain an open receptivity to counterproposals from the union should it seek to alter the relevant economic conditions. If there is disagreement between management and labor as to what constitutes the "necessary facts," the union side might be permitted to file an unfair labor practice charge with the NLRB. The NLRB, or possibly eventually the courts, would decide what constitutes "necessary facts." Similarly, possible dilatory tactics by the union could be overcome by a management initiative.

This proposal is not unlike some interpretations of present U.S. law circumscribing management's right to make unilateral subcontracting decisions (Kujawa, 1972). Key factors in this interpretation include the Supreme Court's decision in the "Fibreboard" case as it interpreted section 8 (d) of the NLRA (relative to subcontracting) to mean that the legal requirement to bargain over conditions of employment ". . . plainly covers termination of employment which . . . necessarily results from the contracting out of work performed by members of the . . . bargaining unit."[18] In implementing this decision, the NLRB in the "Town & Country" case noted ". . . the elimination of unit jobs for economic reasons was a 'term or condition of employment' over which an employer must first bargain with a designated union. . . ." The board explained subsequently that this decision did not constrain management from making economically motivated decisions, but rather that a mutual decision that preserves both a competitive enterprise while preserving unit work can be beneficial to both management and labor.[19]

Skeptics of this proposal may contend it merely legitimizes the union's "whipsawing" of management, a tactic discussed earlier as inimical to labor when practiced by management. This is not the case. "Whipsawing" is often a *fait accompli* with no room for negotiating. This is not envisioned in the present case. Others may argue the proposal is too idealistic, since unions never "bargain down." This is untrue. In 1976, Mansfield Tire secured an agreement with the United Rubber Workers to limit the pay for "downtime" at the plant to 85 percent of "regular" rates, rather than the 100 percent previously paid. The company insisted on this concession so that it could continue to operate an otherwise uncompetitive, aging plant (*Wall Street Journal,* 10/12/76). Similar cases have been reported involving companies across a variety of industries—Frigidaire, Royal Typewriter, McCall Printing Co., P. Ballantine and Sons, and Firestone Tire (*Wall Street Journal,* 11/26/72). Others may feel this proposal holds no benefit for consumers and is thus not a "preferred" solution. This position begs the question of whether or not firms pass on lower costs to consumers in the form of lower prices. The question, in turn, is irrelevant to the proposal, since the "meet and discuss" initiative occurs after management's initial perception of a "need" for the foreign investment. The firm can or cannot pass on cost savings to consumers under either the domestic or foreign production alternative.

Supporters of this proposal see it as a way to enhance productivity of American workers. It may be seen by some as a better alternative to what is felt to be the protectionist proposals of the AFL-CIO to limit imports and to control outgoing investments and technology transfers of MNCs. Some may see it as a preferred alternative to the German and Swedish models for worker participation in a local firm's decisions on foreign investment. While the proposal to "meet and discuss" is in line with present worldwide trends in granting workers a stronger role in management decisions affecting them, in the situation envisioned management still retains the initative, and ultimately its decision will turn on the best set of economic options available to it. Also, the union's interest and jurisdiction is limited to cases defined by a specific set of parameters justifying a direct union involvement. Finally, some may see it as a way to "internalize" the provision of adjustment assistance by reducing the need for governmentally derived funds and the social cost involved in determining the application of such funds. In the proposed situation, "adjustment" would be accomplished by all workers taking "less," at least for some interim period, rather than by a few workers losing jobs, with all the social problems that may imply.

The main feature of the proposal, however, is that it raises a fundamental question that is long overdue for serious debate. Are U.S. labor-management relations to be embraced and controlled within the context of a political consensus; or will time and events be allowed to succeed in apparently destroying what had been a political consensus of the past?

# FOOTNOTES

1. The quotation is taken from the NLRB (1971, p. 1).
2. *National Labor Relations Act,* Title I, Sec. 101, Sec. 1, "Findings and Policies."
3. It is important to recall the focus is on the bargaining power relationship. Other environmental conditions affecting the suitability of the labor response (such as transnational collective bargaining) in reestablishing a power balance, are discussed later in the paper. The present discussion assumes the viewpoint is from the United States. Note, too, the six allegations listed may be similar to those possibly raised regarding operations of multiplant or conglomerate firms in the United States. This does not deny the appropriateness of the allegations to MNCs, however. Indeed, since MNCs function in legal environments outside that of the United States where U.S. unions do not benefit from a legal recognition or prescription on organizing, the allegations (if true) seem much more compelling in the MNC case.
4. U.S. House of Representatives (1970, p. 595). The development of the specific job loss number is described in Goldfinger (1973, p. 35).
5. Dewald (1975, p.4). The Trade Act limits adjustment assistance to workers displaced from jobs where increases of imports "contributed importantly" to the job-loss. Interestingly, this link is apparently impossible given Dewald's own conclusions. See U.S. House of Representatives (1974) Title II, "Relief from Injury Caused by Import Competition," Chapter 2, "Adjustment Assistance for Workers."
6. For a critical review of these studies, see Jedel and Stamm (1973).
7. Since the focus is the "bargaining unit," this conclusion is relevant only at unionized plants or other facilities, and reflects the view that incidence of unionization is lower among "headquarters staff" and professional employees than among production/blue-collar workers.
8. In fact, financial inflows are not necessarily cut off during a strike. Firms still sell to the market from finished goods inventories. However, such inventories are not infinite and need eventually to be replenished. This situation exists whether the firm is an MNC or not. As such, the "inventory" problem cannot be used to differentiate between MNCs and non-MNCs in terms of the issue under discussion.
9. Kujawa (1971). Since this report, Ford initiated a U.S.-Western Europe-Canada production integration scheme for its Pinto automobile.
10. Nearly 40 percent of the firms interviewed, however, had never taken a U.S. strike. The question of dual sourcing to break a strike was thus one of conjecture. Also, several of the firms reported there was no capability outside the United States possessed by the foreign multinational parent to produce for the U.S. market. The shifting production "option" was thus not relevant.
11. Woodcock (1974). An executive of the Ford Motor Company denied the factual accuracy of Woodcock's observation.
12. This proposal was contained in a letter from the Assistant General Counsel of the IUE to the National Labor Relations Board, Region 2 (New York), dated December 12, 1969. The IUE requests for information are delineated in a letter from the Chairman, IUE-GE Conference Board, to the Manager of Employee Relations at GE, dated August 26, 1969. The

decision is "General Electric Company," Case No. 2-CA-11,911, National Labor Relations Board (Region 2). (The original decision was conveyed in a letter from the NLRB Regional Director to the IUE, dated July 9, 1970, and was subsequently upheld later that year by the NLRB General Counsel.)

13. There is a third-type response involving multi-union, transnational action focusing on political action, such as the role of the European Trade Unions Congress in the development of social policy in the European Economic Community. This type response is important, but is not discussed in the present analysis where the emphasis is more on the United States situation.

14. For a brief overview of the "international union structure" and more specific data on the development of the International Metalworkers' Federation, see Kassalow (1975).

15. See Hershfield (1975, p. 28) and Northrup and Rowan (1974 and 1974b).

16. The present analysis does not consider the potential for transnational bargaining on a regional level, such as within the European Economic Community (EEC). For conflicting views on the potential success of transnational bargaining in the EEC, see Roberts (1973) and Frerk (1974).

17. These statements occurred in an exchange of letters between UAW and Ford vice presidents in June 1970.

18. *Fibreboard Paper Products Corp. v. NLRB,* 379 U.S. 203 (1964).

19. *Town and Country Mfg. Co.,* 136 NLRB 1022 (1962).

# COMMENT

## C. FRED BERGSTEN*

*The Issue*

Labor in the United States has four distinct concerns over the multinationalization of business: loss of jobs, redistribution of income in favor of capital, ideological and institutional practices of the firms (such as their alleged proclivity to favor countries which ban or severely limit unionization), and erosion of their bargaining position in labor-management relations. Kujawa focuses on the last of these issues, and has disaggregated the "collective bargaining" concern in an extremely useful way. The labor arguments are unpersuasive, however, in trying to establish that major problems result and that U.S. labor law has therefore become outmoded.

The first contention is that union membership, and hence bargaining strength, has been reduced by foreign direct investment by American multinationals. Even if it is true that white-collar jobs have increased as a result of such investment, however, one cannot thereby infer that blue-collar jobs have been lost. Gross losses of some blue-collar jobs may have been offset by gross gains of other blue-collar jobs. The data on the net

*U.S. Treasury Department

effects of foreign direct investment on American jobs are simply too uncertain to support the conclusion that bargaining units have declined in
size as a result.[1]

Empirically, some of the strongest international threats to unionized
workers have in fact come in industries with very low levels of foreign
direct investment. The most notable include textiles, footwear, steel, and
glass. Conversely, U.S. labor is demonstrably strong in some highly mul-
tinationalized industries (such as autos). There is no clear correlation
between the activity of American multinationals and the strength of U.S.
Labor.

Second, Kujawa notes the view that unions are weakened by their
inability to shut down the total world output of individual multinational
enterprises. It is true that a U.S. strike seldom, if ever, halts the entire
global operation of a firm. The workers would certainly be stronger if they
could do so. But it is not clear how severely, if at all, their position is
weakened as a result. The most important consideration for U.S. labor is
that only a tiny share of foreign production of the firms is (or can be)
exported to the United States. Hence, there is little threat to their U.S.
strikes from the foreign operations of American multinationals.

Indeed, the multinational could be *more* vulnerable than the purely
national firm to national labor disputes. To the extent that the firm is at all
integrated across national borders, it can be jeopardized in several senses.
Corporate goals of portfolio diversification (via geooraphical spread), and
raising or maintaining market share in a variety of countries, suffer from
such disputes. Managers of adversely affected foreign subsidiaries, and of
international divisions, will pressure management of the struck component to yield. It is simply impossible to render an *a priori* judgment as
to whether multinationalization strengthens or weakens national labor,
particularly in a home country (the United States) which accounts
for far more sales for most firms than any other country in which they
operate.

Kujawa's third and fourth points, concerning "whipsawing" and international shifts in the locus of corporate production, are closely related and
indeed are variants of the issue just discussed. He recognizes that "convincing empirical evidence has yet to be developed" concerning the threat
of dual sourcing. Indeed, the bulk of foreign direct investment still aims at
selling in local markets. There are very few corporate networks in which
such sales can be quickly maintained from other components of the corporate family. Spare capacity of the right type seldom exists, and is almost always too costly to establish simply to cope with a single labor
dispute. In fact, Kujawa's report of his own earlier research (with Jedel)
reveals that American multinationals are frequently limited in their ability

to dual source, and thereby to whipsaw. So the practical importance of these contentions, too, remains to be demonstrated.

The unions are on stronger grounds in feeling that they possess inadequate data, and inadequate access to the real decision makers in the multinational enterprises, to effectively pursue their own interests. American unions, if they believe that foreign direct investment by American firms exports jobs from this country, should seemingly believe that the sharp surge in foreign direct investment in the United States by multinationals based in other countries imports jobs and is of benefit to them. Yet the AFL-CIO appears distinctly unenthusiastic about such investments, largely because they imply a need to negotiate with parent firms located outside the United States—and hence outside both the requirements of U.S. law (concerning data disclosure, for example) and the political influence of American labor. It is in these critical areas of data and decision-making, rather than in perceived threats of "runaway plants" and "production shifts to undercut strikes," that internationally immobile labor is truly at a disadvantage vis-à-vis internationally mobile capital and management.

## Labor's Response

Kujawa explicitly discusses only two potential responses by labor to the real and perceived problems posed for it by the multinational enterprise: international collective bargaining, which he views as "impossible" to realize, and changes in home-country labor laws. In additionn several of his comments imply that he might favor a third approach: some form of co-determination, in which workers share management responsibilities and hence deal directly with the whole range of labor problems.

In fact, however, four broad classes of response are available to national labor organizations. They can work both to enhance their own bargaining power and to reduce the bargaining power of the firms, and they can pursue each approach through both national and international means. Several specific steps are available within each of these four categories, as depicted in Table 2.1. U.S. labor has sought primarily to check the flexibility of the firms to invest abroad, via the Burke-Hartke bill in the early 1970s and efforts to increase U.S. taxation of foreign income in each of the last several pieces of tax legislation. It is hardly correct to say, as Kujawa does, that "very little has been done by U.S. unions at the national level in response to multinational enterprise operations."

I believe that Kujawa is also too negative in assessing the prospects for international coordination among national unions to deal with *some* of the more important collective bargaining issues.[2] The international trade sec-

*Table 2.1*    Alternative Strategies Available to Labor to Counter
Multinational Corporations

|  | Reducing the power of multi-national enterprises | Increasing the power of labor |
|---|---|---|
| By national steps | Burke-Hartke<br>Swedish requirement that Swedish firms observe high standards of labor in host countries to qualify for governmental investment insurance | Co-determination<br>Swedish requirement that labor approve foreign direct investment applications |
| By international steps | Codes/regimes to check "multinational enterprise abuses"<br>"International fair labor standards" | International collective bargaining |

retariats in Geneva already provide a good deal of data to their national constituents on the international performance of individual firms. To be sure, however, they are unlikely to cope very effectively with issues of job loss and other direct economic impacts.

For these purposes, labor has to rely on the same approach it used to achieve parity with management at the national level—influencing its own national governments. This was the avenue through which U.S. labor achieved minimum wage legislation, decent work standards, and the requirement that business bargain with it in good faith. Regarding foreign direct investment, one option is to seek legislation that would restrict the international activities of the firms; this has been the major thrust of American unions to date. Another is legislation that would inject labor into the boardrooms themselves; this has been the focus in Germany and other European home countries of multinationals. Swedish unions have pursued both approaches simultaneously.

Kujawa creatively suggests a new way by which U.S. labor could pursue its national option: amending the National Labor Relations Act to require management to "meet and discuss" foreign direct investment decisions. Despite his disclaimer, such an approach at least begins to approach codetermination; it sounds very much like the current Swedish system.[3] That need be no barrier to pursuing the idea, but its full implications should be recognized.

Any such approach toward codetermination, or indeed any movement toward effective international collective bargaining, raises one major policy issue: Would greater cohesiveness between management and labor foster the public interest or threaten it by replacing a present source of contervailing power with a joint strategy that would enhance the oligopoly power of each at the expense of consumer welfare? There are examples of the latter type of development from several specific national industries, even without any formal linkages *à la Mitbestimmung*. More research by labor experts is needed, of both the history of national developments and the international prospect, before such a course of action can be enthusiastically endorsed.

There are several other possible approaches to meeting labor's legitimate concerns about the activities of American multinationals. The United States should institute an "escape clause for foreign direct investment," which, like the traditional trade escape clause, would within a framework of freedom for international flows permit specific groups to avoid injury from specific transactions. One remedy, in cases where the injury contention was sustained, would be adjustment assistance of the type now used to deal with injury caused by increased imports.

To help such an approach to work effectively, the current provision of Section 283 of the Trade Act of 1974 should be made mandatory, as it was in the Senate version of the legislation. This provision calls for American multinationals to provide advance notification to their workers and the U.S. Government prior to a "transfer of production abroad," It would in fact provide a trigger for Kujawa's proposal that the firms be required to "meet and discuss" their foreign investment plans with the unions.

In addition to these steps, the United States should act to check foreign investments triggered solely by tax and other host-country inducements. It should also act against the "performance requirements" through which host countries shift jobs out of the United States (and other home countries) through such measures as value-added requirements and minimum export quotas. The best remedy for both sets of problems is negotiation of new international arrangements that would limit their use by agreement of the countries concerned. Before such arrangements can be put in place, however, the United States may need to act unilaterally against the practices of some host countries.[4]

# FOOTNOTES

1. Kujawa also errs in stating that studies by the Department of Commerce and several business groups "found that foreign direct investment resulted in a concurrent expansion of jobs in the United States." The studies *asserted* such a conclusion, but their *findings* were limited to correlations between rates of increase for domestic jobs and foreign investment. Such correlations are hardly surprising, since the multinationals are the largest and fastest-growing firms on virtually all economic criteria, and add little to the discussion of whether foreign direct investment increases or decreases the level of jobs in the United States.

2. For example, he argues against transnational labor bargaining, from the standpoint of the U.S. national interest, on the grounds that it would *reduce* the competitiveness of U.S. workers. The United States continues to pay the highest wages in most, though not all,

industries, so upward wage/benefit harmonization would *increase* U.S. competitiveness and create American jobs.

3. For example, under this system, Volvo workers fully agreed with the decision of Volvo management to invest in the United States, in contrast to the attitude of Volkswagen workers when faced with a similar situation.

4. These issues and policy recommendations are detailed in Bergsten et al. (1978).


# COMMENT

## RUDOLPH OSWALD*

*The Collective Bargaining Environment*

Collective bargaining takes place in an overall economic environment. Currently that environment has certain elements detrimental to collective bargaining. First of all, unemployment is still at recession levels of nearly 8 percent. Manufacturing employment is down 1.3 million from prerecession levels. This decline is not limited to one or two subsectors of manufacturing, but employment declines have appeared across the board (except for petroleum refining). Construction employment is down by 800,000 to approximately 20 percent below the prerecession levels. Transportation and communication employment is down by 200,000 from levels of two years ago. This is a depressing milieu for collective bargaining. The economy is not growing fast enough to provide jobs for the 1.8 million additional new entrants yearly that are seeking jobs. The unemployment level in October was unchanged from that experienced in January.

Secondly, U.S. economic policy encourages multinational operations by its tax and trade policy. Earnings of foreign subsidiaries are exempted from taxation until such time as they are brought back to the U.S.—and then the profits are further protected from any U.S. tax bite, as MNCs are entitled to a tax credit for any foreign taxes paid. Still another tax encouragement of MNCs is the Domestic International Sales Corporation (DISC) that permits corporations to spin off export subsidiaries in order to defer taxes on export profits. The Trade Act of 1974 also encourages MNCs to expand abroad. Thus the economic climate for bargaining with MNCs in the mid-1970s has been chilly toward unions, and warm and favorable toward MNCs.

Much of the Kujawa paper deals with the effects of multinational operations on bargaining power. This is an important and necessary focus in

*AFL–CIO

terms of effective bargaining; however, it may leave the impression that bargaining is purely an economic power relationship. While that is certainly a part of effective bargaining, it is not the only part of collective bargaining. One of the most important aspects of collective bargaining is its introduction into the workplace of a system of industrial jurisprudence. It assures the worker of his day in court. No longer can the employer take actions against an employee and be judge, jury, and prosecutor in carrying out disciplinary actions. The union has introduced an element of fair treatment. Under this system, the employer retains the role of policeman and prosecutor, but the grievance procedure, with its ultimate steps leading to arbitration, provides for a neutral judge and the union acts as defense counsel for the accused worker. I emphasize this aspect of collective bargaining because it represents not a cost item, but a changed relationship between employers and their employees. It is an important procedural element of collective bargaining in the American system.

*The Effects of MNCs on Bargaining Power*

Now let me address the author's basic analysis of the effects of MNCs on bargaining power. He lists six elements that impinge on union negotiating structure in relation to MNCs. Mr. Kujawa has indeed categorized some of the most serious obstacles thrown into the path of unions as they seek to represent their members in collective bargaining with MNCs. However, these obstacles need not necessarily be insurmountable, nor are they necessarily unique to MNCs. Nearly all of these elements also apply to many union negotiations with domestic conglomerate firms. Many of these same issues and questions could be raised in regard to the Steelworkers' negotiations with Jones and Laughlin, a subsidiary of LTV, or the Meatcutters' negotiations with Armour, a subsidiary of Greyhound, or the Bakery Workers' negotiations city by city with Continental Bakery, a subsidiary of ITT. Let me try to respond a little more directly to each of the six elements.

The first element deals with employment reduction in the parent company of MNCs. Certainly job security is a basic concern of workers. However, as I pointed out earlier, declining employment in the goods-producing industries is a matter of serious concern to unions, whether that decline in job opportunities is caused by a lack of overall demand in the economy or a change in demand for a specific product. Unions also recognize that employment effects flow from technological change as well as from imports. It does not seem worth quibbling over the exact magnitude that each of these factors contributes toward the decline in employment. Rather, the emphasis should be on how to mitigate each of these disemployment effects. Unions recognize that collective bargaining may address some of the symptoms related to disemployment, but the root causes need to be addressed by overall economic policy. Part of that policy approach must take into account the impact on domestic employment that occurs when an MNC moves its production abroad.

In terms of a particular bargaining situation, the threat to a specific bargaining unit of moving jobs can be just as serious when that job leaves the garment district of New York for the barrios of El Paso or Brownsville. Workers have seen their jobs shipped out before, and have not rolled over and played dead. Nor do they intend to now when the job is shipped to Haiti or Korea instead of El Paso or Brownsville. Clearly, for national public policy it makes a great difference whether the jobs go to another part of the country or abroad. For union policy generally, it also makes a difference. But in terms of bargaining, the key element is not the geographic location, but the underlying bargaining relationship.

The author's second element deals with the inability of the union to cut off all financial flows to an MNC during a strike. Certainly the union wants to bring such financial pressure on a company during a strike. For example, during the recent Ford Motor Company strike, no new autos were produced by that company for the duration of the strike. However, if the Meatcutters strike Armour, Greyhound continues to run its buses. When the Bakery Workers strike Continental Bakery in Chicago, they continue to work in Detroit, as that is a separate agreement, and clearly neither of these agreements have any effect upon Hartford Insurance Company, another subsidiary of ITT. Unions have won such domestic strikes and will continue to take this avenue when all methods for peaceful settlement have proved fruitless. Let me add parenthetically that strikes are the exception in American collective bargaining relationships. Less than 3 percent of all contract negotiations end up in a strike, and the total time lost because of strikes amounts to less than ½ of 1 percent of total working time. More work time is lost because of nonjob-related illness, or even alcoholism. Strikes are newsworthy because they are the exception rather than the rule. That does not mean that American workers are ready to give up their right to strike; rather they believe that this is a necessary, inherent right of free workers in a free country. Nor does it mean that the power to strike is not essential. It does mean that U.S. collective bargaining is based on many complex and pragmatic factors.

The third element deals with an MNC's ability to whipsaw a union into lower wages and fringes. Certainly some of these firms try to play this game —as if the unions somehow should equate wage rates and fringe benefits with labor costs. While the worker is interested in the amount of take-home pay he receives, that is not the only part of the labor cost equation. The other half of the equation that measures output per hour is just as important as the measure of hourly wage rates. The *New York Times* (10/29/76, p. D1) highlighted the experiences of an IUE-organized plant in Brooklyn that paid its workers $5 and $6 an hour and was able to compete successfully against similar firms in the Carolinas paying wages of only half that of the Brooklyn plant. The Brooklyn plant was able to pay the higher wages because of its greater productivity. I relate this little example to emphasize that few firms are willing to actually discuss labor costs rather than just wage rates. In terms of whipsawing unions, it isn't only MNCs that try this tactic, but every union firm tries to point out that some nonunion firms pay lower wages. Unions have never accepted that comparison as a basis for bargaining, and aren't about ready to accept that argument from MNCs. Just because a MNC pays 10 cents an hour to its Korean employees, nobody realistically expects U.S. employees to work for 10 cents an hour. Furthermore, an important element in the whipsawing of MNCs is not related to collective bargaining, but rather to the level of exchange rates. Unions have no control over these fluctuations.

The fourth element deals with production shifts to offset strike losses. Let me just say that this same problem exists domestically when a large employer is not totally organized by unions. For example, only 45 percent of the G.E. employees in the U.S. are represented by unions.

The fifth element deals with the locus of decision-making. This issue has plagued U.S. unions in negotiating with many U.S. firms, whether it is A & P with its thousands of stores nationwide, and its hundreds of separate collective bargaining agreements in various locations with such diverse unions as the Meatcutters, Retail Clerks, Teamsters, and Bakery Workers; or Martin Marietta with its activities in such diverse industries as cement manufacturing and aerospace. Similarly the question of locus of decision-making was central to the coordination efforts of some sixteen national unions in their bargaining with G.E. That coordination has been an effective tool in achieving breakthroughs at the bargaining table with G.E.

The author referred to the 1975 Conference Board study of MNCs. This study shows that MNCs control the labor relations of their subsidiaries either directly or indirectly through what they call "consultation" or "managing financial objectives." Whatever it's called, it is clear that the parent retains control over its subsidiary, and unions in collective bargaining will continue to try to establish structures to overcome this challenge to effective bargaining.

The sixth element is inadequacy of data. Again this is a matter of concern even in domestic negotiations. Corporations generally do not provide any data by product line, and balance sheets for conglomerates hide more than they tell. Generally unions are not provided with any detailed financial data, as companies are only required to produce such data if they argue inability to pay. As a result, few companies say they can't afford it, and thus ability to pay does not become a central issue of most negotiations. This doesn't mean that more information wouldn't be useful to collective bargaining. Rather most firms are reluctant to divulge detailed information about their finances, or about their operations.

To summarize, these six elements are indeed impediments to unions in their bargaining—they tend to tilt the power in bargaining toward employers—but they are not necessarily unique in bargaining with MNCs. Unions will certainly adapt some of the tenhniques of coordination used domestically in dealing with conglomerates to the international scene in dealing with MNCs. A few large industrial unions with industry-wide bargaining have more ability to meet some of these problems than smaller, weaker unions involved in only local agreements.

*Public Policy Alternatives*

However, the public policy alternative proposed by Mr. Kujawa seems to be too feeble a step to remedy the imbalance at the bargaining table. The proposal to "meet and discuss" is not strong enough to curb the establishment of a foreign subsidiary or the transfer of work. Early in his paper the author recognized the need of the parties to bargain from strength—but meeting and conferring isn't even bargaining—it is just window dressing. However, the proposal may have some kernels that should be explored further. Maybe the union should be given the power to bargain with a corporation over these issues of establishing a foreign subsidiary or the transfer of work. Then if the parties fail to reach agreement, the company would be barred from such transactions, unless the company could prove to a court that on balance the impact to the workers involved would be less severe than it would be to the company. Certainly this proposal of the author's—translated into real bargaining— should be explored further. In this connection it may be interesting to note that the Metalworkers Union in Germany negotiated a provision with Volkswagen that its new U.S. facility at New Stanton, Pennsylvania, will not export back to Germany without further consultation.

However, the policy proposals of Mr. Kujawa do not go far enough in another sense. They do not affect the underlying economic climate within which the bargaining takes place. In this respect I would like to bring to your attention, and seek your support, for the policy objectives of the AFL-CIO. These proposals as related to MNCs can be summarized as follows:

1. Regulation of the export of American capital and technology which results in the export of American jobs.

2. Repeal of provisions of the Trade Act of 1974 that encourage multinationals to expand abroad.

3. Regulation of foreign investment in strategic industries or investment that interferes with U.S. economic progress.

4. Reporting and monitoring of all international flows in and out of the U.S.

5. Repeal of Sections 806.30 and 807 of the Tariff Code, which encourage foreign production for shipment back to U.S. markets.

6. Elimination of the foreign tax credit, which provides U.S. companies with a dollar-for-dollar credit against their U.S. tax liabilities for their foreign tax and royalty payments.

7. Revocation of provisions for the deferral of tax payments on foreign-earned profits.

8. Establishment of a mechanism to regulate imports and exports.

Enactment of these programs as well as a general full employment program would help provide a favorable climate for collective bargaining in the U.S.

These comments have dwelled somewhat upon the general problems that unions have in negotiations. This emphasis is not to mitigate the importance of the issues involved in negotiating with MNCs, but rather to indicate that unions have long had experiences with some of these same problems. Unions will continue their struggle to overcome these obstacles and improve the lot of the workers they represent. Certainly if this nation subscribes to industrial democracy as well as political democracy, it must be concerned with programs that will protect and enhance the bargaining relationship.

# 3. COMPETITION AND MONOPOLY IN MULTINATIONAL CORPORATION RELATIONS WITH HOST COUNTRIES

Thomas G. Parry, UNIVERSITY OF NEW SOUTH WALES

## INTRODUCTION

The analysis of the effects of international direct investment in terms of its underlying determinants is not new. Thus the classical theory of international capital flows, an extension of classical investment theory across national boundaries, explains both the basis for and the effects of these capital flows in terms of the marginal rate of return on capital (e.g., Iversen, 1936; Ohlin, 1933). Capital will move between countries in response to international interest rate differentials, and the gains from such a movement arises from the resulting improvement in the global allocation of capital.

More recent discussions of the effects of direct international investment

Research in International Business and Finance, Vol. 1, pp. 63–100.
ISBN 0-89232-031-1

(e.g., McDougall, 1960) take a wider view of the relevant benefits of investment for both the home and host countries, but limit the analysis to the framework of perfect competition.[1] Thus McDougall argues that the effects of international investment include a more efficient use of capital globally with a positive net return to the home, investing country and a positive net return to the host country through increased returns to host-country factors. The host-country share of the gains from international investment can be increased via taxation of foreign investment incomes. The most important gains to the host country, according to McDougall, arise from higher tax revenue from foreign profits, and from economies of scale and external economies in general associated with direct investment subsidiaries.[2] Effects on the host country's terms of trade and balance of payments, at least over the longer term, are more problematic. The McDougall analysis does take some account of factors other than simply increased returns to capital in assessing the host-country impacts of international investment. This approach, however, is of limited use in considering the effects of MNC operations on the host economies in which MNCs operate.

The contemporary treatment of the international direct investment associated with the MNC sharply contrasts with earlier treatment of capital flows in terms of international interest rate differentials. International investment in particular, and the operations of MNCs in general, is more properly treated within the framework of imperfect competition. Indeed, it is possible to explain the major groups of international investment theories in terms of various market imperfections and restrictions, both national and international (e.g., Caves, 1974b, and Corden, 1974). Further, the nature of the effects of MNC operations on host economies can largely be explained in terms of those very market distortions that form the basis of international investment and much of the *raison d'être* of the MNC (Parry, 1972).

In terms of imperfect competition within both national and international markets, foreign direct investment can be seen as one of the alternative means of maximizing returns on a firm's assets (Hymer, 1960). In fact, the very evolution of direct investment from trade, especially in manufacturing, can be explained in terms of those market imperfections that affect the timing and location of international production within the product cycle (e.g., Vernon, 1966). The effects of international investment within an imperfect competition framework may be far removed from the optimum global allocation assumed in the classical approach.

A major variant of the industrial-organization or "monopoly advantage" approach pioneered by Hymer specifies technological superiority, rather broadly defined, as the particular asset that the firm exploits via international operations. Thus, the transfer of knowledge within the various parts of a global firm is the crux of the foreign direct investment process, and maximizing the economic rent on that knowledge is the aim of MNCs involved in direct investment operations.[3] There are likely to be considerable economies to the firm in transferring technology, which is costly to produce, within the global enterprise to maximize the returns on that technology (Baranson, 1969). Technology, then, becomes the basis of direct investment rather than just one of the characteristics of the "foreign investment package." And where there are limits on the separability of technology-based direct investment operations, the potential for exercising monopoly power becomes considerable (Vaitsos, 1970).

If we cannot consider the basis of international investment and the nature of MNC operations other than in a framework of imperfect competition, the question arises whether the effects of international investment, globally and on the host and home economies, are the same as in the McDougall-type perfect competition analysis. Are the benefits suggested by the extended classical analysis eroded when account is taken of the fact that the basis of international investment and the MNC operations is imperfect competition? This paper considers this question. In particular, if MNC activities are based on responses to and within imperfect markets, what are the effects on industry structure, conduct, and efficiency? Our concern is essentially with the impact of MNC operations on *host* economies, though there are also important implications for home countries (Horst, 1975a).

# EFFECTS OF INTERACTION

The characteristics of MNCs determine the nature of their effects on host countries. The MNC is a firm having operations in two or more countries on a scale so that growth and success depend on more than one nation, and whose major decisions are made on the basis of global alternatives. It is this global basis of decision making that largely determines the effects of interaction. Decisions within a subsidiary are made on the basis of global firm objectives, and a potential conflict with the perceived best interests of the host nation may result (Parry, 1973). To take one example, the restrictive export franchise may limit one subsidiary's freedom to compete in international markets consistent with some global objective of the MNC. Had the subsidiary the ability to successfully export in the absence of the restrictive franchise, there is arguably a conflict between national (host country) objectives and global (MNC) objectives. The restrictive export franchise is also an example of MNC conduct within the host country that entails adverse effects on industry performance. But one must be careful to distinguish the effects particular to a subsidiary of an MNC from effects that might well arise with any local firm, regardless of ownership (Dunning, 1974).

It may well be that anticompetitive effects are inherent in the very nature of oligopolistic decision making within the MNC (Hymer, 1970). A particularly interesting interpretation of the challenge to competition policy presented by the MNC (Smith, 1974) suggests that the potential conflict is implicit in the nature of MNC functions and operations. It is the power base of the MNC in its global operations, together with its functions of intrafirm and interfirm coordination, which creates monopoly power vis-à-vis the nation state. And to the extent that monopoly power is exploited, the benefits of direct investment from increased productivity and/or lower consumer prices may be eroded or transferred outside the host market.

Transfer pricing practices of the MNC represent a particularly important exercise of monopoly power. And documented evidence of transfer pricing practices and the attendant direct costs may be specifically explained in a theory of monopoly power inherent in MNC involvement in international investment.[4] Thus, transfer pricing in order to shift profits to lower tax subsidiaries, for example, will erode the returns to the host market from taxation. In addition, transfer pricing practices, as one example of the exercise of monopoly power, can lead to distortions in price signals and inefficient resource allocation within the host market. We will examine in greater detail below the conduct-performance effects associated with MNCs's monopoly power. The point to note is that the particular nature of the MNC can affect resource use and the distribution of the joint benefits between the host economy and the corporation.

*Evidence of Imperfect Competition*

There is evidence to support the monopolistic competition view of MNC international direct investment. Some analyses have emphasized the "band-wagon" behavior of MNC direct investment undertaken by international oligopolists (Knickerbocker, 1973, and Polk, Meister, and Veit, 1966). The Polk et al. study stresses the role of market position in the strategy of U.S. firms in their international investment commitments. Knickerbocker's more recent work provides an elaborate demonstration of band-wagon entry characteristics of U.S. multinationals as international oligopolists. Further, certain host country studies have confirmed the importance of monopolistic competition advantages in U.S. inward investments.[5]

On specific features of MNC subsidiaries that may relate to monopolistic or oligopolistic *structures,* there is further evidence supporting this interpretation of international investment. The evidence regarding the relative size of MNC affiliates in host economies, as one indicator of potential monopoly power, seems reasonably conclusive. The affiliates of U.S. enterprises in both developed and developing countries do seem to be significantly larger than domestically owned alternatives (Vernon, 1971a; Horst, 1973; Dunning, 1958). Indeed, the average sales of U.S.-based MNCs in developing nations is larger than in developed host nations (Vernon, 1972a). Further, the average size of all manufacturing MNC affiliates in Canada and Australia appears larger than non-MNCs or locally owned competitors (Rosenbluth, 1970; Parry, 1974b).

On the concentration of activity of the MNC, there is also evidence consistent with the oligopoly approach to international investment. Countries with significant penetration by MNCs, particularly in manufacturing and mining, usually find a high degree of concentration in certain sectors of the economy by foreign MNCs. In particular, MNC affiliates tend to concentrate in high growth, high technology, and export-oriented sectors of the economy (UN, 1973). The structure of those host industries in which MNCs cluster also tends to be highly concentrated, perhaps reflecting the structure of the home-country industry.[6] Indeed, one of the arguments related to the effects of MNCs's structure, performance, and efficiency is that MNC entry often creates adverse "branch-plant" structures within the host market, replicating the structure of the home-country industry. To the extent that foreign ownership is related to concentration in both host and home industries, there is an *a priori* explanation of structural effects. Even if the host industry structure is not highly concentrated, one may still argue that the affiliate's market power lies in being part of a wider, global network with access to those resources not available to local firms.

There is also considerable support for the particular type of imperfect competition associated with technological advantage in international investment. Advantages in technology, as measured by R & D expenditures or personnel, appear to explain both international trade and international investment by U.S. manufacturing MNCs.[7] There appear also to be connections between technology creation, again measured by R & D, and the industrial composition of U.S. direct investment in Europe (Dunning, 1970). The apparent technological basis of U.S. direct investment in Australian manufacturing is reasonably well established (Brash, 1966; Johns, 1967). From the point of view of international production in general, technology is related more strongly to exports *plus* local affiliate sales than to either alone (Horst, 1972a). Horst demonstrates that the apparent technological advantage of U.S. industries explains *both* exports to and affiliate production in the Canadian market, but explains the combination even better.

*Proprietary Technology and Monopoly Power*

The technological basis of MNC advantage, as a specific form of market imperfection, raises special features in the structure-conduct-performance linkages within host industries. Vernon (1974a,b) distinguishes between innovation-based and mature oligopolies as to the advantages each exploits. The innovation-based international oligopolist possesses advantages in introducing new products into world markets and in differentiating old products. Advantages of know-how are embodied in science-based and marketing-based international operations.

With time, these innovation-based MNCs, or at least certain activities undertaken by them, undergo transition to become mature oligopolies, where international market positions are grounded in the more traditional forms of oligopoly collusion and entry restriction. There appear to be important differences in the nature of "effects of interaction" inherent in the innovation-based oligopolist, as distinct from the mature oligopolist. Certain allegations about MNC conduct and impacts on the industry structure in the host country are primarily related to the technology associated with the MNC. One involves the suitability of derivative technology for the host industries; another concerns the monopoly power associated with proprietary technology. What does seem likely is that when the technology or "know-how" associated with the MNC is standardized, *i.e.*, approaches the nature of a public good, the problems inherent in the MNC-host country relationship are quite different.

If technology is one of the main elements in the foreign direct investment package, it is important to assess the net benefits to host countries associated with the entry of science-based MNCs that provide access to technology.

The MNC does provide a highly sophisticated mechanism for technology transfer (Pavitt, 1971). The enconomies of centralized R & D, together with the available financial resources, provide considerable scope for the MNC to develop technology and to use it on a global basis. The foreign affiliate that is a branch of a highly integrated MNC may well have an access to the latest technology through its parent that far exceeds alternative channels for importing technology. However, the conditions attached to that parent technology may entail the exploitation of monopoly power with overall net costs that will be discussed below. Certainly the organizational features of the MNC indicate the relative ease with which technology is freely transferred (Hall and Johnson, 1970), though the operational objectives of the firm raise a number of potential difficulties for the host nation.

Transfer of technology within the MNC may ignore factor proportions, and thus development needs, in host countries. The problem basically stems from the use of equipment developed in (home) markets with one set of factor costs in host countries with quite different relative factor costs. [8] Related to this "appropriateness of technology" problem is the relation between optimum scale of plant from the MNC/technology view, and the market size of the host country. Here also there may be adverse effects on the industrial structure of the host. In some industries, where derivative technology requires large-scale plants and long production runs to achieve minimum long-run average costs, the size of the host market may not be sufficient to sustain optimum levels of output. Where entry by a number of internationally competing oligopolists takes place in these industries, especially behind protective barriers, the resultant industry fragmentation with high-cost, underutilized plants has serious adverse effects on resource use in the host industry. These structure-efficiency problems are examined below, but it is appropriate at this point to indicate the importance of the technology element that is frequently involved.

The nature of the conduct or behavior of the MNC related to technology transfer also affects the benefits or costs to the host country. Fundamental to any assessment of technology associated with MNC operations are the terms and costs applied to the proprietary technology of the MNC. According to the recent U.N. study (1973), the concentration of existing know-how and technological advance in MNCs has become a major source of their monopoly or oligopoly power. In particular, the creation of monopoly rights over proprietary technology, reinforced by existing patent laws, provides a potentially powerful basis for maximizing the MNCs share in host market operations. The problem is especially difficult, since the R & D commitments of MNCs are normally grounded in the expectation of monopoly rents from the new products and processes that result. It is one thing to argue that returns on proprietary technology in any one host market to the MNC needs to reflect past, global R & D commitments by that MNC (Johnson, 1970), but quite another to reward R & D by specifically creating monopoly rights.

The exercise of monopoly power related to proprietary technology may be manifested in transfer pricing practices and various restrictive conditions imposed on the use of technology. The evidence assembled for Colombia highlights some of the problems (Vaitsos, 1970, 1974a). Vaitsos (1970) argues that the resource transfer embodied in direct foreign investment by the MNC takes place in a package of collective inputs. The degree of indivisibility of these collective inputs, particularly with regard to the technology element, creates the monopoly power of the MNC. The collective input package of direct investment effectively limits or excludes potential competition in markets for individual inputs. Thus, for example, the market for management will be limited to the extent that management inputs are part of the direct investment package. Similarly, the Vaitsos' evidence appears to support this for Colombia; the market for imports in areas where MNCs operate is severly limited, thus creating monopoly positions for them in host LDC markets. Indeed, the market for intermediate inputs and capital goods generally is heavily monoplized by the MNC by virtue of the technology embodied in the collective direct investment package.

If technology is embodied and the market for it imperfect, MNCs can exercise considerable monopoly power within host nations. This problem may be compounded by the relative bargaining power of host nations vis-à-vis the MNC, as well as inappropriate government policies that actually validate and reinforce the MNCs monopoly power. The upshot of all this, according to Colombian evidence, is significant overpricing in certain sectors of industry through the transfer pricing practices of MNCs; tie-in clauses placing restrictive requirements on subsidiary purchasing policies and export franchises; and related restrictive conditions on the use of the technology and "know-how" provided by the MNC (Vaitsos, 1970). The implications for net host nation gains vis-à-vis the MNC are made quite clear:

> . . . we can state that the institutional framework, by which technology and/or capital are transferred tied-in to intermediate products and capital goods, result in potentially large monopoly benefits for the supplier of resources (Vaitsos, 1970, p. 39).

Because of these problems, host nations are increasingly attempting to obtain technology from sources other than MNCs. The aim is to obtain technology that yields larger social benefits, preferably replacing imported proprietary technology and associated inputs with local sources. [9]

Two issues arise in connection with the attempt to secure alternative access to technology and related inputs. First, if the MNC loses monopoly rights over new technology and "know-how," will it still emphasize technology creation and, if not, is there an effective alternate source to replace it? In part, the issue involves the relative efficiency of technology creation by MNCs, compared to smaller, national research centers. Also, while the question of the appropriate levels of return to new technology to ensure a constant flow of "appropriate" technological advance is beyond the scope of this paper, it is obviously critical in evaluating policies that seek to bypass the MNC in creating and transferring technology internationally.

The second issue involved in alternative sources of technology, especially for underdeveloped nations with limited indigenous R & D facilities, is whether the terms and cost would be better or worse than those associated with the MNC. While there is clear evidence that MNCs have at times successfully exploited the economic rent accruing to their monopoly positions in technology through restrictive conditions and excessive prices, it is not altogether clear that alternative sources of technology would, *per se,* be preferable or cheaper. For example, the exercise of monopoly power in a market as imperfect as that for''know-how'' does not necessarily require *intra*firm transactions. Depending on the access to information about ''kow-how,'' and the relative bargaining strength of independent firms, *inter*firm transactions could capture the same monopoly rents as the MNC. In the extreme case of highly imperfect information and weak bargaining positions, local firms may pay more for imported technology and agree to more restrictive conditions on its use than would be necessary if it were acquired through an MNC subsidiary.[10]

Any assessment of the relative merits of the MNC as a source of technology depends on how well host goverments can improve the terms on which the collective inputs are obtained, and the extent to which MNCs create and exploit monopoly conditions in the markets for those inputs. The policy choice falls between controlling intrafirm transactions within the MNC by host country governments and encouraging domestic alternatives to secure access to the individual inputs of the direct investment package in the international market. Whatever the decision, it is clear that the monopoly element in MNC technology transfer presents an important constraint on host nation gains from inward investment.

*Effects on Industrial Structure*

Another important effect of MNC interaction with the host nation is its impact on the structure, and hence performance, of the industries in which the MNC operates. The impact of MNC interaction on industrial structure is often identified with the level of industry concentration in host industries. But the issues go beyond simply seller concentration. At this point, there is no conclusive evidence as to how MNC entry does in fact affect seller concentration.

On the one hand, Vernon argues that the mature oligopolies are becoming less concentrated in global markets because the overall world market is growing and the number of new enterprises entering international markets is increasing.[11] The evidence to support this proposition is especially apparent in the automobile, petroleum, aluminium smelting, and pulp and paper industries. On the other hand, there is some presumption that in certain individual host nations, the MNC raises seller concentration. To take the Canadian experience, for example, while there is no apparent correlation between foreign ownership and industrial concentration *per se* (Rosenbluth, 1970), there is evidence that those firms in U.S oligopolistic markets have tended to expand into Canadian industry to a greater degree than firms in less-concentrated, U.S. home markets (Gray Report, 1972;

also Horst, 1975a). The most highly concentrated industries in Canada tend to be those that are most concentrated in the United States. The apparent links between home-industry concentration and MNC affiliate activity should not suggest that MNCs avoid the most concentrated industries in the host country. Some evidence suggests the contrary.[12]

Whether or not the relationship between MNC entry and seller concentration in host industries is causal and, if it is, in which direction the relationship operates, depend on the effects of entry on the number and the size of firms in the host market. In turn, the way in which MNC entry may alter the number of establishments operating in the host-country industry hinges partly on the form of that entry. If the MNC enters an industry via a takeover of or merger with an established enterprise, there is no net change in the number of firms, unless the merger/takeover involves more than one established firm. On the other hand, a green-fields entry by the MNC will, at least initially, increase the number of firms in the industry. What subsequently takes place in the industry is largely independent of the form of MNC entry. Established firms may either be displaced or induced to merge in the face of MNC entry. Marginal firms may well be forced out of the industry and other indigenous firms may be forced to merge in order to compete with the new entrant. Such pressures on rationalization may come from new industry competition or be prompted by government policy designed to promote effective countervailing power to the MNC. Of course, the pressure to merge can effectively arise from the *threat* as well as the fact of MNC entry. European industrial policy appears to have been partially influenced to these pressures.[13]

MNCs seem to have a higher propensity for mergers and takeovers than do indigenous firms in developed host nations. Canadian evidence (Rosenbluth, 1970) confirms that foreign takeovers have accounted for a larger part of total Canadian merger activity than domestic takeovers. More recent Canadian evidence supports this proposition (Gray Report, 1972). While foreign-owned firms may be more active in takeover activity in the host nation than indigenous firms, there is no evidence that this outweighs *de novo* entry by the MNC in its initial establishment. As regards the developing host nations, the principal form of entry by direct foreign investors has been via new green-field entry (Reuber, 1973).

If MNC entry leads to the exit of marginal firms and/or the merger of established competitors, then industry concentration may well increase. The possibility of greater market power within more concentrated industry is thus a possiblity. To the extent that a changed industry structure is related to changed competitive conditions, both as a cause and as a consequence, MNC entry will have some impact on the efficiency of resource use in the industry. By raising monopoly power, it may reduce the efficiency of resource use. But by eliminating inefficient marginal competitors, it may improve allocational efficiency.

A reduction in the number of competitiors in an industry following MNC entry has other implications as well for resource use. In particular, displaced factors of production. If mergers with MNCs displace local factors of production, the net efficiency effects will hinge partially on how these resources are subsequently used. If the new MNC entrant in fact absorbs these factors in activities that entail scale economies, then resource efficiency is enhanced. If, however, displaced factors are taken up by less efficient firms, then resource efficiency is impaired. If displaced factors are absorbed by an MNC entrant that operates at suboptimal size, with excess capacity, or both, then there are adverse consequences for host industry performance. This possibility seems particularly real, judging from existing evidence, in the presence of domestic distortions associated with host-nation protection policies. The problem of inefficient plant operation behind tariff walls in smaller host nations is certainly not confined to instances of MNC entry, but may be compounded by it.

There is considerable interest in the inherent efficiency of the plant associated with MNC entry, not only from the point of view of the suitability of embodied technology, but also from the point of view of the direct effect on host-industry structure. A number of studies have pointed to the inefficient industry structure created by the entry of internationally competing oligopolists behind tariff walls, especially in the smaller developed and developing markets.[14]

. . . the combination of almost any actual or potential barrier to trade with the oligopolistic nature of most of the industries in which foreign investment is important tends to produce a great proliferation of small-scale foreign units, without any real prospect of rationalization or consolidation. *If the units were domestically owned, one would expect market forces to bring about consolidation over a period;* when they are owned by large internationally competing corporations, this is higly unlikely (Brash, 1970).

The large international firm with global financial resources and a commitment to individual market positions can resist normal market forces. This is especially true where any market forces are themselves weakened by tariff distortions that present an obstacle to competitive rationalization that might otherwise occur. Whereas Brash (1970) stresses the combined influence of protection plus international oligopoly, Baranson (1969) considers the problems of derivative technology transfer behind tariff barriers. The argument focuses on the effect of protection in stimulating local production in developing countries using imported technology.[15] Where derivative technology is embodied in a large-scale, high-capital-intensity plant in a relatively small host market, the "branch-plant effect" arises. Encouraged by protectionist policies of host governments, MNC entry results in a proliferation of plants of inefficient scale, high unit costs, and excess capacity. The problem is as much the result of inappropriate host-country policies as of the entry of the internationally competing oligopolists with their "miniature-replica" plants.[16]

There is a case for supposing that MNC entry compounds the problems of industry fragmentation, especially in the case of international oligopolistic rivalry of MNCs. Inappropriate plant size by indigenous firms is certainly possible, particularly behind protectionist barriers, but the crowding practices of MNCs can also lead to or compound excessive industry fragmentation. It is unlikely that the fragmented industry will undergo a competitive rationalization in the shorter term without a change in host-government import policies that would force such rationalization. Of course, it is not always the case that the MNC entrant will introduce inappropriate plant associated with higher unit costs and/or excess capacity. There is some evidence from the experience of foreign investment in the Australian chemical industry that the MNC entrant, even with *existing* tariff protection, will undertake some adaptation of derivative technology to install a smaller-scale, near-optimum size plant with comparable unit costs and little if any excess operating capacity (Parry, 1974a). The extent of adaptation of derivative technology in this way by the MNC entrant was not widespread, but the implications for host-country policy are particularly important.[17]

The operations of the MNC in the host country can have an effect on industry structure through their influence on barriers to entry, including product differentiation.[18] In the first place, it is often only the MNC that can overcome existing barriers to entry in host industries. There are a number of instances cited where MNC entry breaks down the monopoly position of an established firm in the host market (Caves, 1974a; Steur et al., 1973; and Dunning, 1974). The suggestion is that the MNC has the necessary resources to overcome barriers to entry while indigenous firms do not. In particular, where existing industry entry barriers are characterized by large economies of scale, product differentiation, or advanced technology, the MNC has a special advantage. This is because of their usually assumed advantages, discussed above, in exploiting international production based on these particular industry characteristics. Thus, MNC entry that overcomes existing barriers and breaks down established, highly concentrated structures can have a significant, favorable effect on competitive structure in the host industry.

However, just as the MNC can reasonably be assumed to have access to various advantages enabling it to overcome barriers to entry in host industries, the MNC may well create additional or compound existing barriers to entry. If this is correct, then at best the entry of the MNC will simply change the number of oligopolists in the market requiring new entry-forestalling prices to be set. These new entry-forestalling prices may well be higher than pre-MNC entry if the MNC entrant can impose even greater barriers to entry. Further, if the MNC entrants force out established marginal firms and/or stimulate mergers or takeovers among established firms, then the end result may well entail an increase in oligopolistic concentration, particularly if the surviving MNC affiliates establish higher entry barriers. The apparent ability of the MNC in exploiting scale economies, product differentiation and marketing advantages, technological advance, and vertical integration economies suggests that MNCs have the potential to create significant entry barriers, which can only be overcome by other MNCc.[19] Indeed the point stressed by Knickerbocker (1976) is that entry barriers in host industries, particularly based on product differentiation (marketing), R & D, and scale, no matter how high, have not provided any established MNC affiliate with complete protection from *new MNC rivalry*. The problem may be that it is only *new* MNC entry that can overcome entry barriers created by existing MNCs in the market.

On balance, there is good reason for accepting the view that MNCs do have the ability to overcome entry barriers where indigenous firms do not. However, the entry of the MNC, possibly adding to existing entry barriers, may result in a situation of low-level oligopolistic equilibrium with the only pressure coming from potential or actual new entry by other MNCs. Whether this form of competitive pressure produces the desired results for the host nation depends very much on what policies exist to condition the type of entry and determine the nature of "competition" in the market. If protectionist policies stimulate excessive entry, then problems of fragmentation are possible. If there is no effective antitrust policy, then there may be no inducement to "rivalrous" MNCs to do anything other than adopt an "easy-life," market-sharing strategy within an international framework, protected in individual markets by high barriers to entry.

## CONDUCT AND COMPETITION

Whatever the effects of MNC entry on the structure of host industry, the behavior of the MNC and its impact on competitiveness in the industry will be an important determinant of the performance of the host industry. Obviously the conduct of firms in the industry, both the MNC entrants and existing firms, will help determine eventual structural changes in an industry. Similarly, the structure that exists, that is created, or that is reinforced by MNC entry will partly condition the nature of firms' conduct within an industry. The conduct-structure relationship, then, is a two-way interrelationship. In this section, we concentrate on the effects of MNC interaction with the host nation from the point of view of its implications for the conduct of firm—both MNC entrants and established firms—as well as the "competitiveness" of the industry.

The competitive behavior of firms in an industry is a determinant of the "performance" of that industry. Competitiveness affects the efficiency of resource use within firms and the allocative efficiency for the economy as a whole. From the point of view of the competitiveness effects of the MNC, performance determines the distribution of the gains from foreign direct investment among the MNC, the domestic factors of production, and the host government. For example, monopolistic conduct by the MNC in transfer pricing may reduce the net taxes of the host government, as well as the payments to local factors of production if those payments are based on *apparent* host-country value added. In addition, transfer pricing will lead to a distortion in resource allocation if factors respond to incorrect price signals associated with these intrafirm transactions.

In assessing the nature of competition associated with the MNC, particularly with regard to industry performance, account must also be taken of dynamic efficiency considerations. The problem is not confined to judgments about the MNC, but involves the familiar Schumpeterian requirements for the dynamic efficiency of technological advance. What is possibly peculiar to the MNC, though, is that the apparent commitment of the MNC to exploiting technological advance in its international operations, as discussed above, may mean that MNC conduct within any individual host market can only be properly assessed in terms of global criteria. Thus, what appears as a restrictive practice in the individual host market, such as export franchises, may be entirely consistent with global efficiency, both for static resource use and dynamic technology creation. We examine some of these issues below.

While there are certain forms of conduct that are commonly associated with the MNC, it is important to distinguish between restrictive practices potentially employed by any firm, regardless of ownership, and restrictive practices specific to the MNC (Dunning, 1974). Further, any evaluation of conduct or, indeed, structure for industry performance needs to consider the role of domestic distortions that induce inefficient behavior. Much of the criticism associated with the MNC, particularly the Canadian literature, apportions a large part of the blame to inappropriate government policies.[20] To the extent that "undesirable" conduct is evident in MNC operations, the degree to which domestic distortions induce that conduct will have important implications for host-country policy.

Paradoxically, it is because of its greater competitive ability that the MNC may limit overall competition in an industry. Because of special advantages and greater efficiency, the MNC can limit the development of indigenous firms, effectively curtailing rival competition (Reuber, 1973). Some MNCs have advantages over indigenous firms, it is suggested, because of better after-sales services, quality, distribution, and lower prices. The MNC also has advantages in production, especially related to monopoly positions in the global market for factors. Further, the MNC has advantages in management expertise over indigenous firms; and, the MNC has a significant advantage in raising capital both locally and internationally (Macaluso and Hawkins, 1977). Even if the MNC does not rely on predatory pricing and related practices to force out established competitors, the various advantages of the MNC vis-à-vis the indigenous firm may in fact limit the development of a viable competitive alternative. If there is no effective countervailing influence, then there is some doubt as to the source of the pressure, which ensures that any productivity gains are passed on in the market. If the main source of competition is from a potential new MNC entry, as suggested by Knickerbocker (1976), then the nature of competitive conduct may be oriented away from host-nation gains. Other forms of countervailing influence, such as large indigenous firms, have been relied on to provide the competitive balance in a number of countries, though it is not entirely clear whether this does maximize the gains to the host country. This is especially the case where the domestic firm can only compete with large subsidy assistance from the host-country government. What is interesting is the situation where an MNC affiliate is a candidate for subsidy or similar assistance from the host-country government partly to maintain a "competitive" industry.

The MNC's impacts on competition and competitiveness will arise in the first instance via the bypassing of entry barriers in the host market. As discussed above, the MNC has certain advantages that place it in a position to overcome existing entry barriers, thus stimulating competition that would not otherwise take place (Caves, 1974a). The overall effect on competition, however, depends on whether new entry barriers are created which effectively worsen overall competition. In terms of *de novo* entry, there is considerable evidence supporting the view that the MNC does break down domestic monopolies in host markets.[21] Further, there is a strong case for viewing the MNC as a source of continuing competitive pressure within the host market.

According to Caves (1974b) there are essentially three areas of conduct in which the MNC exhibits special features that will bear on competition and competitiveness. First, while it is reasonable to assume that the MNC responds to the same objectives as indigenous firms, *viz.,* profit optimization, the global orientation of that profit optimization may well lead to different conduct (Penrose, 1968). Global profit maximization, according to Caves, will lead to potentially different subsidiary behavior; different global opportunity costs; and different allocative choices, including different risk assessments. Different motivation, therefore, can explain different competitive conduct. Secondly, the MNC has an advantage in access to global information about alternative market sources. and opportunities that will place its conduct on a different footing than that associated with the indigenous firm. Finally, the different opportunity set facing the MNC explains different forms of competitive behavior. In particular, the MNC's inherent advantages in product differentiation result in a reliance on nonprice forms of competition. This has implications both for host industry structure as well as ongoing competitive behavior.

The special conduct features associated with the MNC have direct implications for competitiveness associated with MNC operations. First, because of the special advantages available to the MNC, increased or potential entry by other MNCs will constrain excess monopoly profits. The Knickerbocker argument obviously relies on the threat of potential entry by other MNCs in constraining excess oligopoly profits. As we will see below, there is evidence to suggest that profit levels in industries in which MNC operations are significant are not overtly excessive, though there are difficulties in relying on profitability to measure monopoly power.

Second, because of the MNC's global perspective, its operations in any one national market are likely to be less collusive and restrictive than indigenous oligopolists. A more actively rivalrous behavior is assumed to follow from the fact that the MNC entrant will not have settled into a stable pattern of oligopolistic interdependence or mutual accommodation that may have occurred among existing firms. What happens over time, however, may be quite different. The pattern of oligopolistic interdependence that can emerge between international rivals may have additional consequences for the host nation. The difference between indigenous firms and MNCs enjoying excess profits is that excess profits in the MNC may be transferred out of the host nation, where they are in fact earned.

Third, the MNC's superior access to technology and knowhow suggests that the efficiency of resource use by the MNC in any host industry will be used in competitive pricing and/or improved product attributes. The impact on host-market competitivness is also tied to related effects on other firms in the market. The U.K. experience suggests that U.S. subsidiaries provided increased competition for existing, dominant firms and stimulated an increasing awareness in established U.K. firms generally about the role of R & D and productive management (Dunning, 1958). This demonstration effect was not confined to direct competiors, but carried over to suppliers as well as customers of the MNC affiliate. The effect of foreign technological progress as a factor in the competitive environment of Australian industry has been highlighted in an unpublished paper by Hogan (1962). Hogan argues that the foreign subsidiary's technological superiority will force out higher-cost, marginal firms and introduce a stream of new technical inputs to the host industry. The competitive effect of this technological superiority works through a strong demonstration effect on both rivals and other firms. Even allowing for possible structural problems, notably the excess capacity of fragmented plants, the conclusion is stated in no uncertain terms:

> In the absence of powerful advantages held by domestic enterprises, the foreign sector contributed to increased competition or . . . the amelioration of monopolistic practices especially in those fields where technological innovation is strong (Hogan, 1962, p. 9).

The conduct of the MNC, however, need not be a positive influence on industry competitiveness. Obviously, there are restrictive trade practices common to both the MNC and the indigenous enterprise. There are various practices of an anticompetitive nature, however, that may be either specific to or more commonly employed by the MNC. In particular, the MNC allegedly allocates various markets *globally,* with consequent restrictions on the markets of *individual* host nations. The international allocation of markets, both within the single MNC and between "rival" MNC's, extends to export markets, markets for inputs and markets in raw materials both as inputs and as exports. In addition, the MNC is potentially able to price intrafirm transactions at other than arms-length, a restrictive practice not usually available to the indigenous firm. Furthermore, it is often argued that the degree of product differentiation associated with MNC activities, while not necessarily a restrictive trade practice, may be excessive in terms of resource-use efficiency. We look at each of these arguments in turn.

In general, the *a priori* failures of inadequate competition show up in higher prices, less efficient production, less innovation, and lower responsiveness to consumer "needs." The question is whether the MNC, in its interaction with host markets, is directly responsible for "inadequate competition"? If the MNC is primarily a "mature international oligopolist" in the Vernon sense, then the apparent thrust of conduct is directed to stability within markets behind barriers to entry; that is, a low-level international oligopolistic equilibrium (Kindleberger, 1969). In raw materials, the MNC's aim for growth and stability under international oligopoly conditions does lead to this low-level equilibrium (Vernon, 1972a). Under these conditions, the mechanism that ensures maximum host-country gains is not MNC competition nor competitiveness, but the bargaining positions and relative strength of the host country government *vis-à-vis* that of the MNC (Vernon, 1972a; Mikesell, 1971).

The picture may be different in the manufacturing sector where competition from non-MNCs has some role to play. Further, the science-based international oligopolist is more likely to be providing a competitive thrust grounded in technological advance and a constant stream of innovation. Indeed, it is commonly argued that part of this competitive thrust is directed to international export competition from the host-nation markets. A number of studies point to the export activity of manufacturing MNCs in host nations.[22] The question is whether the export activity of MNCs also involves a restrictive practice in limiting affiliate exports to overseas markets that would otherwise be so serviced, or in engaging in transfer pricing in these transactions. The transfer-pricing possibility must be seriously considered in view of the extent of "tied" exports within the MNC.

The restrictive export franchise is often alleged as a common feature of MNC operations. Evidence regarding the prevalence of this restrictive practice is markedly divergent. On the one hand, some of the earlier questionnaire studies of foreign investment in the developed host nations suggest that the restrictive export franchise is unimportant for the subsidiary (Brash, 1966; Hogan, 1966; Safarian, 1966). In view of the nature of questionnaire responses by subsidiaries, however, this result should not be surprising. On the other hand, evidence for Colombia and India do suggest that the restrictive export franchise may be prevalent in the developing host nation (Vaitsos, 1974a; Frankena, 1972). The difficulty in ensuring adequate government scrutiny and control may explain the apparently different experience of the developed versus the developing host country.

Safarian argues that within the context of demand and cost considerations and the framework of the laws within which the MNC operates, it can be shown that the case for private export restrictions by these firms is, at best, a short-run case (Safarian, 1966). Taking the example of one national subsidiary, it is reasonable to expect that, unless distribution or production costs are lower for the subsidiary, or unless it enjoys a tariff or similar legal preference in third markets, the parent or other subsidiary will export to the third market(s) in order to maximize global firm profits. Should production or distribution costs or other circumstances change so as to favor the subsidiary, the subsidiary should then become the source of exports to the relevant third markets if the corporation is to maximize overall global profits.

These would be the expected patterns if the objective was overall long-run profit maximization. However, argues Safarian, in the shorter term "while existing assets have not been fully depreciated" and where capacity utilization proves important, the result may be quite different. In fact, the location of export servicing in the underutilized plant may simply be the result of its marginal cost being less than for a fully employed plant elsewhere, even though average cost is higher because of output levels below those of a fully-utilized plant. In this case, the behavior of the MNC is profit maximizing and tends towards a more efficient use of resources globally, even though the nation state may see itself as losing out on export markets.

However, not all behavior of the MNC conforms to the profit-maximization assumption. In fact, there probably are instances of the MNC discriminating against the more efficient subsidiary in the short run for reasons other than maximizing profits. On the one hand, simple rules involving restrictive export franchises may be more expedient than examining each new situation from the point of view of contributions to overall profits. This is especially likely in those enterprises that opt for greater autonomy for local management rather than refer every decision to headquarters, or those that impose a set of rules designed to restrict price-cutting competition between autonomous exporting subsidiaries. On the other hand, global profit considerations may lead directly to restrictive export francises for joint-venture subsidiaries. This is especially likely where new technology is transferred to a joint-venture subsidiary: The firm's global profits are greater if exporting is done by a wholly owned subsidary and returns on parent techology are maximized. The same result occurs if the joint-venture subsidiary is charged for access to new technology at "arms-length prices." In this case the joint-venture subsidiary will most likely be priced out of export markets *vis-à-vis* wholly owned subsidiaries with "free" access to technology. If, however, the joint-venture subsidiary is price competitive in export markets despite full charges for new technology (because of, for example, lower labor costs), the MNC's share of export sales plus licensing charges could well contribute to global profits as much as would exports of a wholly owned subsidiary.

Where the firm diverges from profit maximizing behavior and discriminates against a more efficient national subsidiary in favor of another source of exports for third markets, perhaps as a result of a host government's incentives or directives geared to export performance, there is a redistribution of income (and tax receipts) between subsidiaries and the likelihood of a loss of overall efficiency in the location of production. Profit-maximizing behavior of the MNC, via the increased factor mobility associated with international operations, may mean more efficient global resource use. However, as trade and factor movement restrictions imposed by nations further impede the free operations of international markets, the MNC is induced to operate other than as a maximizer and will reinforce any existing distortions.

Another major problem involves the exercise of restrictive practices in the market for inputs, particularly imported inputs, by the MNC in the host nation. The major conclusion of Vaitsos' study of Columbia was that the affiliate firm tends not only to import excessively, but also to pay above arms-length prices for these imported inputs. The exercise of monopoly power in the market for imported inputs is particularly prevalent where the technology element is important in MNC operations. It is difficult to say how widespread is the excessive import propensity by the MNC affiliate. A recent Asian study (Cohen, 1975) suggests that whereas Korean'based subsidiaries tend to import more than the indigenous counterpart, foreign firms in Taiwan import less, and foreign firms in Singapore import about the same as indigenous firms.

However, even if MNC affiliates in host countries do not import more than the domestic alternative, there is still a considerable degree of intrafirm trade in the imports that are directed to the affiliate. The potential use of price manipulation in this trade raises a serious form of restrictive trade practice by the MNC. The manipulation of these prices has income-distribution effects where returns to factors are distorted, and where tax payments are avoided. The issue of arms-length relationships and MNC subsidiaries has been carefully looked at by Edith Penrose (1968).

> All international firms are by definition integrated across national frontiers whether horizontally or vertically or both, for they are conducting similar operations in several countries or are engaged in different stages of the same industry in different countries, or both. A high degree of integration inevitably introduces an important element of arbitrariness in the allocation of overhead costs to different operations and in the setting of prices at which goods and services are transferred between the subsidiary entities of the firm. If we assume that firms attempt to minimize taxes in their efforts to maximize retained earnings, we can infer that they will attempt to use the scope thus provided to allocate overhead costs among their foreign subsidiaries, branches and affiliates, and to adjust transfer prices in order to reduce their total tax outlays (Penrose, 1968, p. 43).

In addition to minimizing global tax outlays, the MNC can use transfer prices as a means of getting profits out of a country where there are controls over income repatriation, or where the existence of minority shareholders in one subsidiary encourages higher charges in order to maximize the international firm's share of profits (Shulman, 1967; Horst, 1971).

While many countries have authorities capable of minimizing distortions in interaffiliate pricing, this is complicated by the difficulty of establishing arms-length relationships. especially for intangible services such as management and technology. Where an effective tax administration system is absent, as in some less-developed nations, the problems of interaffiliate price manipulation are substantially greater. The implications for national policy go beyond any possible balance-of-payments effects of inflated trade prices. More important questions arise as to distortions in income distribution via factor-price manipulation and the optimal taxation of foreign investment, an issue of some importance given the potential benefits of this taxation. Given the tax-avoidance incentive to the MNC and its effect on income distribution, an "optimal" system of taxation would need to take account of the effects of rigged transfer-prices. Ideally, global coordination and supervision among national tax authorities is necessary to avoid distortions caused by the tax-minimizing behavior of the MNC.

Finally, the degree of product differentiation associated with the MNC is often seen as an adverse aspect of the firms' behavior. One of the major advantages of the MNC in its international operations is its ability to create new products and differentiate existing ones both subjectively and objectively. However, the commitment to product differentiation may be excessive. Canadian evidence seems particularly conclusive on this point. Given the high correlation between product differentiation and foreign control in Canadian industry (Eastman and Skyholt, 1967), the conclusion has been that product differentiation was excessive and has entailed resource costs (Gray Report, 1972). This criticism is not confined to Canadian experience with the MNC (Reuber, 1973). And Caves, while stressing the competitive advantages of product differentiation, particularly in overcoming existing entry barriers, suggests that the commitment to product differentiation by the established MNC may become excessive both as a new entry barrier and in terms of resource use (Caves, 1974b).

# THE MNC AND INDUSTRY PERFORMANCE

A number of attempts have been made to assess the performance of the MNC, both in terms of its "efficiency" relative to the domestic-firm alternative and in terms of the overall impact on host industry performance.[23] Unfortunately, the nature of the efficiency considerations or performance indicators has not always been clearly indicated. A firm's productive efficiency, given an objective of profit maximization, may be judged by how low the real costs are for the output the firm produces and distributes. Industry performance, then, in terms of productive efficiency, involves the degree to which the industry's output is produced at minimum attainable cost, *i.e.,* technical efficiency (Caves, 1974b). In turn, industry productive efficency depends on industrial structure and competitive conduct. On the structure side, this involves:

> The horizontal size or scale of the plants and firms in the industry, relative to the scales which would permit lowest unit costs; the degree of vertical integration of plants and firms, relative to the cost-minimizing degree of integration; and, the long-run rate of utilization of existing plant capacity, relative to the most economically feasible rate of utilization (Bain, 1959, p. 343).

As these structural conditions are entirely consistent with, if not more highly compatible with, monopoly, some specification of competitive behavior is also required. Perhaps all that is needed is the condition that the technical efficiency attained under the above structure is not absorbed in above-normal profits by the firms in the industry.

In addition to the technical efficiency aspect of performance, we need to consider the implications for allocative efficiency and dynamic efficiency both of the MNC itself and of the host industry generally as a result of MNC operations. Caves defines "allocative efficiency" as the "appropriateness of the industry's level of output" that can normally be assessed by the presence of other than "normal" profits (Caves, 1974b). "Dynamic efficiency" is concerned with the technology functions, the nature of innovation, both its location and timing, and the diffusion of innovation between and within different markets. We look at each of these three elements of host industry performance, as affected by the MNC's operations.

## Technical or Productive Efficiency

One argument holds that the MNC entrant is not only more efficient in production and distribution, but also raises the efficiency of other firms in the industry (e.g., Caves, 1974b; Knickerbocker, 1976). Because the MNC is likely to have access to the technology associated with minimum-cost plant; is likely to have a greater degree of global vertical integration consistent with cost minimization; and is likely to have access to global markets for the most economically feasible rate of plant utilization, the MNC can be assumed to optimize its own technical efficiency. Further, the MNC will induce a higher level of productive efficiency in established host-market firms, via the demonstration effect and via competitive pressures.

On the other hand, however, one can question whether the MNC does use minimum-cost plant associated with best-practice technique in all host countries. Part of the problem is that the host country may have an insufficient market size or absorptive capacity for best-practice technology. In this case, the feasible minimum cost plant is not necessarily the world-size plant, but one consistent with the host market. If the MNC entrant is using optimum-size plant from the engineering point of view, this need not be consistent with optimum utilization. The problems of fragmentation with multiple MNC entry behind tariff barriers in the small market has often precluded an optimum rate of plant utilization, regardless of how world-size or scaled-down the plant. The cause of fragmentation and attendant excess capacity is more often than not other host-government policies. Even so, the prevalence of this situation must cast doubts on the MNC entrant and the host industry generally being able to optimize productive efficiency.

There is some evidence that the MNC entrant embodies greater technical efficiency[24] and induces this in established firms. Rather indirect evidence, based on admittedly poor data, suggests that direct investment in Australian manufacturing has had a positive effect on technical efficiency in manufacturing industries host to the MNC.[25] The argument is that this has resulted from both a demonstration effect and the direct competitive influence of MNC entry. While there is some case for accepting that the MNC does raise industry productivity both via its own superior technical efficiency and, perhaps more importantly, by inducing greater efficiency in existing firms, this may be a once-only gain from new entry. The gains from any productive efficiency may be eroded by inefficient industry structure, inappropriate plant, and perhaps excessive product differentiation by the established MNC over time (Caves, 1974b).

*Allocative Efficiency*

The way in which the MNC can influence the efficiency of resource allocation in the host economy depends on both structure and conduct impacts. One view is that the MNC entrant that breaks down existing barriers to entry will tend to improve allocative performance by increasing competitive pressures. In other words, by increasing competition, MNC entry will reduce existing monopolistic distortions and raise factor productivity (Knickerbocker, 1976). As with technical efficiency, this may well be a reasonable view of a new MNC entry that overcomes entry barriers.

However, the fragmentation problem has an important effect on allocative efficiency. The extent of excess capacity in established plants as a result of MNC entry is a direct cost in terms of allocative, resource-use inefficiency. A direct measure of the excess capacity associated with foreign direct investment in the Australian chemical industry is given in the increase in per unit costs associated with industry fragmentation (Parry, 1974a). Further, as discussed above, transfer pricing by the MNC can distort the allocation mechanism to the extent that factor use responds to these incorrect price signals.

The transfer-pricing problem is not only relevant to any actual allocative inefficiency, but also makes the identification of allocative efficiency or inefficiency more difficult. The efficiency of resource use is normally assessed in terms of the divergence from "normal" profits in an industry. To the extent that MNCs are shifting profits out of the host country for whatever reasons via transfer pricing, the apparent level of profitability in the host market will be misleading. Thus, evidence that industries in which MNCs are heavily concentrated do not have markedly greater profitability than "other" industries (Johns, 1967; Dunning, 1969) may be unduly influenced by distorted profitability data. Perhaps more important, the MNC and large firms generally may not be profit maximizers. In this case allocative efficiency can only be assessed in terms of the above-normal achievement of whatever objective function the MNC does attempt to maximize.

According to Hufbauer (1975), the efficiency of the MNC, based on technological superiority, need not show up in standard measures of "value of output per unit of input" nor in the relative profitability of MNC and non-MNC subsidiaries. Rather, where the MNC enjoys greater "technological superiority," widely interpreted, then its equilibrium *size* will be, *ceteris paribus*, greater than that of non-MNCs in the same industry. The efficiency of resource allocation is more difficult to define in terms of "normal" size than it is in terms of "normal" profits. But, extending the Hufbauer argument, excessive MNC size, rather than excessive profitability, may indicate a departure from competitive allocation in the market. Evidence from the Australian manufacturing sector (Parry, 1974b) suggests that, whereas there is no marked difference in the profitability of industries in which foreign subsidiaries concentrate and industries dominated by local firms, there is a significant difference between the average asset size of MNC and non-MNC affiliates. The average MNC affiliate is greater in size than the average non-MNC affiliate in ten out of the eleven manufacturing industries examined. Unless size is positively related to dynamic efficiency in R & D and innovation, these data suggest that either the MNC has considerably greater access to static scale economies or attracts a proportion of resources inconsistent with allocative efficiency. What does seem apparent is that profitability may not be an appropriate indicator of allocative efficiency in the presence of the MNC.

*Dynamic Efficiency*

Finally, how does the MNC affect dynamic efficiency in the host economy? Is the MNC in fact a perfector of international markets for technology and know-how, generating an optimum innovative environment in the host market, or is the aspect of monopoly power associated with proprietary technology the determinant of dynamic inefficiency?

Undoubtedly the MNC brings with it access to technology and technological change. Critics, however, argue that the MNC will centralize research and development facilities away from the host nation. Further, the parent will control the size and purpose of any R & D activity that is undertaken by the affiliate. This behavior, it is alleged, is inconsistent with dynamic efficiency in the host market, as it inhibits the development of any domestic technology and the technical, scientific, and management skills that go with R & D.

For the MNC, with an objective of global profit maximization, the economies of centralization give good *a priori* reasons for centralized and shared R & D. What is important is the "suitability" of derivataive technology and the terms of access to that technology. Given the high cost of R & D, it is not altogether clear that the development of national facilities is the best possible means of sustaining dynamic efficiency. However, the evidence regarding inappropriate technology transfer and monopoly practices tied to the use of derivative technology, discussed above, must give cause for some concern. If the problems associated with proprietary technology are in fact tied to the ownership package of direct investment, then dynamic efficiency considerations may make the host nation seek alternative access to technology. In some instances, a nation may have a choice of licensing, joint venture basis, or direct investment as alternative sources of technology. The Japanese case of adopting and adapting derivative technology without foreign ownership but by imitation and development is a proven, if perhaps uncommon, alternative for dynamic efficiency (Ozawa, 1972). The likelihood of access to new and appropriate technology with competitive conditions via the MNC is a rather uncertain aspect of MNC performance. It is clearly an area requiring careful host government scrutiny.

# CONCLUSIONS AND POLICY IMPLICATIONS

The predicted effects of international direct investment by MNCs within the framework of imperfect competition are quite different from those of the classical, optimum global allocation approach. The major effects of interaction between the MNC and host countries can be explained in terms of the very market imperfections that explain international investment via the MNC in the first place. Given the oligopolistic responses of the MNC and the global orientation of their decision making, to what extent are the potential benefits of the "direct investment package" identified in the classical McDougall analysis overturned or eroded? Further, what policy initiatives on the part of host-country governments can maximize the net gains of interaction with the MNC?

It was suggested that the MNC creates special problems for host countries that are based on its multinationality. The problems associated with the MNC arise in both the structure and conduct dimensions of industrial organization. There is also some presumption that the issues are different for the science-based MNC and the "mature" MNC. The elements of monopoly power particularly associated with proprietary technology do seem to give rise to additional avenues for the exercise of various restrictive practices by the MNC (Vaitsos, 1970). In addition, the innovation-based MNC raises the question of the "suitability" of derivative technology both for factor use and host-industry structure. This is not to say that the "mature" MNC is not without potential problems, but rather that the problems take on a different dimension.

As for structure, it is not clear that MNCs have increased concentration in either world product markets individually, or in specific host countries across all industries. The evidence that MNCs tend to move into the more highly concentrated host industries from the more highly concentrated home industries does not establish a *causal* link. Nevertheless, there is ample evidence, from both developed and developing host countries, that under certain conditions MNC entry has created fragmented host-industry structures with attendant excess capacity. The conditions that commonly stimulate this inappropriate entry, however, are related to inappropriate host-government policies, particularly protectionist policies geared to industrialization. The implication for policy initiative is quite clear, as suggested below.

The second major feature of host-market structure affected by the MNC involves barriers to entry. On the one hand, the available evidence does suggest that the MNC has access to various advantages that enable it to overcome established entry barriers in the host markets. In so doing, established domestic monopoly/oligopoly positions are eroded with, at least, a one-shot stimulus to domestic competitive structure. On the other hand, the MNC may create greater entry barriers to protect its established position within the individual market consistent with global considerations. This low-level, international oligopoly equilibrium may well be continually subject to additional MNC entries, but the problem is whether host-nation governments will accept other MNCs as the only source of actual and potential competitive pressure.

In the area of conduct, the first task is to determine which practices are peculiar to the MNC and which are common to oligopolists regardless of ownership. The global orientation of the MNC, associated with global profit maximization and its global opportunity set, leads to specific aspects of restrictive or monopoly conduct. The global perspective may have some initial advantage for the host nation in providing new-entry competition not tied to existing oligopolistic interdependencies. However, the exercise of restrictive practices in export franchises, tie-in import arrangements, and transfer pricing over inputs and exports generally, raises important issues for policy. The extent of such restrictive practices must be weighed against any competitive stimulus from the MNC to the host industry, either via competition or demonstration.

Policies designed to deal directly with, or at least take specific account of, the multinational enterprise are in an exploratory stage in host and home countries. There is not much doubt that both host- and home-country governments have the jurisdiction to control the MNC in its direct interaction with the nation state. Even in the gray area of extraterritorial jurisdiction, a number of government authorities are moving to extend the reach of national or regional legislative control.[26] The immediate need, however, is for some clarification of the jursidictional control of national governments and international agencies as regards the extranational areas of MNC operations.

Turning to some specific policy options relevant to the issues raised in this paper, we can identify a number of potential initiatives involving impacts on structure and conduct. Perhaps the most important point to emerge from the discussion of MNC effects on host-industry structure is the role of inappropriate host-government policy. Many of the structural problems associated with overcrowding, fragmentation, and excess capacity are the direct result of government attempts to induce direct foreign investment as part of industrialization. Though not confined to inducing the MNC responses, tariff policies can be blamed for much of the resultant fragmentation associated with the MNC. Partiuclarly when coupled with bandwagon entry by the several MNCs, tariff protection must be directly blamed as the market imperfection stimulating undesirable structural effects of MNC entry. The policy objective should be to avoid excessive MNC entry into the smaller market, especially in the presence of significant plant scale economies. The problem is how to achieve some balance between the number of firms in the industry and the degree of "competitiveness." A more concentrated industry structure that is appropriate to optimizing costs and capacity utilization can be checked by appropriate antitrust control. Of course, one option in the case of the smaller market seeking entry of large-scale plant is the encouragement of a joint-venture monopoly with an indigenous firm or a nationalized entity. Another option is to retain liberal import policies, which places a further competitive check on a highly concentrated domestic industry.

U.K. experience with the I.R.C. in promoting domestic mergers and rationalization can be interpreted as both seeking to provide a domestic countervailing force to the MNC as well as promoting an appropriate structure for optimum exploitation of economies of scale in general (Dunning, 1974). The conflict with monopolies policy, however, cannot be ignored in this approach. Indeed, part of the problem with the I.R.C. experience in the U.K. was its inherent conflict with the "competition" approach of the Monopolies Commission. Recognizing the need for consistency with monoplies legistlation, rationalization of the fragmented host industry can be achieved either through government initiatives in stimulating mergers, or by reductions in tariff protection, which can have a similar effect on merger and exit activity.[27]

A possible alternative to rationalization policies for fragmented host industries is the encouragement of technology adaptation by the MNC entrant. Technological adaptation in initial plant investment decisions by the MNC entrant involves a smaller, near optimal size plant appropriate to the smaller market with near optimum utilization. Such technological adaptation has been undertaken by the MNC entrant, particularly in response to expectations of tariff reductions (Parry, 1974a). A similar degree of adaptation can be achieved with a deliberate policy to encourage subsidiaries to undertake R & D appropriate to necessary technological adaptation for the smaller market.

Indeed, scientific and education policies can be geared to creating a domestic technical and scientific structure that may serve as an effective counterforce to the MNC. Some evidence indicates that the MNC can erode the existing potential for an indigenous competitive structure (Reuber, 1973). It is often only the government that provides any countervailing power. This can be reinforced by general scientific policies that support indigenous enterprise.

Finally, an area relevant to structure that has seen more active policy response to date, though probably for the wrong reasons, is in mergers and takeovers involving the MNC. The takeover of indigenous enterprise by the MNC has a strong emotive element, and legislation exists in a number of host nations that requires registration and approval.[28] The approval of a foreign takeover depends on some net positive benefits to "national interests," which are inevitably impossible to define. It is not entirely clear whether separate legislation is needed for MNC takeovers/mergers. Rather, general control over merger activity from the point of view of industry structure and "competitive environment" can include the MNC and any special advantages it may possess. Any specific anticompetitive attributes or practices of the MNC are unlikely to be confined to MNC entrants through takeover/merger; these restrictive practices are best dealt with in terms of the MNC and direct inward investment in general.

Policies concerned with MNC conduct need to extend beyond the usual restrictive-trade-practices legislation to take account of the special features of MNC behavior. These particular features involve the exercise of monopoly control over the markets for both inputs and exports. The restrictive export franchise, commonly tied to derivative technology, can lead to a host-nation loss if third-country markets are cut off. Similarly, transfer pricing of exports and, more usually, imported inputs, will have a number of adverse consequences for the host nation.

The policy reaction must, first of all, be based on information about the exact extent and nature of these restrictive practices. It seems clear that a host nation can police transfer-pricing practices if it has information about these practices. The development of a capable taxation and customs authority is needed to police interaffiliate (and, indeed, interfirm) trade. A very troublesome aspect of the information problem is how are arms-length prices to be established, especially in trade in intangible services and technology? The alternative may be simply to establish a licensing procedure over all aspects involved in technology purchases, including service fees, such as the Andean Pact approach. In this way, the prices and conditions of use can be controlled and bargained over by a government body, rather than set by an unbridled MNC or with an independent firm with weaker bargaining power and poorer information regarding alternatives. Such controls can be extended to tie-in clauses over input requirements imposed by the MNC. U.S. legislation on tie-in clauses can be extended to host nations, or, indeed, internationally as a policy of the home country.

Finally, patent laws can be modified to limit monopoly power associated with proprietary technology. Some of the developing countries are experimenting with patent laws to minimize the restrictive conditions associated with this institutional support for monopoly power (Vernon, 1974b). One interesting proposal suggests that host nations could tradeoff the length of a patent life against the restrictive conditions imposed on its use in the host nation (Smith, 1974). Thus, the MNC and host nation could bargain over the duration and extent of monopoly returns associated with innovation.

These examples of policy responses to the special impacts of the MNC on host-industry structure and conduct are by no means exhaustive. Rather, they provide an idea of the possiblilities for policy responses by host nations. On the one hand, policy can attempt to replace the MNC in some or all of its host-market functions. Thus, for example, nationalization of existing MNCs or the setting aside of "key sectors" to which MNCs are barred from entry requires replacing or forgoing the MNC entirely in a sector or the whole country. Alternatively, the MNC can be replaced only in certain functions. Alternative access to various elements of the "direct investment package," notably technology inputs, may bypass the MNC in specific functions. Japanese experience has essentially involved the bypassing of the MNC for most, though not all, inputs. The development of alternative access to technology, however, is not without problems. If the MNC is increasingly bypassed as a source of technological advance, will an alternative, equally "productive," source be developed? Given the MNC's commitment to developing and exploiting new technology internationally, the total erosion of any monopoly profits casts some doubts as to its continuing commitment to technological advance. Perhaps Smith's suggestion that the MNC be allowed to exploit monoply power via patents and associated restrictions for a period of time and in a fashion to be negotiated, provides a fruitful approach to resolve this possible problem.

On the other hand, policies can be geared to modifying and controlling MNC behavior rather than replacing the MNC. The screening and bargaining process over all aspects of specific MNC conduct that affects the host nation is one possibility. The code of conduct presents one set of general guidelines. The joint venture requirement has also been relied on to enforce "good behavior" by the MNC saddled with a local partner (Parry, 1974d). However, joint ventures can often mean poor access to new technology, at higher prices, and with profits potentially channelled out via transfer pricing (Balasubramanyam, 1973). Restrictive trade practices (RTP) legislation may well provide a reasonably efficient approach to the peculiar problems associated with the MNC, without the need for additional measures directed to a foreign firm *per se*. Thus, for example, restrictions over tie-in clauses can apply to imported inputs in intrafirm trade as well as tied, domestic sourcing. Export franchises and transfer pricing can similarly, though with special definition, be controlled, at least with adequate information and administration, via RTP controls in general.

Finally, host countries may rely on some competitive balance found in the countervailing power of indigenous firms. The associated problems are significant, but it may be possible to rely on competitive pressures within domestic markets, provided the special features of the MNC are covered by some countervailing power. There is nothing inherent in competition of this sort that would mitigate the effect of the MNC's peculiar conduct in such matters as transfer pricing and export restrictions, even if structural consequences and general domestic "competitiveness" could be brought under control.

Whatever the policy combination relied on to control the MNC, there is always some danger that excessive control and interference could force the MNC to alternative host markets. Given the competition for industry and employment opportunities, especially in developing host countries, these countries have tended to compete for the entry of the MNC. This competition between host nations has tended to force up the terms in favor of the MNC. As long as host nations compete against each other to attract new MNC entry, relying on domestic policies that exacerbate some of the problems of the MNC, it is difficult to formulate policies, whether unilateral or international, to improve the host country benefits from interaction with MNCs.[29] Some recognition of the mutual interdependence of the host nations, in much the same way that MNCs have recognized their mutual interdependence, is a prerequisite for effective policy response to the challenge of multinational corporations.

# FOOTNOTES

*The author is grateful for the assistance of a University of New South Wales Special Project Fund grant. David Robertson has provided valuable comments.

1. McDougall (1960, p. 203) drops the perfect competition assumption for a part of analysis, but concludes that "imperfect competition does not seem to require much, if any, modification of our previous analysis."

2. McDougall also stresses "know-how" effects in external economies, embodied in the subsidiary as well as in the responses of domestically owned rivals.

3. This argument is developed in Johnson (1970) and Caves (1971a). See also Hufbauer (1975). Caves refers to "intangible assets" rather than technology as such, and stresses "product differentiation" as the appropriate monopolistic-competition advantage on which investment abroad is based.

4. Vaitsos (1970, 1970a); Vaitsos' theory of monopoly power of the MNC is based on the collective inputs of the foreign investment package. In many ways this approach parallels Smith's emphasis on the multinational's power base and interfirm and intrafirm coordination.

5. These include, notably, those by Miller and Weigel (1972) for Brazil, and Buckley and Dunning (1974) for the U.K. Buckley and Dunning's findings support the apparent product differentiation advantages of U.S. subsidiaries.

6. See Vernon (1971a); Dunning (1974); and Parry (1974b). Rosenbluth (1970), however, finds only a weak correlation between the degree of concentration and the degree of foreign ownership in Canadian industry. Recently available data, not yet officially published, on foreign ownership in Australian manufacturing has been compared with concentration ratios. Our results show a correlation of .482 and .508 between the degree of foreign ownership of an industry and the four-firm and eight-firm concentration ratios respectively.

7. See Gruber, Mehta, and Vernon (1967) and U.S. Tariff Commission (1973a). The U.K. experience, however, appears to be somewhat different (Parry, 1974c).

8. See especially Baranson (1969), Chudson (1971), and Governeur (1971). The essential difficulty is that the MNC is normally unwilling to adapt technology that is costly to develop and near costless to transfer within the enterprise.

9. Such host nations include, for example, India and the Andean Pact countries. Japan, of

course, has been doing this with regard to technology for many years, but may well represent a special case.

10. Evidence for India suggests that independent technology and joint-venture technology are less freely available than via the direct-investment package (Balasubramanyam, 1973). However, Vaitsos (1970) maintains that subsidiaries in Colombia paid more for all inputs than independent firms.

11. See Vernon (1974a) and Knickerbocker (1976). Declining concentration in world industry does not conflict with the earlier observation that MNCs tend to cluster in the more highly concentrated industries (Vernon, 1971). Rather, the suggestion is that mature oligopolies are facing increasing competition in international markets in recent years.

12. Dunning (1974), Parry (1974b), Rhadu (1973), and Steur (1973). The recent study by Knickerbocker (1976) suggests that evidence based on the Harvard Multinational Databank " . . . give good reason to believe that foreign direct investment by multinational companies has fostered or at least preserved those conditions of industry structure, in home (cf. Horst, 1975a) and host countries alike, which induce competition among industry members." The evidence regarding concentration at the product-market level is certainly consistent with Vernon's recent observations (Vernon, 1974a).

13. See, for example, Armand and Darancourt (1970), Hellmann (1970), Steur et al. (1971), and Dunning (1974).

14. See, for example, Brash (1970), English (1964), Safarian (1973), Carlos Dias Alejandro (1970), Parry (1974a), and Reuber et al. (1973).

15. The problem of inappropriate derivative technology for market structure is not confined to operations of MNCs. Eastman and Stykolt's work (1967) also concerns the use of derivative technology by domestically owned firms in Canada behind tariff walls. Nor is the problem exclusive to developing countries, even in the case of MNC entry (Parry, 1974a).

16. Canadian experience highlights the role of inappropriate economic policies, notably tariff policies geared to industrial development, in creating these structural distortions (Eastman and Stykolt, 1967; English, 1964; and Safarian, 1973). See also Hogan (1968) on Pakistan's experience with the branch-plant problem and host-nation economic policies. It is also interesting to speculate whether Knickerbocker's detailed evidence about the new competitive entry of rival MNCs into different countries' product markets over the 1950s and 1960s is an *a priori* measure of the market fragmentation associated with that international oligopolistic rivalry (Knickerbocker, 1976).

17. The main reason given for adaptation by the affiliate was to minimize underutilization of installed plant, particularly in anticipation of a reduction in tariff protection.

18. The usual approach to the structure effects of MNC operations is to break down the elements of industry structure into concentration, product differentiation, and barriers to entry. See, for example, Dunning (1974) and Knickerbocker (1976). Product differentiation, however, can be treated as a barrier to entry.

19. Eastman and Stykolt's study (1967) reports a close correlation between product differentiation and foreign control in Canadian industry. In fact, the advantages of the large multiplant company is seen to come from economies of product differentiation, which acts as an important structural entry barrier in the market (cf. Caves, 1971a).

20. See Safarian (1966), as well as the Watkins Report (1968) and the Gray Report (1972).

21. A number of cases are cited in Behrman (1970) and Dunning (1958). Knickerbocker (1976) presents general data on this phenomenon.

22. See, for example, Helleiner (1973), Cohen (1975), and OECD (1974b). A significant proportion of this export activity is "tied" to intrafirm trade (OECD, 1974a, and U.S. Tariff Commission, 1973).

23. See, for example, Brash (1966, Chs. 6–10), Dunning (1970, Ch. 9), Safarian (1966, Chs. 4–7 and 9), Caves (1974c); and Parry (1974a).

24. See Dunning (1970, Ch. 9); and Rhadu (1973). Rhadu found that in thirteen out of sixteen industries examined, foreign affiliates had greater labor productivity than domestically owned rivals.

25. See Caves (1974c). Using unpublished four-digit ASIC data on foreign ownership, we calculated the correlation between productivity (value added per head employed) and the proportion of foreign ownership in Australian manufacturing industries. The simple correlation coefficient is .408, a result not inconsistent with Caves' conclusion. See also Hogan (1962).

26. See, for example, Fulgate (1971) and Horst (1975a) on U.S. antitrust extended internationally and Jacquemin (1974) on the EEC response.

27. This was experienced, for example, in parts of the Australian chemical industry in the early 1970s (Parry, 1974a).

28. This is the case, notably, in Canada and Austrialia. Various countries' approaches are discussed in OECD (1974c) and Wertheimer (1971).

29. The increasing competition between U.S. and Japanese MNCs, at least in Asia and South America, may lead to a better bargaining position for the developing host nation in these areas (Kappor, 1974).

# COMMENT

## RICHARD E. CAVES*

Efforts to integrate the multinational corporation into the analysis of market structure, conduct, and performance have greatly clarified our thinking about the multinational firm as a market participant. Nonetheless, Parry finds, and I agree with him, that we have obtained few unambiguous conclusions for economic policy toward foreign direct investment. Of course, that may not be a bad thing: Well-informed uncertainty is likely to do less mischief than ignorant conviction.

Briefly, the evidence seems to support the following analytical conclusions. Multinational companies tend to be the larger firms participating in any of their national markets, if only because the same firm-specific assets that make them large are likely to make foreign investment profitable for them. Foreign investment tends to occur in concentrated industries, with that correlation arising because foreign investment and concentration share a number of common causes (Caves, 1974d). (We can imagine causal relations running either from seller concentration to foreign investment or from foreign investment to concentration, but neither appears to have been documented from the empirical evidence.) The multinational company enjoys advantages in overcoming barriers to entry, but it may also be a contributor to building those barriers against

*Harvard University

other companies. The MNC is perhaps less likely to join in oligopolistic understandings than a comparable domestic enterprise, but it is also prone to divert competitive strategies toward nonprice activities that may have adverse implications for market performance. Finally, multinational companies tend themselves to be profitable and to operate in industries that earn more than normal profits, but these financial results reflect both efficiency rents and monopoly profits. Thus, at each turn we find our assessment of the multinational company casting up both pluses and minuses.

Parry's paper covers a number of issues that touch on the normative significance of the multinational for market performance. In some cases, opposing views are presented at different points in the paper, leaving one in doubt about how the author resolves them. At some risk of distorting his intent, I shall deal with two aspects of his discussion. First, I shall argue that several of the standard objections to MNC operations are affirmed in the paper without being pursued to their behavioral fundamentals. I shall then also urge some refinements in the paper's policy conclusions.

### MNCs and Market Failure

A chronic difficulty with discussions of policy toward the MNC is that they complain about its behavior without specifying the alternative state of affairs that would be necessary to relieve the complaint. To put it simply, some complaints about multinational companies are really complaints about market power, large corporate size, or even capitalism itself! Although Parry avoids most of these familiar excesses, his analysis needs clarification at some points on the ultimate sources of market failures that may be associated with the MNC.

Before considering the particular instances, let me illustrate the general problem. A proposition currently popular with the Chicago school is that any large firm holding a high market share and earning high profits must simply be collecting rents on something special that it provides to the public (Demsetz, 1973; Magee, 1977a; Mancke, 1974). This view willfully declines to distinguish between unique productive assets that cannot be replicated (and their rents competed away) and contrived scarcities in which the rent is nothing but the reward to the firm's successful action to prevent market rivals from replicating its particular bundle of activities. To oversimplify, if the Chicagoans recognize only the former class of situations, Parry recognizes only the latter.

*Technology and Monopoly Power.*   Parry seems to believe that "the concentration of existing know-how and technological advance in the hands of the MNC has become one of the major causes of monopoly or oligopoly power associated with multinationals." When we assess this asserted relation between proprietary knowledge and market power, two points must be kept in mind. First, the causation runs from the control of proprietary knowledge to multinational enterprise, and not the other way around. Foreign investment is often the most effective way for an enterprise to maximize the returns to its intangible assets; conversely, we have no evidence that the large absolute sizes attained by companies through multinational operations contribute importantly to their rates of investment in the development of new proprietary knowledge. Second, the market failure that is involved here lies in the market for information itself and not in its exploitation through foreign investment. The welfare problem is the familiar one addressed by the patent privilege. Because knowledge is a public good, it will be underprovided unless those who produce it can appropriate and monopolize the product. Property rights in intangible knowledge are potentially a troublesome problem in international economic policy because of the incentive for a country to deny protection to knowledge produced outside its boundaries and become a free rider. However, it does not further clear thinking to suggest that the problem of impacted proprietary knowledge exists because ultinational companies decline to hand their stock out to passers-by.

*Technology and Host-Country Factor Prices.*    Parry repeats with apparent approval the familiar complaint that multinationals fail to adapt their technologies to the factor prices of less-developed host countries. The source and nature of this alleged market failure are not completely obvious. The failure to adopt appropriate technology is a failure to minimize costs, yet we are given no reasons why companies effective enough to attain multinational status should suddenly eschew a routine form of cost minimization. Recent survey evidence suggests that two factors are at work. The technological knowledge proprietary to a company does not include operating capability at every set of relative input prices—all the points on the economist's isoquant map—but only at those input price ratios that are within the company's previous experience. There is a fixed cost of adapting technology to lower relative labor costs and it may exceed the present value of expected cost reductions, especially when the effective unit labor cost of LDC labor to the MNC may be not all that low, and rising rapidly. Furthermore, multinational companies appear to see capital-intensive technologies as valuable for maintaining a uniform standard of product quality throughout their worldwide operations (Keddie, 1975). This objective harks back to the role of proprietary intangibles in multinational enterprise—in this case the trademark or brand identification, which might be impaired if the product's quality is lowered in some production locations. If we object to the MNC's choice of a production technique with an eye to maximizing returns to its intangible goodwill, then the basic problem is not multinationality but the legal protection of trademarks.

*Transfer Pricing.*    Parry repeatedly refers to discretionary transfer pricing as an exercise of monopoly power. Yet any firm controls its internal transfer prices (in the absence of outside intervention), no matter how competitive or monopolistic are the product markets in which it operates. Both competitive and monopolistic firms may be motivated to use non-market transfer prices in order to minimize their global tax burdens. Although the monopolistic MNC will presumably have more profits to move around through transfer pricing, it will be subject to the same incentives as the competitor to manipulate transfer prices. One could argue, though, that the firm with market power may have more opportunities to delude itself by its transfer prices about the true opportunity costs of certain allocations that it makes. Such a firm can believe its own distorted prices without fatally impairing its economic viability, which a firm in theoretical pure competition could not do.

*Product Differentiation, Tariffs, and Efficiency.*    Parry refers to the Canadian model of tariff-protected oligopoly. That model concludes that tariff protection is likely to induce an inflow of foreign investment in the form of inefficiently small-scale branch plants, and that the MNCs are likely to crowd in with such plants until their profits are depressed to normal levels but without any corresponding fall of prices. I believe that this model is both theoretically tight and empirically relevant. However, its necessary assumptions require some careful attention. Given that a multinational company can finance an efficient-scale plant, it would build an inefficiently small one only if production-scale economies are quite large relative to the market or if the individual seller in the market faces a downward sloping demand curve. The latter condition, which is almost necessarily associated with product differentiation, provides the link that integrates the role of the multinational company. Consider the international distribution of production for a differentiated good, and (as we assume) each variety of it is produced subject to the same cost curve and economies of scale, but consumers' preferences are distributed unevenly among varieties. If any production of the good takes place in a small import-competing manufacturing sector, like that of Canada or Australia, it will be of those varieties in relatively great demand, and thus least subject to small-scale disadvantages in local production. Imposing or raising a tariff makes viable the production of brands in less widespread demand, wherefore the average domestic producer's output may shrink even while total domestic production increases. The foreign company that has been exporting successfully to the market is likely to establish production facilities behind the elevated tariff wall and become one of the new small-scale producers. Because facility with product differentiation is one asset that tends to make a company multinational, we expect that the MNC's subsidiary can if anything attract a more price-inelastic demand than the typical domestic producer, in which case the tariff-protected foreign subsidy can be economically viable at an even smaller scale. Thus the multinational company does not create the welfare problem of inefficient production in tariff-ridden industries, which would result in any case if the product is differentiated, but it may worsen the problem by further reducing the average scale of production.

## Public Policy Questions

*Entry by Acquisition.* Public policy toward multinational companies might well attempt to maximize their value as actual and potential entrants into industries otherwise surrounded by substantial entry barriers. U.S. antitrust policy toward conglomerate mergers has been motivated by the goal of scaring large acquiring firms away from buying up companies that are leaders in their industries, and diverting their expansionist zeal toward acquiring smaller and struggling firms, or entering *de novo*. It would be desirable to divert multinationals' entry patterns in the same way. The economic gains from maximizing the supply of effective entrants are perhaps one of the better justifications for the review agencies now screening multinational acquisitions in many host countries. In this context, it is interesting that the initial report of the Canadian government's agency (Foreign Investment Review Agency, 1975) indicates that a large proportion of the international mergers submitted for its approval were initiated by the domestic seller, and involved the disposal of a company that might otherwise have been liquidated.

*Intracorporate Competition.* Parry flirts with, but seems ultimately to reject, the nonsensical proposition that multinational enterprise is bad because the MNC's various subsidiaries do not compete with one another. After all, if the multinational is a global profit maximizer, we cannot expect that it would find the road to riches lying in unconstrained rivalry among its members. To object to the MNC for a lack of intracorporate competition is simply to object to transnational ownership links. Nonetheless, we might consider severing those links selectively in an idealized context where antimonopoly policy could be enforced on an international basis against companies that possess significant market power in international markets. American antitrust policy has never found the dismemberment of going firms by judicial decree an easy matter to countenance. Severing foreign subsidiaries is a less risky remedy, however, because the subsidiary's viability as an independent firm is seldom in doubt. Foreign subsidiaries have occasionally been divested as a result of United States antitrust actions (notably the Canadian subsidiary of the Aluminum Company of America). That remedy might be used more widely, although it, of course, runs into the usual problem of divergent national laws and interests (Caves, 1973).

*Technology Transfer and Joint Ventures.*   Parry recognizes that joint ventures are no panacea to resolve the conflict between foreign investment and the nationalistic feelings of host countries. A company whose multinational status devolves from its control of intangible assets would be expected to have a strong preference for wholly owned subsidiaries, and if forced into a joint venture it will hold out for an arms-length price for the transfer of these assets. Voluntary joint ventures seem to occur mainly where no intangibles are involved and there are large risks to be shared, as in mining and extractive activities. Joint ventures, however they were established, are hobbled entrepreneurial units that can undertake only those activities mutually agreeable to their various parents; and they are unlikely to count for much as competitive forces in the market. We also know that companies transferring technology at arms-length are conscious of the possibility that they are strengthening a future international competitor—this is Joe Peck's (1976) explanation for the rise in the late 1960's of royalty rates on technology transfers, despite the increased number of companies active in supplying proprietary technology on license. And pure transfers of technology seem to work only for production technology or in franchise-type relations, and not where the vendor's intangible assets importantly include marketing knowledge about how to match the company's production to the desires of potential buyers. In short, joint ventures and technology transfer as alternatives to the operations of the MNC are not costless ways to resolve the political acrimony over the multinational company.

# 4.  TRANSFER PRICES, TAXES, AND FINANCIAL MARKETS: IMPLICATIONS OF INTERNAL FINANCIAL TRANSFERS WITHIN THE MULTINATIONAL CORPORATION*

Donald R. Lessard, MASSACHUSETTS INSTITUTE OF

TECHNOLOGY

## INTRODUCTION

The ability of multinational corporations (MNCs) to shift funds and accounting profits among their component units through internal channels raises interesting questions regarding the reasons for and welfare impacts of these firms' operations and, as a result, about appropriate public policies toward them. Popular critiques characterize the MNC as an "octopus," which, through its internal transfers disrupts exchange and credit markets, avoids both home-and host-country taxes, increases its monopoly power, gains an "unfair" competitive advantage relative to local firms, and hides its "excessive" profits to avoid public scrutiny and regulation.[1] While many such charges undoubtedly are overstated and

Research in International Business and Finance, Vol. 1, pp. 101–135.
ISBN 0-89232-031-1

often contradictory, there remain the questions of whether the MNC's ability to internalize financial transactions favors the MNC relative to national firms, whether it has an impact on the location of production, and whether it changes the distribution of income among consumers, suppliers of factors, and governments, both within and among countries. More specifically, each of the following might be asked:

- Do governments intentionally or unintentionally encourage the growth of multinationals relative to national firms by adopting tax policies or financial market regulations that favor MNCs by raising the cost of market transfers of goods, real factors, and especially capital between independent firms and investors?

- Do MNCs shift profits internally and as a result reduce total taxes and/or alter the distribution of tax revenues for a given distribution of real activities? Further, does this profit shifting alter the distribution of real investment, production, and trade itself?

- Do MNCs disguise their true profitability in various countries and as a result distort public policy toward them?

This paper reviews and synthesizes available research regarding the relevance of MNC internal financial mechanisms and the actual use of these mechanisms. Its primary purpose is to determine what, if any, guidance this research provides for policymakers. Since the relevant literature is fragmented, a major part of the paper is devoted to presenting a framework within which the impact of internal financial transfers may be analyzed. Three broad groups of purposes for which the internal financial mechanism may be relevant are identified. These are minimizing taxes, circumventing barriers within and between financial markets, and disguising true profitability as a means to influence public policy.

The internal financial system is deemed relevant if its use increases the value to the firm and its shareholders of a particular operation relative to what it would be if all its financial transactions were at arms-length through external financial channels. By implication, internalizing any financial transfer that can be replicated at no greater cost by an independent single-country firm or individual investor through financial markets will provide no advantage, and hence be irrelevant. Relevant financial transfers may provide MNCs with absolute advantages over national competitors, or in cases where there are unique costs to international financial transfers on an arms-length basis, they may simply offset these costs and put the MNC on equal footing with a local competitor in a particular market.

This review is organized into four parts. The first two sections outline the characteristics of the MNC's financial system and describe the circumstances under which such a system provides significant advantages to the MNC. The third section provides a more in-depth review of theoretical arguments and empirical evidence regarding the role of internal financial systems in minimizing taxes, arbitraging financial markets, and influencing public policy, respectively. The fourth section relates the MNC financial advantages to the "generally accepted" theory of direct foreign investment. And the final section draws conclusions regarding the desirability and feasibility of controlling the MNC's financial system as well as the implications of taking into account its existence in formulating financial, tax, and industrial policies.

## THE MULTINATIONAL FINANCIAL SYSTEM

Rutenberg (1970) and Robbins and Stobaugh (1973) aptly characterize the MNC as a financial system with myriad linkages for transferring funds and/or profits among its various units. Figure 4-1 illustrates the nature of these potential links. All of these links can and do exist among separate, independent firms, but their potential use is very different within a fully *controlled* corporate system. The differences result from two factors; greater discretion in the *choice of channels* through which financial transfers are made and in the *timing of transactions* within a controlled system.

In considering the financial transfers within an MNC, it is useful to also keep track of the internal real transactions that give rise to many of these financial claims. Any transfer of real goods or factors, ranging from

*Figure 4.1*   The Multinational Corporate Financial System

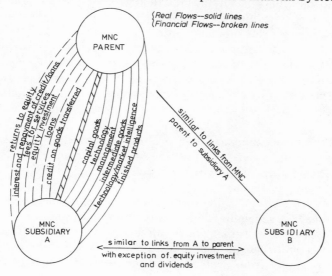

finished product to vaguely defined intangible factors such as management skills, if not paid for immediately at an arms-length (market value) price, is accompanied by a financial transfer giving rise to some type to financial claim. Financial transfers within an MNC also may support real transfers to a component of the MNC from outside the corporate system. In this case, the MNC is acting as a financial intermediary.

*Discretionary Choice of Channels.* The MNC has considerable latitude in selecting the choice of financial channels, especially for transactions that arise from internal transfers of real goods or factors of production. For example, intangible factors of production are transferred to the subsidiary by the parent and can give rise to a wide range of different implicit and explicit financial claims. If sold outright at an arms-length price, no claim is generated. If transferred in return for arms-length royalty fees, then they give rise to an explicit long-term financial contract similar to that which would be entered into by unrelated firms. However, if the cash price or market value of the royalty claims are below an arms-length price, then part of the financial claim will be an implicit (and unregistered) equity claim. If the transferred factors are underpriced relative to the market standards, subsidiary profits (other things equal) will be higher than those of an independent firm, and the parent's equity claim will be more valuable. If overpriced, the parent will be reducing equity by disguising the transfer as a payment on current account for factor transfers.

For financial transfers not arising from internal real transfers, the MNC still has many options. Intracompany financial transfers may be denominated as loans with considerable latitude regarding interest rate, currency, and repayment schedule. They also may be denominated as equity transfers. If the interest rate on a loan differs from market rates for loans with similar risk or if the amount loaned exceeds the subsidiary's contribution to the corporation's total debt capacity, there is an implicit equity transfer. This is also true of parent guarantees of subsidiary borrowing. Implicit or explicit equity claims may be recovered directly through dividend remittances or indirectly through the other types of transfers discussed above.

All of these mechanisms often are lumped together under the term "transfer pricing." Clearly, however, this includes much more than fiddling prices on intracompany transfers of goods.

*Discretionary Timing.* Although certain types of financial claims incorporate a specific schedule of payments, many mechanisms used by the MNC allow for leading or lagging of intracompany transfers. Trade credit, on open account, can be used quite flexibly. The flexibility of fees or royalties resulting from previous or concurrent transfers of factors of production may be limited by the contractual terms, but since both parties are related, the terms often can be altered. The most flexible of all, of course, are the equity claims. The MNC parent has considerable discretion regarding remittance of its equity claim or "rolling it over" into a new larger claim by reinvesting profits.

Even when timing is limited by contractual terms or government regulations, there is almost always a degree of latitude over the exact nature and timing of the flows. This flexibility is enhanced by the discretion the MNC has regarding the timing of internal transfers of goods and real factors of production.

## The Relevance of Internal Financial Systems

While much has been made of the MNC's ability to select channels for and change the timing of internal financial transfers, little has been done to identify expressly those conditions under which these degrees of freedom represent an advantage for the MNC relative to single-country firms operating on an arms-length basis. After all, a purely domestic firm with several operating units has a similar system; yet such systems generally are not the object of the same type of criticism leveled at the MNC. For a domestic firm it does not appear that such a system provides an advantage relative to a set of smaller firms relying on arms-length external financial transactions. For example, for a multi-unit firm operating within a single country to engage in leading and lagging of intracompany payables would provide no special advantage, since the same results could readily be obtained by short-term external borrowing or lending transactions by the various units. Similarly, for one unit to borrow funds and relend them to another would have little economic impact. The ability to internalize financial transactions is relevant only to the extent to which there are barriers or costs to transfers of funds through external channels or differences in taxes depending on how revenues and costs are allocated among the various subunits of the firm.

The internal financial system of a multidivision firm within a single country such as the U.S. is largely irrelevant for two reasons. First, financial markets are quite efficient. Thus the cost of funds (equity and debt) for any particular investment can be expected to reflect the risk of the investment rather than whether it is being undertaken by a large diversified corporation or a smaller firm operating in a single industry. Further, transactions costs for transfers via financial markets will not exceed the costs of comparable internal transfers. Under such circumstances, mechanisms that allow for internal transfers of funds between operating units of a firm provide little or no advantage, since similar transfers could be replicated by independent firms or investors at little or no additional cost. In fact, most corporate financial transactions, including decisions regarding the structure of claims issued by the firm and whether earnings are retained or paid out as dividends, are shown by Modigliani and Miller (1958, 1961, 1963) to be irrelevant in efficient markets. Specific features of the tax system provide the strongest exceptions to the irrelevance arguments in the domestic case,[2] and even some of them are eliminated if *both* corporate and individual taxation is considered (Miller, 1976).

Second, the taxes associated with a particular operating unit are, under most circumstances, independent of whether it is part of a large conglomerate firm or separately incorporated. A single tax rate applies to the profits of all major corporations. Although the system is asymmetrical with respect to tax losses, these can be carried backward or forward, and besides, there exists an external "market" for tax losses through leases and other tax shelters. In extreme cases, unusable losses can be "sold" by merging the losing firm with a profitable one. As a result, there is little to be gained from spreading losses throughout a series of related firms.

There are several reasons for believing that the internal financial system is more likely to be relevant to a firm operating internationally. Often there are tax costs and other restrictions to financial transfers across national boundaries and many governments impose restrictions on domestic financial transactions. Both provide advantages to firms that can circumvent them through internal financial transfers. Tax rates differ across countries. Conflicting claims by various governments sometimes give rise to double taxation and there are limits to which losses or taxes paid in one country can be applied against profits or tax liabilities in another. As a result of these factors, the ability to allocate revenues and costs internally will affect global tax payments, as well as the distribution of these payments. Thus the value of a venture may depend on the nature of the firm that owns it.

*Financial Tariffs and Quotas.*   One way to view the conditions under which having an internal financial mechanism will make a difference is to think of the multinational financial system as a network of linkages (as depicted in Figure 4-1) where transfers along some or all of the channels face tariffs or quotas. For example, within the accepted rules of the game for the international payments system, capital account transfers may be restricted (they may face quotas) while current transactions such as payments for goods or intangible factors of production are unrestricted. In such a case, there is a clear advantage to a firm having discretion over the type of channel through which it operates. In other cases, financial transfers classified as capital account transactions will face tariffs (transfer taxes or dual exchange rate systems) while current transactions will not.

Access to particular domestic financial markets also may be restricted to local firms. The MNC, through its local subsidiaries, can gain access to these markets and shift the funds elsewhere within its global systems through one of the many available mechanisms. In this way, it circumvents a barrier that would prevent international financial transfers by national firms or individual investors based in other countries.

Most importantly, by appropriate internal transfers the MNC can reduce overall taxes and can avoid taxes on specific financial transfers. This may bring them below the level that would have to be paid by national firms or individuals operating at arms-length, or it may simply offset double taxation, putting it on par with local competitors. In the case of the U.S. deferral provisions, for example, to the extent that the parent can shift funds from one subsidiary to another without passing them through the U.S. as remitted profits, taxes are postponed and hence their economic impact is reduced.

The major types of costs or restrictions that make internal financial transactions attractive are summarized in the box below.

---

Formal Barriers to International Transactions

- Quantitative restrictions (exchange controls) and direct taxes on international movements of funds.
- Differential taxation of income streams according to nationality and global tax situation of the owners.
- Restrictions by nationality of investor and/or investment on access to domestic capital markets.

Informal Barriers to International Transactions

- Costs of obtaining information.
- Difficulty of enforcing contracts across national boundaries.
- Transaction costs.
- Traditional investment patterns.

Imperfections in Domestic Capital Markets

- Ceilings on interest rates.
- Mandatory credit allocations.
- Limited legal and institutional protection for minority shareholders.
- Limited liquidity because of thinness of markets.
- High transaction costs attributable to small market size and/or monopolistic practices of key financial institutions.
- Difficulty of obtaining information needed to evaluate securities.

---

Gains to MNCs from being able to circumvent these barriers can be grouped under two headings: *financial market arbitrage* and *tax system arbitrage*, although there clearly is an overlap between the two. Further, the ability to shift profits internally and thus disguise true profitability may be advantageous to the MNC in cases where profits are a function of bargaining or regulation, rather than competitive forces. Such potential gains do not appear to fit readily into the framework outlined above, but as we shall show, they are similar in nature to those resulting from tax system arbitrage. We shall refer to this class of gains as *regulatory system arbitrage*.

# STUDIES OF MNC FINANCIAL BEHAVIOR

The questions of ultimate interest in this review are to what extent real investment, production, and trade decisions and the distribution of benefits resulting from these decisions are changed because of the MNC's ability to shift funds and profits internally. There are few studies that provide any direct evidence on these questions. As a result, we are forced to rely on less direct evidence, either in the form of models that show what behavior we should expect from MNCs under certain conditions or on general observations of the financial behavior of MNCs and its apparent impact on their real decisions.

In the following three sections, we review models and empirical observations of MNC financial behavior in terms of minimizing taxes, circumventing financial barriers, and disguising true profitability. A few of these models have been developed in order to draw positive inferences about MNC financial behavior and its impact on real variables, but the majority are normative models focusing either on the optimal exploitation of a firm's financial system, generally taking real variables as givens, or on the evaluation of individual investments, taking into account the impact of the financial variables. Although the former are of more direct interest, the latter also are of interest, since they typically involve more detailed and complex treatments of corporate financial behavior.

Both types of models serve two basic purposes in the study of the relevance of MNC financial systems. First, they provide concrete specifications of the nature of advantages provided by such systems and of the conditions under which they are relevant. Second, they provide some idea of the importance of these effects relative to other factors that influence real decisions. Given the difficulty of empirically verifying the role of various factors in the expansion of multinational enterprise, this is very important.

Empirical studies of MNC financial behavior face many problems. In particular, most are plagued with measurement difficulties. This is to be expected, since the essence of exploiting an internal financial system involves using internal channels for transferring funds and profits, many of which are unregistered either in the firm's reported results or in country data.

## The MNC Financial System and Tax System Arbitrage

Clearly, differences in tax systems among countries have an impact on decisions regarding the location of production. Interactions exist between host-country income and withholding taxes, home-country corporate taxes on foreign source income including the effects of credits and deferrals, and home-country taxes at the investor level on either distributed or undistributed corporate profits. Thus total taxes paid on the profits of a particular venture will depend, to some extent, on the nationality of the investing firm. To that extent, taxes become relevant to the ownership decision. These effects have been reviewed by Horst (1975, 1977b), Hufbauer and Foster (1976), Kopits (1976a), and Musgrave (1975), among others. The scope of this review is more limited, concentrating on changes in the effect of taxes on location and production decisions that result from the MNC's ability to engage in internal transfers. We begin with the positive models that incorporate real decisions.

*Positive Models of MNC Tax Arbitrage.* Horst (1971) provides one of the first concrete models of direct foreign investment that takes into account the impact of the MNC's ability to manipulate transfer prices. He focuses on the production (and hence trade) decision of a monopolistic firm selling the same good to two different countries, allowing for various combinations of scale economies and ability to price independently in the two markets. Since the only financial transfer he allows is manipulation of transfer prices on intracompany trade, such transfers will have an effect on the tariff as well as tax bill. As a result, he concludes that the firm will always be choosing between the largest and smallest possible transfer price for its exports, pricing goods as low as possible when

$$\pi_2 > \frac{t_2 - t_1}{1 - t_2} \tag{1}$$

where $\pi_2$ is the tariff rate charged by the importing country and $t_1$ and $t_2$ are the total tax rates (including home-country taxation of foreign source income, etc.) imposed by the exporting and importing countries, respectively. He further argues that since tariff rates generally will exceed tax differentials, both because tax systems appear to converge around a common rate and because U.S. firms can consolidate income from high-tax and low-tax countries and thus diminish any remaining differentials in effective tax rates, minimum transfer prices for exports to affiliates will be the rule. As a result, he concludes that tax increases by high-tariff countries will have little or no impact on the real decisions of firms, but will change the distribution of tax revenues in favor of these countries. If he had allowed for internal profit transfers that have no effect on tariffs, such as royalties on intangible factors of production or internal financing, this latter question would have been much more complicated. One would expect even less impact of taxes on real decisions, but conclusions regarding the impact of tax changes on the distribution of tax revenues would be much harder to draw.

In his most recent research on this subject, Horst (1975, 1977b) concentrates on the potential impact of changes in U.S. tax laws, such as the elimination of deferral, requiring country-by-country computation of the credit, and replacing the credit with a deduction, on the real investment and production decisions of U.S.-based MNCs and on the distribution of income between firms and the tax authorities of home and host countries. His model incorporates several financial variables that have an impact on taxes: headquarters charges (royalties and fees), the proportion of earnings remitted as dividends, and the debt/equity mix in intrafirm financing. For purposes of exposition, he concentrates on the effect of changes in the intrafirm debt/equity mix, taking dividend remittance and headquarters charges as fixed. However, since their profit-shifting effects are for the most part similar to those of royalties and fees, his results can be interpreted as if they apply to the full range of profit-shifting techniques. He concludes that certain changes in tax policy such as eliminating deferral or grossing-up LDC-source income would have little impact on real MNC activities, although they would shift revenues to the U.S. because they would remove old and create new incentives for profit shifting. If this profit shifting is unconstrained, he finds that even such drastic change in U.S. tax policy as replacing the credit with a deduction would have little impact on the real decisions of multinationals, but would have drastic effects on the distribution of tax revenues. His analyses and conclusions are much too complex to discuss in detail here, but they provide a strong case that the MNC's ability to make internal financial transfers must be taken into account in any analysis of the effects of current or proposed taxation of MNCs or their activities on various countries' tax revenues. Hufbauer and Foster (1976), and Sato and Bird (1975), in exploring similar issues, also conclude that internal financial transfers must be considered in examining tax effects.

Vaitsos (1974a,b) provides an extensive and provocative discussion of the welfare impact of MNC's ability to set nonmarket transfer prices for internal transfers of goods and services. He focuses on a seeming anomaly—the overpricing of goods and services to LDC manufacturing subsidiaries by their developed country parents in spite of the fact that most of these subsidiaries face relatively low local tax rates, liberal deferral provisions *vis-à-vis* home-country taxes, and, in many cases, relatively high tariffs. These factors, as shown by Horst and others, would be expected to result in a shift in reported taxable profits from parents to subsidiaries and not the other way around! He identifies a set of possible explanations, including transfer pricing as a means for: disguising local profitability to decrease political exposure and improving the firm's position in bargaining for tariff, subsidy, and other benefits; minimizing global taxes *even if* local tax rates are lower than parent rates; bypassing restrictions on remittances; and taking advantage of local joint-venture partners.

Vaitsos' tax argument is that a firm whose revenues from home and unaffiliated export sales are smaller than its costs in the home country, including those of supporting the global operation, will shift profits "upstream" to the parent in order to avoid tax losses. This undoubtedly is true. However, Kopits (1976a, p. 27) points out that there are few firms in this situation. A more likely scenario is that U.S.-based firms would shift profits "downstream" to use up excess foreign tax credits generated from operations in relatively high-tax countries. Clearly, generalizations are dangerous, but it appears unlikely that the phenomenon observed by Vaitsos can be explained in terms of tax minimization.

*Normative Models of MNC Tax Arbitrage.* Rutenberg (1970) provides a general model for optimizing MNC financial transactions, but he excludes from his model most real investment and production decisions, assuming that these have already been made. His aim is to show how the general tax minimization (and financial arbitrage) problem can be formulated as a linear program incorporating a host of constraints on the extent to which transfer prices, fees, royalties, and financial charges can be manipulated. As such his model sheds little light on the impact of these transfers on real decisions, but it does serve to make explicit many of the different channels available. He does discuss one real decision, the location of production for "high-margin" products, focusing on products with low transportation costs where current production costs are low relative to selling price, as a result of rents from previous R & D, advertising, or a monopoly position. Implicitly, what this involves is an unregistered transfer of the "patent" or "market franchise" at a zero price.

Robbins and Stobaugh (1973) employ a linear programming model developed by Daniel Schydlowsky to trace the potential benefits to a hypothetical firm of exploiting different aspects of the internal financial system. In their example, they vary constraints to allow for: alterations in transfer prices on intrafirm product flows by plus or minus 20 percent; shifting internal credit terms from 0 to 180 days with interest rates varying from 0 to 8 percent; varying maturities and rates on intracompany loans; and varying both the timing and amount of royalty and fee flows. They conclude that by optimizing, their hypothetical firm could increase the parent firm's profits by 16 percent from the base level where each unit is financially autonomous. While most of this gain is attributed to financial market arbitrage, a point we discuss below, tax minimization also plays an important role. The critical determinants of the extent of gains are the volume of intrafirm transactions of all types and the leeway the firm has in altering the terms on each transaction.

In addition to external constraints on "transfer pricing," firms may place internal constraints on such manipulations either because of considerations of social responsibility or because of distortions that such practices introduce into internal control systems. Shulman (1967), for example, stresses the costs in terms of internal distortions of altering transfer prices for tax purposes. However, Arpan (1971), Salma (1975), Nieckels (1976) and others show that firms can and many do have separate transfer-pricing systems for internal and external purposes. Of course, this increases the complexity of international management and, presumably, gives an advantage to those firms with scale and experience sufficient to cope with it. Both Salmi (1975) and Nieckels (1976) develop optimizing models for tax-oriented transfer pricing that are quite rich in operational detail. There appears to be little question that under realistic assumptions tax arbitrage should provide advantages to the MNC.

Other normative models that one would expect to incorporate tax considerations are those focusing on MNC investment decisions. In reviewing the capital budgeting literature, however, we found that while tax factors were included, differences in taxes for MNCs and national firms were not treated explicitly. Exceptions are Adler (1974) and Adler and Dumas (1976), who focus on differences between required returns for MNCs and national firms. They show that taxes are relevant, but they emphasize distortions in financial markets as the basis for most of these differences.

*Empirical Studies of MNC Tax-Related Behavior.*   Kopits (1972, 1976b) concentrates on a limited but complex set of internal financial decisions—the choice of royalties or dividends for remittances to the parent firm. In the 1972 paper, he estimates the reaction of dividends to differentials between home- and host-country tax rates and to split-rate tax systems in host countries that discriminate between retained and remitted earnings. He finds that taxes did have a significant effect on dividend remittances from developed countries and from this concludes that taxes may have a substantial influence on real investment flows. However, these results cannot be interpreted as showing whether the tax effects differ for MNCs, nor that they change real decisions. At best they show that taxes affect the percentage of profits remitted as dividends, and, without including other transfer channels as well as explicit estimates of the firms' investment opportunities, provide only limited evidence in this regard. In the later paper, Kopits (1976b) focuses on royalty remittances. He shows that the choice cannot be based simply on the relative tax rates in the home and host country, but also on the firms' ability to offset excess tax credits in high-tax countries against income generated from low-tax countries, a point also made by Ness (1972). Kopits again obtains significant results for developed countries, lending support to the notion that taxes do matter. To the extent that royalty arrangements are more flexible among related firms than unrelated firms, these results have a more direct bearing on the issue of whether taxes have a differential impact on MNCs. The results are again limited by the fact that the set of financial variables considered is small, a point that Kopits recognizes. Kopits (1976a) reviews a variety of similar efforts by other authors and concludes that there is some support for the notion that MNC financial decisions reflect tax factors. In general, however, he concludes that most tests are of limited value given the complexity of the underlying behavior and the extreme difficulty of capturing the effects empirically.

*Descriptive Studies of MNC Tax Arbitrage.*    Robbins and Stobaugh (1973) provide an extensive description of MNC practices based on interviews with thirty-nine U.S.-based MNCs. In describing corporate transfer-pricing behavior, they conclude that tax minimization is an important consideration, but that exchange-rate restrictions provide even stronger motivation. Citing published figures on intracompany trade, they argue that by varying transfer prices by only 10 percent, U.S. MNCs would generate financial transfers larger than total actual royalty payments and approximately equal to actual dividend remittances. They believe that financial transfers are smaller than this figure, but nevertheless of considerable importance. One of the major points addressed by Robbins and Stobaugh is whether the extent to which a firm exploits its internal financial system is a function of firm size. Using a logistic regression model, they conclude that it is, with small firms making relatively little use of the system, medium firms substantial use of the system, and large firms moderate use of the system. They conclude that the reduced integrative focus of the large firms reflects external and internal constraints resulting from firm size.

Arpan (1971, 1972) reports on transfer-pricing practices of U.S. and non-U.S. MNCs. For most firms, he finds that managements viewed transfer prices as mechanisms for minimizing taxes and/or circumventing remittance restrictions. Effects on the degree of management control also were considered to be important, but many firms avoided conflict between the two objectives by using different transfer-pricing practices, apparently as the result of incentives provided by home-country tax systems.

*The MNC Financial System and Financial Market Arbitrage*

In this section, we focus on the circumstances in financial markets that would present MNCs, with their internal financial systems, with advantages relative to national firms or individual investors. In order to do so, it is necessary to identify in each case the nature of the advantage to be gained, the mechanism through which the MNC gains it, and the reason the same advantage is not generally available to non-MNC investors. The latter consideration is particularly important, since, as noted above, any access to financial markets that can be replicated readily by firms not possessing extensive internal mechanisms for transferring funds and/or profits or to individuals operating through financial markets is irrelevant to the differential valuation of the firm and its activities. For purposes of discussion, we divide MNC behavior aimed at profiting from financial market distortions into *exchange control arbitrage, credit market arbitrage,* and *equity market arbitrage.*

*Exchange Control Arbitrage.* If a country imposes exchange controls in order to maintain its exchange rate at a particular level, firms or investors able to circumvent these controls can engage in profitable arbitrage. One would expect MNCs, with their multiple channels for funds transfers to be favored in such cases. In a project valuation model, such gains would appear as a higher cash flow for the MNC than for an alternative investor firm lacking the mechanisms to circumvent the barriers. This source of gains appears to be a major element of MNC transfer pricing behavior *vis-à-vis* LDC subsidiaries as observed by Vaitsos (1974a, b) and Lall (1973). Both Arpan (1971, 1972) and Robbins and Stobaugh (1973) confirm this with their surveys of MNC behavior.

Leading and lagging is a major factor in exchange control arbitrage in those cases where governments intervene in exchange markets or impose restrictions temporarily to stave off a devaluation or revaluation. Firms that can accelerate or delay financial transfers clearly can gain. MNCs often will have a unique advantage, since they can alter current account transfers so as to avoid capital account restrictions. This type of exchange arbitrage is most likely under an exchange rate system with occasional large changes in currency parities. In fact, this ability of MNCs to beat the system may be a strong argument in favor of flexible exchange rates.

While exchange controls are generally thought of as binding on profit remittances, they also may interfere with the ability to invest in a particular project, as was the case with the U.S. OFDI controls. The MNC's ability to underprice real transfers and to guarantee external borrowing by foreign subsidiaries, both of which amount to unregistered outflows of equity, undoubtedly were a major factor in reducing or eliminating any impact of the controls on their real investment patterns.

*Credit Market Arbitrage.* A closely related potential source of gains is the ability of MNCs, through internal financial transfers, to take advantage of distortions in interest rates or escape the effects of restrictions on the availability of credit. Distortions in interest rates may result from a failure of market rates to adjust to an international equilibrium level due to (1) restrictions on the rates themselves—presumably resulting in credit rationing and allocation through nonmarket channels; (2) restrictions on access to domestic markets that shift the domestic equilibrium; and (3) restrictions on international financial transactions, including but not limited to exchange controls, that prevent international forces from acting on the domestic equilibrium.

The MNC, possessing at once the nationality of its home country and of the country in which the investment is located, will at worst have no disadvantage with domestic firms in obtaining subsidiary financing and gaining access to local financial markets. It should have a clear advantage in circumventing restrictions in international financial transactions, enabling it to borrow funds where available and shift them to countries where national investors face credit rationing.

Robbins and Stobaugh (1973) describe various mechanisms available to MNCs to circumvent restrictions separating capital markets. However in demonstrating these mechanisms, they employ the optimizing model discussed above in an unrealistic fashion. They assume that the firm knows future exchange rates with certainty, but that interest rates in various currencies do not reflect this knowledge. Thus their model generates large, sure gains from shifting currencies, gains that are limited only by restrictions placed on external corporate borrowing in various countries. Such a situation could only persist because of effective barriers to capital transfers, in which case the MNC would have to possess mechanisms for circumventing the barriers not available to others.

Macaluso and Hawkins (1977) provide some evidence that MNCs are able to avoid domestic credit restrictions to a greater extent than domestic firms. In four out of the six countries they examine, the MNC share of total investment rises when credit is tight. They also show that in tight credit periods, the share of MNC investment financed from internal sources increases, adding further credence to the view that MNCs actively circumvent domestic financial policies.

*Equity Market Arbitrage.* An argument similar to that applied to credit markets can be made for equity markets. Again, the MNC can engage in arbitrage if it has an advantage relative to domestic firms or investors in overcoming explicit or implicit barriers or minimizing taxes on international transfers of capital. The source of gains to equity market arbitrage is the reduction of risk through diversification. In the presence of barriers that inhibit international portfolio diversification by individual investors, the required rate of return for a given project may be lower for the MNC than for the national firm.

The logic of diversification is well known. Since the outcomes of different projects are not subject to exactly the same risks—i.e., the returns generated by several projects are not perfectly correlated—the risk of a portfolio of projects or securities will be less than the average risk of the individual projects. Lessard (1976) and Solnik (1974) show that the benefits of international diversification of equity securities investments are particularly strong. Equity returns within individual countries exhibit substantial covariation, placing a lower limit on the risk of a diversified portfolio of equity holdings. For large developed countries, this lower bound is around 50 percent of the risk (measured in terms of standard deviation) of the average individual security. However, since variations in returns on equity in various countries are substantially less than perfectly correlated, this lower bound falls to roughly 30 percent for an internationally diversified portfolio.

In an integrated international capital market without barriers or costs to capital transfers, individual investors can diversify their holdings of securities broadly, thereby averaging out much of the risk of individual projects themselves. As a result, the rate of return required on a particular venture will reflect only its contribution to the risk of a fully diversified portfolio, which is substantially smaller than its total risk. Since investors can diversify their own portfolios readily, firms need not concern themselves with their degree of diversification and can judge a venture's expected rate of return in relation to its systematic risk. As Adler and Dumas (1976) show, diversification at the corporate level will be relevant only when there are costs or barriers to such diversification at the investor level.

Many discussions of the diversification motive for DFI, including Prachowny (1972) and Stevens (1973), overlook this point, concentrating instead on the risk-reducing benefits of diversification without specifying why these are uniquely realized through the MNC. Ragazzi (1973), in contrast, stresses imperfections in non-U.S. equity markets, arguing that these may make the MNC the preferred channel for international diversification by U.S. investors. These considerations suggest that MNCs should not be concerned with forming corporate portfolios of activities with efficient mixes of total risk and return. Rather, they should seek to extend the frontier available to individual investors by investing more heavily, relative to the level justified by real and tax advantages, in those countries where investors cannot readily diversify for themselves. There are no direct tests of the relevance of the diversification motive for MNC expansion. Agmon and Lessard (1976b) suggest this is because of the difficulty of separating its effects from those of real market imperfections. Partial support, however, is provided by Hughes, Logue, and Sweeney (1976) and Agmon and Lessard (1977), who show that MNC security price behavior does reflect corporate international diversification. In order to confirm or reject the equity arbitrage hypothesis, empirical tests are required that relate direct foreign investment flows as a proportion of total investment flows between pairs of countries to differences in barriers to portfolio capital flows.

### Internal Financial Transfers as Means to Disguise Profits and Influence Public Policy

Several authors, including Robbins and Stobaugh (1973), Lall (1973), and most notably Vaitsos (1974a,b), argue that MNCs often use internal transfers to disguise the profitability of local operations for political or social reasons. If a country pursues an industrial policy that explictly or implicitly focuses on profit rates, there clearly is a motivation to do so. This is likely to be particularly important for LDCs that seek to develop local industry by granting monopolies protected by high tariffs and often supported by direct or indirect subsidies. Profit-maximizing MNC behavior in such a case calls for shifting profits out of the local subsidiary, similar to that motivated by limitations on profit remittances. Further, although it might appear that such a strategy would increase an MNC's global taxes, since the LDCs in question often have relatively low tax rates, the tax effects can be offset if the profits are shifted to another low-tax jurisdiction. Therefore, determining which factors dominate is as yet an unanswered empirical question. Vaitsos' results for Colombia, for example, which showed a pattern of overpricing by MNCs in the pharmaceutical industry, could have reflected the considerations of either circumventing exchange controls or influencing industrial policy. A similar analysis for another country with a similar industrial policy but no exchange controls, such as Venezuela, could be extremely instructive.

A related argument is that MNCs use discretionary transfer prices as a means to increase monopoly gains by allowing them to either undercut competition or gouge consumers. There appears to be little direct basis for this argument, since the MNC's ability to discriminate between countries in its pricing depends upon tariff barriers and other forms of market barriers. Weston (1973) discusses this point at some length and dismisses it as having little merit. On an indirect level, however, if reported profitability is a factor in the determination of tariff protection, internal profit shifting will affect consumer prices as well as government revenues.

# FINANCIAL MARKET IMPERFECTIONS AND THE THEORY OF DIRECT FOREIGN INVESTMENT

It is generally acknowledged that in order to justify foreign investments, the multinational corporation must have some advantage relative to local firms in the countries in which it invests that allowed it to overcome the costs imposed by cultural and geographical distance not borne by them. Most economists have argued that the primary sources of advantages by MNCs relative to local firms are imperfections in markets for products and factors of production.[3] Financial factors generally are excluded, presumably because financial markets are deemed to be more efficient than markets for real goods and services and hence less likely to give rise to advantages from internal transfer mechanisms. However, the above discussion suggests that imperfections in financial markets, including the ability to arbitrage tax systems, do exist and hence may give rise to an advantage for MNCs relative to local firms. In order to illustrate the potential relationship of these gains to the more traditional advantages of multinationalism, we outline the key factors affecting the value of investment projects facing the MNC in a partial equilibrium setting.

*Project Valuation in a Multinational Context.*   The pattern of international investment, both in terms of the location of production and the ownership of firms, can be viewed as resulting from the interaction of a supply of investment opportunities occurring through time in different countries and the demand of potential bidders for these opportunities. The successful bidder can be either a domestic firm, defined as a firm located in the country where the investment takes place, or a foreign firm. Assuming complete information about the prospective return on investment opportunities, the successful bidder will be the one to whom the project is worth most. Successful bidders will be those who can generate larger or less risky cash flows over time from a given investment opportunity. This superiority may arise primarily as the result of imperfections in goods or factor markets. But it also may reflect some financial market imperfections. Alternatively, the successful bidders may have been able to capitalize the uncertain future cash flows at relatively lower required rates of return, again the result of imperfections in financial markets.

One firm may have higher cash flows than another because it has lower current costs because of control over intangible factors of production such as special knowledge not available in the market, a preferred market position, or other mechanisms that generate rents.[4] It may have lower total risks because of its control of the market, its special knowledge, and many other of the factors that also produce higher returns. Direct investment, foreign or local, can be viewed as a way to capitalize on these potential advantages either in the absence of markets in which the source of the advantage can be sold and the capitalized value of rents obtained directly or in the case where the "sale" of the advantage would destroy its rent-producing character.

Financial factors that could increase real project cash flows for the MNC relative to the level obtainable by a domestic firm include the ability to circumvent exchange rate barriers that maintain the exchange rate at a disequilibrium level and the ability to reduce total taxes by appropriate choice of the channels through which the flows are transferred to the parent.

These same financial market imperfections may result in lower required rates of return for a given level of total project risk. Risky projects are most attractive to those investors able to diversify the largest proportion of the project's total risk. When there are costs or barriers to portfolio capital flows, MNCs are able to accept lower rates of return on projects than single-country firms because of their ability to diversify investment risks internationally.[5] A closely related potential financial advantage of the MNC is its ability to engage in arbitrage between financial markets where restrictions on capital flows or direct government intervention distort the cost of debt capital.

The value of a project from the perspective of a particular firm is the present value of estimated future cash flows discounted at the required rate of return which reflects the project's risk:

$$V = \sum_{t=0}^{\infty} \frac{CF_t}{(1+\rho_*)^t} \qquad (2)$$

where:     $V$ = total project value

    $CF_t$ = annual after-tax project cash flow to parent firm (prior to financing charges and related tax adjustments)

    $\rho_*$ = the overall cost of capital reflecting the required rate of return on equity, an opportunity cost, as well as the explicit costs of other sources of funds.

If the cash flows are perpetual and equal in all years, this reduces to:

$$V = \frac{\overline{CF}}{\rho_*} \qquad (3)$$

In general, real imperfections will be reflected in the cash flows, while financial market imperfections will be reflected in the discount rate.

The various financial effects can be made more explicit by using a more generalized present-value formula where the tax impacts of the discretionary use of alternative financial channels, the financial structure, and other financial effects are treated individually.[6] The value of the project can be viewed as the sum of the present values of the project cash flows to a single-country firm located in the same country as the project after taxes but prior to financing costs, discounted at a rate reflecting the business risk of the project; the present value of tax savings relative to the taxes paid by the domestic firm as the result of internal financial transfers within the MNC; and savings resulting from being able to exploit specific distortions in credit markets:

$$V = \sum_{t=0}^{\infty} \frac{CF_t}{(1+\rho)^t} + \sum_{t=0}^{\infty} \frac{\Delta T_t}{(1+r)^t} + \sum_{t=0}^{\infty} \frac{\Delta I_t}{(1+r)^t} \qquad (4)$$

where:  $V$ = total project value

$CF_t$ = annual after-tax flows of the project if all-equity financed by a domestic firm (*i.e.*, prior to any financing effects).

$\rho$ = discount rate appropriate from parent perspective to the entire after-tax cash flow stream prior to any financing effects.

$\Delta T_t$ = tax savings (penalties) relative to the level which would be paid by a domestic firm if the project were financed entirely by equity.

$\Delta I_t$ = annual savings (penalties) on interest costs of debt financing due to direct subsidies, differential access to repressed markets, or international arbitrage relative to what the firm would have to pay for unsubsidized borrowing obtained on an arms-length basis.

$r$ = interest rate on debt as approximation to relevant discount rate for relatively certain streams of tax shields and interest savings.

Thus, differences in project value as a result of financial factors will be captured by differences in $CF$, the after-tax project flows; in $\rho$, the discount rate appropriate to the all-equity stream; by differences in $\Delta T$, reflecting tax effects of the MNC's integrated financial system; and by differences in $\Delta I$, reflecting differential abilities of firms to take advantage of financial market distortions. Of course, MNCs commonly possess other advantages *vis-à-vis* local firms resulting from imperfections in the markets for technology and managerial skills, but they also face the disadvantage of operating at a distance without an intimate knowledge of the domestic, political, social, and economic setting. Thus at times the financial advantages of MNCs may be the decisive factors.

# IMPLICATIONS FOR PUBLIC POLICY

The studies reviewed in the third section, although not conclusive about the magnitude of internal financial transfers within MNCs or their impact on real decisions, leave little doubt that there are incentives for such transfers and that they do take place. Few aspects of MNC behavior evoke as much outrage as transfer pricing, broadly defined, and there are numerous proposals for cracking down on these practices and enforcing arms-length transfers. However, many profit-shifting practices are not heinous deeds, but are legal and would be considered by many as ethical. Further, even when this is not the case, the difficulty of controlling profit-shifting behavior would appear to argue in favor of reducing incentives for internal transfers rather than trying to control them directly.

If tax and financial systems provide incentives for certain types of behavior, MNCs should respond accordingly, within ethical and legal bounds. If they fail to do so, they are not behaving economically, at which point their very existence should be called into question. Of course, some profit-shifting practices involve misrepresentations of fact and violate the letter as well as the spirit of the law and should not be condoned. Many, however, are legal in a literal sense and many fall within the range in which reasonable observers would disagree as to whether they were ethical or unethical. Almost by definition, the activities of an MNC involve transfers of intangibles or even goods that have no objective arms-length price. Many of these are joint products and often their costs cannot be defined with certainty even within the firm. Further, in many cases the intangible factors, in particular technology and managerial knowhow, are goods that can be applied in one unit of the firm without detracting from their value elsewhere. Thus, in many cases, there is no objective economic solution and the allocation of profits within the MNC is totally arbitrary.

Financial transactions within the firm can be denominated in a variety of currencies and, given the illusion implicit within most tax systems that the national currency has constant purchasing power, a firm can reduce taxes by careful use of this mechanism. Is this illegal? Clearly not. Immoral or unethical? I do not know. And the list of such possibilities goes on.

Another argument in favor of concentrating on reducing incentives for internal profit transfers as opposed to controlling transfers themselves is that anything less than perfect control will favor MNCs relative to national firms. In fact, the recognition that differences in tax systems, barriers to capital flows, and regulated economies often provide advantages to MNCs able to take advantage of or circumvent these factors gives rise to a number of public policy considerations.

*Implications for the "Efficiency" of MNCs*

The central issue in the broad debate surrounding MNCs is whether they are vehicles of international economic efficiency, facilitating transfers of goods and factors of production that otherwise would not take place, or whether as suggested by Hymer (1970) they are vehicles for extending monopoly power, by removing from market channels transfers in certain critical goods or factors. Stated another way, the issue is whether the imperfections in goods and factor markets that are the sources of MNCs's advantages are "natural" barriers (largely due to the difficulty of transferring certain specialized intangibles) or are barriers created by the MNCs themselves to gain and hold monopolistic advantages. In the former case, the argument is that MNCs are "good," since they enable exchange, and hence welfare gains, that otherwise would have been impossible. In the second case, they are "bad," since they simply represent an extension of monopoly power. Since the two are difficult to distinguish in practice, the conclusions of most students of MNCs follow from their prior beliefs regarding the importance of "natural" and "created" barriers.

The recognition that the internal financial system of an MNC also may provide it with advantages further complicates the debate. To the extent that multinationalism is encouraged by tax systems that impose higher taxes on independent ventures than on the same ventures when part of an MNC, it does not represent an increase in efficiency, but neither can it be considered a monopolistic act. Rather, the MNC is largely a passive beneficiary of goverment policies and, to the extent that there are economic or political costs to corporate bigness, the costs are borne by society at large. Of course, it is possible that one country gains politically while others lose. This will be the case if economic control is shifted to MNCs based predominantly in one country. U.S. tax policy, in fact, appears to encourage such concentration.

If MNCs gain from their ability to circumvent barriers in financial markets, it might be argued that they contribute to a more efficient allocation of capital and risk. However, the barriers they overcome are in large part created by national governments to serve some social objective. The end result of the barriers and of MNC efforts to circumvent them is unlikely to be efficient from a domestic or international perspective. Nor is it likely to be politically desirable, since it implies greater concentration of economic activity (Agmon and Lessard, 1976a).

It is ironic that many barriers erected by countries to increase their economic independence may encourage the growth of MNCs which can bypass the affected markets. Similar arguments apply to incentives to multinationalism created by regulatory or bargaining situations which favor firms able to disguise profits through internal transactions.

The literature reviewed in this paper provides little hard empirical evidence regarding the importance of financial factors as incentives for multinationalism. However, the arguments presented suggest that these factors must be given greater weight in future studies, both because they provide a potentially important motivation for multinationalism and because they distort reported flows of investments and profits that form the basis for many conclusions regarding the desirability of MNCs.

## Implications for Tax Policy

The discussion of tax policy toward MNCs by either home or host countries typically is couched in terms of economic efficiency, although it sometimes boils down to a "neo-mercantilist" approach of maximizing revenues for the country in question with little regard for international efficiency or equity. The typical efficiency criteria, capital import neutrality and capital export neutrality, seek to avoid tax-induced distortions in the international allocation of investment, production, and trade. A type of tax-induced distortion missed by both criteria is the favoring of MNCs relative to national firms or individual investors in those cases where internal profit transfers or global consolidation will reduce total taxes. This suggests a third efficiency criterion, which might be termed "octopus neutrality" or, more seriously but somewhat less accurately, "transfer price neutrality." Basically, it would call for the same tax treatment for a particular investment regardless of whether it was part of a multinational conglomerate or a stand-alone venture owned directly by individual investors. Examples of departures from this criterion from a U.S. perspective include the current system of limiting foreign tax credits to the U.S. tax that would be due on the foreign-soure income, but allowing firms to use an overall limitation. This clearly favors those U.S. firms with low-tax foreign operations to offset against operations generating excess credits. It would appear that this advantage could be eliminated by requiring a country-by-country computation of tax credits. However, this would increase the incentives for profit shifting among high- and low-tax countries and would continue to favor the MNC—Catch-22. Only in the case where tax authorities are able to enforce arms-length prices for all transactions would this not be the case. Further, although the U.S. firm with an extensive system of high- and low-tax operations has an advantage over the U.S. firm with few overseas operations, both will be at a disadvantage relative to domestic firms in the low-tax country and, at best, will be only on par with domestic firms in the high-tax country. Thus, transfer-price neutrality will conflict with the other efficiency criteria.[7]

The one case in which transfer-price neutrality will always coincide with both capital import and capital export neutrality, of course, is when all countries employ the same tax system, including a common unit of account. Several studies reviewed in this paper provide support for moving in this direction. They suggest that the effect of internal financial transfers, if unconstrained, is to neutralize the influence of tax factors on real decisions, but to magnify the effects of differences in tax systems on the distribution of tax revenues. It is precisely in such a world where countries would retaliate quickly against any competitive tax change, and the only stable solution would be a common system. Such a step would also eliminate all tax-related incentives for profit shifting, thus reducing the need for controls over intracompany transactions.

## Implications for Financial Policies

A similar set of conclusions can be drawn regarding the implications of the MNC's internal financial system for a particular nation's financial policies. We assume that a country does not wish to restrict MNC operations if these are viewed as contributing to efficiency, but that it does not want to encourage growth of the MNC where this is not justified by natural conditions in goods and factor markets. In this case, the country will attempt to insure that national firms can bid successfully against MNCs for projects where they expect at least the same operating cash flows. Thus, the government will wish to insure equal access to credit resources and to world equity markets where the project's risks will be evaluated in the context of well-diversified portfolios. Elimination of financial restrictions of all sorts would appear to lead to this ideal, although for a variety of institutional reasons which are beyond the scope of this review, additional intervention on behalf of national firms in LDCs might be required.

## Implications for Regulation and Bargaining

This is the area in which conclusions appear to follow most clearly. As stated by Streeten:

> The allocation of large overhead and joint costs . . . is bound to be arbitrary within wide limits and a policy of maximizing global post-tax profits from the world-wide system of operations of the firm will greatly reduce the significance of declared prices, capital values and rates of return for purposes of national policy (Streeten, 1974, p. 264).

Little more need be said, except that the comment is applicable to developed countries as well as to LDCs. Vernon (1971a) makes this point, and it has been reiterated by many others, yet researchers continue to draw conclusions based on reported financial flows which tell only part of the story. One presumes that policymakers are not significantly different in this regard.

In all three areas—tax policy, financial policy, and regulatory policy—the ability of MNCs to shift funds and profits internally represents a constraint on national policies, a constraint that must be observed if governments do not wish to encourage the growth of MNCs beyond levels justified by natural conditions in goods and factor markets. In this regard, at least, MNCs do challenge national sovereignty.

## FOOTNOTES

*The author is grateful for the comments of Gene Carter, Ian Giddy, Thomas Horst, and Jim Paddick.

1. Barnet and Muller (1974) provide a provocative but often contradictory recital of the key charges leveled at MNCs for their financial behavior.

2. The major exception within the U.S. is the differential tax treatment at the investor level of dividends and retained earnings, which favors internal transfers from "cash rich" to "cash poor" operations as opposed to transfers through financial markets that would entail payment of dividends by one firm and the issue of new securities by another.

3. Reviews of the theory of direct investment are provided by Dunning (1973), Kindleberger (1969), Ragazzi (1973), Stevens (1974). The "generally accepted theory" appears to be that direct foreign investment can be explained in terms of wealth-maximizing behavior by firms that derive advantages from imperfections in markets for intangible factors of production. These imperfections may be "natural," reflecting special characteristics of the factors being transferred (Magee, 1976) or may be created by the firms themselves through monopoly power (Hymer, 1960; Vaitsos, 1974a).

4. These rents, of course, may represent returns on previous R & D investment as suggested by Magee (1977a).

5. The benefits of international diversification to lower risk were extended to direct foreign investment by Ragazzi (1973), Rugman (1975), and Stevens (1974). Aliber (1970) also presents a financial rationale for direct investment, but bases it on a preference for the currency of the base country firm.

6. This approach is similar to that of Myers (1974), who shows that the additive relationship will hold within an integrated, efficient capital market. It will not hold strictly in the more general case where markets in different countries are to some extent segmented by barriers and where there are distortions within particular markets. Nevertheless, it is a useful way to identify the various elements in the process.

7. I am indebted to Thomas Horst for bringing this point to my attention.

## COMMENT

### GERALDINE GERARDI*

The multinational corporation (MNC), with its ability to shift funds across national boundaries through internal channels, presents challenges for the governments of home and host countries. Lessard questions whether tax policies and financial market regulations encourage the growth of MNCs

*U.S. Treasury Department. The views expressed are not necessarily those of the Department.

relative to national firms, and whether the MNC's profit-shifting capability alters either the intracountry distribution of tax remenues for a given distribution of real activities, or the distrubution of real investment, production, and trade. He also discusses the MNC's ability to disguise its true profitability as a means of influencing public policy.

Although Lessard points out that studies of the internal financial transfers of MNCs provide no conclusive evidence about the magnitude of these transfers or their impact on the firm's decisions, he suggests that there are incentives for the use of these transfers and that they do take place. Some empirical support for the incentive provided by taxation for MNCs to shift profits to tax haven jurisdictions was provided by Gerardi (1976). An analysis of tax return data indicated that, as the foreign tax burden increased, a larger percentage of the total profits of a U.S. parent corporation and its controlled foreign corporations were declared in tax-haven countries. However, the results of this study were inconclusive in determining the extent to which discretionary transfer-pricing practices on intracompany transactions were used to shift profits to subsidiaries in tax-haven countries.

Because of the difficulty of controlling profit-shifting behavior, Lessard argues for a reduction in transfer-pricing incentives currently provided by taxation and financial market regulations rather than direct controls of transfers. He points out that the influence of tax factors on real decisions can be neutralized if all countries adopt a common tax system and unit of account. Although Lessard's suggestion may well contain the long-run solution to the transfer-pricing problem, feasible short-run solutions are also necessary and desirable. I agree with Lessard on the difficulties involved in directly controlling transfer prices. Although U.S. tax authorities have attempted to control the use of transfer pricing for profit-shifting purposes by issuing detailed regulations for the calculation of an arms-length price on intracompany transactions, in a large number of cases no single objective standard has been applied by tax administrators for determining the appropriate price on intracompany transactions. Hammer (1972) reports that in two cases U.S. federal courts found that a 50/50 profit split between parent and subsidiary was reasonable. The court did not address itself to the question of why this split was reasonable.

One may speculate that the judge, in viewing the parent and each subsidiary as an active, viable company making its respective contribution toward earning the income in question, concluded that they were entitled to share the profits equally.

However, Hufbauer (1975b) reports that in many instances the subsidiary owns less than 50 percent of the combined capital stock (including goodwill and know-how), so that the result of following this approach is that profits that are attributable to the parent may be sheltered in the subsidiary.

In order to prevent the artificial shifting of profits between parent and subsidiary, more objective methods for the calculation of the arms-length price are needed, as well as more vigorous tax administration. Not all countries enforce arms-length pricing with the same degree of vigilance. For example, Hufbauer (1975b) reports that enforcement of Section 485 of the United Kingdom's tax law concerning transactions between related parties depends on negotiation rather than directives; that prior to 1972 German authorities had no statutory power concerning the allocation of income between related firms; and that although the French tax code provides French tax authorities with the power to adjust income, it was only applied in a few cases.

One approach often recommended for dealing with potential transfer-pricing abuse is to allocate income on the basis of a formula containing some combination of property, payroll, and sales.[1] This formula, called the "Massachusetts Formula" is often used in the United States to allocate profits of firms engaged in business across state lines.

Distinctive problems are associated with profit allocation in a multinational world by contrast with a multistate federation.[2] States do not have complete sovereignty in the tax field as nations do. In the United States, the Federal tax system provides a standardized method of tax accounting, and states usually follow the Federal lead. But no similar uniformity of tax accounting exists at the international level. The degree of international cooperation required for the adoption of a profit allocation formula is not likely to be achieved in a near future.[3] Indeed, despite years of effort and Congressional prodding, even the states have not agreed on a common allocation formula.

Nevertheless, Brannon (1974) and Gerardi (1976) have argued that formula apportionment could be used to determine "safe-haven rules" that might be used to supplement an arms-length transfer-pricing standard. Transfer prices that yielded a taxable base within a certain range of the base that would be generated by strict application of an allocation formula would not be subject to conflicting claims by national tax authorities. For example, a firm's profits would be subject to change to the formula profit only if:

$$P_i > \P_i \, (1+s), \text{ or if}$$
$$P_i > \P_i \, (1-s)$$

where $P_i$ is the reported profit of firm $i$, $\P_i$ is the profit allocated to firm $i$ on the basis of the formula, and $s$ is the safe-haven percentage.

Whatever the merits of this approach, or any other suggestion, it is worth noting that the national debate on the proper allocation of profits between the various establishments of a multistate firm has engaged U.S. scholars, legislators, and judges for at least ten years without a final resolution. By these standards, the international debate has just begun.

## FOOTNOTES

1. The rationale for this formula is that business earnings are determined by both supply and demand for the product. Since both sides of the market should be reflected in an equitable allocation of the tax base, payroll and plant are used to stand for the supply side and sales for the demand side.

2. A detailed discussion of the similarities and differences in the state taxation of multistate corporations and national taxation of multinational corporations is beyond the scope of this paper. See Marcia Field (1974) and Charles E. McLure, Jr. (1974).

3. According to Musgrave, part of the problem is that the relative weights assigned to each factor in the formula are a matter of judgment. These weights would be of considerable importance for the assignment of tax base between developed and developing countries. See Musgrave (1972.)

# COMMENT

## RICHARD M. HAMMER*

## INTRODUCTION

The contribution of MNCs to the economic development and welfare of the countries in which they operate has generally been recognized. In my view, it would be difficult even for critics of the international business community to deny the fact that these large business enterprises have on balance made positive contributions. Both developed and developing countries offer incentives to encourage MNCs to make investments in their countries in the hope that they will increase (or continue to increase) the country's levels of industrial development, technology, management skills, employment, and foreign exchange.

Nonetheless, in this age of cynicism born of Watergate and subsequent disclosures, the MNCs (in fact, the business community as a whole) have fallen into disfavor as a new critical attitude toward traditional institutions

*Price Waterhouse & Co.

has been manifest. This new critical attitude, particularly toward multinationals, is based in part on political factors, such as the alleged interference of multinationals in the domestic affairs of host countries, and based in part on economic factors stemming from the recent recession that encompassed virtually all the economies of the world.

It is alleged that MNCs, because of the economic might inherent in their huge and far-ranging financial resources, have greater power than many sovereign states around the world. For example, in the area of taxation, it is often alleged that MNCs arbitrarily manipulate transfer prices on transactions between entities within their group to maximize profits in low tax or nil rate areas. Or, it is often alleged that MNCs take unfair advantage of such devices as tax havens and tax holidays to maximize their after-tax rate of return. Whether or not the use of such devices is logically in the best interests of the MNCs (to maximize their rates of return), it is the opinion of this writer that too many exogenous forces exist today to allow full flexiblilty and latitude to the MNCs in structuring their transactions solely with profit maximization in mind.

## International Organizations

The new anti-MNC mood manifested itself in the middle 1970s in nationalistic and protectionistic attitudes around the globe, and has resulted in a proliferation of studies and reports by international agencies and regional groups, such as the European Economic Community (EEC), the Andean Pact countries, the Organization for Economic Cooperation and Development (OECD), and the United Nations (UN). The organizations have in general concluded that multinationals should be subject to stricter supervision, regulation, and control, with a view to making them more responsive to the needs of the countries in which they operate. Attempts to devise international guidelines on a voluntary or enforceable basis are under consideration by several international organizations. Multinationals themselves, and business organizations representing them, are also formulating voluntary codes of conduct.

## The United Nations Report

The United Nations issued the report of its Group of Eminent Persons on multinationals in June 1974. It was slanted toward the problems of host (capital importing) countries, and more particularly toward the developing countries of the world. These were the countries most prone to the type of abuses alleged against MNCs. The report expresses the concern of various governmental authorities with the ability of multinationals to arrange their structure and financing in such ways as to enable them to avoid taxes or divert income from high to low-tax countries or tax havens, and generally to take advantage of the diversity among national tax systems.

*Intercompany Pricing.* In particular, these governments are concerned with intercompany transfer pricing and the UN report notes that one quarter of the world's international trade in goods is between related companies. The report recommends that home and host countries should enforce arms-length standards and that guidelines and rules of behavior should be developed. It is interesting to note that the United States was awarded an honorable mention for the way it has dealt with the intercompany transfer pricing problem in Section 482 of its Internal Revenue regulations. It would seem that the rest of the world has evidently learned a considerable amount from the U.S. experience. Although not all the problems that can arise in intercorporate relationships have been resolved in the U.S., nonetheless, Section 482 issues seem to be much less in the news today than was true a decade ago, obviously because more taxpayers are making efforts to comply with the now long-standing rules.

The message that can be clearly discerned from the UN report is that there will be a greater awareness and enforcement by foreign governments in the intercompany pricing area in the years to come. At the moment, governments apparently consider themselves severely hampered by lack of information. This presages even greater emphasis in future on disclosure and exchange of information through informal government-to-government exchanges or under tax treaties or other types of formal international agreements.

While it is likely that solutions based on concerted international action may be slow in coming from an enforcement point of view, there is no doubt that the governments of the developed countries will be taking steps to enforce arms-length pricing standards and will use all means at their disposal to obtain the information needed to accomplish this goal.

*Tax Havens.* A second area of concern expressed in the UN report relating to taxation is the use of tax havens by MNCs to completely avoid or defer the payment of taxes to their home countries. The issue arises because many countries do not tax foreign income (*i.e.,* income earned by controlled foreign affiliates) until it is repatriated to the parent company as, say, dividends or interest under the so-called *deferral privilege.* Other countries have territorial concepts such as the *exemption system* under which they do not tax foreign income at all. The deferral system tends to encourage the accumulation of funds in tax-favored holding companies.

In principle, the UN report favors the taxation of foreign income in the home country under a modified version of a current *accrual* basis, with a credit for current *accrued* foreign taxes, thus in broad outline leaning toward terminating deferral provisions. However, for political reasons, it suggests a variation from a true current accrual basis through delaying the taxation of profits until they are remitted abroad by the affiliate in the host country, at which time tax would be assessed whether the profits or dividends are paid directly to the parent or to an intermediary holding company. The report appears somewhat reluctant to recommend a complete end to deferral, presumably in deference to the developing countries who offer tax holidays and other tax concessions, which would be nullified by a full current-accrual basis for taxation of foreign income. Furthermore, it is recognized that tax havens are sometimes necessary to avoid double taxation and the UN report does not express strong condemnation of them *per se*.

*Tax Incetnives and Tax Holidays.*   A third area covered in the UN report deals with the practice of (primarily) developing countries in offering tax holidays or tax incentives to encourage foreign investment, thus permitting MNCs to play one country off against the other. The report, however, does not condemn all tax holidays and tax incentives which, it is recognized, have their place in the industrial development of less advantaged nations. And furthermore, it suggests that the home country should give credit for taxes spared (a concept which has been anathema to U.S. policymakers for many years).

## Transnational Commission

Following the recommendations contained in the UN report, the U.N. Economic and Social Council (ECOSOC) approved in December, 1974 the establishment of two new institutions to deal with issues relating to multinational enterprises: the Commission on Transnational Corporations and an Information and Research Center on Transnational Corporations.

The Transnational Commission, which was established in 1975, is an intergovernmental body, composed of representatives of 48 countries. It calls on spokesmen from business, labor, and the universities for assistance in its studies. Its mandate is to act as a forum for conducting studies on the political, economic and social impacts of transnational corporations on the countries in which they operate. The commission is to assist ECOSOC in developing a set of guidelines for a code of conduct to be observed by transnational corporations.

The Information and Research Center is to obtain information on matters pertaining to transnational enterprises and to conduct research that might be useful in the formulation of the code of conduct. It will in effect be the research arm of the Commission.

## OECD

The OECD has been studying many of the same areas that were covered in the report of the UN Group of Eminent Persons. One of its study groups (working parties) is looking at all the parameters of the subject of intercompany transfer pricing (in its broadest sense) and has thus far issued a pronouncement covering only intercompany loans. This pronouncement embraces the arms-length standard for interest payments and eschews any adoption of safe haven concepts, such as is contained in the U.S. rules governing intercorporate indebtedness. Recently a draft directive on treatment of intercompany transfers of intangible property and research and development has been exposed. This directive, in addition to embracing arms-length considerations on the transfer of intangible property, also encourages recognition of cost-sharing arrangements to be used in the development of intangible property. It seems clear that the OECD will continue to adhere to the arms-length standard except where a viable alternative exists.

The OECD has *also* been looking at tax havens, tax holidays, and exchanges of information. As to tax havens and holidays, the OECD is essentially against such artificial devices it deems to be non-neutral, but recognizes (and accepts) that certain countries may have to use tax incentives, for a limited period of years, to accomplish desirable economic and fiscal policy goals.

The OECD devoted a great deal of time to the development of a "code of conduct," *i.e.*, a set of guidelines for standards of corporate behavior abroad, which culminated in their adoption by the Council of Ministers at their Paris meeting in June, 1976. The U.S. business community and the U.S. Government consider that such codes should be broad enough in scope to apply not only to multinationals but also to purely domestic corporations, as well as to the governments of host countries and home countries alike. Also under consideration are questions of whether such codes should be voluntary or mandatory, and whether they should be the subject of multinational agreement by international agencies or bilateral treaties. The U.S. view is that they should be voluntary and between the companies and the national governments.

There are many instances of individual corporations having voluntarily formulated their own guidelines of corporate behavior and issued them to their employees and to the public. Countries such as Canada have published guidelines for foreign-controlled firms in Canada. Business organizations such as the International Chamber of Commerce have developed guidelines for multinationals and home and host governments. In addition to the OECD, the UN is also in the course of developing guidelines. Moreover, Senator Proxmire has advocated that the U.S. adopt, by legislation, a mandatory code of conduct for its MNCs, which has been triggered by recent disclosures in the area of sensitive payments.

Some of the more important issues which are the subject of codes of conduct and guidelines are the following:

*a. Expropriation:* whether national or international law should apply on questions of compensation and arbitration.

*b. Taxation:* intercompany pricing, tax incentives and tax havens.

*c. Local ownership in foreign-established enterprises:* the rights of host countries to take control of their natural resources and to demand substantial equity in local investment opportunities for local nationals.

*d. Labor relations:* the training and promotion of local nationals.

*e. Transfers of technology:* giving the host country access to foreign technology.

*f. Financing and source of capital:* foreign capital investment and retention of earnings for further development.

*g. Support of national plans and policies:* in the area of exports, market development and technological development.

*h. Fair treatment of foreign-controlled companies:* nondiscrimination for multinationals.

*i. "Good citizenship" of foreign-controlled companies in the host country:* compliance by the multinational and its employees with the tax laws, business ethics and practices of the host country.

*j. Disclosure of information by multinationals:* the adequacy (or inadequacy) of data supplied to host countries' tax authorities.

Finally, the OECD has investigated the question of deferral, *i.e.,* whether the home country of the parent corporation or an MNC group should tax income at all earned by the MNC's overseas affiliates. Unlike the UN, the OECD is in favor of retaining deferral, but with a strong bias against tax havens as being non-neutral.

# FORCES LIMITING MNC FLEXIBILITY

I am of the opinion that today no single or group of MNCs has the ability or potential exercise of power to challenge the authority of the sovereign states in which they operate. As long as the world community is governed by the rule of law, no corporation can with impunity disregard the legal code of any nation in the furtherance of its goal of profit maximization. Indeed, the nations of the world are becoming more sophisticated in this electronic/atomic age and are able to effectively regulate or control, to a greater or lesser degree, the local impact of the international business community. Admittedly, this may not have always been true, but many forces put into motion in recent years have created the present situation.

## Intercompany Transfer Pricing

In the taxation area, as mentioned earlier, one of the charges against MNCs is their ability to structure intercorporate dealings so as to shift profits artifically to low-tax areas from high-tax areas. There is a good deal more emotionalism and politics in this indictment than fact. For one thing, tax rates around the world have increased in the last decade or so with the result that most countries assess corporate income taxes at rates close to 50 percent, thus removing any incentives for wholesale profit shifting. Even the developing countries of the world, despite offering tax incentives such as temporary tax holidays, have imposed a higher burden of direct taxation on corporations operating within their borders.

But levels of taxation are only half the story; the other half is enforcement. In my experience, the enforcement efforts of both the capital exporting countries and the major capital importing countries have now advanced to the stage where one might call them quite sophisticated, particularly in the intercompany transfer-pricing area. Although some of the developing nations are not quite so far advanced, they are fast learning appropriate enforcement techniques, many of them with the assistance of task forces from our Internal Revenue Service. Clearly, the developed nations of the world, which probably account for more than two-thirds of the world's trade and production, have signaled (by action rather than rhetoric) the MNCs of their intentions in this regard—a signal that has not been ignored.

The almost universal standard that has been adopted by various enforcement authorities in their approach to the intercompany transfer-pricing problem is the arms-length standard. This is the cornerstone of our own Section 482 regulations. In applying this yardstick, enforcement agencies require data. In most cases, the data comes from the taxpayer itself, as few companies would seriously challenge a request for data emanating from a country in which it operates. However, the network of bilateral tax conventions that exists today, as well as multilateral and regional treaties, and the activities of international governmental bodies such as the OECD have provided the wherewithal for one country to provide information to another regarding MNCs operating in both of their countries. Moreover, national tax authorities are availing themselves of this facility more and more frequently.

*Tax Havens*

Although tax-haven countries do continue to exist and attempt to attract investment, the advantages of their continued use are fast disappearing, except for special-purpose vehicles like captive insurance or finance companies. This is in part because of anti-avoidance legislation in certain key capital exporting nations (*e.g.,* Subpart F in the U.S.A., FAPI in Canada, and Aussensteuergesetz (ASTG) in Germany), which eliminates some or all the traditional tax-saving opportunities in the use of havens. It is safe to prophesy that other capital exporting countries may relatively soon enact similar anti-avoidance legislation. In addition, strict enforcement of the arms-length principle on intercompany transactions often results in reallocating income of a tax-haven entity to the entity in the group (usually operating in a high-tax country) that actually earned it. Based upon these relatively recent developments from legislative and administrative points of view, it appears that the use of tax havens (except as noted above) will become a less significant factor in international trade and income flows in the future.

### Non-Tax Factors

Other types of national and nationalistic legislation impose restraints on the activities of MNCs. Many countries have relatively recently adopted foreign investment control laws (*e.g.,* Argentina, Australia, Brazil, Canada and Mexico); still others control inflowing foreign investment through administrative procedures that generally require registration of the investment through the central bank with at least implicit governmental approval (*e.g.,* several European countries). More countries impose exchange control requirements regulating both inflow and outflow of currency. Together these rules are designed to monitor and promote the host country's financial and economic well-being and tend to diminish the flexibility with which an MNC can move funds from country to country. This is not to say that total funds mobility has been eliminated, but certainly some restraints have been invoked.

### Attitude

Probably the most important of all factors in today's environment is attitude. In light of recent disclosures and other developments, the managements of the world's MNCs are fully aware that good "corporate citizenship" in the host countries in which they operate, as well as in the home country, is as important a consideration as squeezing the last cent of profit out of a particular operation by whatever means available. In other words, short-run profit maximization *per se* is no longer the sole yardstick by which to measure success for an MNC, but rather the achievement of maximum profitability commensurate with the social and economic policy goals of the host and home countries. The advent of the OECD Code of Conduct, together with the development by other national and international organizations of such standards of corporate behavior, signal the desire of the free world for self-restraint in the international business community. Certainly the agreement to abide by these guidelines by most MNCs, as seems sure to transpire, will represent the business community's acknowledgement and acquiescence of the new morality. On balance, it is undoubtedly in the best interests of all concerned.

# 5. TECHNOLOGY CREATION AND TECHNOLOGY TRANSFER BY MULTINATIONAL FIRMS

Arthur W. Lake, CAMBRIDGE UNIVERSITY

## INTRODUCTION

*Basic Issues*

United States industries have to a significant extent been the world's leading creators of new technology and, thus, often possessed a substantial competitive advantage in world markets. The transfer of technology worldwide through the multinational firm (MNC) and its impact on industries of host countries has increasingly been thought to be associated with a comparative deterioration in U.S. technological performance (Brooks, 1972). Observations of both trade patterns and growth of productivity for Japan, West Germany and, to a lesser extent, the United Kingdom,

Research in International Business and Finance, Vol. 1, pp. 137–187.
Copyright © 1979 by JAI Press, Inc.
All rights of reproduction in any form reserved.
ISBN 0-89232-031-1

suggest that their high-technology industries have actively been catching up, or, through U.S. direct investments, reducing the U.S. technological lead. Moreover, improvements in communications have increasingly internationalized the scientific systems of host countries and have made them more responsive to scientific developments in the United States and elsewhere. Adding to this the introduction and diffusion of new technology on a worldwide scale within MNCs, we find it increasingly difficult to distinguish the leaders from the followers in the creation and adoption of new technology.

The research and development expenditures in 1966 of individual United States manufacturing industries, presented in Table 5.1, dem-

*Table 5.1*   R & D Expenditures in All Firms and in MNCs,
United States, 1966
*(Amounts in millions of dollars)*

| Industry | 1966 | | |
|---|---|---|---|
| | All firms | MNCs | MNCs as percent of all firms |
| *All manufacturing* | *14,656* | *7,598* | 52 |
| Food products | 153 | 136 | 89 |
| Paper and allied products | 88 | 64 | 73 |
| Chemicals | 1,461 | 1,258 | 86 |
| Drugs | 318 | 303 | 95 |
| Industrial chemicals | 955 | 777 | 81 |
| Other chemicals | 188 | 178 | 95 |
| Rubber | 178 | 127 | 71 |
| Primary and fabricated metals | 386 | 312 | 81 |
| Nonelectrical machinery | 1,300 | 743 | 57 |
| Electrical machinery | 3,586 | 1,814 | 51 |
| Radio,TV.,comm.equipment, andelectroniccomponents | 2,216 | 685 | 30 |
| Other electrical machinery | 1,370 | 1,129 | 82 |
| Transportation equipment | 6,786 | 2,537 | 37 |
| Textiles and apparel | 51 | 29 | 57 |
| Stone, clay, and glass | 128 | 103 | 80 |
| Instruments | 434 | 371 | 85 |
| *All other manufacturing* | [1]105 | 104 | [1]100 |

[1]Estimated

*Source:* All firm data from National Science Foundation, *Research and Development in Industry,* 1969 (NSF Publication: NSF 71-18), Washington, April 1971, and Highlights (NSF 71-39), Dec. 10, 1971; MNC data are from U.S. Department of Commerce, Bureau of Economic Analysis, International Investment Division, United States Tariff Commission, 1973, p. 561.

onstrates with few exceptions that MNCs have undertaken a major share of U.S. technology creation (52 percent in 1966) and, in some cases, almost all. For example, 95 percent of R & D spending by drug companies in the United States was carried out within MNCs. Since we shall examine the participation of foreign MNCs in the U.K. drug industry, this fact is particularly interesting. Furthermore, even in an example of a major exception to the rule, the electronics subsector of the electrical machinery industry, where MNCs represented 30 percent of R & D expenditures, the extremely fast rate of diffusion of technology among competing firms means a very high level of imitative product introductions worldwide without each firm carrying out its own extensive research and development. Thus, through its effect in triggering technology creation in this industry, the role of U.S. MNCs may be substantial, and we shall examine the bearing that this aspect has to technology creation and transfer in the U.K. microelectronic components industry.

There are many interesting issues from which to choose given the subject of this paper. Three will be examined in some detail: the novelty of R & D by MNCs, the speed of MNC technology transfer, and the impact of the MNC on host-country industry. These have been selected because of their general relevance to studies of MNCs in light of the OECD consultations (OECD, 1969, 1976) regarding guidelines for international investment and multinational enterprises. Furthermore, the author's research has analyzed the market-entry activity of U.S. and other foreign companies in the U.K. drugs and microelectronic components industries (Lake, 1976a, b).

The first issue, the novelty of R & D by MNCs, requires an examination of factors influencing the quality and character of research within MNCs, the strategy of their R & D programs, and their capacity for R & D. Moreover, consideration is given to the microeconomics of technology transfer and market entry and to the competitive pressures inducing innovation and imitation. The second issue, the speed of MNC technology transfer, relates to the length of time taken before a technology gap is closed, or more specifically, the impact of MNCs on the rate at which technology has been diffused and has affected the market, production, and R & D levels in the host country. The third issue defines the impact of MNCs on host-country science and innovation, and seeks to establish the effects of MNCs on the scientific and technological performance of host-country firms.

## Approach and Definition of General Concepts

The analysis of MNCs with respect to their creation and diffusion of technology is, by its very nature, a complex task because of the extensive technical background needed. Thus, the researcher must frequently depend on the opinion of technical experts to distinguish, where possible, those technologies that represent a discrete jump over those that were primarily imitative or more obvious derivatives of previous work. Moreover, to build up a dynamic picture of technology creation and transfer, data must often be collected to cover a time span of sometimes more than a decade. Due consideration should therefore be given to major changes in the conditions affecting the supply of new technologies, e.g., in the drug industry, to the legislation regarding quality and testing needed before introducing new products.

The term *technology* is used throughout this paper to denote that body of knowledge that enables the ideas, inventions, concepts, or techniques of science to be applied for commercial purposes. Thus, one may distinguish between creative activity in pure science, which seeks the general progress of science; and technology, which seeks the application of science to readily useful and primarily commercial ends (Dunning and Steuer, 1969, p. 9). Hence, the term *technology creation* refers to the work companies carry out to bring a new product onto the market as well as the related work involved in developing and altering the product throughout its subsequent forms and improvements. Sometimes the concept of a single technology may be used in reference to a body of knowledge or know-how that can be readily distinguishable from others owing to outstanding characteristics. It becomes apparent that an individual product may include several technologies. Moreover, the term technology may also be employed to distinguish a set of product markets related by a strong thread of association with a readily definable technology (Ansoff, 1958, pp. 392–414; 1965, pp. 103–121).

The term *technology transfer* is used to convey a generally, though not necessarily, commercial activity that brings about a wider application of a single technology. Technology transfer takes place in a territorial sense as well as in a technological sense. For example, firm A may transfer a technology to country B, meaning that it applies the technology in country B. Subsequently, the application of a technology in country B may be further extended with its use by a local firm. Furthermore, the local firm may use the technology in a new application or extend its use among a wider population of users.

These varied forms of technology transfers may be distinguished by the major commercial levels at which they take place. One such level is the *market level,* whereby use is extended to a population of individuals or firms through a reproducible package of goods or services, a commodity, or a service. A second is the *production level,* where the spread in use of a technology is primarily related to a firm's in-house activities, although the source of the technology may be external. A third level is the *research and development level,* where the application of a technology can be used to create products imitating those already using the technology. Alternatively, it can be used either to create new products, thereby fostering the development of new markets, or to create a new body of technology through the application of the existing technology. These three levels of technology transfer are representative of the depth, or degree, to which a body of knowledge becomes part of the fabric of the commercial and scientific system of its users.

Technology creation and technology transfer are most readily analyzed when know-how representative of a technology can be defined discretely. However, technology creation is often not reflected in a single end product and the new technologies become hazy or indistinguishable in application. But, for the drug and microelectric industries, technology creation and transfer can be analyzed with respect to discrete products or processes, which we shal term *innovations,* and which are representative of significant departures in scientific application and know-how. Hence, the definition of an innovation is rigorous in the sense of measuring a new and commercially viable technology. For this paper, imitations, which may in other studies have been termed innovations, are representative of a body of related knowledge and primarily reflect technology transfer as it has been defined above.

The general approach we have adopted is to relate technology creation and transfer activity to the imitation cycle, which is defined in the following section. In this way, the analysis can be conducted along the lines suggested above, and consideration given to technology transfer on the three levels of diffusion—market, production, and R & D.

# A MODEL OF THE IMITATION CYCLE

The technological infrastructure of the United States has been the world's most prolific source of MNCs. Within Europe, which account for almost one-half of U.S. foreign direct investment, the United Kingdom is the single most important host country. The analysis that follows is primarily based on the market entry and technology transfer activities of U.S. companies in the United Kingdom. In order to examine the performance of host-country and foreign companies within the U.K. market, the analytical framework of the imitation cycle was developed. The imitation cycle reflects a frequently observed pattern of competition within industries in which the pace of technical improvement is very rapid.

The imitation cycle varies slightly in description, depending on the specific technology on which it is based, though it generally emerges from a major technological breakthrough or innovation. The technology transfer that occurs following the commercial establishment of a new technology, *i.e.,* innovation, leads to rival introductions of substitutes by competing firms. However, limitations in terms of readily available improvements or substitutes for the innovation, and the ceiling imposed by market size, mean that the burst of new competitive activity from additional firms following a significant breakthrough always peters out. The frequency of new firms introducing the technology diminishes while the time elapsed between new entries increases.

This plateauing aspect of the frequently observed imitation cycle can be well represented by a model characterizing the frequency or time pattern of entries on a skewed bell-shaped distribution, as illustrated in Figures 5.1 and 5.2. We have made use of the log-normal model, since aspects, such as the clustering of market entries and compression of lags between entries at the beginning of the imitation cycle, can be readily measured by estimates of various statistical parameters. Furthermore, the log-normal model presupposes a skewed-left distribution. In addition, the statistical estimates of the parameters developed from the model can be employed in subsequent econometric analysis. The log-normal model, which thus forms the basis of the analysis of imitation cycles, may be defined mathematically (Aitchison and Brown, 1957) as:

$$\Lambda(t/\mu,\sigma^2) = {}_0\!\int^t \frac{1}{(2\pi\sigma^2)^{1/2}\theta} \exp\left\{\frac{-1}{2\sigma^2}(\log\theta - \mu^2)\right\}d\theta \tag{1}$$

and

$$N_t = N^* \left\{\frac{1}{(2\pi\sigma^2)^{1/2}\theta} \exp\left[\frac{-1}{2\sigma^2}\ [\log\theta - \mu]^2\right]\right\}d\theta \tag{2}$$

where:

$N_t$ = the number of market entries at time t,

$N^*$ = the eventual number of market entries,

$\mu$ = mu, the parameter measuring the mean between time of the original innovation and lag before market entry of the individual firm in natural logs,

$\sigma$ = sigma, the parameter measuring the dispersion around $\mu$ in natural logs,

$\theta$ = theta, the basis for the log-normal distribution, which can be arbitrarily defined, *e.g.,* as time in months or years.

The cumulative log-normal distribution, which is defined by equation (1), is illustrated in Figure 5.1, while the frequency distribution of equation (2) is presented as Figure 5.2.

The values of mu, sigma, and $N^*$ determine the shape and height of

*Figure 5.1*    The cumulative log-normal distribution applied to the market entries of an imitation cycle giving the parameters $\mu$, $\sigma$ and the variable N*.

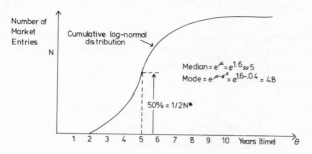

both the cumulative and the individual frequency distributions. An additional parameter $\delta$ (delta) was used in the study of the microelectronics industry as a measure of the time taken between the innovation's first market introduction anywhere in the world and its date of introduction in the U.K. In the case of innovations occurring in the U.K., the value of delta is zero. Detailed information regarding the sources of the data are given in Lake (1976a, b).

### The Interpretation of Parameters

Figures 5.1 and 5.2 illustrate a single case of an imitation cycle. However, the shape of the cycle tends to vary depending on various factors determining the speed and extent of technology transfer. For example, a semiconductor technology, which is not broadly extended to potential users, will have a lower value of $N*$ relative to other technologies where utilization is more widespread. If the technology is applied in a larger number of uses, *i.e.*, the scope of application is enlarged, this is likely to

*Figure 5.2*    The frequency of market entries measured in natural logs or absolute terms. Note that the frequencies making up the log-normal distribution are distributed normally with respect to 1n (time).

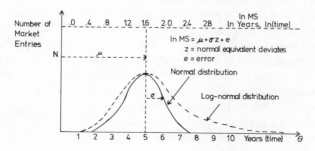

be reflected in the number of firms seeking to imitate the technology, hence in $N^*$.

Furthermore, the transfer of technology to and within a given group of firms, for example, host-country firms, may occur less rapidly than, say, the transfer between parent companies and their foreign subsidiaries operating in the host country. The rate of technology transfer is, thus, somewhat dependent on who the eventual recipients are. Since this may be quite variable, the values of $N^*$, delta, mu, and sigma, may also vary widely.

In cases where values of mu and delta are low, the diffusion of the technology is more rapid. Moreover, if sigma is low, the concentration in terms of numbers of imitating firms and the extent of the similarity in time required by firms before market entry are both higher. A technology that brings with it distinct competitive advantages is likely to be transferred under more competitive conditions, possibly resulting in lower values for mu and sigma. Nevertheless, a larger population of users may also tend to modify the values of mu and sigma.

*The Results of Estimation•*

Imitation cycles were estimated for twenty semiconductor (of which many were microelectronic) component innovations and forty technical or therapeutic areas of pharmaceuticals. The following equation was used:

$$ln\ MS = \mu(mu) + \sigma\ (sigma) + e \qquad\qquad (3)$$

where:

$ln\ Ms$ = The lag between innovation anywhere and market entry in the host country by host-country firms or the subsidiaries of foreign firms.

In the case of the pharmaceuticals industry, the lag measured was between the innovation in the U.K. and subsequent introductions. Typical imitation cycles are illustrated in Figures 5.3, 5.4, and 5.5 for transistor-transistor logic in microelectronic components, anti-Parkinson drugs, and non-thiazide diuretics in pharmaceuticals. It is readily apparent from these examples that values of the parameters for different cycles vary. Moreover, an examination of individual introductions will show that variations also occur in the number of U.S. subsidiaries, host-country U.K. firms, European and other subsidiaries, entering the market. For example, in both the microelentronic components and the anti-Parkinson drug examples, European firms entered later than many U.S. subsidiaries.

Summaries of the results of estimation of twenty imitation cycles in

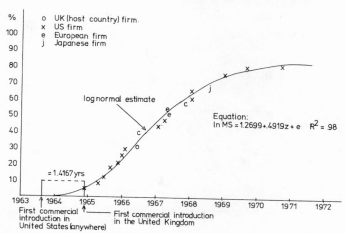

*Figure 5.3* T²L (Transistor Transistor Logic)

semiconductor components and forty in pharmaceuticals are given in Tables 5.2 and 5.3. The statistical fits for the equations were generally good and on average $R^{-2}$ exceeded .86 with only slight variation. The fits were fractionally better in pharmaceuticals and the range of variation tended to be small for $N^*$ and for the parameters. On average, both industries, despite their differing levels on MNC participation in research and development, which was apparent from Table 5.1, had a similar average number of participants (i.e., 16) within imitation cycles.

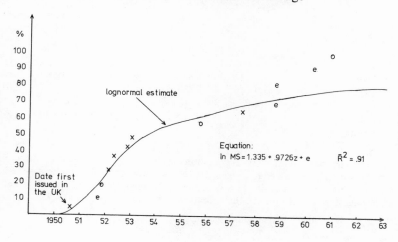

*Figure 5.4* Anti-Parkinson Drugs

*Figure 5.5*   Diuretics (Non-Thiazide)

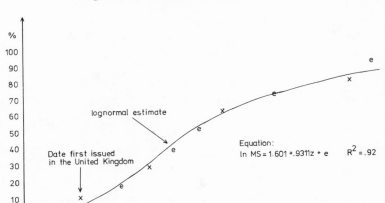

Comparisons of the averages for parameters of the imitation cycle of integrated microelectronic components and discrete semiconductor components suggest that the average numbers of participants may have increased marginally, since innovations in the integrated components group tend to be more recent and the average $N^*$ for them is 18 compared to less than 16 for discrete components. Furthermore, it has been found that the numbers of eventual firms in imitation cycles in the U.K. semiconductor

*Table 5.2*   Summary of Results
Parameter Estimates of 20 Initation Cycles
in the U.K. Semiconductor Industry

| Group | $N^*$ number | Delta years | Mu years | Sigma years | $\bar{R}^2$ |
|---|---|---|---|---|---|
| All twenty imitation cycles 1950–1973 | 16.10 (8.81) | 1.6958 (1.6306) | 3.2247 (1.6517) | 1.9552 (1.4086) | .8759 (.1161) |
| Discrete components[1] 1950–1973 | 15.57 (9.44) | 1.8556 (1.8501) | 3.1756 (5.2158) | 2.0013 (7.2261) | .8773 (.1066) |
| Integrated microelectronic components[2] 1961–1973 | 18 (7.11) | 1.2167 (.5157) | 3.3734 (1.4067) | 1.8230 (1.2599) | .8715 (.1556) |

[1] Point contact transistor (Ge), alloy junction transistor (Ge), diffused transistor (Si), diffused mesa transistor (Ge/Si), epitaxial devices, planar transistors (Si), junction field effect transistors, alloy junction diode (Si), power rectifier (Si), zener diode (Si), tunnel diode, unijunction transistor, varactor diode, light emitting diode, schottky-barrier diodes.

[2] DCTL logic, DTL logic, ECL logic, p-MOS.

*Table 5.3*   Summary of Results
Parameter Estimates of 40 Imitation Cycles
in the U.K. Pharmaceuticals Industry

| Group (number of cycles) | $N^*$ number | Mu years | Sigma years | $R^2$ |
|---|---|---|---|---|
| All imitation cycles (40) | 16.48 | 5.38 | 2.41 | .89 |
| | (6.76) | (1.34) | (1.14) | (.07) |
| Cardiovascular system (6) | 17.50 | 5.97 | 2.39 | .88 |
| | (3.0165) | (1.35) | (1.14) | (.07) |
| Central nervous system (11) | 14.36 | 5.77 | 2.36 | .86 |
| | (6.28) | (1.36) | (1.16) | (.07) |
| Hormones (7) | 18.29 | 4.89 | 2.50 | .90 |
| | (6.80) | (1.27) | (1.07) | (.08) |
| Infections and infestations (8) | 19.00 | 5.51 | 2.48 | .92 |
| | (9.36) | (1.32) | (1.22) | (.03) |

industry has been strongly associated with the number of firms selling in the United States, $N^a$, and the number of firms participating that have had previous experience in the U.K. market, $N_e$.

$$N^* = - \underset{(-1.67)}{2.208} + \underset{(2.51)}{.103 \, N^a} + \underset{(12.41)}{1.313 \, N_e} \qquad \bar{R}^2 = 0.93$$

Thus, as the population of experienced firms grew, so too did the potential for technology transfer and imitation. Moreover, since American firms formed an important source of technology transfers to the U.K. industry, the progress of market entry in the United States has important implications for U.K. industry. In addition to technology, the structure of the U.S. industry in terms of numbers of competing firms would seem also to be transferred.

## THE NOVELTY OF RESEARCH AND DEVELOPMENT

Despite the fact that sales of MNCs outside the home country may often represent a large share of total sales, the propensity to locate technology creation activities in the home country has generally been very high. Definitive estimates of the level or share of spending on core or basic research are not available, but Table 5.4 shows total R & D expenditures for U.S. firms in 1966. It is readily apparent that with 94 percent of U.S. MNC's research and development in 1966 carried out in the U.S., the proportion of basic or core technology creation carried out in the home country must also be extremely high. For example, in electronic components only about 4 percent of total research and development spending of

*Table 5.4*   R & D Spending by Multinational Firms in Manufacturing
*(Amounts in millions of dollars)*

| Industry | 1966 spending | | | | |
| --- | --- | --- | --- | --- | --- |
| | | | | Percent of total | |
| | In U.S. Amount | Abroad Amount | Total Amount | In U.S. (percent) | Abroad (percent) |
| *All manufacturing* | *7,598* | *526* | *8,124* | *94* | *6* |
| Food products | 136 | 18 | 154 | 88 | 12 |
| Grain mill products | 41 | 2 | 43 | 95 | 5 |
| Other | 95 | 16 | 111 | 86 | 14 |
| Paper and allied products | 64 | 3 | 67 | 96 | 4 |
| Chemicals | 1,258 | 74 | 1,332 | 94 | 6 |
| Drugs | 303 | 25 | 328 | 92 | 8 |
| Soaps and cosmetics | 66 | 13 | 79 | 84 | 16 |
| Industrial chemicals | 777 | 8 | 785 | 99 | 1 |
| Plastics | 31 | 12 | 43 | 72 | 28 |
| Other | 81 | 16 | 97 | 84 | 16 |
| Rubber products | 127 | 4 | 131 | 97 | 3 |
| Primary and fabricated metals | 312 | 10 | 322 | 97 | 3 |
| Primary (excl. aluminum) | 130 | 5 | 135 | 96 | 4 |
| Fabricated (excl. aluminum, copper, and brass) | 138 | 5 | 143 | 97 | 3 |
| Primary and fabricated aluminum and other | 44 | 0 | 44 | 100 | 0 |
| Nonelectrical machinery | 743 | 90 | 833 | 89 | 11 |
| Farm machinery and equipment | 119 | 13 | 132 | 90 | 10 |
| Industrial machinery and equipment | 184 | 44 | 228 | 81 | 19 |
| Office machines | 108 | 5 | 113 | 96 | 4 |
| Electronic computing equipment and other | 332 | 28 | 360 | 92 | 8 |
| Electrical machinery | 1,814 | 103 | 1,917 | 95 | 5 |
| Electrical machinery and equipment[1] | 1,100 | 13 | 1,113 | 99 | 1 |
| Radio, TV, electronic components | 685 | 28 | 713 | 96 | 4 |
| Other | 29 | 62 | 81 | 23 | 77 |
| Transportation equipment | 2,537 | 134 | 2,671 | 95 | 5 |
| Textiles and apparel | 29 | 0 | 29 | 100 | 0 |
| Lumber, wood, and furniture | 25 | 61 | 86 | 29 | 71 |
| Printing and publishing | 17 | 0 | 17 | 100 | 0 |
| Stone, clay, and glass | 103 | 4 | 107 | 96 | 4 |
| Instruments | 372 | 21 | 393 | 95 | 5 |
| Other | 61 | 4 | 65 | 94 | 6 |

[1]Includes household appliances.
*Sources:* Table 5.1, and U.S. Department of Commerce, Bureau of Economic Analysis.

U.S. MNCs was for work abroad, and in pharmaceuticals this proportion was only 8 percent.

The internationalization of a company's activities often brings with it problems as well as advantages (Hopper, 1969; Stopford and Wells, 1972; Hulin-Cuypers, 1973), and this is also the case with research and development. Moreover, there would seem to be very little association, in the example of U.S. MNCs, between the proportion of research and development of an industry carried out abroad and the proportion of the research in the industry conducted by MNCs. Furthermore, this suggests that the propensity for locating research and development abroad was determined at that time by forces other than the mere fact of being an MNC or of being in a research-intensive industry.

The factors influencing the novelty of research and development in the MNC include those which reinforce the pressure or objective of the firm to be innovative (perhaps to maintain a monopoly position, Dunning, 1969, p. 25), and those which make it feasible to carry out novel R & D (company size or management, Johnson, 1970c; Hopper, 1969). Consideration is first given to those factors that may be thought of as coming primarily from within the firm, which are aspects of the motivation, strategy and coordination of technology creation, and which influence the propensity of the MNC and host-country firm toward innovation. Consideration is then given to external factors that exert pressure on the firm to strengthen its efforts at technology creation.

## The Organization of Technology Creation

Although it is sometimes said that, given sufficient spending, a company can buy its own inventions, this requires qualification, especially for truly innovative technology creation. While invention may be the result of independent inspirations of brilliant people, companies may surely establish suitable conditions for such creative activity and its application. The relationship between R & D spending and product novelty may be more consistently positive considering the support a company can give in applying a new idea once it has emerged and through the imitation or extension of proven technology. In permitting a higher quantity and quality of R & D support, a company, whether large or small, may be able to raise the quality and suitability of its products and possibly gain entry to the market sooner than with lower levels of R & D.

Two aspects of technology creation can frequently be distinguished: the creation of useful ideas out of fundamental or inspired research, and the utilization of the ideas to create commercial products by the application of skills and experience in technological development. These two aspects may be carried out by the same individuals or divided among different specialized personnel at various stages in the idea-to-product sequence.

Companies may prefer to have their idea creators—the inventors—combine their innovative work with a managerial role such as the development of a specific project. Thus, some companies expect the senior scientist to assume a management role and interact with a participant in the application of the idea to final products. Others prefer to have the scientist remain predominantly a scientist and idea and project creator, but avoid the role of manager and applications participant. The coordination of a number of projects is sometimes assigned to a professional manager or to a senior scientist from the research staff, who may be expected to assume a greater coordination role in his later years.

Scientific advance is frequently related to outstanding achievements of specific individuals. Thus, the creativity that is important to a firm within a technologically competitive industry is often not as readily accessible or reproducible as a company's ability to utilize it. Thus, technological firms, whether international or not, frequently emphasize the search for truly ingenious or brilliant scientists for their core research staff. Such brain trusts may provide the companies with the novelty of research effort required for new and path-breaking products and processes. Such research groups in MNCs may have the advantage over those of national firms of having access to ideas from several national scientific cultures. The international firm seeks to combine these through its superior "brain trust," or scientific core, to give it a definitive technological lead.

Management of research on an international scale within an MNC normally requires broader coordination then would normally occur within a centralized national firm. In theory, a large MNC could have several optimal-sized research units in separate countries. But for most MNCs, management control tends to be exercised from the source nountry in a less independent, and more centralized, arrangement. A minority of MNCs, with decentralized management structures, may prefer research units that are largely self-sufficient and carry a project through from original idea to final marketing. The evolution of a decentralized R & D structure, with self-sufficient research units, may emerge through historical accident or as a deliberate policy to emphasize the cultural and scientific difference among countries and thus to bring the benefits of a full product creation cycle to self-sufficient units abroad.

*The Hierarchical Structure.*   The organization of research and development in the majority of MNCs is hierarchical. Functions involving research of a fundamental nature are highly centralized, while the functions in the later stages of the idea-to-marketing cycle may be distributed worldwide to satellite research, development, or production units. In the hierarchical structure some of the R & D to adapt technology to specific markets is decentralized. But for defensive reasons, foreign units are sometimes limited in the self-sufficiency of even their adaptation capabilities.

Adherence to a hierarchical structure may result from the need for close managerial control and to retain control over proprietary rights. Centralization may also help to retain people within the company. Since its full research and development program may be centered around a single outstanding scientist or small group of specialists, the more closely these can be coordinated, the less the risk of their loss to rival firms. Moreover, the continuous search by companies for gifted people is often frustrated by competition from universities and other scientific institutions. The centralized research core, sometimes based on a small group, may be required to achieve the critical minimum mass to provide the new knowledge and ideas that are subsequently developed, refined, and perfected by scientists and specialists performing a support function. For early phases of a technology creation, only a few mutually reinforcing scientific employees capable of sparking technological development may be involved. When a discovery is made, a support program is required and additional personnel are employed. This support staff may consist of less innovative specialists, who provide a more predictable and more consistent service to the company's overall technology creation.

Research and development within a hierarchical structure is normally organized into programs of research guided by the scientific core of the research staff, which may emerge with identifiable projects for development and application. The list of potential avenues of development, to be carried out by the support staff, is permitted to grow as long as manpower permits. Otherwise, those projects of lesser potential are either shelved or subjected to longer and less concentrated programs of support.

Since the MNC generally begins with its core of scientific research in the source country and does not find additional groups of outstanding individuals in host countries, it is natural that the R & D organizational structure follows hierarchical lines, with support and application work—especially that at the later stages of product development and dependent primarily on marketing needs—carried out in affiliates in host countries.

*The Parallel Structure.*   A life cycle hypothesis for MNCs may predict that multinationality and general decentralization of control is associated with company development, its maturity, and its increasing need to sustain company growth in the face of declining rates of expansion in existing markets. Irrespective of the validity of the life cycle hypothesis, parallel or semi-independent research centers in several countries present an interesting feature of MNCs. Since a creative research and development program could provide a basis for an independent product market with separate production and marketing strategies, its influence in determining policies and control within the multinational firm may be substantial. A structure of parallel R & D activities involving two or more independent units in various countries, each capable of executing the full idea-to-market sequence, occurs very infrequently in firms where unambiguous centralized control is preferred.

The nature of technology creation in organizations with parallel R & D structures finds that both the core and support activities are contained within several units in two or more countries. Moreover, core activities may vary between areas of scientific research in different countries according to the special skills of the principal researchers. Nevertheless, it is unlikely that work within a scientific area can be as effectively coordinated between parallel structures as within a hierarchical one. This, however, does not exclude the possibility of complementary and effective research programs among parallel groups. Support work in the parallel structure of organization may be carried out within any national unit, since each unit will have the capacity to do most types of work itself.

An advantage of the parallel structure is its capability for carrying through a project from birth of the idea to final product in more than one country. In gearing up for and in launching an innovation, both units can simultaneously coordinate efforts to reach a wider market from the start and thus preempt rival activity to a greater extent.

## The Capacity for Innovation and Its Strategy

A measure of the capacity for innovation of MNCs is their frequency of participation within well-defined imitation cycles. As Figure 5.6 shows, U.S. MNCs in the U.K. drug industry generally outperformed their rival U.K. firms. This is illustrated by the clearly higher distribution of the number of market entries by U.S. firms. For forty imitation cycles analyzed, the U.K. distribution has a smaller number of outstanding companies (for example, with a frequency greater than 12) and also fewer "medium performers" (between 5 and 12). Moreover, the population of U.K. firms with multinational as well as multitechnical capacity is clearly smaller than that of U.S. MNCs operating in the U.K. markets. A similar story emerges for the U.K. semiconductor industry, which in recent years has been virtually overwhelmed by the numbers of strongly competitive transnational U.S. companies. This fact is readily apparent in looking at the example of a single imitation cycle in Figure 5.3 (p. 147). Given such examples of U.S. technological superiority, what are the prospects for the U.K. industries and what explains the U.S. leadership?

If the technologically-based multinational firm is to grow, it usually requires a continuous expansion of its activities into new territorial or technical markets and the successful protection and extension of existing markets. The strategy and capacity for technological and territorial

*Figure 5.6*    The numbers of market entries per company in forty imitation cycles in pharmaceuticals presenting firms with highest frequency in first rank. U.S. subsidiaries as a group had more firms entering more markets than the U.K. firm group. For example, U.S. subsidiary of rank 5 made fifteen market entries. While the U.K. firm of rank 5 made twelve market entries.

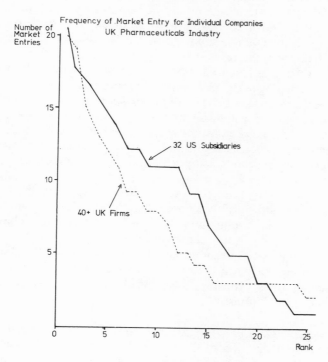

growth of individual firms varies through time and among the industries in which they are active. For example, a company that has successfully developed a major new product will probably seek to swing a substantial proportion of its R & D resources toward downstream support of that product in the research-to-sales cycle. The emphasis would be on activities such as marketing with a view to extending sales geographically or intensively within a territory. In contrast, the company that has a significant technical gap to bridge, owing to its products being superseded by cheaper and better quality imports, may increase core and upstream R & D efforts to improve the technical content of existing products or to create new products. In the former case, the strategy of the firm emphasizes an increased internationalization of company activities to derive a technological rent from territorial expansion. In the latter case, it emphasizes innovation and technical development. Although the overall strategies need to maintain a balance between the two objectives, a firm in a given period may need to emphasize one or the other.

An R & D program that consistently keeps a company in the vanguard of its industry with regard to the technological nature of its products requires a continuous and significant level of research and a substantial outlay in addition to that which may be required subsequent to the discovery of a viable project. Furthermore, a firm that wishes to remain at the frontier in a specific technology runs the risk of losing its leadership if it cannot cover new and related areas as these develop. Thus, sustaining the core of a leading research program is costly. A small firm that has succeeded in keeping in the forefront of a technical area may have insufficient financial resources for the required support activity at the point when this becomes most necessary; *i.e.*, in the period when no rival products are on the market. Moreover, market entry based on the novelty of a company's products depends on its ability to manufacture and market the product on an ever-increasing scale. Firms that cannot match the rate of increase in demand from internal sources run the risk of unbalancing the market and giving greater incentive to rival firms at the periphery, some of which would possibly ignore the market if adequate supplies were available. For example, innovating U.S. semiconductor firms have sometimes found themselves short of supplies when demand was rising rapidly, thus encouraging competition. A small company may reach the market early but subsequently run the risk of losing control over technology by subcontracting to (or licensing) a firm which has the available marketing or production capabilities.

## Internationalization and the Microeconomics of Technology Transfer

The internationalization of a company's operations will generally involve several forms of technology transfer. For our purposes, three main categories of transfer are of primary importance: market-level, production-level, and research-level transfers. The training and movement of people provide one vehicle by which new technology is diffused and applied. The economics of such activities depends upon how this is organized and the type of specialized knowledge being transferred. For example, in the case of the training of personnel for marketing abroad, indigenous trainees may travel to a training center located in a central location, since this would be less costly than the movement of the training group to several widely separated foreign locations. But if the trainees are concentrated in one area, it would be less costly for the trainer to travel to the trainees. In any event, the movement and training of individuals to effectuate the transfer of technology is likely to be designed so as to minimize costs of coordination (including costs of transportation, communications, training and administration). Similar costs and similar economic considerations will govern the microeconomics of technology transfer in the form of physical capital, plant, and equipment. For example, a highly fragmented international geographic market would make a bulk material manufacturing plant, even with significant economies of scale, in each territorial market economically unfeasible. Rather, the plant would be located proximate to a number of markets with consideration given to the relative size of each, to the economies of scale, and to distances involved in trans-shipment. Similarly, the widespread transfer of packaging, formulation or assembly activities may be dictated by the economics of location so as to minimize costs.

With the internationalization of company activities, the economics of marketing, production, and development activities determine to a great extent the form and mode of international technology transfer within overall corporate strategy. In moving from the marketing, to production, to research levels, considerations of the protection of proprietary rights become increasingly important in decision making, since these, as fixed overheads, eventually permit reduced costs. Even at the marketing level the loss of trademarks would increase the company's costs of promotion. Similarly, in production and development research, companies may guard their proprietary rights jealously in order to keep control over long-term costs.

## Innovation and the Microeconomics of Market Entry

In designing its research program, the MNC may place initial emphasis on the development of its research core. But while few companies admit that they have too many good ideas, an overproductive core without adequate support tends to dilute market entry for individual products despite expansion on a broad technical front. This may carry the danger of attracting rivals in several prospetive product areas, leaving a firm without the necessary support to resist stiffening competition. Too many good ideas may thus spread the company programs too thinly and projects that would otherwise succeed tend to fail through lack of adequate support. Nevertheless, some innovative companies engage in core research activity, sometimes for very long periods, to seek an eventual discovery that can provide a strong basis for future expansion, both technical and territorial.

The nature of the optimal balance between a company's technological and territorial activities varies considerably among companies and industries, and generalizations are obviously difficult to substantiate. Writers such as Ansoff (1965) have suggested that the strength of individual corporate strategies frequently lies in choosing those technologies that are most complementary to the firm's existing facilities and its desired direction of movement. The synergies arising from complementary technologies may thus shape corporate strategy. On the other hand, a firm with adequate cash flow may utilize a part of it to branch out into new technologies so as to achieve a stronger overall approach to technical markets and territories and retain its advantages over rivals and sustain its company growth.

Figure 5.7 illustrates these two major elements of corporate strategy, the technological and territorial, for three hypothetical companies—A, B and C. Company C illustrates a firm that balances its diversification pro-

*Figure 5.7* Company strategy and capability toward technological and territorial diversity. In Company B's case, the company appears to control or reach limits to its technological expansion and concentrates on reaching a wider territorial market. Company A, after pursuing several technological initiatives initially, in the second period appears to follow a similar strategy with Company B, but is capable of extending its several technologies in several markets simultaneously. The progress of Company C illustrates simultaneously expansion of territories and technologies on an ever-increasing scale.

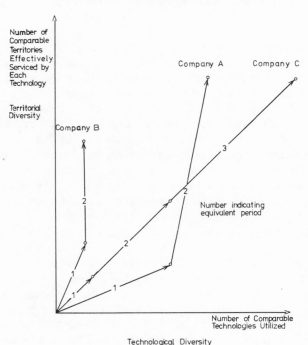

gram across technologies and markets, with sufficient resources to develop and apply the promising new technologies. Company A is a firm that succeeds in straddling several technologies in period 1, emphasizing the core R & D; and subsequently expanding territorially in period 2 as the period 1 technologies are exploited and developed. Company B shows a firm that is capable of only limited technical diversification in the first period, and that focuses narrowly its territorial growth in the second. While these are simple illustrations, they do raise the question of which factors limit corporate diversification, and what is the optimal strategy for an individual MNC.

The doctrine that MNCs tend to incorporate technological advantages in their products and operations is now well established (Vernon, 1966; Caves, 1971a,b; Hufbauer, 1965; Horst, 1972a,b). However, it is by no means clear to what extent the fact of operating multinationally represents a proactive strategy of extending these advantages and technological intensities, or alternatively represents a defensive and reactive strategy that might eventually dilute the technological advantages. Moreover, the inducements or pressures under which both small and large companies initiated and sustained transnational operations in the past may have changed as a result of the greater proportion of trade conducted on a worldwide basis by large, established MNCs.

In the U.K. industry, operations of U.S. foreign subsidiaries have been a productive means whereby the parent company was able to realize a rent on its technology owing to the novelty of its products. The company thereby increases its total revenues from which to finance either a further expansion of its operations, additional R & D to improve its products, or both. Hence, the factors that govern the value of foreign companies in securing and maintaining an MNC's technological lead are not independent of the forces that determine how multinational a firm will become. To understand the extension of a firm's operations in the international sphere, analysts need to establish which factors are the important determinants of company strategy and behavior. This is especially important in those industries in which the full production sequence of a commodity is highly internationalized, and where technological advances have influenced considerably the inducements for the worldwide diffusion of various parts of the cycle.

In multinational companies with parallel R & D structures, the determination of territorial and technological priorities for market entry presents a facet of the general problem of corporate control also evident in firms with hierarchical managerial structures. In hierarchically organized firms, the priorities established in the centralized control of the bulk of R & D work may be considerably influenced by the fact that other support programs are decentralized. Centralized control becomes important to the

*Figure 5.8*   The conceptual trade-off with respect to the magnitude and timing of support given to individual projects. In the case of Project A, support is given earlier and larger overall. These two elements form crude "measures" of the "quality" of support given to individual projects. A higher quality support program is often associated with the size of a company, especially in the case of MNCs.

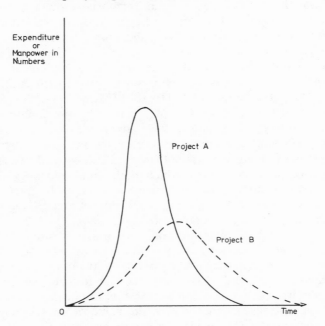

MNC in establishing an appropriate level of support for specific market entries in source and host countries, at which time the magnitude and timing of resources utilized need to be decided. The individual project thereby becomes subjected to an evaluation of time-cost trade-offs as well as to an assessment of overall prospective revenue-profit yields from market entry in different territories. This simple choice can be illustrated using Figure 5.8. In the case of Project A, a higher quality research program, measured by the magnitude and timing of resource utilization, is carried out in comparison to Project B, which is given lower priority. Moreover, it may be suggested that larger companies, or smaller companies that have a manageable core productivity, can allocate more funds sooner to a winning project when this is identified. However, the definition of a project's viability and prospective yield may involve a substantial element of risk, which again tends to favor the larger MNC that has reserve resources and a more diversified portfolio of projects.

## Competitive Factors Inducing Innovation and Imitation

A company, whether confined to a local market or selling worldwide, derives its technology rents from the scarcity of the technological advantages it is able to offer the user through its product. A completely novel product, for which no technical substitutes exist, will have a market and market price dependent on the extent to which the innovating firm creates and meets the needs of actual and potential users. An initial imbalance of supply and demand, governed largely by the scarcity of the new product and the technolgy it embodies, may not only have provided the inducement for the innovator to create the new technology, but the incentives for its rivals as well. With the introduction of its product, the innovator starts from an initial position of a monopolist. Thus, the innovating firm can have considerable influence over the early price of the innovation and thereby influence supply and the incentives for potential rival companies. Misjudging the prospective demand for a new product may add to a supply imbalance and raise price expectations, thereby providing a signal to potential rivals that imitation would be profitable. Thus, market entry with technological leadership sometimes entails substantial risk and uncertainty over whether to gear up sufficiently to avoid a potential market imbalance or to maintain a supply price sufficiently low to dissuade potential entrants. The firm, of course, seeks to achieve both objectives. In markets that are worldwide, the successful pursuit of this strategy is very much the domain of the large MNC, which need not invest physically in any specific territorial market in order to serve it.

The time lag between the innovator's first introduction of a new product and its subsequent imitation by rival firms is an important aspect of market entry conditions, which is influenced by the internationalization of activity through MNCs. Furthermore, the extent to which host-country firms are represented in the imitating group often reflects the degree of technological dependence produced by the technical advantages of MNCs. An absence of host-country firms would suggest technological dependence. Moreover, the conditions under which host-country firms are able eventually to imitate MNCs's technology reflect the general availability of technologies through alternative channels such as international licensing or host-country R & D. An important factor determining the inducement of market entry by host-country firms is the duration of demand and supply imbalance following innovation. The company wishing to deter imitation is likely to approach the market intending to limit demand growth (*e.g.*, through high prices and limited promotion) to that which it can readily meet, or intending to meet a "fully created" demand by maintaining adequate supplies of the new product at a price low enough to deter potential competitors. In either case, the imbalance created in the market by introduction of a new product can be minimized and the inducement to rival firms to imitate the product is correspondingly lessened.

The fact that innovators often create the demand for their new products means that to some extent they may control the imbalance between demand and supply through their own marketing efforts. It is frequently postulated that market expansion is subsequent to technological development. However, MNCs may find conflicting priorities. On the one hand, they are encouraged by the potential growth of technological rents on existing products through the opening of new territorial markets (requiring a marketing effort). On the other hand, they may face pressures in the source country for improvements to the existing technical position where innovation may have already induced competitive imitations from rival firms. The size of an MNC and its international marketing capability are important determinants of the extent to which both priorities can be met simultaneously. A large international company may have the distinct advantage of a supply network already in operation, while a smaller company may have to rely on a foreign firm to do its marketing, and possibly receiving a lower rent on its technology and a less effective marketing effort with the higher risk of the technology being copied by a potential rival. Protection of the home or base market is frequently given priority over foreign expansion (Caves, 1971a); hence, the increase in domestic capacity or the creation of an improved technology receives a greater amount of resources from the small firm when facing competition in the home market.

The internationalization of an industry means that, worldwide, host-country firms responding to the penetration of MNCs are alerted sooner to the possibilities of subsequent technological innovations to which host-country firms in other territories can respond more effectively. For the small innovating company seeking to expand in overseas markets (and protect its home market), the potential sources of rivalry have grown to include MNCs from other source countries, other firms from the same source country, and even from host-country firms. The increasingly competitive international environment within industries, together with the emergence of MNC activity, makes a less fertile ground for international expansion by relatively small national companies. Thus, firms innovating from the strength of a worldwide network have a distinct competitive advantage.

The ability to sustain a market imbalance for any innovation will be higher the better able the innovator to meet competition when it arrives. In this regard, the MNC often has the advantage of working from territorial or market strength as well as technological strength. The creation of technology, even without its actual application, means that it has a "technological reserve capacity" in case its markets are challenged. Furthermore, the speed with which it can respond to an actual competitive threat in specific markets with an improved technological alternative of its own is related to the strength of its existing facilities in those markets. Just the threat of mobilizing its potential may deter entry by smaller companies. A plan of tactical defense by the MNC in the event of challenge is frequently embodied in reserves of technology that remain underutilized until required. Size is a significant element in the speed and the intensity at which the response can be made. It is frequently within the scope of the large MNC to maintain both its technological and market leadership position. The factors that determine the speed with which new technology is introduced come primarily through rivalry among those firms that succeed in becoming international and manage to sustain a sufficient technical reserve.

While obvious problems exist for the small host-country firm, including the increasing national dependence on large MNCs for technology, a major innovation by a small firm does create an imbalance of supply that remains as a route for market entry. Though limited, this route has frequently led to a competitive international environment conducive to a rapid pace of technological creation and diffusion.

To summarize, the novelty of a company's research and development may be reflected in three important aspects of its market entry activity. First, there is the territorial aspect, which concerns the time that transpires between innovation and the firm's market entry in different territories. Then there is the technical aspect of whether or not the product introduction represents a significant technical advance on products already offered in the market. Finally, there is the intertemporal aspect of whether or not the introduction of the product represents a significant intertemporal transfer of resources toward the earlier development and application of technology than would otherwise be the case.

# THE SPEED OF TECHNOLOGY TRANSFER

The MNC can influence the speed of international technology transfer by its decisions governing the international application of its own factors of production. It can also influence it indirectly by stimulating the creation, development, or application of similar or imitative technology by rival firms, from either the source, host, or third countries. Should the impact of technology transfer by an MNC fall primarily on host-country firms, the rate of technology transfer would then depend on the capacity of the host country to create, develop, and utilize new technology that is competitive to that transferred within the MNC.

The speed of the technology transfer process depends upon the rates of change on three levels. At the market level, the product innovations of the MNC shape the utilization of resources in the host country directly through their influence on international patterns of competition, consumption, and production. At the production level, the technical ideas, methods, and skills of the MNC stimulate technology directly by changing the processes and organization of production in the host country. Finally, at the R & D level, the host-country firm or foreign subsidiaries are capable of pursuing parallel and competitive R & D programs.

The analytical approach adopted for the analysis of international technology transfer is dictated by the need to account for additional factors relating to the international nature of the transfer, and which would not be adequately identified by the methods used in the analysis of technology transfer in a domestic context (Toulmin, 1968; Mansfield, 1963, 1968; Globerman, 1973a; Ray, 1973; Finan, 1975; Stobaugh, 1971a, b; Tilton, 1971). Measures of the intensity of technology transfer between countries can be based on the extent to which consumption patterns and resource utilization patterns are changed through the introduction of new technology and the extent to which its utilization invokes the absorption of new methods and techniques into the fabric of economic activity. Alternatively, the level may be measured in terms of the utilization of new technology for market entry in the host country—the method used in this section.

## Market-Entry Lags and Imitation

The transfer of an innovation to a host-country market by an MNC generally initiates a burst of competitive activity similar to that represented in Figures 5.3, 5.4, and 5.5. The speed of the technology transfer is reflected in the parameters mu, sigma, and delta, which have been estimated for innovations in the semiconductor and pharmaceutical industries. Averages and standard deviations of these parameters were presented in Tables 5.2 and 5.3. It was noted that variations tended to be fairly large, particularly in the semiconductor industry. In Figure 5.9, three imitation cycles have been drawn to illustrate how differences in the parameter values and the value of $N^*$ can be reflected in the pattern of market entries in the host country. If it is assumed that cycle A represents an "average" imitation cycle, such as given in Tables 5.2 and 5.3, then cycles B and C are deviations form the average. These deviations can be associated with factors related to the technology itself, firms applying it, the time taken before it was introduced, the scope for its application, and so on. This section develops a method by which the influence of some of these determinants can be assessed.

Before presenting the results of the analysis, various factors that may condition the speed of transfer should be considered. For example, the

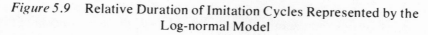

*Figure 5.9*    Relative Duration of Imitation Cycles Represented by the Log-normal Model

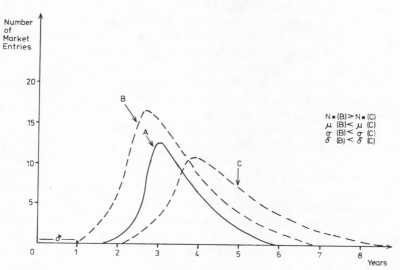

competitive response to foreign entry in the host country might be assumed to depend on the degree to which the existing industrial structure is challenged. The successful entry into a new market requires that the innovator meet the new demand from that market. But to minimize the potential host-country challenge to foreign entry, the innovating MNC may initially adopt a low-profile strategy so that it may effectively increase the size of its market while reducing the speed at which established firms are aroused to compete. A strategy involving a sizeable challenge to the host-country firms would likely initiate a competitive reaction and possibly increase the costs of entry. A quiet entry strategy may, on the other hand, make established host-country firms adopt a wait-and-see attitude and later to find the technology of the MNC more competitive than they had initially expected. Moreover, diffusion at market level may also be reflected at the product level. Territorial distribution of product units within the MNC may occur, depending on its marketing strategy and the need to proceed more slowly in the beginning stages in sensitive markets. Notwithstanding the above comments, rivalry with other source-country firms would limit the effectiveness of a low-profile strategy and hasten technology transfer.

During the early phases of the development of a new market, shortages are likely to be related to the monopoly supply position of the innovator. Furthermore, during its initial phase the imitation cycle may exhibit a slow pace of participation and limited technological choice. But, as the market expands and the rate of market entry rises, the development of the technology becomes more rapid. Market level diffusion thus brings on the transfer of technology at the other levels and leads to a more reliable supply, an increasing diversity of alternative products, and improvements to existing products and high degrees of product differentiation. However, the advance of any given imitation cycle may be reversed by the launching of a major superceding innovation. Among the diverse products from the superceded technology, many become redundant and the pace of the technology's development peaks, as firms scramble to acquire and utilize the superceding state-of-the-art techniques.

Because of their size and the control that they can exercise over individual markets, large MNCs may also be capable of exerting some influence over the pace at which rival technologies are able to gain a market foothold. Their extensive marketing arrangements, the great diversity of their products, and their ability to reduce costs while maintaining supply may grant a range of options to MNCs that would give them advantages over smaller innovating firms. Furthermore, while host-country firms may not be able to reduce prices during the plateau period or mature phase of an imitation cycle, since economies of scale of host-country manufacture are less attractive, the MNC can sometimes draw on its foreign sources to provide a lower-cost product. The severity of the impact of a superceding technology on host-country firms is augmented by the fact that MNCs in the plateau period are able to draw on a greater diversity of products developed from the obsolescent technology in other countries.

A new technical breakthrough with a substantial local MNC presence places greater pressure on host-country firms to acquire each superceding technology sooner than would be the case in the absence of a transnational link. This could even lead to a strategy of reciprocal investment on the part of host-country firms in the parent countries of rival MNCs. But, to be successful, this approach to technology acquisition needs to be timed so that the subsidiary may benefit by being in on the early phases of a new technology cycle emerging in the source country. It would also seem that the host-country firm would have to prepare its technology for market entry in the other source country well in advance of its intended application in the host country, although the ultimate effect of reciprocal investments may be to reduce the technology transfer lag between different countries.

Although reciprocal investment may characterize many industries, the pace at which it takes place appears to be related to the need of the host-country firm to maintain similar technological advantages to those enjoyed by the MNC or foreign firm sourcing its technology abroad. For example, in the semiconductor industry, U.S. firms such as Fairchild, National Semiconductor, and Intel have been able to draw on the large electronics community near San Francisco. If a British competitor wants to keep up with the technical developments of the area, it may feel the need to source some of its technology there also. Moreover, in the pharmaceutical industry, British companies have enjoyed a different culture of academic and industrial drug research, which can be tapped by U.S. firms establishing research and other facilities in the U.K. The two industries, however, differ in the extent to which the research into technologies can be advantageously sourced internationally, and also in the extent to which the technology transferred is based on intensive research and development. Furthermore, the comparative advantages enjoyed by firms in one British industry may be related to the level of sophistication of its research while in another it may be based upon the characteristics of its markets.

The analysis conducted on the two industries found a significant difference between the industries both in the extent to which the competing firms were MNCs and in the manner in which the technology was transferred and imitated within the industry. In the case of semiconductors, many innovations originated in America outside of established MNCs, and the speed and frequency with which firms subsequently entered the U.K. market was increasing through time. In the pharmaceuticals industry, it was found that most innovators were large MNCs and these recently have tended to introduce products first into the United Kingdom rather than United States. Furthermore, the evidence did not necessarily show that the speed of technology transfer was increased by an MNC presence, owing possibly to the effect that differences in government regulatory systems have had on innovation.

The study of the semiconductor industry (Lake, 1976a) suggested that in imitation cycles where the number of experienced firms was higher (*i.e.,* those which had been in an earlier imitation cycle) ([*Ne*]; of newly entering firms [*NE*], or of firms conducting research and development in the host country [*RD*]), the initial lag ($\delta$) between innovation in the United States and introduction in the United Kingdom was shorter. The regression results for the analysis of 20 innovations were as follows:

$$\delta = +3.29 \quad -.26RD \quad -.10NE \qquad \bar{R}^2 = 0.05 \qquad (4)$$
$$(-.1.28) \quad (-.1.03)$$

and

$$\delta = +2.66 \quad -.816Ne \qquad \bar{R}^2 = 0.03 \qquad (4a)$$
$$(+3.22) \quad (-1.3)$$

Although the coefficients were not very significant, they were of the correct sign. Thus, the fact that innovations were made in the United States would seem to have some marginal effect on technology transfer or imitation of state-of-the-art technology in the United Kingdom through the participation of experienced and technically progressive firms.

In contrast, new products in the pharmaceutical industry tended to be late arrivals to the United States rather than to the United Kingdom (Lake 1976b). Almost 70 percent of the drugs taken from a sample of 74 out of 150 new chemical entities issued in the United States (and listed by De Haen) during 1963–1972 were introduced first into the U.K. market. It is shown in Table 5.5 that the average lag of introductions to the United States for these was about 2½ years, increasing in cases where transfers were made within or between European companies to around 3¼ years. The averages for all 74 drugs given in Table 5.6 illustrate that, while the average lags for drug transfers within U.S. companies were shorter than for British and European companies, they were still more than six months, and that the overall average was a lag of 1⅓ years. The presence and market entry activity of U.S. MNCs in the pharmaceutical industry would thus seem to have pushed forward the state-of-the-art in the U.K. industry.

It has been suggested that one effect of market entry of MNCs might be to bring about increased competition, and thus a clustering of market entries within a shorter time period than would otherwise be the case. The analysis of imitation cycles of the semiconductor industry suggested that the presence of higher numbers of large firms, measured by size of sales in the U.S. *(SS)*, and of firms licensed for U.S. semiconductor technology *(LT)*, and a smaller proportion of newly entering firms *(NE/N\*)* (*i.e.*, from

*Table 5.5*   Average Leads for Drugs Introduced First into the
United Kingdom[1]
1963–1972 (52/74 Drugs)

Years

Subsequent Introduction into the United States by

| Introduced First into the UK by: | U.S. firm | U.K. firm | European or other firm | All firms |
|---|---|---|---|---|
| U.S. firm | 2.14 | — | .08 | 2.21 |
| | 48.1% | | 1.9% | 50.0% |
| U.K. firm | 2.82 | 2.29 | 4.17 | 2.85 |
| | 11.5% | 3.8% | 1.9% | 17.3% |
| European or Other firm | 2.04 | — | 3.37 | 2.67 |
| | 13.5% | | 19.2% | 32.7% |
| All firms | 2.23 | 2.29 | 3.26 | 2.47 |
| | 73.1% | 3.8% | 23.1% | 100.0% |

[1]Lake 1976b

*Table 5.6*    Average Leads (+), Lags (−) for Drugs Introduced into the
United States[1]
1963–1972 (Sample 74 drugs)

Years

| Introduced first by | Then Introduced Abroad by | | | |
|---|---|---|---|---|
| | U.S. parent or subsidiary firm | U.K. firms | firms | All firms |
| U.S. parent or subsidiary firm | −89 55.4% | +1.7 1.4% | +1.47 4.1% | −.69 60.8% |
| U.K. firm | −2.89 8.1% | −2.29 2.7% | −4.17 1.4% | −2.85 12.2% |
| Other firm | −2.04 9.5% | +1.58 1.4% | −2.35 16.2% | −2.05 27.0% |
| All firms | −1.25 73.0% | −.46 5.4% | −1.75 21.6% | −1.34 100.0% |

[1]Lake 1976b

the periphery), tended to increase the clustering of market entries, as measured by $\sigma$ (sigma):

$$\sigma^* = 2.833 - \underset{(-.45)}{.068\,SS} - \underset{(-.1.72)}{.141\,LT} + \underset{(+.61)}{.99\,NE/N^*} \quad \bar{R}^2 = 0.12 \quad (5)$$

where

$\sigma^* = e^\sigma$, *i.e.*, in years.

Similarly, in the pharmaceutical industry, sigma may have been slightly influenced by the participation of MNCs whether measured by the presence of large U.S. MNCs *(USFS)* (the number present from the group of the ten U.S. firms with the largest foreign sales in 1971), or of large MNCs in general *(WLF)* (the number present from the group of the world's twenty largest firms by sales 1971):

$$\sigma = \underset{(16.93)}{.55} - \underset{(-1.11)}{.009\,USFS} \qquad \bar{R}^2 = .06 \qquad (6)$$

and

$$\sigma = .56 - \underset{(-1.60)}{.007\,WLF} \qquad \bar{R}^2 = .04 \qquad (7)$$

Again, the regression coefficients, although suggestive, were not very significant. Thus, the participation of MNCs may have only a marginal effect accelerating the rate of technology transfer through the rivalry within this group, which tends to lead to a clustering of new introductions.

The analysis of the impact of MNCs on the speed of technology transfer at the market level also included an examination of their effect on the median or average length of time taken for imitation. In the semiconductor industry, it was found that the increased participation of the innovative firms $Ne^*)$ was negatively associated with $\mu^*$:

$$\mu^* = \quad 4.62 \quad - \quad 0.47\ Ne^* \qquad\qquad\qquad \bar{R}^2 = 0.12 \qquad\qquad (8)$$
$$\quad\quad (4.616) \quad (-1.87)$$

However, in the pharmaceutical industry, an increased participation of large MNCs *(WL)* (the number participating of the world's largest ten firms by 1971 sales), or of host-country firms *(BF)* tended to have a slight positive association with $\mu$:

$$\mu = \quad 2.044 + \quad .0135\ BF + \quad .0210\ WL \qquad\qquad \bar{R}^2 = 0.11 \qquad\qquad (9)$$
$$\quad (27.33) \quad (1.908) \quad\quad (1.792)$$

There would thus seem to be no pronounced effect resulting from increased participation of MNCs on the overall rate of market entry within the imitation cycles of the pharmaceutical industry, although the number of introductions being made was higher. Nevertheless, it was subsequently found, from an examination of the rank correlations of positions of U.S. MNCs within imitation cycles of new chemical entities introduced in the United States during the 1963–1972 period, that early market entries in the United Kingdom tended to be associated with MNC company size and the "quality" of its research program in the United States, as measured by the ratio of R & D personnel.

*Technology Diffusion at the Production Level*

The increased territorial or technical utilization of a technology generally represents the transfer of technology at the production level and can take place within or between companies. If successful, it generally means increased sales and larger markets. Moreover, firms that have the capability to carry out technology transfer may be expected to exercise a leadership role within their respective industries.

Since sales of highly technical products such as made-up pharmaceuticals or semiconductor markets are generally related to the innovativeness of the firms forming the population of participants, the size of individual companies, both relatively and absolutely, may be related to their capacities for technology creation and technology transfer. Moreover, the statistical association between innovative performance and sales comes out strongly in both industries. Thus, in semiconductors, an index *W,* which measured individual innovative performance of fifteen companies in terms of their frequency of participation in twenty imitation cycles, weighted according to the firm's position in the sequence of market entry within the cycles, was strongly correlated to the size of sales in the host country ($S^h$):

$$S^h = -.95 + 0.0863\ W \qquad\qquad \bar{R}^2 = 54 \qquad (10)$$
$$(5.88)$$

Similarly, in pharmaceuticals, the innovativeness of sixty individual companies within forty imitation cycles was strongly associated with their size of sales:

$$S^h = +.23 + .18\ W \qquad\qquad \bar{R}^2 = 54 \qquad (11)$$
$$(8.44)$$

The implication of these results is that, if a company is to grow, it needs to be competitive technologically, not only by increasing its frequency of entry within imitation cycles, but also by participating sooner relative to other companies within imitation cycles.

While technology transfer and technology creation may lead to larger sales for individual companies, these may permit the same companies to sustain their innovative performance, since increased sales generally mean increased savings for technological as well as for territorial expansion. In the case of seventeen U.S. semiconductor firms operating in the United Kingdom, innovativeness with the twenty imitation cycles, as measured by $W$ as the dependent variable, was strongly associated with worldwide company sales ($S$) (in 1973 in U.S. £ million), and with the length of time the companies had been selling in the United Kingdom ($A$):

$$W = -41.90 + .19\ S + 5.3\ A \qquad \bar{R}^2 = .75 \qquad (12)$$
$$(2.316)\quad (4.536)\quad (4.906)$$

A similar relationship for seventeen U.S. pharmaceutical firms was found between $S$; $E$, the size of establishment in the United Kingdom measured by number of British employees; and innovativeness in forty pharmaceutical imitation cycles:

$$W = +.034\ S + .032\ E \qquad\qquad \bar{R}^2 = .57 \qquad (13)$$
$$(2.64)\quad (4.95)$$

Moreover, it was found that, in the semiconductor industry, shorter entry lags ($T$, in years), between the innovation beginning the imitation cycle and the firm's market èntry were associated with the frequency of market entry within the twenty imitation cycles ($F$) and the length of time the company had been selling in the United Kingdom *(A)*, although for the latter variable the association was not very strong:

$$T \text{ (in years)} = 5.26 - \underset{(-2.87)}{.13\, F} - \underset{(-.69)}{.03\, A} \qquad \overline{R}^2 = .27 \qquad (14)$$

Thus, some feedback from a company's total size and experience and its experience in the U.K. market to its innovativeness in the United Kingdom may be suggested from the results for both industries.

### The Transfer of Research and Development

Since the host country can initially lag in the creation of a new technology, the transfer of technology may represent a method of substituting foreign for domestic technology creation and thus bring about both a saving of resources in the host country and a faster international pace of technology diffusion. Furthermore, the economics of international transfers within companies may, owing to factors such as more effective organization, mean that such transfers are made sooner and at a lower cost within MNCs than between unaffiliated companies. In both cases, the transfer of technology may be made under a licensing agreement with the licensee paying royalties, generally based on sales for a stipulated period.

Host-country firms in the U.K. semiconductor and pharmaceutical industries have generally found that licensing agreements have permitted an earlier entry into new product markets, which has sometimes been the only feasible method of entry. The decisions related to licensing are made within the context of the expected sales and profitability that an agreement could bring to the licensee. This is illustrated in Figure 5.10, which shows the discounted prospective revenue curve related to the time elapsed from initial technology transfer. The discounted prospective cost curve for technology transfer within an MNC, from the time that market entry is to be made, is represented by *CC*, while that for a host-country licensee is *BL*. The curve *CC* lies below *BL* owing to synergystic economies of intrafirm transfer compared to interfirm transfers. The host-country firm, if it should attempt to create the technology itself, could expect to find that the costs lie along *BB* and that they also depend on how soon market entry is to be made. From the way that the cost curves are drawn in Figure 5.10, it is apparent, for example, that the host-country firm could earn a higher prospective profit as a licensee providing royalty payments were not greater than that represented by the vertical distance between *BB* and *BL*.

The optimal timing of market entry, given the prospective cost and revenue curves illustrated, occurs when profits are most likely to be maximized, which is where the vertical distance between *DD* and the cost

*Figure 5.10*   The options open to a host-country firm either to license a new technology or to carry out research and development itself. Both operations are subject to time-cost trade-offs, as embodied in the shape of the illustrated cost curves.

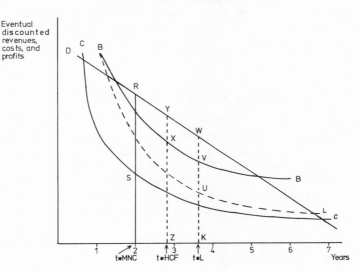

curves is the greatest. Suppose that this occurs at $t^*$ MNC for the MNC; at $t^*$ HCF for the host-country firm that carries out technology creation internally, and at $t^*$L for the host-country firm that is licensed by a foreign company. The licensee is better off provided that *WU* is greater than *YX*. Moreover, if the host-country firm decided to go it alone, its timing of market entry should be earlier than if it operates under a license.

Although Figure 5.10 illustrates an example where the MNC holds a comparative advantage in terms of cost and optimal date of market entry, in practice licencees of foreign technology are still given some considerable advantage. This is readily apparent from the examination of the imitation lags occurring in the semiconductor industry (over twenty imitation cycles) for U.K. licensees, which averaged about four months earlier for technology transfer than in the case of the transfers to wholly owned U.S. manufacturing subsidiaries. Moreover, the average innovativeness from transfers to licensees as measured by index *W* was around 20 percent higher. These results are all the more remarkable given the extremely good record of several U.S. pioneering companies such as Texas Instruments, Fairchild, RCA, Westinghouse, General Electric (U.S.A.), and General Instruments. Furthermore, in the pharmaceuticals industry, U.K. firms have also made considerable use of licensing agreements. One estimate (Lake, 1976b) puts this as high as 41 percent in the case of 137 new chemical entities introduced in the period 1950–1972. The highest proportion of licenses in the case of agreements with American firms (34 percent) were made in the central nervous system drug group, as was the case of agreements with European firms (29 percent). Thus, in both industries, licensing has been an important and early method of transferring technology at the research and development level.

# THE IMPACT ON THE HOST COUNTRY

The activities of MNCs affect the structure of host-country industry and the performance of host-country firms with respect to technology creation and transfer at three levels of operation: market, production, and R & D. Moreover, the influence of MNCs from any one source country may extend to the performance of third-country firms, thus reinforcing their impact through influences on a wider group of companies. One ultimate effect on host-country firms may be a heightened response at the international level to innovation.

*Impact at the Market Level*

The influence of MNCs at the market level extends to the users of products based on new technology as well as to host-country suppliers. On the supply side, three general areas of impact may be identified (Dunning, 1975). First, MNCs influence the ability of host-country suppliers to remain innovative and to compete effectively. Second, MNCs affect the extent to which local suppliers can become independent of foreign sources of technology in order to remain competitive and to exercise an "acceptable" degree of local ownership and selective control over operations. Finally, MNCs help determine the general effect on the resource utilization of local suppliers and users that may alter the balances of local application of resources and the ability of these to meet requirements. The influence of transnationals on the structure of supply extends across all of the above considerations and may initiate and accelerate changes in the size, distribution, number, degree of diversification, internationalization, and integration of local suppliers.

On the demand side, the users of new technology may be significantly moved from existing patterns of consumption, through changes and extensions in the mix and diversity of products in the market. The patterns of consumption brought about by MNC activity may thus increasingly parallel patterns in foreign countries. Besides this, they may be made more receptive to foreign supply and, as in the case of semiconductor components, lead firms downstream in the production process to make greater use of certain foreign inputs.

The creation of a new technology that is subsequently transferred at the market level by the MNC induces a series of perhaps diverse responses from the competing source-country and third-country firms. The technology itself, particularly if its primary use is as an input into production in the host country, may have varied effects. It may extend integration of the industry vertically owing to its effect on the technological character of the final product, *e.g.,* as with microelectronics having an interpretation bias that permits firms upstream to diversify downstream. Alternatively, it may enable foreign users of the technology to compete more effectively in the host country. Furthermore, the introduction and utilization of the product may invoke a closer interface between the foreign supplier and local users, thereby reinforcing the transnational market and technological links.

The impact of an innovation and its subsequent transfer at the market level may begin slowly with the activities of a leading foreign company. This, however, may rapidly induce a competitive reaction on the part of other foreign suppliers; force local firms to alter their marketing activity, perhaps initially to deter foreign entry, but eventually to match the entry of new products through imitation; or bring about a competitive response from third countries where the technology is sufficiently advanced to enable entry. Thus, at the market level, the number of competing firms may rise, as may the diversity of sources of supply, and the host-country firm (and perhaps the source country MNC) may face an increasingly competitive environment.

A number of factors that contribute to the host-country firm's ability to survive competitively and match foreign technologies, and at the same time bring about an effective utilization of domestic resources are increasingly influenced by technology transfer activities of MNCs. In the past, host-country firms that foresaw local market entry by MNCs often had time to respond and initiate their own R & D. But, the emergence of the MNC marketing capabilities with the associated shortening of lags between sales in source and host-country markets means that host-country firms are given shorter advance notice and market information. Hence, the time available to respond is shortened. Host-country firms may thus need to seek clues of possible market entry through the acquisition of knowledge about what is possible rather than what is actually practiced elsewhere. This need for a proactive attitude toward technology may become a requirement for survival as the internationalization of industry progresses. In other words, the host-country must increasingly behave and respond as though rival MNCs were capable of instantaneous transfer. Moreover, the need for the host-country firm to establish the capability for entry is raised, with the result that it is more likely to establish a foreign marketing capacity or arrangement.

This suggests that the eventual impact of MNC activity on technology diffusion at the market level will be to reduce the transfer lag between source and host country. MNCs may bring closer together the imitation cycles in source and host countries in terms of the timing of market-entries. The impact of MNCs on the structure of host-country industry is one of limiting the indigenous firms to those that are sufficiently large to sustain their own foreign marketing operation. MNCs's effects in the host country may tend to raise the level of foreign involvement and direct investment by domestic firms so as to match the transnational operations of foreign companies. In becoming MNCs, host-country firms would enter more readily into international sourcing and utilizing of resources, which would also have effects on the host-country.

*Impact at the Production Level*

The influence of MNCs at the marketing level often necessitates adjustments in the production process in host-country firms. At least three areas of production may be affected. First, the processes or techniques of production may or may not be economically efficient in the host country, owing, for example, to changes in the required scale of production caused by increased market size for some products and diminished size for others attributable, for example, to product differentiation. Second, transnational marketing may also make certain types and stages of production activity even more advantageous for local firms in the host country, principally through the availability of different types of labor and materials suited to newly introduced state-of-the-art technology. Third, MNCs affect the mix, types, and sources of inputs for their more diverse and differentiated products.

With the introduction of product or process innovation and its subsequent imitation by local and foreign companies, the need for modification at the production level emerges through the basic requirements of the innovation itself. The more rapidly the market increases in size, the greater and sooner are pressures exerted on host-country firms to scale-up their production methods to create their own in-house (imitation) production methods or import foreign machinery. The utilization of foreign techniques may be so postponed by a slow rate of domestic market growth, or by the possibility of production methods being rapidly superceded, that improvements in the host country may fall significantly behind those carried out in MNCs with their international sales and operation.

The locational divisibility of stages in the production cycle is a characteristic of microelectronic manufacture, making foreign production of various stages advantageous, but a part of the production sequence is usually retained in the source country. For example, at least three stages of the production cycle for integrated circuits require substantial labor inputs for which the costs of foreign operation are generally not greater than the cost of source-country manufacture, for the present at least. These are systems design, components testing, and systems assembly. The first requires skilled design technicians, which are found in the U.K. or Europe and probably eventually in Asia, costing one-half the American rate. The low-cost semi-skilled labor suitable for the other two stages can be found in offshore locations such as Taiwan. A schematic representation of the costs for locating various stages of the production cycle offshore is shown in Figure 5.11. Those stages of the production cycle that are labor intensive with a cost curve such as *cc'* can be transferred offshore to locations where the required labor is readily available at low cost. This results in a cost curve below *cc'* and represented by *oo'*. However, the availability of skilled engineers in the source country presents the possibility of automating the stage of production that is labor intensive. Consequently, when the high costs of developing automation methods can be offset by large vol-

*Figure 5.11*

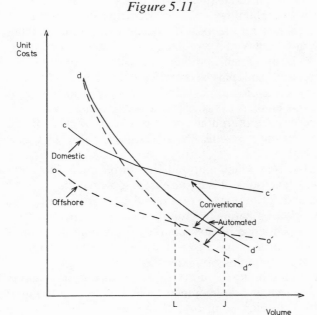

ume, firms once again may locate the activity in the source country. The costs of production by automated methods are gradually reduced through learning economies, *i.e.*, represented in the above figure by the shift from *dd'* to *dd''*, and the initial volume requirement is cut, as by *LJ*. The crucial factor behind the use of automated methods is the time that is needed to develop them. There is the further problem of debugging such systems so that they become an attractive proposition for smaller firms.

*Impact at the Research Level*

To be innovative, companies generally need to sustain a program of research over the long term. This implies ongoing R & D core and support programs. If the firm has a strategy of keeping R & D personnel secure and productive in their jobs, then sharp variations in the size of a company's overall research program would be avoided and R & D would be regarded as a fixed cost. However, for host-country firms, the initial impact of competition from MNCs might be to reduce both revenues and profits and thus create pressure for cuts in overhead such as R & D. The impact of MNCs might thus be to reduce the overall effectiveness of host-country research to the extent that this is determined by the provision of research funds on a continuous and increasing basis.

In addition, competition from MNCs at the market level most probably influences the required quality of the research program of local firms to keep pace with technology transfer occurring through the MNC. It then becomes necessary for the local firm to both differentiate its products and provide a sufficient variety of them to remain competitive. The host-country firm is, as a result, probably pressured into shortening lead times between research and market entry for individual products, and to place greater emphasis on support and less emphasis on core research. Moreover, this emphasis is reinforced by the company's need to compete in the variety and differentiation of products offered. If the impact of MNCs is sufficiently severe, the host-country firm may cease core research altogether.

A second area in which multinational firms can influence host-country research and development is in the extent to which they are able to rely on local ideas and technology. For example, where a particular culture of scientific work (originating in a foreign country) supercedes local technology, the independence of host-country firms may be diminished as the host-country firm may have to relinquish some of its independence and acquire foreign technology by licensing.

At the extreme, a host-country firm, because of its inability to finance adequate research and development, may be forced into liquidation or be acquired by a foreign company. If the acquisition is to gain access to technology owned by the host-country firm, a "parallel organization" for research and development might be used by the expanded MNC.

*Summary*
   The increasing importance of creation and transfer of technology by MNCs poses many questions for analysis within a dynamic international framework. Technology creation is important, because some industries and even economies depend on new technology to grow and survive within the competitive international environment. The large MNC has several objectives as parts of its strategy, and thus is not necessarily the best institution for technology creation from the national perspective. Yet, MNCs are the preeminent institutions for assembling ideas and people on a worldwide basis to create a most productive environment for technology creation. The small progressive firm, which may be receding as an agent of technology creation, provides a challenge to the large MNCs from the periphery and plays an extremely important competitive role. But such firms often have insufficient resources to propel them into the MNC group. The predominance of technology transfer through MNC activities means that corporate advantages play an increasingly important role in the creation of the wealth of nations. Although countries may have the resources for independently creating technology, their economies may not be suited to utilize it on an internationally competitive basis. Hence, in the international competitive context, corporate objectives concerning the transfer of technology may conflict with national objectives, but only through its full international role can MNCs be competitive and efficient.
   The diffusion of technology, which occurs at least at three levels of activity—the market, the production, and the research and development level—can be studied within the framework of the imitation cycle developed in this paper. The analysis considered two industries, semiconductors and pharmaceuticals, which are different in the extent of MNC involvement. The rate of diffusion or imitation of technology may marginally have been influenced by rivalry among MNCs in the industry. The MNC thus may influence not only the novelty of R & D, but the rate at which its results and operations are transferred internationally. Moreover, rivalry among companies within the same country may affect international transfers as well as does competition among companies in different countries. Therefore, the impact on host countries of the MNC may be considerable, since local companies, to survive, must compete locally with rival foreign firms, which base their activity on technologies for larger and more highly developed markets. It seems likely that, to survive, even the smallest domestic firms have to seek technology and markets outside local sources.

# COMMENT

## INGO WALTER*

The determinants, characteristics and consequences of technology transfer probably represent one of the most poorly understood dimensions of international economic relations. This is especially true if we adopt—as I believe we should—the broadest possible definition of technology. That is, we define technology as "useful knowledge" incorporating product, process, management, and marketing knowhow—anything that can lead either to perceived new or better products or to increase the efficiency of producing entities.

International technology flows clearly take place in a wide variety of ways, both as disembodied knowledge and embodied in people and products, both externally via the market and internally between units of multinational enterprises. Their effects on the location of production and trade, on employment and productivity, on international financial flows, and the like are sometimes ambiguous and usually complex and difficult to analyze. While conventional economic models of international trade and production can handle a part of this issue, particularly in identifying some of the possible economic consequences, the analyisis and its predictive value has necessarily been partial. Concern with the underlying *determinants* of technology transfer, its *characteristics* and the *channels* it takes has been intermittent at best. And yet the thinness of the state of knowledge in this area has hardly discouraged policy planners in developed and developing countries, and in international organizations, to continue to act as if we really knew what we are talking about. The bottom line, at this stage, is likely to be bad policy.

Arthur Lake, in his paper, has attempted to advance the discussion in a similarly partial way—in my opinion successfully—by focusing specifically on product innovation, and tracing through the "newness" of research and development on the part of MNCs in the pharmaceutical and semiconductor industries, the speed and time-pattern of technology transfer, and the impact on some aspects of the host country's economy. His concept of an "imitation cycle" as a technique for assessing the role of interfirm rivalry in each of these areas is, I think, a useful one, and the empirical results seem to support the behavioral model he has proposed. It begins to get at the underlying causes of technology transfer in two high-technology industries, as well as the channels involved in the transfer process. Especially interesting is the intercountry transfer of oligopolistic competitive structures that apparently has accompanied the

*New York University

technology flows. Equally interesting is the symbiotic relationship between a creative core "team" of researchers on the one hand and the firm's access to markets for the end-products of innovation on the other. The MNC's institutional structure provides both the markets to absorb new technologies and the need for technologies to serve those markets. While some general principles along these lines do seem to emerge, the apparent interindustry differences are perhaps even more illuminating: innovation external to MNCs coupled to technological diffusion via the MNC in semiconductors, versus intra-firm innovation *and* diffusion in pharmaceuticals, for example.

In attempting to develop the implications for MNC host countries of technology transfer in the industries studied, Lake focuses on market impacts, on production processes and organization, and on qualitative and quantitiative dimensions of the research and development effort. Unfortunately, the impact of MNCs on *production* technology is given short shrift, with a virtually exclusive focus on product-related innovation. Surely advances in production techniques and equipment introduced from abroad that lower costs or enhance product quality might have led to imitative reactions by local and third-country firms not unlike those associated with product innovations—albeit perhaps less dramatic and more difficult to identify. Similarly, imitative R&D by local firms is discussed all too briefly, even though the implications for host-country science and technology policy and for national resource allocation may be substantial indeed. And so the trade-offs involved between technological dependence and independence in these sectors remain unexplored. But, of course, there are limits to what can be accomplished in a single study, and in my view Lake succeeds very well in what he has set out to do.

The paper certainly raises a number of interesting questions which seem worth pursuing:

—What explains the apparently high degree of interindustry variance in the location of basic research—that is, inside or outside the structure of the multinational firm?

—What role does government support of basic and applied research play in the respective innovative and imitative performance of U.S., British, and third-country firms in the two industries studied?

—What effects did the technology transfers under examination have on the MNC *home* country's trade, employment, and resource allocation?

—What were the implications of the technology transfers studied for profitability of the U.S. multinationals involved?

—How did the apparent speed of the technology transfers and its repercussions affect the social and economic costs of adjustment in both home and host countries?

All of these questions, of course, are subject to the usual difficulty of having to run the world twice—of trying to figure out what might have happened in the absence of technology transfer, or in the absence of the MNC as an institutional innovator and as a conduit for international technology flows. The results of such an exercise, in turn, depend critically on a series of assumptions about the alternative course of events that are sometimes hard to defend in an area as complex as this.

It seems to me that useful empirical studies of technology transfer generally have to be undertaken, as this one is, at a fairly high level of specificity. The variegated nature of technology flows and their industry-specific packaging often mandates this approach, and sometimes a useful analytical concept such as the imitation cycle results. Clearly, the causes and consequences of the kind of product-technology transfer discussed in this paper can be entirely different from those related to a transfer of production, application, marketing, and management technology, for example, even in the same industry. This does not mean that comprehensive examinations of intra-MNC technology transfers cannot tell you something about what kinds of technologies are flowing in what direction, the underlying motivations, and the economic consequences. Neither does it doom to failure attempts to forge conceptual links between the existence of the MNC as an institutional form and the importance of development, internalization, and application transnationally of useful knowledge in the contemporary international economic order.

One rather promising approach to the interaction between technology and the multinational enterprise is being taken by Jean Hennart(1976). In this particular view, there are three principal ways of organizing transactions in the international economy: through markets, through long-term contracts, and through firms as essentially permanent institutions that operate transnationally with more or less unified and hierarchial managerial structures. Just as nations are subject to some fundamental economic principles in the determination of world production and trade patterns, so each of these three types of institutions is subject to important economic advantages and limitations in the determination of relative efficiency in international transactions.

Markets work best (a) when there are a large number of buyers and sellers, (b) when transactions costs are low—i.e., the cost of information, measurement, bargaining, and enforcement—and (c) when the products or services to be exchanged are relatively homogeneous. Markets do not work so well when they are subjected (a) to a high degree of uncertainty, (b) to small numbers of transactions among comparatively few buyers and sellers, and (c) to complex and heterogeneous products or services, as a result of which the bounded rationality of individual participants combines with opportunism to produce high transactions costs. Under such conditions the system tends to drive a wedge between what the seller receives and what the buyer pays, and fails to maximize the joint welfare of the two parties to the transaction.[1]

Our second transactions medium, contracts, serves to reduce the costs of exchange by specifying precisely the rights of buyer and seller over the life of the agreement, by outlining specifically those actions by either party that would be in violation of the contract, and setting forth terms of compensation in case this happens. Because all eventualities have to be specified in advance, along with the requisite contingent behavioral adjustments by buyer and seller, long-term contracts tend to be relatively costly when aplied to various types of international transactions.

The multinational firm, as a third alternative, involves internal centralization of information and decision-making. Because of its institutional structure, the MNC is able to reduce transactions costs by (a) not having to disseminate information to all parties of an exchange, and (b) avoiding contracting and enforcement costs, since bargaining and cheating behavior by parties to the transaction can be curbed directly within the firm's management structure. On the other hand, the multinational firm as a transaction medium does incur internal organization costs that may well rise with the overall size of the enterprise and the number of hierarchial decision and control levels involved. Hence, at some point the internal costs associated with an additional transaction will tend to exceed the alternative external transaction costs, and thus help to delineate the role of multinational firms, contracts, and market in international exchange.

Technological innovations (broadly defined) related to efficiency of the internal workings of the multinational company, together with increasing complexity in the character of international transactions, are held responsible for a growing *transactions cost advantage* of the MNC over both long-term contracts and markets—and, hence, provide an important reason for the emergence of the multinational corporation as a fact of life in the international economy. Note that technology plays a dual role in the rise of the MNC's *institutional* comparative advantage, by increasing the relative efficiency of the firm over contracts and markets as a transaction medium and by influencing the kinds of transactions undertaken internationally toward precisely those most suitable for internal organization via the firm.

Whether related to products, processes, or applications, international transfers of technology do involve a great deal of uncertainty, recurrent and varied transactions, extended periods of time, and poorly defined and enforced property rights between a small number of buyers or sellers. Useful knowledge is often embodied in products or people, and even in disembodied or "pure" form, its value is sometimes difficult or impossible to assess without having to reveal its substance. Channels of technology transfers are diffuse and difficult or impossible to control. All of these are characteristics that tend to limit the comparative usefulness and efficiency of conventional market transactions, and at the same time tend to confine the suitability of long-term contracts (*e.g.,* licensing) to a specific subgroup of technology flows. Instead, the organizational relationship that exists between the MNC and its employees does away with many of the transactions costs involved in both of these, wherein not least important is the existence of an institutionalized environment within the firm of cooperation and efficient information exchange. As we have noted, the MNC incurs monitoring and administrative costs, to be sure, but these tend to fall well below the alternative transactions costs associated with the market (Dunning, 1976).

Technology transfer and the multinational firm are thus viewed as being fundamentally complementary in nature. On the one hand, the contemporary importance in a technical age of international transfers of useful knowledge has favored the development of the MNC as an organizational form more efficient as a transaction medium than either the market or long-term contracts. On the other hand the existence of the MNC as an efficient technology conduit has greatly enhanced transfers of knowledge between nations. The proprietary nature of much of this knowledge, coupled with the continuous lines into sources of market intelligence, costs of inputs, and similar information (each potentially saleable via the market) in turn, has further reinforced the global competitive position of the multinational enterprise.

A number of hypotheses fall out of this rather general concept of the MNC as a virtual "creation" of technology:

—Intrafirm technology transfers will tend to exceed international transfers between nonaffiliated firms.

—MNCs will tend to pay more for acquisitions of existing companies in host countries than competitive local firms because joint operation of the acquired firm as part of the MNC network is more profitable than separate operation via the market.

—The innovation process within the firm will itself tend to be vertically integrated.

—The economic importance of MNCs traced over very long periods of time will vary with changes in levels of internal organizational efficiency in relation to the costs of selling knowledge in the market.

—Differences in both internal organization costs and the state of home-country technology help to explain apparent differences in the relative importance of U.S., European, and Japanese MNCs.

—Attempts by MNCs to organize interaffiliate transactions according to the rules of arms-length pricing is inherently inefficient and hence self-defeating, and will tend to raise costs.

—MNCs will try, whenever possible, to avoid joint ventures that threaten to drive up internal organization costs and erode the advantage that the firm has over the market.

It seems that this rather sweeping view of the multinational corporation as having an inherent comparative advantage as an *institutional form* in an age of technology has a great deal of merit. The hypotheses it throws up appear eminently testable, and the model itself may well have useful predictive properties. To a considerable extent, Lake's findings fit nicely into the overall concept. The model also identifies resource-allocation and efficiency gains to the international economy associated specifically with the institutional existence of the MNC, as distinct from the corresponding gains associated with conventional international trade and investment.

Few would contest that international flows of useful knowledge today represent one of the most important, yet least well understood, dimensions of international economics. Because such flows frequently—some would argue predominantly—occur through channels other than the market, they do not necessarily fit well into our inherited models of international economic relations. It may be argued that the rapid growth of nonmarket (government) interventions in businesss operations around the world now require MNCs to develop a new kind of technology to deal with the potentially costly external conflict that can and does result, and that failure to develop such a technology may will erode the aforementioned comparative advantage of the MNC as a institutional form. Studies like Lake's, perhaps because they make the economist uncomfortable about the rather elegant view of the world he has been taught, promise to force some rather important changes in our thinking.

## FOOTNOTES

1. A similar concept of market failure and its relationship to the development of intrafirm transactions has been developed by Stephen P. Magee (1976).

## COMMENT

### ROGER SEYMOUR*

On the subject of technology creation and transfer, the academic community has made tremendous progress toward the postulation of practical hypotheses and the establishment of a lexicon with which all parties can work. This is significant, because it brings coherence to "a very large

*IBM Corporation.

something,'' to quote Winnie-the-Pooh, which people have otherwise assumed to be "just the way it's done." A parallel example exists in the
efforts to establish computer programming as a "science."

Note that I do not mention multinational firms in my reference to the
subject. This is purposeful—to underline the fact that, today, it is virtually only the MNCs that have state-of-the-art technology and the means of
transferring it.

Arthur Lake's paper is useful in suggesting how technology creation
and transfer can be analyzed. A singular contribution is the identification
of levels of transfer, including the market level. This recognizes
downstream effects involving the user or customer. There is a distinct
correlation between the user's role in the transfer process and the manner
and form of technology transfer. An overwhelming tendency has been to
focus on R & D and production as the principal, if not the only, transfer
process to consider. This has produced a distortion of perspective, especially outside the nations of the OECD, which manifests itself in a passion
to obtain factories with local equity control, and for unbundling technology transfers to confine the transfer and the rewards for it to the manufacture of the existing product line.

But the user virtually always plays a role in the process. Lake notes this
downstream effect in the case of semiconductor marketing. It may be
minimal, as in the case of a tractor—operating instructions and a number
to call for maintenance—but that is a bit of technology passed on to the
user. It may be substantial as in the case of computers where there is not
only a substantial flow of technology to the user, but where the user may
also create and transfer technology back to the MNC in a feedback loop.
This facet of transfer needs illumination so that the developing countries
do not strangle user application of technology by cutting off the flow
"ex-factory."

Another contribution of the paper is the recognition that the transfer
process may continue with respect to a product already introduced or
already produced. Lake speaks of "subsequent forms and improvements," which is a way of life in high-technology industries. A reactor, an
airplane, or a computer is subject to continual modification and upgrade
*after* it has been placed in operation. Akin to the user's role in the process
of transfer, this is a significant variant, which may wreck attempts to
legislate from generalizations.

One should be cautioned against an assumption of a hand-in-hand relationship between research and development. One problem is semantics.
One man's research is another man's development.

Is there a useful relation in technology creation between the "R" and
the "D". If by "research" we mean "basic research," one will find a

number of large MNCs with significant rates of technology transfer who do not have enough "research" activity to even warrant a departmental title. They wait for others to discover and define the phenomenon; then they ram it into development. Crudely put, how many semiconductor firms operating in the U.K. invented the transistor? How many computer firms operating in the U.S. created the concepts of an Atlas or a Gamma?

This relates to another point noted by Lake, on the novelty of R & D, and emphasized by Professor Michalet of the University of Paris-Dauphine. This is the "propensity of MNCs to locate the core activity of technology creation in the source country." In the case of research, and often in the case of development, splitting the activity between the source and another country may result in both facilities falling below the critical mass required for viability.

Another aspect of this point relates to the markets addressed by the MNC. A company addressing a single marketplace, let us say high-voltage power gear, would not be inclined to split the creative effort among countries. Doing so would add the problem of coordination without any likely increase in results. Splitting may be advantageous where several markets are in question; *e.g.*, research in materials for semiconductors in one country and research in mathematics for programming in another. Yet, even here the minimum critical mass problem may arise from the need for adequate intermixing of scientific disciplines and the lower variable cost for technical and administrative support in one location. Whatever the cause, splitting or paralleling R & D seems more the exception than the rule, The U.N. estimates that 98 percent of the R & D is performed in the developed countries. Only about 5 percent of R & D is performed by MNCs in countries other than their homelands.

I might note an argument sometimes made that the establishment of an off-shore R & D facility by an MNC results in a brain-drain from the host country and is therefore detrimental. The laboratory sucks up scientific resources, cloaks its technology and output with secrecy, and exploits that technology outside the host country. This curious twist makes the MNC damned if it does distribute R & D worldwide, and damned if it concentrates it in the home country. Suffice to say that I have not yet heard of a nation rejecting the implantation of a foreign-owned laboratory.

I would quarrel with the idea that MNCs can pull their punches when entering the market in a host country so as not to create too much competitive reaction. I do not think most companies would want to do that or are capable of managing such a "half-a-loaf" objective. Rather, my experience indicates that companies maximize whatever investment they can afford to put offshore and do their best to put the competition in a catch-up or chase-up mode. The game is one of staying ahead of the other company on the learning curve. Nowhere is this more crucially evident than in the semiconductor industry, and I truly regret the emphasis some governments have placed on emulating the "big grey box" when instead, as has become painfully obvious, they should have concentrated on the specks of silicon that make the box work. But the idea of MNCs pulling punches leads to another significant point in Lake's paper, as illustrated by such phrases as "analysis within a dynamic international framework" and "the large MNC has many priorities." The latter points to a basic fact in today's world: Transfer of technology takes place as a result of the international investment decision, not without it and not in spite of it. Entire papers could, and I hope will, be devoted to the content and form of transfer as a function of the magnitude and kind of international investment that accompanies it. The proposals of the Group of 77 ignore this connection and raise the possibility that their policy proposals would slay the goose to get at the golden eggs.

The reference to dynamism is the key point I would close on. R & D and technology transfer is a moving target, a very rapidly moving one. Among many actions bearing on the subject, perhaps two stand out. In the developed nations, we are seeing whole sectors of industry be made components of national economic policy for sustaining or increasing employment and export receipts. To the extent that the transfer of technology appears to aid or harm these objectives, it will be regulated accordingly. Freedom of enterpreneurial decision resulting in transfer is decreasing, as the objectives of local employment and output in specific industries are raised in national priorities.

The other action involves proposed codes of conducts for MNCs, by LDCs, which they feel will enhance the transfer of technology. The general feeling among MNCs is that such codes, if implemented, would be counterproductive for the developing lands, because dynamic technology transfer would be vitiated if not brought to a standstill. A few nations within the group are "jumping the gun" and implementing portions of the proposals unilaterally.

These two trends are, unfortunately, complementary in the wrong direction. In a time when many developed countries would withhold technology transfer if it were to impact on local employment and export earnings, the developing countries propose disincentives to the transfer of such technology that would otherwise be made. To cap it off, even where no braking effect is applied by an MNC's home government, the uncertainties engendered by the developing countries' actions are slowing the investment that must underlie technology transfer and diverting it to other developed nations. All this does not imply that we should cease our efforts because we cannot "beat city hall." It does suggest that we redouble our efforts to obtain understanding before it is too late.

The dynamic international framework referred to by Lake in his summary should tell us that the treatment of the subject of technology transfer in a static international context will be sterile, and I believe that our government, academic, and industrial communities can and must work together to turn the dynamics in a positive direction.

# 6. THE COST, CONDITIONS, AND ADAPTATION OF MNC TECHNOLOGY IN DEVELOPING COUNTRIES

Richard W. Moxon, UNIVERSITY OF WASHINGTON

## INTRODUCTION

As the debate on development policies has shifted in recent years, so has there been a change in the perceived role of the MNC in LDCs. While economic growth was the dominant policy objective and capital and foreign exchange gaps were the major perceived obstacles to growth in the 1950s and 1960s, analysis of the MNC emphasized its effects on capital formation and the balance of payments. As the major development goal has shifted toward increased employment and income redistribution, the MNC's role in contributing jobs and products for the poorer segments of developing societies has become of greater concern. Thus, the appro-

Research in International Business and Finance, Vol. 1, pp. 189–233.

priateness of MNC products and manufacturing technologies to meet these goals is currently a subject of considerable debate. Furthermore, LDCs have learned from OPEC that, at least in some cases, it is possible to rearrange relationships with the MNC by 'unbundling" the package of resources and abilities offered and bargaining for each component individually. It may then be possible to obtain the technological component of the MNC contribution on better terms than in the past. Thus, they are concerned with alternative sources of technology and their relative costs.

The two questions that have received the most recent attention, and will be the subject of this paper, are:

—How appropriate is MNC technology for LDCs, and can other sources, or the MNC itself, be induced to provide more appropriate technology?

—How costly is MNC technology for LDCs, and can the MNC or other sources supply technology at lower cost?

Answers to these questions require clear definitions of a number of terms. As in any such debate, these differences may influence the answers to the questions, or at least the way the questions are addressed.[1] The meaning of "appropriate" technology is open to economic and political debate, but it certainly goes beyond the criterion of labor intensity. This issue, and the evidence on the appropriateness of MNC technology, will be discussed in the second part of this paper. Defining the cost of MNC technology presents conceptual and empirical difficulties because of the arbitrary and sometimes hidden ways of pricing technology and the problems in evaluating these costs (and associated benefits) in comparison with alternatives. The issue of costs and conditions will be discussed in the third section. A further definition required is that of technology itself, and of what is meant by technology transfer through the MNC. These questions are discussed below.

*The Nature of Technology*

Most studies of technology transfer through the MNC concentrate on technology in the manufacturing industries, rather than in mining, agriculture, or services. This will be the focus in this paper, although studies are needed on other sectors where MNCs are important. But beyond this focus, studies vary in the breadth of definitions used. All include production methods and process know-how as the most obvious form of technology, but most broaden the definition to include product designs and sometimes managerial systems.

The inclusion of product design in the discussion of MNC technology is now common among writers on the subject. Thus, one study refers to "the design of industrial plants, products and processes" (Wells and

Chudson, 1974, p. 2). Another defines technology very broadly as "the ways in which commodities are produced, and the nature of the commodities being produced" (Stewart, 1973, p. 236). Another uses the term "consumption technology" to differentiate product design from "production technology" (Helleiner, 1975). Including the product itself in the definition of MNC technology is consistent with the popular notion of technology (each new product improvement is labeled a technological advance), as well as with the common association of technology with research. Evidence shows that most industrial research is intended to develop new products rather than new processes, although processes must later be changed to manufacture these products (Stewart, 1973, p. 240). Much technology transfer to LDCs through the MNC is a result of the introduction of new products, and part of the payments of LDCs for MNC technology is in the form of product trademark royalties.

Writers who have examined specific cases of the process of technology transfer through the MNC in detail tend to use the broadest definitions of technology, possibly seeing better than others the complexity and interrelatedness of various product, process, and managerial aspects. Thus Baranson includes managerial systems for production planning and control in his discussion of the transfer of technology (Baranson, 1969, p. 28). And Behrman and Wallender (1976) include in their case studies the planning, implementation, and follow-up of a project, as well as product and process design. But both studies exclude general management, marketing, and financial skills, and focus only on management directly associated with the design of products and processes, and the control of production. This seems to accord with recent U.N. guidelines, which include the "skills necessary for manufacturing a product and for establishing an enterprise for this purpose" (UNIDO, 1973, p. 1). Thus the definition of *technology* used here will include the design of products, plants, and processes, as well as the managerial systems needed to establish plants and keep them operating efficiently.

*Technology Transfer through the MNC*

The MNC transfers technology to developing countries in many ways: by exporting its products, by exporting its patents and technical knowledge through licensing or technical assistance contracts, or by exporting itself through direct investments (Wilkins, 1974). The last of these often includes the first two and is the form of most interest in this paper. Most concern in LDCs is directed at technology transfer *through* the MNC system of owned affiliates, rather than at purchases of machines or technical know-how *from* the MNC by independent parties. In fact, the first two forms, although still presenting problems to LDCs, are often seen as attractive alternatives to the complete control of the transfer process within the MNC.

Technology transferred within the MNC takes many different forms, and for a typical parent-subsidiary relationship may involve the following mechanisms: (1) *documentation*—manuals, specifications, and drawings describing the product, production processes, and managerial control systems; (2) *visits and exchanges of personnel*—visits by parent company personnel or consultants to the subsidiary to implement the technology or train local people, and visits by subsidiary personnel to be trained in other facilities of the company; (3) *memoranda and other communications* to exchange information; and (4) *machines*—in which the technology is embodied in the equipment (Behrman and Wallender, 1976). These exchanges may take place under formal contracts, such as licensing of trademarks or patents and technical assistance contracts, or in more informal agreements. Since the parent controls the ownership of the subsidiary, a legal contract may not be needed, or may be used only to comply with foreign exchange regulations or other laws rather than to insure that the subsidiary does not violate the agreement.

Some of the technology transferred may be patented know-how, other may be proprietary unpatented know-how, such as trade secrets, and other may be unproprietary know-how, *i.e.*, it is known to others outside the firm and usable by them. Even this unproprietary know-how may not be freely available to all potential users, however, especially those in an LDC. There is some evidence that unpatented know-how is more important than patented know-how in transfers to LDCs, both in the value to the receiving country and in terms of payments made to foreign companies (Helleiner, 1975, p. 163).

It is also important to note that technology transfer through the MNC is a process involving activities occurring over an extended period of time. For a typical case, it will involve the analysis of the feasibility of a project, the design of the plant and product (these may sometimes be simply copies of already existing designs), plant construction, the design and implementation of control systems, and the training of employees and sometimes suppliers. After the plant begins functioning, there will be product and process improvements (sometimes as a result of local research), troubleshooting, and continued training of personnel. The various mechanisms of technology transfer would typically have different relative importance at different stages. The inflow of documents, machines, and personnel would typically be heavy at the initial stage of introduction of a new technology, whereas at later stages these would be replaced in importance by memoranda and other communications. And while patented know-how and other proprietary knowledge may be important initially, much of the later transfers may be of a nonproprietary nature. This "cycle" of technology transfer should be studied more carefully, as it has obvious implications for the relative bargaining strengths of the MNC and LDC, and for the feasibility of alternative channels of technology transfer.

*Alternatives to Technology Transfer through the MNC*

Conclusions as to the costs and appropriateness of current forms of technology transfer through the MNC depend considerably on the alternatives to which these forms are compared. The main dimensions of alternatives to current forms are: first, how adapted is the technology to the local economic conditions; and second, who controls and uses the technology in the host country. Thus four basic alternative forms of technology transfer are:

—Technology controlled by the MNC in the host country and not adapted to the local environment (assumed by MNC critics to be the current state of affairs, although evidence on adaptation by MNCs is presented below).

—Technology controlled by the MNC in the host country, but adapted to the local environment.

—Technology controlled by a local enterprise in the host country, but not adapted to the local environment. In this case the technology could be locally generated or imported, possibly from a MNC.

—Technology controlled by a local enterprise and adapted to the local environment. Again, the technology itself could be local or imported.

The following sections will examine the feasibility and cost of these alternatives.

# APPROPRIATENESS OF MNC TECHNOLOGY

The adjective "appropriate" has replaced such alternatives as "labor-intensive" or "intermediate" in many discussions of technology in developing countries. It has the virtue of allowing the user to define what "appropriate" means in the context of the technology and countries of interest.[2] This section will discuss the criteria of appropriateness and the evidence on the appropriateness of MNC process and product technology. The first part will focus on appropriate production technology. assuming that the product design is given. The second part will examine the appropriateness of the products themselves, given what is known about their production proceses and other characteristics.

## MNC Production Technology

The MNC is accused of importing to LDCs the production techniques it has developed for indusrial countries without adapting them to differences in factor costs and other conditions. The question of what is appropriate production technology is examined below, after which the available evidence on the adaptation of technology by the MNC is summarized, and the alternatives open to host countries in attempting to insure that appropriate technology is used in their manufacturing industries is evaluated.

*What Is Appropriate Production Technology?*   Most studies of the appropriateness of technology in developing countries have focused on the *choice* of technology and have defined technology in terms of the ratio of labor to capital used. This emphasis is insufficient for judging appropriateness for two reasons—labor intensity is an inadequate description of a technology, and appropriateness should be judged not only in terms of the product (the technology itself), but in terms of the process (the transfer of technology).

Labor intensity is an insufficient criterion for appropriateness for a number of reasons:

—Labor is not a homogeneous factor. The focus should be on the use of unskilled labor, presumably the relatively most abundant labor in developing countries, rather than on all categories of labor.

—Capital is not the only scarce resource in developing countries. Some categories of labor, some materials, foreign exchange, or organizational and enterpreneurial ability may be equally or more scarce. So the focus should be on the efficient use of all of these scarce resources, not just capital.

—Even if only labor and capital are considered, the most labor-intensive method may not be appropriate. Sometimes one production method saves both labor and capital as compared to another, and a developing country would waste both resources if it chose the inefficient method. One study found for rice milling in Indonesia, for example, that the most labor-intensive method was only used if the opportunity cost of labor were virtually zero (Thomas, 1975). And Indian cottage industry has been criticized as being wasteful of capital *and* labor (Strassmann, 1968). Rather than use labor intensity as the measure of appropriateness, a more useful definition is "the set of techniques that makes optimum use of available resources" (Morawetz, 1974).

But efficiency of use of existing resources is insufficient as a criterion, for countries are not content to simply follow the dictates of comparative advantage, but attempt to improve their factor endowments. Some technologies, and some processes of their transfer, may prvide more training for local workers in useful skills, more development of the capabilities of local suppliers, and more of other such linkage effects than alternative technologies and transfer processes. So an *appropriate technology transfer* is one that makes efficient use of available resources and also enhances these resources.

*Adaptation of Production Technology by the MNC.* It is clear that the environment of LDCs calls for the use of technologies quite different from those used in industrialized countries. Markets are generally smaller, productive factors differ in availability and cost, and cultural factors inhibit the use of the methods of industrial countries. Yet the MNC is often accused of not adapting its methods, and instead, imposing inappropriate technologies on LDCs. In particular, the MNC is said to use too much capital and too little labor, thus contributing to the unemployment problem. This lack of adaptation is said to result from the lower capital costs and higher labor costs presumably faced by the MNC, from the company's sunk investment in capital-intensive technologies, its excessive concern for global technological standardization, its greater familiarity with the management of capital-intensive facilities, and its monopoly position, which allows it not to be concerned with maximum efficiency.

Studies that attempt to measure the degree of adaptation of technology by the MNC in response to factor price differences compare capital-labor ratios either between MNC plants in developed versus developing countries, or between MNC-owned plants and locally owned plants in LDCs. These studies face serious problems in the measurement of capital-labor ratios, and in isolating the causes of measured differences (Mason, 1971). The scale of operations is generally different. Capital stocks are difficult to value and are not necessarily good measures of how much capital is used per unit of output. And many studies suffer from serious aggregation problems, even when narrow product categories are used, as plants differ in the degree of vertical integration. If a foreign plant is only assembling imported components, while the home-country plant fabricates components before assembling them, it is not surprising that the foreign plant is more labor intensive. Studies that examine specifice industries in detail, and supplement statistical data with interview and direct observation, are generally more convincing. Some of the most thorough studies of different kinds are summarized below:

—Strassmann (1968) found many examples of adaptation by foreign companies in Mexico and Puerto Rico. After adjusting for scale of production, he found that foreign companies seemed to adapt more than private local firms to factor price differences. They were, for example, more willing to use second-hand equipment and multiple shifts. But from interviews he found no big difference between locals and foreigners in the stated importance of capital cost differences; neither group considered them very important.

—Mason (1971) found only slight differences in capital intensity between U.S.-owned and locally owned companies in Mexico and the Philippines. In fact, on some of his measures, local firms appeared to use more capital than U.S. subsidiaries. He found adaptations to smaller scale and to skill shortages, with the latter sometimes leading to more capital-intensive methods.

—Reuber (1973) found that there was adaptation of production equipment in 22 of the 77 MNC projects in developing countries that he studied, and in 27 of 77 there were changes in production techniques. Low production volume was much more important than low labor costs as a cause for adaptation, and some changes were in response to low skill levels, raw material differences, and government regulations. Of course, the majority of firms reported no adaptation.

—Wells (1973) found that MNC affiliates in Indonesia used more capital-intensive techniques than local companies, but explained this on the basis of their ability to avoid price competition rather than on the fact that they were foreign.

—Courtney and Leipziger (1974) found significant technology differences between developed country and developing country affiliates of MNCs in six of eleven industries, but the differences were not systematically toward more labor intensity in LDCs. Furthermore, although their sample size was large and they controlled for scale effects, the aggregation of products and process levels makes direct comparison impossible.

—Morley and Smith (1977 and forthcoming) found differences in capital intensity between MNC plants in the U.S. and Brazil, but found that the scale of production was the most important reason for the difference. Interviews revealed that if the Brazilian plants were to have the same volume of output, most companies would use U.S. technology without adaptation. They also found much more adaptation for certain parts of the production process (*e.g.,* material handling) than for others. (See also Yeoman, 1968.) They found also that U.S. and other foreign affiliates were more capital intensive than local Brazilian firms, and that not all of the difference was accounted for by scale. They note, however, that differences in product mix may affect their findings, and the problem of extent of vertical integration could also have an effect.

—Behrman and Wallender (1976), in a number of detailed case studies of technology transfer in Ford, Pfizer, and ITT, note many cases of adaptation. Ford was reported to use older technology in some plants than in the United States or Europe, in some cases technology that was several decades old. Similar examples were noted for Pfizer and ITT. The reasons for adaptations were not always specified, but there seemed to be an emphasis in most cases on using less "skill-intensive" methods, and on "scaling-down" processes because of small markets. But other adaptations, such as Ford's use of more inspectors and single-head versus multiple-head wrenches, seemed to be in response to lower labor costs. The case studies also note many instances of adaptation to what might be called cultural factors rather than economic factors (*e.g.*, methods of training may have to be changed as a result of educational levels and traditional learning habits). But although such adaptations are evidence of flexibility of the MNC, they are not of primary interest in our discussion of the appropriateness of technology.

The studies that have been summarized here show that there is no overwhelming evidence that the MNC adapts less to the local factor prices than do local companies, but neither is there strong evidence that MNC affiliates use the most appropriate technology. Several authors state that the potential for adaptation has not generally been approached, but there are few quantitative indications of this intuitively plausible conclusion.[3] More studies are needed of actual adaptations compared to potential adaptations. Nevertheless, the conclusion of virtually all studies on the subject is that there is great potential for further adaptation. This has led to a search for the obstacles to the adaptation of more appropriate technologies.

*Obstacles to the Use of Labor-Intensive Technology.*   A long list of obstacles has been offered to explain why companies, both local and foreign, fail to adopt more appropriate production technologies. Earlier studies focused on the alleged fixity of factor proportions or distortions in factor prices, while most later studies have emphasized problems in the decision process itself. The following identifies the major potential obstacles and presents the available evidence on their importance.

*Technological alternatives* may be limited, or occasionally there may be no alternative set of factors allowing a given volume of output to be manufactured economically. Econometric studies that have attempted to measure the elasticity of substitution of factors of production are subject to many statistical difficulties, and have in fact provided widely different conclusions (Morawetz, 1974). But a number of more disaggregated studies indicate that, for most industrial products, numerous alternative production methods are possible. Tokman (1972) found that some industries in Venezuela were naturally very labor intensive or capital intensive, but that in others substantial possibilities for substitution existed. Pack (1974) found wide substitution possibilities in Kenya, especially outside the core of the production process, and Wells (1973) found a wide range of techniques being used side by side in Indonesia, with striking differences in relative factor use. Other recent detailed case studies document the availability of a wide range of technologies for many products (Baer, 1976; Pickett et al., 1974).

Nevertheless, once the volume of production is specified, substitution possibilities are reduced. Boon (1964), in his detailed study of machining processes, found that the optimum technology for some tasks is sensitive mainly to the scale of production, with capital-intensive methods dominating labor-intensive ones at any factor-price ratio once a certain scale was reached. Morley and Smith argue that this price-sensitive range is very narrow for some processes, with some clearly labor intensive or capital intensive optimum for most factor-price ratios. They found that this accounted in some cases for a perceived lack of adaptation where in fact adaptation possibilities did not exist—for some processes labor-intensive methods were used both in the U.S. and Brazil, and the same was true of capital-intensive methods for other processes.

Some operations, especially materials handling, packaging, and clerical tasks, seem very adaptable in response to factor-price differences, and it has been noted that U.S. firms tend to adapt these tasks (Yeoman, 1968). Strassmann noted that substitutability was less in making powders, liquids, and other nondurables than in durable goods. Boon too found fewer adaptation possibilities for certain tasks on parts that were complex, large, or required great precision. Furthermore, where quality requirements are high, old methods may not work (Morawetz, 1974). As stated by Strassman (1968):

> Science allows voltages, pressures, temperatures, speeds and sensitivities beyond the reach of man. Volume allows and prescribes their use in production. Volume also favors use of equipment over men because of geometric scale effects and because more machines become easier, and more men harder, to coordinate. Science, quality, and volume therefore combine in the course of development to lower the substitutability of hand workers for machines. Where labor-intensive operations remain, they should be welcomed, yet be recognized as silver linings that are nevertheless part of the cloud of backwardness.

More disaggregated studies are needed, but despite the very important effects of scale, it appears that technological fixity is not common unless product specifications are rigid. On this point, the MNC may play a negative role. Baranson (1970) found that many MNCs insisted on maintaining uniform quality worldwide. For example, it was reported that IBM worked on the principle of technological parity worldwide. But Thomas (1975) and Wells (1973) found that in many cases quality was equal with labor-intensive methods, and in fact was in some cases perceived as better by consumers. The MNC may be more interested in reliable quality than in top quality (*e.g.,* a Macdonald's hamburger rather than a French wine).

Hand-made may signify top quality, but may not be as reliably good quality as machine-made.

*Factor prices* may be so distorted from social opportunity costs as to inhibit the choice of appropriate technologies. There is a long list of such distortions and their effects in raising the labor costs and lowering the capital costs facing enterprises in LDCs.[4] Such distortions include over-valued exchange rates and preferential duties that encourage the importation of capital equipment, and labor laws or union movements that discourage increased hiring of workers. It seems clear that these distortions affect the choice of technology by both the MNC and the locally owned enterprise.

It is, furthermore, possible that the factor costs faced by the MNC are different from those of local firms. Studies of the pay practices of the MNC generally show that it pays more than local firms (ILO, 1976), but these results are difficult to interpret because of aggregation problems. The studies that have tried to make comparisons among similar foreign and local firms for specific job categories show that MNCs pay more, but the differences are modest, and may still be compensated for by lower turnover and higher quality (Mason, 1971; Wells, 1973).

In terms of the capital costs of the MNC versus local firms, it seems clear that the size of the MNC results in a lower cost of capital. But no study is available comparing capital costs and showing a systematic effect on the choice of technique. More frequently cited is the influence of the availability of capital on choice. Wells (1973) notes that state firms in Indonesia had access to capital and used capital-intensive methods, while for some small local firms the absolute lack of capital restricted capital intensity. But Strassmann found no significant difference between local and foreign firms in terms of the availability and cost of capital.

Several recent studies support the conclusion that although factor price distortions have some effect on choice of technology, the elimination of such distortions would not greatly modify the degree of adaptation (Baer, 1976; Pickett et al., 1974). Other causes must be found.

Poor *labor productivity* could eliminate the undoubtedly much lower labor costs of LDCs. Many studies have attempted to measure labor productivity differentials. Those that have done so using aggregate data for industries have had the usual problems of aggregation and the isolation of effects of separate variables. More convincing are studies in which executives have been asked to compare labor productivity among countries, assuming similar amounts of capital per worker. These studies show that labor-productivity differences may exist, but are much smaller than wage-rate differences.[5] For some tasks, particularly those in labor-intensive export operations in the Far East, workers in LDCs are sometimes reported to be more productive than their industrial-country counterparts. Thus the conclusion must be that labor costs, even adjusted for productivity differences, are very large. Again, it is possible that workers in foreign firms are less productive than in local firms, thereby leading the foreigner to use more capital, but this does not seem likely, and there is no evidence to support such a conclusion.

Labor-intensive techniques may require *complementary resources* that are scarce in LDCs. Mention was made earlier of company attempts to de-skill production operations, and that this sometimes resulted in greater labor intensity. In export-oriented operations, it was found that U.S. companies sometimes introduced more automated test equipment in order to avoid the need for inspectors with refined judgmental skills (Moxon, 1974). Baier (1976) cites skill scarcities as inhibiting the use of second-hand machinery and multiple shifts, either of which would increase the labor intensity of a production process. Strassman has developed very thoroughly the proposition that labor-intensive methods often require better supervisors and managers, and he and Mason (1971) cite this as a reason for lack of adaptation. Here the MNC may have an advantage over local companies if it has better management systems. In fact, Mason found that the MNC tended to use more unskilled labor than local firms, together with more supervision. But others argue that local companies may have more ability in managing large groups of workers. On this point there is little empirical evidence.

Besides requiring complementary skills, labor-intensive methods may require the use of other scarce resources. Raw materials may be wasted by less precise or unreliable hand methods, and in process industries it is plausible that continuous flow saves material as compared to batch processes. But Wells (1973) found that labor-intensive methods were material-saving in the companies he studied. Boon also mentions that labor-intensive methods, while saving on fixed capital, may require more working capital because of greater needs for in-process inventory. Again, detailed empirical studies would be needed to support this as an important factor.

The MNC may not be completely rational in its *choice of production techniques*. Several recent studies note that various characteristics of companies' decision-making process may result in less adaptation of methods than is economically justified. There appears to be a lack of systematic consideration of alternatives, a tendency to accept suboptimal methods if satisfactory profit levels can still be achieved, and an engineering bias in favor of the most modern methods. But many such features of the decision process seem to apply equally well to local and even government-owned companies as to MNCs.

The almost automatic use by foreign firms of familiar methods is noted by several authors.[6] Morley and Smith found that foreign firms of various nationalities in Brazil relied on their home-country experience and habitually chose capital equipment from their home countries. This may be rational in many cases, as the use of a new technique may involve extra development expenses or result in inefficiency until the method becomes familiar. Such expenses may not be justified if the market for the technology is small. Or limited search for local alternatives may result from the lack of time to conduct an adequate search (Thomas, 1975). Also, some risks are involved in the use of labor-intensive methods. Managers may perceive the threat of labor unrest or difficulties in quickly expanding or contracting the work force in response to demand fluctuations.

An alternative explanation is that firms may be engaged in "satisficing" behavior rather than in profit-maximizing. Morley and Smith offer a number of examples suggesting that managers do not pay much attention to the choice of techniques as long as profits are at a satisfactory level. Yeoman (1968) found that MNCs did not adapt unless production costs were a large percentage of the sales price, making production efficiency important. Other studies[7] point out many instances where a manager's life is simplified if he just has to manage a few machines instead of a large number of workers (or a small number of capital-intensive projects rather than a large number of labor-intensive ones). It is, of course, difficult to separate the effects of "satisficing" behavior from the quite legitimate costs of search or the risk of using untried methods.

There also appears to be a bias in many selection procedures in favor of modern techniques. Wells found that even when a more efficient labor-intensive technique was known (and, in fact, already being used by the company) more capital-intensive techniques were chosen "to keep up with the competition" or to achieve top quality, even when the quality change was not perceived by the consumer. He calls this the choice of technique by engineering man rather than economic man. He notes that engineers wish to avoid operating problems, and have more confidence in machines than in people in this regard. He even cites one case in which the engineers used U.S. wage rates when calculating costs of different methods of production in Indonesia. Since equipment decisions are often made by engineers, these biases lead to capital-intensive methods. A study of the choice of rice milling techniques in an LDC also found this kind of engineering bias (Timmer, 1975). Another argued that the decision often is "an engineering one subject to a broad economic constraint" (Pickett et al., 1974).

In some cases, excessive capital intensity may result from inefficient allocation of an organization's available capital to units making decisions on choice of technique. Wells notes that if a manager is allowed to reinvest his cash flow, he may choose a new machine rather than a risky investment in another line of business. Morawetz (1975) points out a case of a government enterprise in Columbia investing in capital-intensive ventures since it was allowed to reinvest its cash flow. And Timmer also found that the cost of capital as perceived by different government ministers did not correspond to that of central government planners. So a decision maker is not likely to make the best choice for a company or country unless he has an adequate picture of the relative costs of capital and labor for the whole organization.

Evidence is not conclusive on whether the MNC is worse or better than local companies as to its willingness to consider various alternative technologies and to make rational choices. On the one hand, the MNC is more exposed to different technologies worldwide and is closer to the international market for second-hand equipment. It can also amortize development costs for innovative technique over a large number of developing country markets. But, on the other hand, some studies report that local companies are more flexible, at least in their choice of machinery (Morley and Smith, forthcoming; Mason, 1971). The MNC's reporting system may put undue emphasis on output per worker as a measure of productivity, or otherwise inhibit technological adaptations. The MNC central staff often carefully screens technological choices by subsidiaries, and may not be the best channel for encouraging imaginative adaptations (Behrman and Wallender, 1976).

This evidence of irrationality provokes a search for its causes. Most authors feel that the culprit is the lack of competitive pressure that would force companies to be more cost conscious and to use more labor-intensive methods where appropriate. Yeoman (1968) found that in industries where the cross-elasticity of demand was low, there was less adaptation than in ones where price was an important competitive tool. Wells found that companies selling branded products, and thereby able to compete on a basis other than price, were less likely to adapt, whether they were foreign or local. He argued that all companies are pushed toward capital intensity, but that only those with sufficient market power could afford this luxury.

The existence of companies, often foreign-owned, in positions where competitive pressures are weak is often the result of protection offered to import-substituting industries. Export industries could be expected to be more conscientious in searching for efficiency, thus, adapting more than others, but international quality standards are likely to be a serious offsetting factor. For example, Motorola was reported to ship machinery to its export-oriented plant in Korea from an identical production line in Phoenix (Behrman and Wallender, 1976). Export-oriented plants of MNCs may be more labor intensive because of the nature of the products and processing stages selected for transfer to LDCs, but it seems unlikely that they will make significant adaptations in overall production technology.

*Enhancement of Local Resources by the MNC.* The arguments and evidence presented so far have concerned the extent to which the MNC is biased against the use of the abundant unskilled labor in LDCs. But technology transfer through the MNC may also affect the quality of resources available for future use by the countries. The question here is whether the MNC does a good job of enhancing the countries' labor skills, entrepreneurial abilities, and research capabilities, and whether such skills and abilities are transferable to other uses in the economy. Here there is evidence to indicate considerable effort on the part of the MNC to enhance resources but little comparing such efforts to those of local companies.

The MNC often engages in extensive training of the workers in its affiliates in operative and managerial skills. These training programs are undertaken sometimes because of government requirements, but usually to further the company's productivity and sales. Teams of specialists from company headquarters or other affiliates give formal courses or on-the-job training, and local employees are often sent to affiliates in other countries for training (Behrman and Wallender, 1976). Many companies provide training to suppliers in order to insure that they will meet their quality and delivery goals (Reuber, 1973). And the MNC is sometimes an important source of training of the users of new technology. It has been estimated, for example, that IBM alone accounts for about half the training of computer users in Latin America. Still it is difficult to know how the MNC compares with local companies in the frequency of training programs. One study found that there was no big difference, although the MNC tended to have somewhat larger programs (Mason, 1971).

It has sometimes been alleged that the training provided by the MNC is for skills that are not transferable to other parts of the economy, and that key managerial and entrepreneurial skills are not provided. This may be true in some cases, such as some very esoteric skills in export-oriented electronics plants, but most of the training is in skills such as welding and mechanical work, which seem very appropriate to the needs of LDCs. Indications are that the MNC loses many of the workers that it has trained to other local enterprises (Behrman and Wallender, 1976). The MNC also provides considerable training in managerial skills and most companies seem to attempt to replace expatriate managers with locals.

The MNC may also affect a country's capabilities in research and development. Although most fundamental research of the MNC is concentrated in a few countries, considerable product development and support research is carried out in LDCs (Duerr, 1970). It is often necessary or more economical to do adaptative research close to customers or sources of materials, and this is the first step in building an infrastructure of research capabilities. There are increasing examples of companies that are establishing research laboratories in the larger LDCs to serve regional or world markets.[8] The MNC certainly enhances local resources with training and research programs, but it is difficult to assess the costs of these programs for LDCs relative to other alternatives.

*Alternatives to MNC Technology.*   There is little evidence that the MNC performs worse than local enterprises, even local state enterprises, in the introduction of appropriate production technology. But much could be done to encourage the MNC to further adapt its technology and to use its ability to enhance local resources. Of course, other alternatives are available—the government itself can import more appropriate technology, or it can be generated locally, but here the main question is relative cost, the subject of a later section.

The MNC and local enterprises can be encouraged to adopt more appropriate technologies by the following measures:

—Encourage or require consideration of alternative technologies in the approval process for new investments, and attempt to reduce the cost of search for new technologies, perhaps through a government-supported information service. It appears that entrepreneurs will not otherwise systematically consider alternatives. One suggestion for encouraging consideration of alternative technologies has been to require joint ventures, as local partners are presumed to be more sensitive to local factor prices. But the evidence presented above does not support this presumption as a general case.

—Reduce distortions in factor prices and give clear government guidelines to encourage adaptation. Incentives for the use of second-hand equipment, intensive use of capital, and other capital-saving innovations might be advisable.

—Encourage the upgrading of local resources, especially those that are complementary to the use of unskilled labor, for example through required training courses for supervisors and skilled workers.

—Move toward a more competitive environment in which the use of efficient labor-intensive methods is required by pressures in the market.

—Allocate resources to those products and production processes that are inherently labor-intensive. Production technology depends to a large extent on the product being manufactured. Thus choice of appropriate products is crucial.

## MNC Product Technology

MNCs are accused of selling products in LDCs that have been developed for affluent consumers in industrial countries and charging premium prices for these largely superfluous products. This section of the paper will consider what products are appropriate, the evidence on MNC adaptation or innovation of products for LDCs, and how countries can encourage the introduction of "appropriate products." In this discussion, as before, a part of the problem may be unique to the MNC, but a large part of it may be explained by the more general situation, common to local companies and MNCs, reflecting the income gap between rich and poor countries. The MNC may be only the tip of the consumer society iceberg.

*What Is Appropriate Product Technology?*   One criterion of appropriateness is cost. Given two similar products, the one that costs less is clearly more attractive to a consumer in an LDC. Since the MNC may be able to charge more than its competitors for similar products, because of heavy advertising and established brand names, this becomes an important consideration in evaluating the appropriateness of MNC products. The question of costs and prices will be dealt with below.

Most discussion of appropriate product characteristics has focused on two criteria: first, that they should be manufactured with a labor-intensive technology, and second, that they should not incorporate "luxury" features, but should instead have only "essential" features, especially those of special necessity in an LDC. It is clear, however, that these two criteria may sometimes be in conflict, and international trade presents the possibility that the products consumed in a country need not be manufactured there.

Stewart (1973) notes that a given product can be characterized as a bundle of characteristics that fulfill a number of different needs of consumers. As consumers get richer, they spend proportionally less income on satisfying "essential" needs, thus demanding products with more "luxury" characteristics. Poor consumers of LDCs would presumably be better off if offered more products with only "essential" characteristics rather than fewer products with more luxury characteristics. These presumed welfare effects of given products are, of course, difficult to measure through any kind of consumer research, and most pronouncements on this score are therefore made by planners or other government officials on the basis of their own subjective values. Given the disenchantment in industrial countries with the proliferation of seemingly superfluous products, however, there is an even stronger case against such products in poor countries.

Products with more of the "essential" characteristics do not necessarily use appropriate production technology. Indeed, some luxurious products may be among the most labor-intensive, e.g., all kinds of services and hand-made products, while some of the most essential products may be capital-intensive (Morawetz, 1974; Helleiner, 1975). Indeed, concentration of a countries' manufacturing industry on efficient production of a small number of standardized, high-volume products could lead to more capital intensity. So, although it is preferable to find appropriate products with appropriate manufacturing processes, this may sometimes be contradictory.

However, in some cases it may be possible to find alternatives that combine desired product characteristics and manufacturing techniques. Baranson proposes the following criteria for appropriate transportation vehicles: low initial cost, easy maintenance that avoids use of scarce skilled labor, ruggedness and reliability sufficient to endure poor roads and other adverse conditions, and simple manufacture that allows use of general-purpose machines. These criteria formed the basis for the development by U.S. automobile companies of vehicles for LDCs.

International trade offers, of course, the possibility of exporting products that have an appropriate production technology and importing those with an appropriate consumption technology. There is evidence, for example, that MNC export-oriented plants are more labor-intensive than import-substituting plants (Helleiner, 1973). The recent shift in development priorities to favor manufacturing exports is based partly on the employment implications of such a move.

*Product Adaptations by the MNC.*    It is clear that a need exists in LDCs for products that will satisfy basic human needs of affordable food, clothing, shelter, and health care. The MNC makes undoubted contributions in some of these areas, particularly in pharmaceuticals, but is accused of doing too little innovation or adaptation of products for LDCs. Little research has been done on this subject, so that most evidence is in the form of examples and counterexamples.

Many examples are available of efforts on the part of the MNC to develop and promote products adapted to LDC markets.[9] The vehicles developed by Ford and General Motors, Ford's small-scale tractor, Northrup's low-cost communication system, the development and promotion of high-protein foods, and Pfizer's "East Coast Fever" project in Africa are a few examples. Quite frequently, the MNC has research laboratories both in the home country and host countries working on the development of products for local markets (Behrman and Wallender, 1976). But it is undoubtedly true that much more innovation and adaptation could be done. One study of marketing policies of U.S. and European companies producing consumer packaged goods for various U.S. and European markets found that most companies made few product changes to serve individual markets, although they did change prices, sales promotion techniques, and advertising much more frequently (Sorenson and

Wiechmann, 1975). The conclusion of the authors was that there was too much standardization. While this study did not include LDCs, it indicates the reluctance on the part of the MNC to modify product designs.

*Obstacles to Product Innovation and Adaptation.*    Many of the obstacles to product adaptations are similar to those inhibiting process adaptations. New products require *development expenses* that may not be justified by small markets. Consumer needs are not translated into effective demand because of low per capita incomes, so the most attractive market in many LDCs is the upper class. Even products developed for the poor, such as high-protein supplements, may end up being consumed mainly by the rich, because of an inability to manufacture the product at a low enough cost. The development of simple products which may be easily copied, will probably not lead to the high returns on investment typical of heavily promoted differentiated brands. Since the MNC has a sunk cost in developing a product for industrial countries, the development of an alternative product for the LDC market may not be attractive. Development of standard products with standard advertising worldwide may lead to efficiencies and to simpler control systems, although these savings may not always be as great as sometimes supposed (Sorenson and Wiechmann, 1975).

Again, the case against the MNC as being particularly biased against product adaptations is not strong. Local companies too may find it more attractive to copy existing MNC products than to develop their own. And the MNC may be more likely to be able to justify development of an appropriate product that can be introduced in several countries, thus spreading development costs. This seems to have happened in the automobile and pharmaceutical industries in some cases.

The MNC may have an *irrational bias against appropriate products* for LDCs, with the resulting reduction in profits covered by a monopoly position in the market. There may exist an engineering bias in favor of excessive quality, and a desire to be perceived by governments as offering nothing less than top-quality products. Sometimes such questions become quite controversial, as in the case of a pharmaceutical company offering to LDCs what may be a very appropriate product for their needs, but which has not been approved by health authorities for use in the home country. Whose criteria of appropriateness should be used in such cases?

*Alternatives to MNC Product Technology.*    Evidence on the effect of the MNC on product technology in LDCs is, thus, not very convincing. The MNC is strong in only a few industries that are oriented to the most "essential" needs, such as food processing and medicines, so its role in fulfilling all such needs is only marginal. Governments can take some steps to encourage the MNC to develop more appropriate versions of some of its products, mainly by removing disincentives that may prevent production for regional markets. The MNC has an important role to play in the manufactured exports of LDCs. But insuring the marketing of appropriate products is more a question of income distribution and a political willingness to limit consumer choice, two areas where governments must take the lead.

## COSTS AND CONDITIONS OF MNC TECHNOLOGY

There is widespread agreement that determination of a fair price for technology is very difficult, since it is sold in a market that is complex and imperfect. "Knowledge, it seems, is not only not free but it is not even available on competitive markets" (Helleiner, 1975, p. 161). The market is often characterized by oligopolistic sellers and poorly informed buyers with the "products" for sale being difficult to compare. Furthermore, technology often is provided in a package with other resources or goods, making it difficult to evaluate the price of the technological component and leading to hidden costs. Furthermore, the "price," as expressed in the direct costs, may be a small part of the full cost as the sale is often conditioned on the acceptance by the buyer of restrictive conditions that may substantially increase the true costs.

Analysis of the cost of MNC technology to LDCs requires a clear definition of the alternatives to which this option is compared. These range from foregoing the acquisition of the technology, to generating a similar technology locally, to acquiring it through a different channel in which a local enterprise will exert more control. The last of these alternatives will be the focus here. It will be assumed that the foreign technology is desired and that local generation of the technology has been determined to be unfeasible or too costly. Although many LDCs are at a stage in development in which some industrial technology is generated locally, all face many situations for which other countries have a decided comparative advantage. One author states, "Other countries may well resent this, but it is questionable whether their own market sizes, income levels, and availabilities of scientifically trained personnel would permit them to invest with profit in the development of rival advanced technologies" (Johnson, 1970, p. 42). Thus the comparison here is between importing technology through subsidiaries of MNCs and importing it through other channels.

The discussion is organized into two parts. First, the characteristics of the technology market are described, including the products, the buyers and sellers, and the price mechanism. Then the alternative transfer channels are described and their benefits and costs to both buyers and sellers are evaluated in theoretical and empirical terms.

## Price Setting in the Technology Market

*The Technology "Product".* As described earlier, the 'products" being offered in the technology market are of many different kinds. The most important distinction here is between proprietary and nonproprietary technology, as the markets for these two types are quite different. *Proprietary technology* is that which is unique to a given enterprise, while *nonproprietary technology* is available on a competitive market, or may even be freely available. There are, of course, infinite variations between these two extremes. Technology may be proprietary because of legal protection through patents and trademarks, or it may simply be that the technology has been kept secret but unpatented by its creator.

While technology in the sense of knowledge is always created and stored by people, the technology may be sold (transferred) in various forms. The owner may sell it in the form of machines or products that have been manufactured using the knowledge, or it may be transferred in the form of documents describing the knowledge, or in the labor of persons possessing the knowledge. These different forms may have very different consequences in terms of the costs and benefits to both the seller and buyer of the technology.

In practice, these different forms of technology—proprietary and nonproprietary, embodied and disembodied—are often sold in combination and the sale is usually accompanied by the sale of a number of other types of goods and services. It may, therefore, often be difficult to determine the price of an individual element in the transaction. And the transfer of technology may be accompanied by restrictions on its use that may imply indirect costs to the buyer. Of particular concern are restrictions on exports, on the source of inputs, and on the internal management of the buying enterprise.

*Market Participants and Their Objectives.* The cost of technology transfer by an MNC to an LDC is often determined by bargaining among the MNC, the government of the country, and sometimes a local company. Each has its own view of the value of the technology, and its own preferences as to how it should be transferred. The objectives of each participant and how these influence the price of technology are discussed first. The effects of alternative channels on price will be discussed subsequently.

The MNC possesses technology and is constantly acquiring or generating more, often at considerable expense. The markets of LDCs offer an opportunity to help recoup these expenses and increase the return on its R & D investments. The company has various alternatives for earning a return from its technology in a given market, ranging from licensing it to an independent company to transferring it through a wholly owned subsidiary. Its choice will depend on which alternative offers the promise of the best long-term returns. Included in this calculation will be the return to be earned from the technology itself, plus the return earned from other sales that can be tied to the sale of technology. It will also include an estimate of the effect of each alternative on costs and revenues of other operations of the company throughout the world, as well as a guess as to the long-term effect of each on the company's ability to generate and sell additional proprietary technology.

An independent local company has a need for technology to be used in local or export markets. It may have a number of alternative sources including the MNC. Its choice will depend on which alternative will have the most beneficial impact on its profitability, including in this calculation not only the direct costs and benefits of the technology, but also the effects of other resource transfers that may be tied to the purchase of technology. In particular, the local company may be interested in access to an MNC trademark, or to foreign capital or markets that accompany the technology sale (Cilingiroglu, 1975).

The government of an LDC, while having in common with the local company the desire to acquire technology at low cost, should make its calculations in a different way. It should be measuring the social costs and benefits of each alternative, calculating what resources each alternative will provide, and what local resources will be used. Its calculation of benefits and costs may differ substantially from that of the local company. It will not, for example, count the monopoly power provided to the local company by a foreign trademark as a benefit, whereas this may be an important gain from the local company's viewpoint. And it may count training by the local company of workers to use the technology as a benefit to society, while the company sees it as a cost.

The country will be concerned with the direct, visible costs of the technology (royalties, etc.), but also with hidden costs, such as possible overpricing by the MNC of inputs to the local company. The licensee, on the other hand, may not be overly concerned with overpricing, if the extra cost can be passed on to the consumer, or if it can serve as a channel for transferring funds out of the country. Moreover, the country will be especially concerned not only that the technology is transferred, but that it is absorbed. That is, not only should the technology be used, but eventually local companies should develop the ability to make efficiently products of good quality without outside assistance (Wilkins, 1974).

Another difference between the country and company approaches may be in the wider range of alternatives considered. Not being committed to one local company, a government may reject a negotiated contract between MNC #1 and local company A, in favor of a better one between MNC #2 and local company B. Although the first contract may show a favorable benefit-cost ratio, the country will want to see which of many alternatives shows the best ratio (Vaitsos, 1974).

Thus, a detailed benefit-cost analysis of the technology by the country may yield an evaluation quite different from the value seen by the MNC or the local company. For this reason, governments can not rely simply on local companies to obtain the best bargain on foreign technology, however good at bargaining such companies might be.

*Determination of the Price of Technology.* The mechanism for determining the price of technology depends very much on the degree to which the technology is proprietary. For nonproprietary technology the mechanism is that of a relatively competitive market, while for proprietary technology it is closer to a bilaterally monopolistic bargain, in which the relative strengths of the MNC and the country determine the outcome (Vaitsos, 1974).

Proprietary knowledge is expensive to generate, but once generated, its application may involve very little incremental cost. However, the seller will be concerned with recouping the initial expenses through a price much higher than the marginal cost. The value of the technology in a given foreign market may be difficult to estimate, but the owner presumably will have reasonably good estimates based on its use elsewhere.

To the LDC, on the other hand, a price based on sunk development costs will seem unreasonable, especially since the technology was probably developed for use mainly in industrial countries. It will be reluctant to contribute much to the MNC's development expenses, especially since development laboratories are located somewhere else and much of the research is not applied in the particular country. Thus, for the recipient country, the value of the technology may be difficult to estimate until it is actually acquired and there may be few readily comparable alternatives.

The seller and buyer will, thus, have very different views of what constitutes an equitable price, the seller emphasizing the high development costs and high use-value and the buyer emphasizing the low marginal costs and uncertain value in the particular country. The price will, therefore, tend to be set in accordance with the relative bargaining strengths of each party, with the bargaining strength of each being a function of the alternatives open to it and its knowledge of the options open to the other party. A country will be in a better position if: first, it has a large and growing economy, and an attractive investment climate; second, it knows the terms of agreements made by the MNC in other countries; third, it understands the benefits and costs to the MNC of the sale of this technology; and fourth, it investigates other alternatives that it may have open. If the country is badly informed, it will clearly be at the mercy of the MNC.

In the market for nonproprietary knowledge, on the other hand, the two parties will be likely to come to similar estimates of the value of the technology. A much greater proportion of the price charged by the MNC for such technology will represent the incremental costs of applying the knowledge, rather than the allocation of past expenditures. More comparable alternatives will be available to the buyer, and application of the technology in other countries will have provided good estimates of its worth. Thus, the price for such technology should more closely reflect competitive forces.

### Alternative Channels for Transfer of Foreign Technology

*The Case for Unbundling the MNC Package.* Several United Nations studies have examined in detail the alternative channels of technology transfer open to LDCs.[10] The purpose has been to evaluate the feasibility of unbundling the package of resources typically provided by a foreign direct investor and to determine the costs and benefits of buying each component separately. These studies and others have revealed the wide variety of restrictive business practices associated with technology transfer, and have improved the understanding of the often hidden and indirect costs of foreign technology. But they have neither shown clearly that one channel or another is best, nor that unbundling should be pursued in all situations. Rather they have reinforced the conviction that LDCs must improve their ability to negotiate with the sellers of technology, both by understanding feasible alternatives and by developing mechanisms to evaluate the social costs and benefits of each.

Foreign technology will usually be imported by an LDC for use on a specific project. The project may be small, *e.g.,* a program to improve efficiency in one department of a manufacturing plant, or it may be very large, *e.g.,* the installation of a petrochemical complex. A typical project, however, will require unpatented know-how (not necessarily all foreign) for: project planning, product design, plant design and construction, control and support systems design, start-up of operations and implementation of systems, and continuing management including product and process improvements (Behrmann and Wallender, 1976). This know-how will usually have to be supplemented by access to patented technology in the form of documents, equipment, or material inputs. In addition, the project may require access to foreign resources other than technology, especially capital or markets.

A number of alternatives are available for acquiring all or some of these foreign resources. The following table lists three of the most important ones and what each alternative typically provides. There are, of course, many variations of these basic options, and not every agreement of a given type will provide all the resources listed in the table. The foreign-controlled subsidiary, of which the majority joint venture is one example, provides the most complete package of resources, including patented and unpatented know-how and other resources. Licensing agreements usually provide only know-how (sometimes only access to patents without assistance in applying it), and generally do not provide aid in project planning, systems design, management, or other resources. Turnkeys provide a complete package of technology, but generally do not provide continuing management assistance or resources other than technology.

Comparing the costs to an LDC of these different channels is clearly quite difficult. Since each provides a different package of resources, the country should attempt to establish the cost of each part of the package or devise combinations of channels that will provide comparable packages. For example, it is not sufficient to compare the foreign-controlled subsidiary to a simple licensing agreement. Adjustments must be made to make them comparable. One might compare the cost of the licensing agreement with the cost of only a part of the foreign investment package

*Table 6.1*  Resources Provided by Alternative Channels for Acquisition of Foreign Technology

| | Foreign-controlled subsidiary | Licensing agreement | Turnkey agreement |
|---|:---:|:---:|:---:|
| Unpatented know-how | | | |
|   Project planning | x | | x |
|   Product design | x | x | x |
|   Plant design | x | x | x |
|   Systems design | x | | x |
|   Construction and startup | x | | x |
|   Continuing management | x | | |
| Patented know-how | | | |
|   For product design | x | x | x |
|   For process design | x | x | x |
|   Proprietary machinery | x | x | x |
|   Proprietary material inputs | x | x | x |
| Other resources | | | |
|   Capital | x | | |
|   Contact with foreign markets | x | | |

comparable with the resources supplied under the license. Alternatively, one might add to the cost of the licensing agreement the costs of capital and other resources that will be needed to supplement it to make it comparable with the benefits supplied by an MNC affiliate. Another difficulty in comparing the alternatives is that each gives rise to payments of characteristically different kinds, and each is also associated with a number of hidden or indirect costs and benefits to the developing country. The evidence, both quantitative and qualitative, on their relative costs and benefits is discussed below.

In the following discussion, the case for unbundling the technology component of the foreign direct investment package will be described and then, using the foreign-controlled subsidiary as a base, the cost of other alternatives will be evaluated. The theoretical case for unbundling has been made most strongly by Vaitsos (1974b) and Streeten (1971, 1974), who have argued that the packaging of resources is a major source of the MNC's monopoly power. By conditioning access to its proprietary technology or other monopolized resources on the purchase by the buyer of other parts of the package, it reduces its competitors to those able to supply the whole package. Such tying may operate in various ways: tying old technology to new, tying access to technology to accepting capital contributions, or tying technology to the acceptance of export controls or the use of company-controlled raw materials. As Streeten argues in referring to the operations of the MNC in the export processing zones in LDCs:

> The packaged nature of the contribution of the MNC, usually claimed as its characteristic blessing, is in this context the cause of the unequal international distribution of the gains from trade and investment. If the package broke or leaked, some of the rents and monopoly rewards would spill over into the host country (Streeten, 1974, p. 263).

Of course, there are limits to unbundling the package. Sometimes alternative sources of parts of the package may not be available, either because of reluctance on the part of sellers or weaknesses on the part of the buyers. Many have noted that access to patented technology is insufficient without knowledge about how to use it (Behrman and Wallander, 1976; Helleiner, 1975). Indirect transfers of technology through MNC affiliates, rather than directly from the MNC to the host country, is partly in response to this lack of capacity to apply available knowledge (Cooper, 1971).

And some MNCs with proprietary knowledge may not make it available except in packaged form. A number of studies have examined the choice by the MNC among the different forms of exploiting its technology in foreign markets.[11] The conclusions are that a company will be most likely to insist on control (a wholly owned subsidiary or majority-owned joint venture) when:

—It is large and experienced in international operations, thus having the resources necessary to exploit foreign opportunities.

—It emphasizes either rationalization of production among several countries (typical of companies with narrow product lines) or heavy advertising efforts. In either of these cases a foreign partner seems to cause considerable problems for an MNC in coordinating its international strategies.

—It has a unique product or significant technological edge, thus being concerned about the loss of this technology. Again, those companies with a narrow product line will have more concern in this regard.

This suggests that firms having such characteristics may not be willing to unbundle their technology, or may do so only if they can receive very high fees or impose restrictive conditions. This may not, of course, be of great concern to LDCs in some cases. For example, The MNC characterized by a strategy based on heavy advertising, as are cosmetics and soap manufacturers, may be seen as a company contributing relatively little to an LDC in terms of appropriate technology and the country may forgo its contributions. However, production rationalizers, such as automobile companies, may offer excellent export possibilities under wholly owned subsidiaries while being completely unwilling to provide export markets to a licensee. Some large, technologically sophisticated companies, like the computer manufacturers, may offer significant technological contributions to a country if allowed to retain control.

> The limits to unbundling are nicely summarized as follows: The ability to purchase the information separately will depend on its separate transferability. Where the advantage lies not in any special formula, but in a complex network of information gathering, filtering, processing, feedback and application, a separate transfer may be impossible. When parting with the knowledge would be detrimental to the company, a separate transfer would be possible but will not occur (Streeten, 1970, p. 241).

The foreign-controlled subsidiary is tied to the parent in a number of ways, many of which give rise to financial flows. It is generally impossible to determine how much of any given payment corresponds to a given contribution. The parent company is interested in the total returns from the subsidiary, but the mix of flows will depend upon such factors as taxation, exchange controls, and the requirements for managerial control.

The foreign-owned subsidiary thus has the most potential of any channel for increasing the hidden costs of technology transfer.

A typical parent-subsidiary relationship will involve:

—Licensing of patents and trademarks to the subsidiary, giving rise to royalties, the most obvious form of payment for technology.

—Provision of technical and managerial assistance, headquarters services, and access to the parent's expertise, giving rise to direct fees and the allocation of a portion of the parent company's overhead to be charged to the subsidiary. Again, a part of such payments is for technology.

—Sales and purchase of goods between the parent and the subsidiary, giving rise to payments in both directions. Since the goods, especially intermediates sold by the parent to the subsidiary, may embody technology, part of the price of such goods is a payment for technology. These transactions offer the potential for disguised payments in the form of overpricing of the intermediates.

—Equity investments by the parent in the subsidiary, giving rise to subsequent flows of dividends. These investments may be financial contributions, they may be in the form of machinery and other goods, or they may represent the capitalization of intangible know-how and good will. Thus dividends may represent in large part a payment for technology.

—Loans by the parent to the subsidiary, giving rise to interest payments. Such payments, if above market rates, may represent a disguised form of payment for technology.

The determination of which of the flows corresponds to payments for technology, and which for management, for goods, or for entrepreneurial risk-taking is virtually impossible.

The parent-subsidiary relationship likewise involves control of the subsidiary by the parent, which gives the parent the ability to restrict the subsidiary's behavior. Such restrictions may have the effect of increasing the benefits of the subsidiary to the parent, and of increasing the costs to the host country of this channel of technology transfer. Of particular concern in this regard are restrictions on exports, on the source of inputs, and on the internal management of the subsidiary. Some of these restrictions are inherent in the international patent and trademark system, while others reach far beyond these legally sanctioned controls.

Many of the costs and restrictions described above are common in technology transfers between independent parties, but others are unique to the parent-subsidiary tie. This says nothing, however, about the relative costs of different channels, as the magnitudes of each cost or restriction in each alternative channel must be determined. The limited evidence available on this point is summarized below.

*Royalty Payments and Other Charges For Technical Assistance.* Licensing agreements are common between parents and subsidiaries, as well as between independent foreign and local firms. Payments under both kinds of agreements take many forms, usually being calculated as a percentage of sales, but sometimes involving initial lump-sum payments, minimum payments regardless of sales, additional charges based on services rendered, and so forth. A number of studies by the U.N. and others have examined the terms of licensing agreements (UNIDO, 1973; UNCTAD, 1974a). They have found that licensing agreements typically involve payments averaging around five percent of sales, but with significant differences among industries. They have not found evidence showing a major difference in royalty rates between parent-subsidiary agreements and those between independent parties and, since many parents do not explicitly charge royalties to their subsidiaries for technology, a more complete study would probably reveal lower average loyalty charges to affiliates. In fact, one study found that parents charged more for technology to their joint venture affiliates than to their wholly owned subsidiaries (Stopford and Wells, 1972, p. 162). A U.S. Department of Commerce study noted that parents sometimes do not charge affiliates for technology, even if they charge others. The study noted, however, that there may be a trend toward more formal agreements between parents and affiliates (Teplin, 1973).

Despite a lack of clear evidence that parents systematically overcharge their affiliates for technology, it is obvious that the charges for technology do not relate very well to the worth of the technology. One study found, for example, that royalties were charged to foreign affiliates in Argentina on almost all their sales, regardless of whether the technology utilized was old or new, and that the rates on old and new technology were similar (Chudnovsky, 1975, p. 457). Another found that many U.S. multinationals had very poor systems of control for their technology contributions and receipts from affiliates, often not charging anything to a subsidiary for many parent company contributions (Lovell, 1969). A number of case studies have revealed that much technology to affiliates is provided free of charge, but with payment presumably reflected in increased dividends or in other forms (Behrman and Wallender, 1976).

*Pricing of Intermediate Goods From Parents to Subsidiaries.* Another way that an MNC may extract a return on its technology is to overcharge its subsidiaries for materials used in the production process. Vaitsos (1974b) found striking examples of this in Latin America, although the extent of the overpricing varied greatly among industries, being by far the highest in pharmaceuticals. There is reason to believe that pharmaceuticals represent an extreme case since: first, it is an industry where host-country price controls limit the profitability of local subsidiaries and encourage taking profits in other ways; second, it is the industry *par excellence* with high technology development costs and low incremental costs for application of the technology; and third, there are a number of companies in the international market, especially those in Italy, that copy patented products without paying development costs and are able to undercut the prices of other companies. Using their prices as a basis for comparison, as Vaitsos often did to conclude that there is overpricing by the parent company, it is plausible to conclude that, in fact, the price may be a fair reflection of the company's costs. Nevertheless, overpricing of intermediates has been found by others (Cilingroğlu, 1975; Chudnovsky, 1975), and there is some evidence that it is worse in parent-subsidiary relationships than in agreements among independent parties. Vaitsos found that when independent licensees were required to buy materials from a licensor, there were often clauses stipulating that the prices charged be close to international prices, while such clauses were less common in parent-subsidiary relationships. Another study found that joint ventures paid less on their purchases from parent MNC's than did wholly owned subsidiaries (Stopford and Wells, 1972, p. 160).

Although inflated transfer prices have received much attention, the potential for manipulation is limited to certain industries and countries where imports by foreign-owned subsidiaries are large. And although tax-rate differences and exchange controls may provide reasons for raising transfer prices to LDCs, not all considerations point in this direction. In particular, tariffs reduce the desirability of such a practice and management control and administrative difficulties may argue for maintaining uniform arms-length transfer prices worldwide.

*Dividends and Interest on Loans From the Parent.*   Dividends and interest payments may also disguise payments for technology. There is little reason to believe that dividends are inflated, however, as governments often limit these payments, and companies may be especially careful in limiting the visibility of their profits. Interest payments, on the other hand, offer more attraction for extracting funds from a subsidiary. Such payments may be deductible for tax purposes in the host country, exchange controls may not be as strict, and home country tax laws may favor interest payments over dividends. Whether the potential for manipulation is used to any great extent has not been studied, but presumably some charges for technology are hidden in these payments.

Summarizing the evidence above, it is clear that a potential exists in the MNC to disguise charges for technology in other payments and, thus, to facilitate overpayment by an LDC for some technology. But, except for some overpricing of intermediate goods, there is little evidence that such potential is in fact systematically realized. It will, of course, be very difficult to prove the case one way or another because of the difficulties in evaluating the worth of individual, and in fact total, contributions by an MNC. Vaitsos, for example, calculated the total effective returns on investment to the parent companies in his study, including all payments and all overpricing. He again found very high returns, mostly because of the overpricing of intermediates. But his calculations did not show the market values of all contributions by the parent, many of which are not reflected in specific payments. A more relevant calculation would compare the market value of all contributions with the total payments.

*Restrictive Business Practices.* A hidden payment by an LDC for foreign technology may be implied by restrictive business practices which sometimes accompany the technology.

> The indirect cost is the sum of the advantages the purchaser accepts to sacrifice as a result of the particular agreement. For example, when a licensee agrees not to export, or not to expand beyond a certain market, he agrees in effect to lose all benefits derived from export or an expansion of his business (Cilingiroglu, 1975, p. 79).

Various studies have revealed the widespread existence of such practices in the licensing of foreign technology, the most prevalent being those restricting a licensee's right to export, requiring the use of raw materials provided by the licensor, or giving the licensor control of various aspects of the licensee's operations (UNCTAD, 1972a, 1974a). It is naturally very difficult to determine the costs to the country of such limitations. An export restriction, for example, is not the only barrier to an aspiring exporter in an LDC. The question, therefore, is what would have happened in the absence of the particular restriction.

Again there is little evidence showing that technology transfer through the MNC implies more such restrictive practices. Studies by UNCTAD and others find widespread restrictions in licensing agreements between independent companies, and it has generally been found that contracts between parents and subsidiaries contain fewer restrictions.[12] Nevertheless, what is explicit in an arms-length contract may be implicit in intracompany transactions. Parents certainly do not give complete freedom to subsidiaries, but neither does this mean that the interests of the LDCs are poorly served. There is ample evidence, for example, that the MNC does a good job, relative to local companies, in exporting certain manufactured products from LDCs, especially in those cases where foreign marketing barriers would be substantial for a local company (de la Torre, 1972).

One implicit barrier to exports, even in cases where they are not explicitly prohibited, is the international patent and trademark system. A licensee aspiring to export may find his markets closed by this system even if his agreement allows exports. There is a strong argument that the international patent system does not benefit LDCs (UNCTAD, 1974b; Penrose, 1973). Foreign companies have been shown to dominate patent filings in LDCs, with only a small percentage of patents actually worked there, the rest being intended often to preserve an export market. But, again, this is an issue that goes well beyond arguments about the MNC.

Thus, the empirical evidence so far available is inconclusive on the costs of buying foreign technology through the MNC. Instead, what is needed is an evaluation of individual agreements on a case-by-case basis to see what is provided and what it costs under each potential transfer mechanism.

Most of the discussion above has compared technology transfer through the MNC versus licensing agreements. But a similar approach is needed to evaluate management contracts or turnkeys. Both of these mechanisms attempt to overcome the shortgage in LDCs of management skills, but they have similar deficiencies. First, unless there are explicit agreements, they do little to upgrade the management skills of local personnel (Behrman and Wallender, 1976). Second, they may have insufficient incentives for good performance. Turnkey contractors are responsible for designing, building, and starting up a plant, but may not be responsible for keeping it going later. Management contract fees will typically be based mainly on the amount of work and not on the success of the project. On both these counts, either the wholly owned subsidiary or joint venture may provide better value for the costs incurred.

*Host Country Policies on Alternative Channels of Technology Transfer.* Several LDCs have begun programs aimed at reducing the costs of foreign technology (Driscoll and Wallender, 1974). These efforts have been aimed mainly at increasing their bargaining power in dealing with the sellers of technology and at eliminating restrictive business practices associated with the transfer of technology. There are now also proposals for an international code of conduct for such transfers. There is evidence that if such efforts are pursued in a flexible way, they may increase the benefits and decrease the costs of foreign technology.

Reports from several countries indicate that careful screening of technology-licensing agreements can reduce their costs. Examples from Colombia and Mexico show that even with a relatively modest effort, royalty rates have been reduced substantially (UNCTAD, 1974a; Camp and Mann, 1975). More elaborate procedures, involving systematic screening of alternative sources of technology, and possibly the generation of technology locally, might produce even better results. These programs may, of course, be expensive, and their effectiveness will depend on careful coordination of government efforts with industry needs, a task presenting considerable difficulties. But such programs are being implemented in one form or another in Mexico, India, and the Andean Group.

Of course, reductions in royalties and fees is not a sufficient indication that the costs of technology have gone down, as other financial flows may offset these reductions, especially in the case of contracts through MNC affiliates. Control of technology payments, therefore, requires a broad program of control of all flows associated with technology (material inputs, dividends, etc.) such as that contained in the Andean Group's foreign investment code. Royalty reductions will be of little use if needed foreign technology is not available at these lower prices. On this point, the evidence so far does not justify firm conclusions (Camp and Mann, 1975).

Restrictive business practices should be eliminated where feasible, both in agreements within the MNC and with other foreign sources of technology. But flexibility is needed in the application of rules concerning such restrictions. Tie-in clauses, for example, may in some cases be reasonable for reasons of quality. Export restrictions imposed by an MNC on its licensee may be acceptable if the company provides large offsetting benefits to the country.

The most effective policy for an LDC is to establish a systematic mechanism for evaluating the social costs and benefits of foreign technology on a case-by-case basis. Such an analysis would look not only at royalties and restrictions, but also at the appropriateness of the technology provided. Good guidelines, rather than absolute prohibitions, are needed to make such a procedure effective. The country should be especially sensitive to the possibilities for trading off restrictions or costs in one area against benefits in another, thus finding the best package. The first attempts at the control of foreign technology have appeared to be rigid, but as countries gain more experience, flexible guidelines hold the promise of obtaining for LDCs the benefits of MNC technology at reasonable cost.

## FOOTNOTES

1. OECD (1974, Chapter I) contains a discussion of the influence of definitions on the technology transfer debate.

2. Two useful references for discussions of appropriate technology in a context broader than that of the MNC are Jequier (1976) and Stewart (1974).

3. See Morley and Smith (forthcoming), Yeoman (1968), and Wells (1973).
4. See Strassman (1968), Mason (1971), Thomas (1975), Wells (1973) for examples and evidence on this point.
5. Strassman (1968) summarizes some of these. A more recent study is Basche (1975).
6. See especially Morley and Smith (forthcoming), Mason (1971), and Wells (1973).
7. Particularly Timmer (1975), Wells (1973), Strassmann (1968).
8. Behrman and Wallender (1976) describe ITT's efforts in Mexico and Pfizer's in Brazil and Kenya.
9. Most of these examples come from Baranson (1969), Behrman and Wallender (1976), and Wells and Chudson (1974).
10. Examples are Cooper (1971); UNCTAD, *Guidelines* (1972a); UNCTAD, *Major Issues* (1974a); Chudson (1971).
11. See especially Stopford and Wells (1972), Baranson (1970), and Stobaugh (1971).
12. See UNCTAD (1974a), Gilingiroglu (1975), Chudnovsky (1975).

# COMMENT

## JACK N. BEHRMAN*

Professor Moxon's paper is an excellent collation of the literature on this subject and provides a useful structure for analysis of the issues faced by policymakers. I would like to sharpen and expand some of the points I think may not be adequately understood by some readers.

The basic thesis of this paper can be summarized as follows: Although some of the indictments of the MNCs as transferers of technology are undoubtedly accurate, many examples can be shown of the opposite activities or effects. Therefore, regulation of the process by host countries, though necessary, should be done in a highly flexible manner so as to gain the maximum benefits. Despite his careful balancing of the pros and cons on every aspect that he examines, Professor Moxon does not raise the arguments against the flexibility he recommends. Where governments are unstable and rules tend to be rigidly stated, flexibility places the foreign company in a tenuous position. For example, if an agreement is flexibly negotiated under fairly strict regulations, a succeeding, opposing government has an opportunity to charge "favoritism" or fraud. Resulting penalties may be severe. If regulations are to be applied flexibly, it must be understood that this is a policy decision and the process of approval must be clarified so that the foreign company is not held culpable later.

### Appropriate Technology

In his concept of appropriate technology also, Moxon does not push an already complex subject quite far enough. Moxon asserts correctly that

*University of North Carolina

emphasis on the ratio of labor to capital used is insufficient for judging the appropriateness of technology and accepts the definition of Morawetz that appropriate technology is "the set of techniques that makes optimum use of available resources" in a given environment. But this concept is also inadequate, for it assumes knowledge of some fairly precise goals in terms of specific products as well as either a static environment or known changes in the future. Neither assumption is likely to be accurate in a developing country. The difficulty of defining the concept is illustrated by the fact that the National Academy of Science and the National Academy of Engineering have had a joint panel working on *appropriate technology* for over two years and they have not yet published an agreed text. A study for the Agency for International Development has attempted to be fairly specific, providing the following summary definition:

> In terms of available resources, appropriate technologies are intensive in the use of the abundant factors, labor, economical in the use of scarce resources, capital and highly trained personnel, and intensive in the use of domestically-produced inputs.
>
> In terms of small production units, appropriate technologies are small scale but efficient, replicable in numerous units, readily operated, maintained and repaired, low-cost and accessible to low-income persons.
>
> In terms of the people who use or benefit from them, appropriate technologies seek to be compatible with local cultural and social environments.

This definition also is inadequate, at least from the standpoint of developing countries. They are seeking through industrialization to change not only industrial structures and economic growth, but also the cultural and social environment; and those who are aware of the problems of industrialization recognize that it involves cultural and social change. Therefore, what is appropriate technology for one year may not be appropriate two or three years hence.

If one is trying to manage change, one should search for technologies that are appropriate for periods in the future as well as the present. To determine this level of appropriateness, the government needs to look at several factors: the anticipated division between agricultural and industrial activities in the country, the selection of specific industries to be promoted, the types of commodities that are to be produced in each industry (luxury versus mass consumption goods), the ability to train manpower to use the particular technologies (even if that manpower is scarce at present), the relationship of the technology to stimulation of local R & D activities, and the relationship of the technologies to the need to produce lower cost products for a local mass-consumption market or for export (if for export, quality constraints are also imposed).

In addition, appropriateness would have to consider the impact of the technologies on the conditions of work as well as on the living conditions in the community—that is, all of the social costs imposed by it. Appropriate technology is too often seen as an "input-output" problem, whereas, it is also a sociopolitical problem. For example, the problem of appropriate technology in transportation in the Andean countries is better posed in terms of whether mass transportation should be provided by means other than the auto rather than in terms of the best technology for producing automobiles. The question should not even be posed in terms of automobiles, but in terms of how to move people and goods most effectively in line with wider objectives of urbanization, community lifestyles, political freedom, etc.

Not wishing to push the concept this far, Professor Moxon permits the narrowness of the literature to dictate the scope of his own paper. Thus, he states, since "Most of the empirical studies on the appropriateness of MNC technology has focused on labor intensity, . . . a disproportional amount of this paper is also on this aspect." This may be an interesting question for economists, with their narrow view of the way in which decisions should be made, but it is not very useful for the governmental policymaker.

*Alternative Technologies*

Even within the narrow confines of the labor-intensity question, the usual analyses leave something to be desired in their assertion that companies did not adopt alternative technologies in many cases where they have existed. Moxon cites Tokman, Pack, and Wells to the effect that substitute technologies existed in the countries they studied; but he fails to indicate *why* the particular technologies used were decided upon and the others rejected. To know why would require information as to the alternatives open to the companies (the information available to them) and the costs of obtaining or using them. Of course, the cost to the companies is different from the cost to the economies, as Professor Moxon notes on several occasions in the paper. But if the company does not assess the cost in the best way from the standpoint of the host economy, it is up to the government to shift the factors on which the companies base that particular decision.

Professor Moxon's collation of the studies, which show that these decisions by both companies and governments are complex, is useful in cautioning that there are no easy answers. His emphasis on the question of control or maintenance of quality is to be welcomed, since this is so frequently overlooked. It is quite important for an MNC concerned with maintaining its good name or serving worldwide markets from multiple production locations. Even in mass consumption goods, the reduction of rejects from the production line becomes important in keeping costs down and reaching the local or foreign market. This objective may be obtainable only through high capital-labor ratios.

Moxon recognizes that MNC decisions may be tied to profit-satisficing and therefore are not "rational" in the sense of profit-maximization. This insight should be stressed, for this approach is not unique to the MNCs. All critics should recognize that companies make a quick and ready trade-off of the costs of gathering information, or of violating existing methods of decision-making, against alternative technologies or modes of production. When all production phases are tied into a single engineering concept, permitting quick rectification of difficulties from a central technical staff, corporate decision makers are not likely to seek alternative technologies (especially if substantially different) in the hope of achieving marginally greater sales or profits. Such a shift would introduce too much uncertainty. This situation reflects, as Moxon notes, an engineering bias on the part of many MNCs.

The paper emphasizes the numerous things that companies do and do not do in technology transfers, providing evidence as to why they do what they do, but not why they avoided specific alternatives. Though he suggests some policy constraints, what is needed for decision-makers is specific evidence of the reasons why they rejected alternatives available to them. This, of course, is difficult to do, and not enough of this type of research has been done. There are obvious difficulties in trying to research something that was not done, but where recommendations are to be made that alternatives be adopted, just this type of research is needed.

He argues that MNCs might be encouraged to adopt "more appropriate technologies" by several measures, one of which is to require joint ventures—since "local partners are presumed to be more sensitive to local factor prices." Though he states quickly that there is insufficient evidence to support this recommendation, he does not present the arguments that would raise serious doubt that such a measure would in fact improve the technologies. Not only is there serious question as to whether the locals know anything more about alternative technologies than the foreign partner, but also the requirement of a joint venture is likely to reduce the flow of technology and to constrain the alternatives available to the local partner—if fewer MNCs offer to negotiate, the opportunities are reduced. We have little knowledge of the companies that decided not to enter such negotiations and why.

The second measure suggested—the use of second-hand equipment—is an old recommendation soundly trounced by the developing countries themselves in every U.N. forum in which it has been raised. The recommendation that a "more competitive environment" be created so that more "efficient labor-intensive methods" will be required through pressures in the market is simply inappropriate for many small-sized economies. It does not address the question of "appropriate technology" for future growth, for the market does not record preferences beyond today.

### Costs and Conditions

Turning to the cost and conditions of technology transfers, Moxon tries to recognize the complexity of licensing agreements, but again he does not go far enough. Technology agreements range from fairly simple contracts to very complex ones; an examination of an average agreement would show at least thirty provisions that are directly traded off against the price of the technology to be transferred. It is, therefore, virtually impossible to determine what the appropriate price of a given technology is, unless one examines thoroughly all of the provisions of the licensing contract. It is for this reason that much of the discussion of transfer pricing is irrelevant. No licensor will agree to the cost provisions in a contract before all of the rest of the provisions are nailed down. Even in the standard contract used by RCA, the costs provisions were closely related to all of the other standard provisions of the contract; the only items that were negotiated were which particular patents were to be covered and the precise technology support to be given, which then dictated the numbers filled into the cost provisions.

What many of the codes on technology transfer do not understand, and government officials do not want to appreciate is that each technology transfer bears a total cost that has to be covered; however it is calculated (or estimated) by the licensor, it will be met one way or another or the contract will not be signed. Since the cost of the technology itself and even the cost of transfer are indefinite, the problem is one of negotiation. Singling out one provision—be it quality control, export restrictions, equipment purchases, or intercompany transfers—is an ineffective way of handling the problem, because one does not know where the impact of any one restriction will fall. If the licensor must give up on one desired provision, he will exact a "fee" somewhere else in the agreement or in performance. The licensing arrangement should be looked on itself as a package with the recognition that the objectives of the licensor and licensee may be different from that of the host government.

This same view of a package should be applied to the proposal to "unbundle" technology transfer from the investment package. Unbundling this large package is much more likely to raise the prices paid by the host country than to reduce them. The view of Vaitsos and Streeten quoted by Moxon that this " . . . packaging of resources is a major source of the MNC's monopoly power" is erroneous both analytically and actually. Power does not come from packaging; it comes from the ownership of a key factor. Packaging is the result of having the key factor, which permits other factors to be tied to it. Unbundling is not going to reduce the monopoly rents desired by the MNC, and if it cannot obtain the rent through selling the entire package, it will seek to gain the same rent on the few factors to be sold—unless, of course, there are other uses for the parts not sold in this package. The monopoly power attaches to the single factor, rather than to the package. If monopoly power does not exist with reference to the key factor, then it does not exist for the package either, and no excessive price is extracted by bundling.

Pressures to unbundle also do not recognize the many ancillary contributions provided by the MNCs through close ties of ownership and control over affiliates. The widespread lack of understanding of this point was the reason why Wallender and I studied transfers *within* MNCs. One of the conclusions reinforced by that study is that there is no way to cost technology transfers. The relationship is much more like a marriage contract; any effort to nail down all of the contributions and to put a cost or price on them is to undercut the agreement from the beginning. Governments can appropriately lay down the rules as to what will be recognized as a marriage under the law, but they have wisely refrained from stipulating precisely what the partners shall do to fulfill that contract. There is no reason why governments cannot do the same for licensing agreements or investment arrangements. But, any effort to stipulate the precise actions will have unanticipated impacts on the behavior of the parties. This lack of knowledge of the results of restrictions makes it extremely difficult to implement any policy of discovering and obtaining "appropriate technology."

Similarly, calculations, such as those done by Vaitsos demonstrating wholly inappropriate returns under licensing arrangements, have been based on a separation of elements within the contract and an application of calculations that are inappropriate or irrelevant if not inaccurate. As Moxon points out, one would have to show the market values of all contributions, provided freely or for fee, by the parent through and outside of the licensing agreements during the period of the contract in order to be able to determine whether the costs were excessive—to the licensee or to the host country itself.

## Restrictive Business Practices

This difference between the advantages to the licensee and those to the host country shows up pointedly in the discussion of restrictive business practices. Many of these practices are desired by the licensee as well as by the licensor; they are not forced upon the licensee at all. Even if the licensee might not like to comply with some of them—such as the purchase of particular raw materials—he will accept them as part of the price of the license and may be able to bargain down the royalty by arguing the availability of cheaper materials elsewhere. However, if the materials did in fact affect the quality of the output and, therefore, the salability of the product, even if he wished by buy inferior materials, it might not be to his advantage. Similarly, quality control requirements may be necessary in order to expand sales into foreign markets—unless they are less-discriminating countries, which might well be the case. Each of the so-called restrictive business practices is merely a negotiating point, unless the host country wishes to establish firm guidelines for *all* companies in the economy. What one finds instead in the Code on Technology Transfer proposed by the Group of 77 is that "all restrictive business practices are undesirable, unless they are to the advantage of the developing countries." This negotiating stance is highly unlikely to produce appropriate technology, appropriate licensing arrangements, or an appropriate flow of technology.

I conclude, along with Professor Moxon, that flexibility is desired, but I would also argue that a much more specific understanding of the channels of technology transfer, seen in the behavior of different types of companies, is as necessary as an appreciation of the types of technologies that are deemed appropriate. Economists and government officials have given too little attention to the institutional mechanisms within which technologies are generated and through which they are transferred. A better understanding of the decision criteria, the information constraints, the imperfections of markets, the myopia of government officials, and the trade-offs between present and future needs should leave us a bit less critical and frustrated by the present inadequacies in the identification and transfer of appropriate technologies.

# COMMENT

## NORMAN HINERFELD*

My interest in this paper stems from several sources. First, Kayser-Roth Corporation is a leading manufacturer of wearing apparel and specialty textile products employing 26,000 people in the United States. In addition, we manufacture abroad products that are shipped into the United States market, including manufacturing in several LDCs—Jamaica, Dominican Republic, Hong Kong, Taiwan, and Korea. In addition, we manufacture on an indirect basis for export to the United States in several

*Kayser-Roth Corporation

other countries, including Spain, Italy, Malaysia, Thailand, and Brazil. We also license overseas manufacturers who produce for consumption in foreign markets. These licenses, which encompass manufacturing technology, marketing know-how, and the use of established trademarks, are located in a total of 96 different countries. Finally, the subject matter is of special interest, since I have served as Chairman of the U.S. Chamber of Commerce Task Force on Technology Transfer, from which a report has been published. That report argues that the United States no longer holds a world monopoly on available investment capital and is no longer the unchallenged low-cost manufacturer selling in world markets. As a result, we must recognize that this country's key resource, underpinning its position in international trade, is its technology base. Further, this technology base must be buttressed by a coherent national policy for its proper deployment.

I turn now to Professor Moxon's paper. Moxon has made an evenly balanced presentation of the role of the MNC in adapting technology to the economic and social environment of the LDCs. Leaving aside differences in emphasis, there is little in the paper with which I would disagree. However, I must take exception to the basic premise underlying the paper: namely, that the phenomenon of the appropriateness of technology transfers and the resultant pricing of these transfers is a problem directly related to the role played by the multinational corporation. Rather, I believe that the problem of technology transfer is part of a much broader question. Are *intellectual property rights* (owned by anyone) to be treated differently than *tangible property rights*?

The MNC is now in the world spotlight. The issue of technology transfer, however, goes beyond the scope of the MNC, important though it may be, to include all private firms and governments, large and small, who own know-how, patents, and trademarks. Among the real questions to be faced are:

—How will technology property rights be maintained and exploited by the owner?

—How will societies in developing countries gain maximum access to the benefits of this constantly evolving technology, given the fact that the bulk of this technology is now owned by private firms located in the industrial nations?

I don't believe we can produce a blanket theory under the MNC banner to describe behavior under all conditions for the technology transfer process. While relative bargaining positions are sometimes affected by the fact that the owner of the technology is a large MNC, often the controlling factor is the attitude, law, or customs of the host country, regardless of who is the donor. Further, the attitude of the host country on matters of technology transfer is often the same even if the technology is owned by domestic firms within that same country. Professor Moxon cites examples of this phenomenon.

I think the following analogy is pertinent. In the early history of the United States, the American Indians took the position that if the oceans and the air are free, why does the white man think anyone owns the land? The LDC's attitude is similar. Why do industrial nations believe that they own technology? God made ideas freely available to everyone; therefore, international law should insure that technology is freely available to all. In stating this analogy, I am perhaps overstating the case to emphasize a point. However, I believe the core of the LDC position is based on such thinking.

This attitude on the part of LDCs ignores the basic fact that, in the industrialized nations of the western world, most technology is owned by private firms, not by governments. Therefore, the governments of the industrialized nations are not in a position to compel free or even bargain-priced distribution of technology as demanded by the LDCs. A further unrecognized obstacle is created by organized labor in the industrialized countries. Their objection to the proliferation of technology in the hands of low-wage competitors in the LDCs could prove to be the ultimate stumbling block. The governments of the LDCs must recognize that this fear of loss of domestic jobs can prove to be an even greater barrier to the transfer of technology than the lack of appropriateness of the technology being transferred, the related "restrictive practices" of the MNCs, or the actual prices placed on the sale of technology.

The basic mechanism to promote the transfer of technology involves the development of proper incentives both for the owner and for the potential receiver of the technology. Not only must the product of the technology be appropriate, the price paid for it must also be appropriate for technology transfer to occur. Consequently, the appropriateness of technology is criticized by the developing countries on incorrect grounds.

Firms owning technology, to the extent they act logically, will voluntarily provide appropriate technology and appropriate products. They do this to maximize their own return on investment. Further, they price technology taking into consideration at least the following:

—Competitive sources of technology, whether the competition comes from other high-technology corporations or from more labor-intensive, less-sophisticated technologies.

—The total (average) cost of technology, pricing not on the margin, but on the basis of the "sunk costs," including "sunk costs" incurred to develop nonproductive processes en route to achieving the technology that is finally capable of commercialization.

It is my opinion that technology will be transferred only if four precon-
ditions exist:
—The host country believes that the technology being acquired is appropriate to their needs.
—The host country, given the state of competitive sources, believes the
technology is priced at a level they can afford.
—The owner of technology believes that a reasonable profit will be
earned by transferring the technology.
—The domestic political pressure groups in the source country will not
veto the transaction.

The appropriateness of technology depends upon its purpose. If a manufacturing operation is set up in an LDC to make products for the world
export market, then the technology must be price competitive in the world
market and the product quality must be acceptable for that market. If, on
the other hand, the manufacturing facility is set up to produce for the
domestic market in an LDC, then the type of technology that will be
employed must produce a product that is salable at a profitable price and
at an acceptable quality level within that domestic market. This price
could be higher than the world market price if the government of the LDC
protects domestic industry. Therefore, the trade-off between the use of
foreign exchange, scarce capital resources, and the availability of under-
employed labor will determine the appropriate level of technology. Nothing in this argument states that the decision is made unilaterally by the
owner of the technology. Further, as Professor Moxon points out, the
utilization of less sophisticated, less capital-intensive technology will be
adopted only if the host government has agreed to the social goals of
training and employing large segments of its population, and is not en-
amored with utilizing capital-intensive technology merely as a "fad."

My company's experience in the apparel industry indicates that there is
no single underlying principle that determines the level of technology
appropriate for every instant case. When we manufacture overseas for
export to the U.S. market, with very few exceptions we must use the
latest technology and very heavy capital investment in order to compete
pricewise and qualitywise. The absence of an appropriate infrastructure in
the LDC limits our ability to train and control large groups of people,
particularly in the initial stages of development. As a consequence, we
must send technicians to the LDC during the early stages of an operation;
and we do whatever we can to establish manufacturing methods that
"deskill" the manufacturing operation.

However, there has been an important exception to this scenario in our
own experience. Many years ago, when we started to manufacture in
Hong Kong, we found that there was an abundance of skilled labor and

skilled management which had emigrated from Shanghai during the 1940s. The large reservoir of skilled personnel permitted Hong Kong apparel and textile manufacturers to compete on the world market with labor-intensive rather than with capital-intensive operations. However, this is a very special case of a developing country having the personnel infrastructure at the very start of its development of manufacturing capability.

Today, even Hong Kong has turned to the utilization of the latest capital equipment in order to overcome the major advance in labor costs experienced in that country during the past decade. Most apparel factories in Hong Kong today are no more labor intensive than their counterparts here in the United States.

Our experience in Jamaica, on the other hand, indicates that after seventeen years of manufacturing in that country, we still have not developed a level of labor productivity equivalent to that of the United States. Despite the big wage gap of approximately £2.00 per hour, compared to the United States, our factories in Jamaica must employ the latest technology in order to operate competitively for the export market. There, the problem involves the great difficulty of developing a technical infrastructure that could effectively utilize a more labor-intensive mode of manufacture. In Jamaica, the appropriate technology is also the most advanced state of the art.

When we look at our company's licensees in the LDCs who manufacture for their own domestic market, we find a different set of circumstances. In every case, the domestic markets in these LDCs are thoroughly protected from import competition. Therefore, the appropriate technology in these countries is to employ more labor-intensive, less capital-intensive manufacturing processes. The decision as to the type of technology to employ and the type of products to manufacture in each of these cases is an economic, not a political decision. Clearly the decision is not thrust on these licensees by our firm, which "owns" the needed technologies. Given the state of the protected economies in which these firms find themselves, and given the availability in these countries of low-cost labor, it is clearly to these firms' economic advantage to use a labor-intensive technology. This choice would not be to their economic advantage if these licensees were attempting to develop an export industry.

I conclude, based upon our company's experiences and upon the experiences reported by the many firms participating in the Chamber of Commerce Task Force on the Transfer of Technology, that we must not permit bureaucrats, at home or abroad, to set up fixed guidelines specifying appropriate technologies, appropriate products or appropriate prices for the transfer of technology. Such a rigid system, by ignoring the give and take of the marketplace, would serve only to create disincentives to the free flow of technology from country to country. Once these incentives have been removed, the flow of technology—appropriate or otherwise—would cease, mutually denying the benefits of such transfers to both the donor and the donee.

# 7. ECONOMIC DEPENDENCE AND ENTREPRENEURIAL OPPORTUNITIES IN THE HOST COUNTRY—MNC RELATIONSHIP*

James Riedel, JOHNS HOPKINS UNIVERSITY

## INTRODUCTION

One of the striking manifestations of the rise of MNC investment in the last two decades has been the growing concern over the issue of economic dependency. The issue of economic dependence is not a new one, nor does it pertain exclusively to the phenomenon of international investment. A condition of dependence can be said to exist whenever the development and expansion of one economy is conditioned by that of another (Dos Santos, 1970). This is a condition that can result as well from reliance on international trade in goods and services as from the acquisi-

Research in International Business and Finance, Vol. 1, pp. 235–268.

tion by foreigners of domestic resources of production. All countries that participate in the international economy are "dependent" to some extent, although, like the fabled equals, some are bound to be more dependent than others.

That a system of balanced interdependence does not exist can be attributed to the skewed distribution of the world's resources among nation states. Countries poor in resources and small in size rely on trade to a greater extent than larger, more endowed countries; they are, in other words, more dependent. Dependence is the price a country pays for the benefits of participating in the international division of labor. Whether or not the price is justified can only be assessed according to the circumstances and objectives of a given country. Other things being equal, one might expect the gains from participation—or the opportunity cost of autarchy—to be greatest for those countries at the unfavorable end of the world's resource distribution. Other things, however, are rarely equal; and while this view of dependency is at extreme odds with the Marxist view that dependence results from the material needs of international monopoly capitalism, it does not imply that many Marxist concerns, including the possibility of exploitation, are not valid. No doubt in some instances the cost of dependence are excessive and unjustifiable, and demand some form of international intervention in lieu of which a more autarchic position might be preferred (Cohen, 1973). The issue of relative benefits and costs of pariticipation in the international economy, either through trade or investment, is not, however, the concern of the present paper.[1]

The principal question addressed in this paper is whether multinational corporate investment is merely a symptom of dependence, or if it is a cause. It has been suggested that countries that are poorly endowed with production resources are prone to dependency as a result of reliance on international trade and investment. It should follow that the forces that promote economic growth and development at the same time reduce dependence, at least up to the point at which nonreproducible resource constraints become binding. A distribution of resources that maximizes growth in the early stages of development might well entail a relatively heavy reliance on trade or foreign capital if, for example, economies of scale are important. It is conceivable, therefore, that a dependent position at one stage of development might be a necessary condition for a more self-reliant position at another. In order to draw this conclusion, however, it is necessary to assume that reliance on trade or foreign capital does not independently affect domestic savings or investment behavior in a way that might mitigate the growth-dependency relationship. With regard to foreign capital, this assumption has come under considerable attack in recent years. The evidence emerging in empirical studies suggests that although foreign capital may have positive growth effects, it tends at the same time to perpetuate and reinforce dependence as a result of an unfavorable behavioral relationship *vis-à-vis* domestic savings. Foreign direct investment, it is alleged, usurps scarce investment opportunities and as a result causes governments as well as the public to consume more and save less than they otherwise would.

The third section of this paper summarizes and evaluates this literature to determine how strongly empirical evidence supports this contention. In addition to discussing some notable methodological shortcomings, it is argued that recent empirical studies are not adequately formulated to provide much insight into the impact of multinational corporate investment on either domestic savings or investment behavior. An attempt is made in the fourth section to provide a framework that allows one to evaluate the impact of foreign direct investment on domestic entrepreneurial opportunities. Some hypotheses concerning the relative impact of different types of foreign investment are developed in the following section. Problems concerning the empirical investigation of the relationship between foreign direct investment and domestic entrepreneurial opportunity are briefly discussed in the final section. The main thesis of this paper is that the relationship between foreign direct investment and domestic investment opportunities defies generalization, and can be reliably established only by considering prevailing circumstances of host countries and the nature of different types and forms of foreign investment.

# FOREIGN CAPITAL, DOMESTIC SAVINGS AND ECONOMIC DEPENDENCE

Ever since Rostow (1956) coined it, the term "self-sustained growth" has been bandied about by laymen and economists alike. In its most common form it is taken to mean a state of affairs in which a country can achieve continued growth by relying on domestic savings to finance a desired level of investment. Since savings are functionally related to the level of income, whatever causes income to increase might likewise be thought to contribute toward the achievement of self-reliance. The inflow of foreign capital constitutes a net addition to resources available for investment, and hence future expansion of income and increased savings. The notion that foreign capital might instead contribute toward the perpetuation of dependence stems from empirical evidence that the immediate, direct effect of foreign capital on domestic savings is negative. Foreign capital, it is alleged, induces public and private sectors to save less and consume more domestic income. Which is the predominant influence, the indirect positive effect via increased income or the direct negative effect deriving from a negative behavioral relationship? This is an issue that has been argued back and forth in the literature with a great deal of confusion. Only in a very recent paper (Bhagwati and Grinols, 1976) has the relationship between the two opposing influences been precisely spelled out. Before going on to evaluate the empirical basis of the claim of a negative behavioral relationship between domestic savings and foreign capital, it is worthwhile to see how such a relationship, assuming it does exist, might affect a country's ratio of domestic savings to income.

Bhagwati and Grinols (1976) formulate the problem in terms of a simple Harrod-Domar model, modified to allow domestic savings to be functionally related to foreign capital inflow and the level of exports.[2] The effect of an assumed behavioral relationship between foreign capital and domestic savings on the level of income, the level of savings, and the savings-income ratio is expressed in the following three equations that derive from a standard Harrod-Domar model (Bhagwati and Grinols, 1976, pp. 6–7):

$$Y_T^F = Y_T + \frac{F(1 + c)}{b}\left[(1 + a\,b)^T - 1\right] \tag{1}$$

$$S_T^F = S_T + F(1 + c)\left[(1 + a\,b)^T - 1\right] + c\,F \tag{2}$$

$$\frac{S_T^F}{Y_T^F} = \frac{S_T}{Y_T} + \frac{c^F}{Y_T^F} - (a + cF + dE)\left[\frac{1}{Y_T} - \frac{1}{T_T^F}\right] \tag{3}$$

where $Y_T^F$ and $S_T^F$ are income and savings levels in period $T$ after a constant level of capital inflow, $F$, over $T$ periods; $Y_T$ and $S_T$ are the levels of income and savings that would prevail in the period had there been no capital inflow; $E$ is the level of exports (determined exogenously); $a$ is the output capital ratio and $a$, $b$, $c$, and $d$ are parameters of the *domestic* savings function,

$$S = a + b\,Y + c\,F + d\,E \tag{4}$$

Assuming $-1 < c < 0$, $d > 0$ and alternatively, $b \gtrless S/Y$, Bhagwati and Grinols derive the following conclusions from the above equations:

— From (1): it follows that $Y_T^F$ will always be greater than $Y_T$.
— From (2): one sees that $S_T^F < S_T$ for small $T$ so long as $-1 < c < 0$, although there is some point in time at which $S_T^F > S_T$.
— The relationship between the (domestic) savings ratio with and

without capital (equation 3) depends on whether $b$ (the marginal propensity to save is $\gtreqless S/Y$ (the average propensity to save). If $b < S/Y$, $S_T^F/Y_T^F < S_T/Y_T$ forever. However, if $b > S/Y$, it is possible, though not inevitable, that $S_T^F/Y_T^F$ can eventually overtake $S_T/Y_T$. The sufficient condition, Bhagwati and Grinols show, depends on the size of the export sector relative to the economy.

The model clearly demonstrates that " . . . whether capital inflow creates dependence [assuming $-1 < c < 0$] will depend on the assumed parameters of the model as well as the targeted level of savings rate and the time by which it must be achieved" (Bhagwati and Grinols, 1976, p. 2). It is also evident from the model that foreign capital will always lead to declining dependence (so defined) so long as $c \geq 0$ and $b > S/Y$. To test the relevance of the dependency hypothesis, Bhagwati and Grinols simulated the model for various countries, using previously estimated values of the parameters of the savings function, and noting that "the basic finding $c < 0$ remains, to date, unrefuted." While this observation is certainly true, a survey of the empirical literature suggests that it is of little consolation.

## EMPIRICAL EVIDENCE ON THE FOREIGN CAPITAL– DOMESTIC SAVINGS RELATIONSHIP

Empirical analysis of the effect of foreign capital on domestic savings has emerged only in the last ten years. Prior to that time, the relationship was established by assumption, the predominant assumption being that each dollar of (net) foreign capital inflow results in one dollar of investment and imports, domestic consumption and savings remaining unaffected (*e.g.*, Rosenstein-Rodan, 1961; Chenery and Strout, 1966). Since there is little theoretical justification for this assumption, which in fact traces back to the classics of Ricardo and Mill, the only very recent empirical work on the issue would seem long overdue.[3]

A summary of empirical studies of the foreign capital-domestic savings relationship in LDCs is presented in Table 7.1.[4] On the face of the evidence it would appear that the "classical" assumption is quite unjustified. The unanimous conclusion of empirical analysis is that a negative relationship exists between foreign capital inflow and domestic savings, implying that foreign resources are used only in part to augment investment and in part to finance additional consumption. However, there is little agreement among the various studies as to how the shares are divided between competing uses. These results provided support for several authors' negative impressions of the benefits from foreign capital in LDCs and have led in some instances to somewhat premature conclusions. For example, Griffin, citing the results presented in 1970, states " . . . if our hypothesis that capital imports lead to lower domestic savings is correct, a country that relies upon foreign assistance to achieve growth may become permanently dependent and incapable of self-sustained growth" (Griffin, 1969, p. 122). Weisskopf (1972, p. 37) contends that his results "support the hypothesis that the impact of foreign capital inflow on ex ante domestic savings in underdeveloped countries is significantly negative." As Bhagwati and Grinols' model makes clear, both of these conclusions require qualification. Weisskopf's contention that foreign capital lowers the level of domestic savings is valid, even if $-1 < c < 0$ only in the "short" run. Griffin's claim that foreign capital lowers the domestic savings ratio is also not necessarily implied by the results that $-1 < c < 0$, but rests on the value of other parameters in the economy. However, the question being addressed at this point is not whether valid conclusions have been drawn from the empirical results presented in Table 7.1, but rather whether the results themselves are reliable indicators of the behavioral relationship between foreign capital and savings.

An assumption that has been in good standing for more than 200 years cannot be expected to fall without protest, and indeed the empirical results summarized in Table 7.1 have elicited a good deal of criticism. Criticism has been leveled on grounds of both method and concept, though in both areas the main source of trouble can be traced to the problem of aggregation. The dependent variable analyzed has without exception been either domestic savings ($S$) or gross domestic investment ($I$), which given the definition of the former

$$S = I + X - M$$
$$S = I - F$$

is the same as total (foreign and domestic) savings.[5] This definition follows the standard practice of deriving domestic savings as a residual by deducting from gross capital formation ($I$) the current account deficit ($X - M = -F$). However, most empirical studies have departed from the accepted accounting practice by deducting the deficit on trade account from gross capital formation, lumping net unrequited transfers together with the balance on capital account.

Attempting to assess the behavioral relationship between domestic savings and foreign capital inflow, so defined, involves several notable conceptual problems. First, consider the practice of excluding net unilateral transfers from national income and domestic savings. Principally this has been done for reasons of convenience, since it allows one to derive $F$ from trade statistics without recourse to balance-of-payments data, which prior to 1960 were generally not uniformally available for LDCs. Some conceptual justification for this practice might nevertheless be made on the grounds that resources made available by transfer payments (public or private) originate abroad after all, and entail, therefore, no domestic savings initiative. This reasoning, however, defies the logic of national income accounting, which distinghishes transfer payments from capital account transactions in that the latter entail an obligation of repayment whereas the former do not. It makes some sense to deduct the capital account balance from gross investment in deriving domestic savings, because, although capital inflow constitutes an addition to resources currently available for consumption and investment, it gives rise to claims of an equal amount on future savings for servicing the external debt. No such claim is involved in transfer payments. Therefore, although such resources originate abroad, since they involve no claim on future (or past) savings, they should be treated as essentially a domestic resource, particularly if the object of analysis is to assess the issue of dependency.[6]

A further conceptual limitation is involved at the level of aggregation employed in most of the studies. When $F$ is used as an explanatory variable of $S$, only net capital inflows are apparent, which are offset by an equal and opposite transaction in the current account, thereby giving rise to a net claim on *future* savings. Ignored at this level of aggregation is a multitude of capital transactions that may be offset by changes in claims on *past* savings. Analogously, a deficit on current account may also not be financed out of future savings (*i.e.*, direct foreign investment or governmental borrowing), but rather out of past savings by liquidating foreign assets or drawing down exchange reserves. Of course, no conceptual problem would be involved in the process of netting were one able to assume that all forms of "foreign capital" exhibit the same behavioral relationship to domestic savings. Since such an assumption is most unreasonable, and indeed in surveying the literature no such assumption is ever made explicitly (although at this level of aggregation the assumption is implicit), the results summarized in Table 7.1 thus defy the drawing of meaningful policy conclusions. Although several studies have analyzed somewhat disaggregated capital flows (Areskoug; Papenek; Gupta), none have delineated "direct foreign investment," which is, of course, the variable most relevant in an examination of the impact of MNCs.

One of the most fundamental points of criticism raised in the literature is the problem of confusing correlation with causality (*e.g.*, Kennedy and Thirlwall, 1971; Papanek, 1972, raise this point). Are savings low because foreign capital inflows are high—or vice versa? The necessary assumption in order to interpret the regression results directly is the "foreign capital" inflows are exogenous. Weisskopf, whose results are considered

*Table 7.1* Summary of Major Findings of Empirical Studies of the Effect of Foreign Capital on Domestic Savings in LDCs

| Author | Cross country (C) or Time series (T) | Number of observations | Estimated equation and results with respect to the effect of foreign capital |
|---|---|---|---|
| 1. Rahman (1968) | C | 31 | $S/Y = a - .25^* F/Y$ |
| 2. Griffin (1970) | T | 14 (Colombia) | $S/Y = a - .84^* F/Y$ |
| 3. Griffin & Enos (1970) | C | 32 | $S/Y = a - .73^* F/Y$ |
|  | C | 12 | $S/Y = a - 1.14^* F/Y$ |
| 4. Chenery & Eckstein (1970) | T | 16 LDCs, 13–14 obs. | $\bar{S} = a + b\,\bar{Y} + d\,\bar{E}/Y + \left(\begin{matrix}-1.15\\ \text{to}\\ +.64\end{matrix}\right)^{v} \bar{F}$ |
| 5. Weisskopf (1972) | T,C pooled | 17 LDCs, 10–12 obs. | $\bar{S} = a + b\,\bar{Y} + d\,\bar{E} - .23^* \bar{F}$ |
| 6. Papanek (1973) | C | 85 | $S = a + bE_p + dE_o - 1.00^* A - .65^* P - .38\,R$<br>$S = a + bE_p + dE_o + e\log Y/N + f\log N - .64^* F$<br>$S = a + b\log Y/N + d\log N - .73^* F$ |
| 7. Areskoug (1969) | T | 21 LDCs, 12–15 obs. | $I = a + bY + \left(\begin{matrix}-.71\\ \text{to}\\ +4.29\end{matrix}\right)^{w} B' + \left(\begin{matrix}-.32\\ \text{to}\\ +1.70\end{matrix}\right)^{v} F'$ |
| 8. Areskoug (1976) | T | 21 LDCs, Appr. 21 obs. | $I = a + bY + \left(\begin{matrix}-.39\\ \text{to}\\ +1.16\end{matrix}\right)^{v} B'' + \left(\begin{matrix}-3.03\\ \text{to}\\ +3.31\end{matrix}\right)^{z} F''$ |
| 9. Gupta (1975) | C | 40 | $S/Y = a + bY/N + dG - 1.19\,F$<br>$S/Y = a + bY/N + dG + eD - .78A - 1.47P - 1.05R$ |

10. Chenery and Syrquin (1975)   T,C pooled

$S = a + b\,Y + d\,(\ln Y)^2 + e\,T - .82\,F$
$S = a + b\,Y + d\,(\ln Y)^2 - .65\,F$   1432
$I = a + b\,Y + d\,(\ln Y)^2 + e\,T + .16\,F$
$I = a + b\,Y + d\,(\ln Y)^2 + .34\,F$
$S = a + b\,Y + d\,(\ln Y)^2 + e\,T - .56\,F$   820
$I = a + b\,Y + d\,(\ln Y)^2 + e\,T + .45\,F$

Definition of Variables:

$S$  : Domestic savings
$Y$  : GNP
$F$  : Net capital inflow, *i.e.* current account deficit
$E$  : Total exports
$E_p$  : Primary exports
$E_o$  : Non-primary exports
$A$  : Net transfers received by government plus official long-term borrowing
$P$  : Foreign private investment including private long-term borrowing and private direct investment
$R$  : Other foreign inflows including net private transfers, net short-term borrowing, other capital and errors and omissions
$N$  : Population
$B'$  : Net government external borrowing
$F'$  : Net private capital outflow plus change in reserves less net transfer payments
$B''$  : Net official borrowing plus net transfer receipts less change in official reserves
$F''$  : Total net capital inflow into the private non-monetary sector
$G$  : Growth in real GNP
$D$  : Dependency rate defined as percentage of population between 0–14 years of age
(*NB* : A bar over variable indicates measurement in constant prices)

Notes:  *  indicates statistical significance

v. Negative coefficients in 11 of 16 cases.

w. 6 of 21 were negative some of which were significantly different from zero, but two of which were significantly different from +1. 6 of 21 were positive, but significantly less than +1.

x. 6 of 21 all positive were significantly different from zero, 4 of which were at the same time significantly less than +1.

y. 4 of 21 all positive were significantly different from zero, 3 of which were at the same time significantly less than +1. No significant negative coefficients were found.

z. 2 of 21 were found to be negative and significantly different from zero, 1 was found to be significantly greater than +1 and 4 were found to be significantly less than +1.

243

"the most comprehensive and sophisticated ones available to date" (Bhagwati and Grinols, 1975, p. 88), states that "there is good reason to believe that foreign aid and private investment are not exogenously related to any variables in the model" (*i.e.*, investment, income, exports, imports). The "good reason," he maintains, rests on Griffin and Enos' (1970, p. 315) claim that a cursory examination of the motives for "aid" shows that "how much a country lends another will not be determined by its need. . . , but by the benefit it yields (the donor)." However, as "aid" in the majority of the studies (including Weisskopf's and Griffin's) is measured by the deficit on trade account, such a cynical assessment of development assistance, however valid, seems quite out of place. As Papanek (1972) points out, there are a host of exogenous factors such as war, political upheaval, abrupt shifts in terms of trade and weather that can give rise to trade deficits, simultaneously causing foreign resource inflows to increase and domestic savings to fall. Without isolating such factors, one must conclude, as do Kennedy and Thirlwall (1971, p. 136), that the negative correlation between $S/Y$ and $F/Y$ is "as much a vindication of the present pattern of aid flow as a condemnation of capital imports because they are 'consumed.'"[7]

The empirical studies summarized here have made little effort to develop the hypotheses that underly the presumed negative relationship between foreign capital and domestic savings. Griffin (1971, p. 230) has been most explicit, offering two basic premises, the first of which is implied in the studies of Weisskopf and Rahman:

—Government responds to capital inflow by either reducing taxes or making less effort to collect taxes, thus leading to declining public savings.

—Foreign capital lowers private domestic savings, because if it participates with local entrepreneurs " . . . it will supply at least some capital that indigenous entrepreneurs would have saved themselves (and thereby) . . . reduce the incentive of local investors to save." Alternatively, if foreign capital establishes wholly owned enterprises they may "pre-empt the most profitable investment opportunities and the strong direct competition faced by local investors may tend to reduce the supply of indigneous entrepreneurship."

Both hypotheses assume that investment opportunities are given (or fixed by government-planned targets) and that they would be fully exploited by domestic investors in the absence of foreign capital inflow. This implies that at least some of the resources that complement capital would be fully utilized (in the absence of foreign capital) and that the elasticity of their supply or substitutability, at least in the short run, is zero. The basic primary factors that complement capital are labor, foreign exchange, and managerial ability. The first we know too well is anything but fully utilized in most LDCs. The second and third are precisely those factors that are often believed to accompany foreign investment. Thus, it would seem equally as plausible to hypothesize *a priori* a positive relationship between savings and foreign capital as a negative one. Furthermore, one should perhaps question the appropriateness of Griffin's first premise on the grounds that it is probably as much an expression of bad policy as of an unfortunate behavioral relationship associated with foreign capital. Accepting this argument, the issue of dependence would seem to hinge principally on the extent to which foreign investment supplants or crowds out domestic private investment. Previous empirical studies provide little conclusive evidence on this question one way or another, focusing as they have on domestic savings and given the definition of foreign capital inflow employed. It would seem far more fruitful to focus analysis on the relationship between domestic and foreign private investment rather than to look at domestic savings with all its attendant problems of concept and measurement. In any case, as Houthakker (1965) argues, savings in LDCs are very much dependent on the availability of investment opportunities.

## FOREIGN DIRECT INVESTMENT AND DOMESTIC ENTREPRENEURIAL OPPORTUNITIES

The question of whether direct foreign investment (DFI) supplements or supplants domestic investment is crucial not only to the dependency issue, but also to any broader evaluation of benefits and costs associated with DFI. In order to assess the impact of DFI, one must establish a standard of comparison based on what would or should occur in the absence of DFI. A decision on the substitutability between DFI and domestic investment establishes the basis for such calculations. Previous benefit-cost studies of DFI have relied very little, if at all, on empirical estimates of the relationship in making such a decision. They have instead set the standard for comparison by assumption, testing the sensitivity of benefit-cost calculations under alternative situations (e.g., Hufbauer and Adler, 1968; Lall, 1975). Following this approach, most benefit-cost studies have been concerned very little with the mechanisms by which DFI might affect domestic investment opportunities. It is clear, however, that without considering such mechanisms it is all but impossible to establish which among alternative assumptions is likely to be most "reasonable." Moreover, empirical relationships between direct foreign investment and domestic investment, no matter how statistically sophisticated, are of little value without a theory to explain them—or, as Hawkins (undated) has put it, "a fact without a theory is no fact at all."

It has been suggested that "the analysis of direct investment as a response to foreign opportunities in imperfect markets . . . can be a powerful tool for analyzing the question of 'pre-emption,' or of foreign industrial domination" (Moran, 1976, p.8). The argument is that the basic nature of MNCs, the fact that they invariably possess some form of monopoly asset (technological or managerial know-how, trademarks, patents, or some other intangible asset) explains how and why foreign investors are able to crowd out or preempt local investment opportunities. It is, of course, these traits of MNCs that in fact make foreign investment possible, since without some form of competitive edge the foreign firm would otherwise be at a disadvantage by the mere fact of its foreignness. That MNCs tend to be larger, more established firms in the most dynamic industries of the home country implies that they are likely to be the strongest competitors local entrepreneurs may face. However, it should be recognized that the competitive presence of the MNC may not be contingent upon its location of production facilities within a given country, since local entrepreneurs may be intimidated every bit as much by competition with MNC exports. This point is qualified by Thomas Horst's finding that "when American firms invest abroad, they not only produce goods which hypothetically might be produced in the United States, but they also undertake a wide variety of non-manufacturing activities to expand the foreign marketing for their products" (Horst, 1976, p. 150). Their competitive presence, according to Horst, is thus enhanced by the location of production facilities within the boundaries of a given country. This qualification notwithstanding, however, the oligopolistic nature of MNCs, including their technological advantage, does not explain how their presence *per se* in a foreign country might lead to the crowding out or preemption of local investments.

A more appropriate approach is to examine the impact of foreign competition throughout the economy: in factor markets, markets for intermediate goods and raw materials, foreign exchange markets, as well as in those markets in which local and foreign firms compete for sales. In fact, the impact of foreign firms in input markets might be the most relevant consideration concerning the question of preemption, since only in these markets (as opposed to the markets in which MNCs sell) is the competitive presence of the MNC directly contingent on its location of production facilities within the local economy. Whether or not DFI supplants, supplements, or possible even stimulates local investment opportunities can only be deduced by summing the net effect of foreign competition on local investment plans throughout the economy.

A firm's investment plans are generally formultated in terms of expected profitability of investment, which in turn is determined by expectations of future costs, prices, and sales volume. An investment may be considered profitable whenever its yield, defined as the rate of discount that makes the sum of expected future net revenues ($R$) equal to the value of the investment, exceeds the rate of return or yield on the next best alternative (which may include consumption). Net revenue ($R$) can be expressed as

$$R = S \cdot p_s + E \cdot p_e \cdot r - (L \cdot p_l + K \cdot p_k + M \cdot p_m + N \cdot p_n \cdot r)$$

where $S$, $E$, $L$, $K$, $M$, and $N$ are local sales, exports, labor, capital, domestic raw materials/intermediates and imported inputs, respectively, $p$'s refer to prices, and $r$ is the exchange rate.

Direct foreign investment by expanding supply in the domestic market, altering the balance of payments, and making additional demands on primary and intermediate inputs can be expected to influence each price element of the revenue function. The magnitude of the influence, however, will depend on the type of the foreign investment and the prevailing circumstances within the host country. The impact of a given DFI on domestic prices ($p$'s) will depend, other things being equal, on the size of the market at which the investment is aimed, and the price elasticity and cross-price elasticity *vis-à-vis* all substitute and complementary goods. The impact on domestic costs of production ($p_l$, $p_k$, and $p_m$) will hinge on the investment's technological factor requirements, the relative scarcity of factors of production, the elasticity of factor supply, and the technological limitations for factor substitutability. Of course, holding those factors constant, the impact on domestic production costs will depend crucially on how extensively foreign investors rely on local sources of scarce factors of production, principally capital, skills, and managerial talent. A given DFI might be assumed to have a negligible effect on world prices ($p_l$ and $p_m$), although the initial inflow of capital as well as subsequent demand for imported inputs, export sales, and the repatriation of earnings will influence either the exchange rate ($r$) or, in the case of fixed rates, the general price level of the economy.

Analyzing the impact of DFI in this framework, it becomes apparent that general propositions concerning the issue of preemption are all but impossible to establish *a priori*. Instead, the net effect of a given DFI on local investment opportunities will depend on the interaction of a range of variables concerning circumstances within the host country and the motivation/type of foreign investment (*e.g.*, import-substituting vs. export-oriented).

John Dunning (1973, p. 296) has further suggested that the form of the foreign investment is a crucial factor: "The implications of an investment to finance a take-over are different from those of the setting up of a 'green field' venture; an investment to supply a completely new product will have a different effect than one to replace an existing product." Takeovers would not be expected to influence cost and revenue parameters to the same extent that new investments might, since they constitute no net increase in demand for inputs or supply of output. By the same token, takeovers make no direct contribution to capital formation, although they will indirectly contribute to capital formation if domestic entrepreneurs eventually reinvest the capital imported to finance the take-over. Ultimately take-over investments could have as great or greater impact on local investment plans as "green field" investments, depending on the extent to which local entrepreneurs reinvest and the way in which they reinvest. Thus, although Dunning is undoubtedly correct in pointing out that different forms of investment will entail different implications for domestic capital formation, it is difficult to determine, *a priori,* what the differences might be.

## HYPOTHESES CONCERNING THE DFI-DOMESTIC INVESTMENT RELATIONSHIP UNDER DIFFERING CIRCUMSTANCES

The conclusion that emerges from this discussion is that hypotheses concerning the DFI-domestic investment relationship should be formulated on a country-by-country, case-by-case basis. Empirical studies of the relationship that fail to account for even the broadest divergencies in country situations and investment types are bound to be of little practical value. For even if one makes broad generalizations about the economic circumstances of country groups (developed countries vs. less developed countries) and investment types (import-substituting vs. export-oriented), different implications regarding the relationship between foreign and local investment become apparent.

One of the fundamental differences between developed and less-developed countries in terms of economic policy is that, whereas the former are primarily concerned with managing demand, the latter's major problem is mobilizing supply. It should follow, therefore, that the influence of DFI on domestic investment prospects in developed countries is more likely to be determined by demand variables, while in LDCs it's more likely to be influenced by supply variables. The first half of this hypothesis is supported by Caves and Reuber's (1971) study of United States investment in Canada, which found that during periods of strong aggregate demand DFI had in fact a very *positive* impact on domestic investment in Canada, while in periods of decline the impact of a given amount of DFI on capital formation was much weaker. Caves and Reuber's finding that "a dollar's worth of direct investment can be associated with about two dollars of capital formation'' (p. 194) during periods of strong aggregate demand suggests that, in at least this one developed economy (Canada), input supply is sufficiently elastic to accommodate expanding foreign investment without seriously deteriorating the profitability of domestic investment opportunities.

In the less developed countries, the potential negative impact of DFI on domestic investment prospects may result less from the foreigner's absorption of limited market opportunities than from their claim on scarce resources of production, the supply of which may be very inelastic. The obvious exception to this proposition would seem to be import-substituting (i.e., host-country, market-oriented) foreign investment in LDCs, which appears as a clear case of foreigners "robbing" market opportunities created specifically by governmental policy for local investors. However, the main thrust of the heavy criticism that has been leveled against import-substituting DFI in LDCs has focused not on their domination of local markets, but on their inefficient use of the scarcest factors of production. Once foreign investors have managed to circumvent trade barriers erected with the intention of cultivating domestic entrepreneurship, they have found little motivation to adapt production techniques to local conditions. As theory and evidence suggest, import-substituting DFI tends to concentrate in those industries in which the MNC's competitive position is secured by the possession of some form of monopoly asset. As a result of this key characteristic of import-substituting DFI, foreign firms have been able to transplant production techniques from home, which are typically capital- and skill-intensive, and given the lack of complementary industries in the LDCs, have made strong demands on foreign exchange in order to acquire needed intermediate inputs from abroad. There is little question that import-substituting DFI, in making relatively heavy demands on the scarcest factors of production in LDCs, has acted to frustrate local investment by driving up production costs. That they may have at the same time usurped market opportunities created by government policy (tariffs and quotas) is somewhat academic, since evidence suggests that opportunities so created might better have been avoided altogether (Little, Scott, and Scitovsky, 1971).

Export-oriented DFI in LDCs, which has gained momentum in the last decade, is by nature very different from the import-substituting variety. This is hardly surprising, since the latter is motivated by barriers to trade, while export-oriented DFI in motivated by specific considerations of comparative advantage. Since wage costs have been identified as the major determinant of export-oriented DFI (Helleiner, 1973; Riedel, 1975a), one would expect, and evidence bears out, that export-oriented DFI tends to concentrate in relatively labor-intensive branches of industry and uses techniques of production that appear no more capital-intensive than those employed by local counterparts.[8] Although export-oriented DFI tends to rely heavily on imported inputs (Reuber, 1973; Riedel, 1975), it nevertheless makes a net contribution to foreign exchange and should as a result ease investment constraints imposed by the availability of foreign exchange. The fact that export-oriented DFI does not compete directly with local firms in domestic markets and that it tends to employ technology consistent with prevailing factor endowment situations in LDCs suggests that it should have somewhat less of a negative influence on revenue and cost parameters faced by local entrepreneurs. On the other hand, the fact that this form of investment tends to be relatively "enclavish" implies that it might have less positive external influence in generating investment via backward or forward linkages as compared to the import-substituting variety.

The approach to analyzing the DFI-domestic investment relationship suggested here recognizes the need to account for indirect as well as direct influences. That the total impact of foreign investment must take into account forward and backward linkages associated with investment is not an uncommon notion, although it has yet to be formally incorporated into an empirical analysis of the relationship. It is not, however, a universally shared notion. In suggesting guidelines for appraising foreign investment, Lall (1975, p. 75) eschews Hirschman's externalities, arguing:

> Hirschman's backward and forward linkages are really concerned with the overall inducement to invest in the economy, and not with the optimum allocation of given resources, . . . The inducement to invest aspects would be relevant if aggregate investment in the economy were not limited by the availability of savings.

Although Lall's contention that the availability of capital (i.e., savings) constitutes the single constraint to investment is somewhat naive and outdated, his general argument that the problem of LDCs is one of generating supply, and not demand, is consistent with the argument developed here. Of course, Hirschman emphasized linkages not only because they generate demand, but also, and perhaps more importantly, because they might induce latent entrepreneurs to come forward to take advantage of investment opportunities made obvious by the creation of bottlenecks. Thus, whereas Lall emphasizes capital, Hirschman emphasizes decision-making ability as the key constraint on investment. In assessing the impact of DFI on suply constraints, a more general approach is suggested here. Moreover, it should be recognized that demonstration effects emanating from DFI may also constitute an effective inducement to local investment in LDCs.

To summarize, DFI affects domestic investment opportunities through its impact on casts and prices. In developed countries, the influence is likely to be felt primarily on the demand side as factor supplies are generally relatively elastic. In developed countries, the impact of DFI is determined primarily by the size of the market at which the investment is aimed, the state of aggregate demand, and the extent of linkages or indirect demand generated in other sectors. In LDCs, where factor supplies are much less responsive to price incentives, the impact of DFI on domestic investment opportunities is most likely derived from the former's absorption of scarce resources. In this regard, the brief summary of various types of DFI suggests that the export-oriented variety is likely to have less of a negative effect and may even provide a positive stimulant to domestic investment by lowering the cost of foreign exchange and providing demonstration effects for local investors. Import-substituting investment, by comparison, is likely to absorb relatively more scarce resources, driving up production costs and thereby potentially frustrating domestic investment plans. It is to be reemphasized, however, that these generalizations are derived from very naive assumptions about the nature of broad country groups and investment types. That discussions of the relationship between foreign and domestic investment have rarely attempted to distinguish the characteristics of host countries, and the nature of foreign investments, even at this very high level of generalization, reveals perhaps most clearly the very primitive stage of the discussion on this important issue.

## EMPIRICAL INVESTIGATION OF THE IMPACT OF DFI ON DOMESTIC INVESTMENT OPPORTUNITIES

Most attempts to verify empirically the hypothesis that foreign capital creates economic dependence by supplanting domestic investment have focused on the relationship between domestic savings and foreign capital inflow, defined as the balance of payments current account deficit. Because these studies generally fail to differentiate between foreign capital obtained through transfer payments, portfolio investment, or direct foreign investment, it was argued above that they provide little if any insight in the relationship between MNC investment and domestic investment opportunities. However, if one considers the mechanisms by which foreign investment affects local investment opportunity, it becomes apparent that balance of payments data, no matter how disaggregated, are unlikely to be of any significant value in analyzing the issue. In order to evaluate the full impact on the cost and revenue parameters of the host country, one must have an index that reflects the total magnitude of foreign investment activity. Balance of payments data would be able to provide such an index only if MNCs relied exclusively on capital exports to finance their overseas investments. Since evidence suggests that this is not the case, the studies summarized in Table 7.1, including those that attempted to disaggregate balance of payments data (Areskoug, 1976; Papanek, 1973), are further undermined.

In order to get an idea of just how inappropriate balance of payments data are for analyzing the issue, Table 7.2 presents statistics on the sources of funds for capital expenditures of U.S. MNC foreign affiliates in 1972. As the table reveals, foreign affiliates of U.S. MNCs in developed countries relied on sources external to the firm (the affiliate) for over one-third of the total finance of capital expenditure. Of this sum, over two-thirds was provided by foreigners. In the less-developed countries, however, the reliance of U.S. MNCs on foreign (i.e., host-country) sources of finance was even greater. Sources within LDC host countries appear to have financed approximately one-third of the total value of U.S. MNC affiliate capital expenditure in 1972. Moreover, further evidence reveals that reinvested earnings constitute the greatest source of funds internal to the firm, leaving net capital flows across national boundaries to account for a relatively small share of the total amount of foreign direct investment.[9]

To my knowledge, the only published study of the relationship between foreign and domestic investment to avoid balance of payments data in favor of data on the total value of DFI is Caves and Reuber's study of U.S. DFI in Canada. The approach developed there is to first construct a

*Table 7.2*    Sources of Funds for Capital Expenditure of Majority-owned Foreign Affiliates of U.S. MNCs: 1972
(U.S. $ millions)

|  | Developed Countries | | Developing Countries | |
|---|---|---|---|---|
|  | All industries | Manufacturing | All industries | Manufacturing |
| 1. Total Sources | 9416 | 5184 | 3477 | 1073 |
| Internal | 6079 | 3963 | 1662 | 378 |
| External | 3337 | 1221 | 1815 | 695 |
| 2. External Sources | 3337 | 1221 | 1815 | 695 |
| U.S. | 1155 | 346 | 747 | 300 |
| Foreign | 2182 | 875 | 1068 | 395 |
| 3. Foreign Sources | 2182 | 875 | 1068 | 395 |
| Financial Institutions | 208 | −330 | 120 | 178 |
| Other Foreign Residents | 1974 | 1205 | 948 | 257 |

Source: Ida May Mantel, "Sources and Uses of Funds for a Sample of Majority Owned Foreign Affiliates of U.S. Companies, 1966–72," *Survey of Current Business*, 55, No. 7 (July 1975), pp. 29–82.

regression model that reliably explains domestic capital formation in the absence of DFI. DFI is then entered as an explanatory variable in the model; if it is found to make a statistically significant contribution to the explanatory power of the model, the hypothesis that DFI is strictly supplementary is rejected. If the DFI regression coefficient is found to be significantly positive (negative), the interpretation is that DFI stimulates (supplants) domestic investment.

Although this approach involves several notable econometric limitations and fails to reveal the channels through which DFI affects domestic capital formation, it does nevertheless provide a means of measuring the overall impact, particularly if one is able to incorporate lagged responses. The basic minimum requirement, however, is the availability of time series data on DFI over a sufficiently long period of time. This is a requirement that, unfortunately, is difficult if not impossible to fulfill for most developed countries, much less for developing countires. In view of the fact that the issue is essentially empirical, the collection of data on DFI and analysis of the relationship for a broad sample of countries would seem to be a research area of great priority.

# FOOTNOTES

*I am grateful to the Institut für Weltwirtschaft and the Deutsche Forschungsgemeinschaft for partial support of this research.

1. A concise discussion of some of the issues raised by the *dependentistas* concerning the distribution of gains between MNC and the host country, and the inherent political and economic distortions introduced by MNC investment is found in Moran (1976).

2. The level of exports was included as an argument in the savings function, despite the lack of any theoretical or empirical basis, in order to keep the analysis consistent with previous empirical work by Weisskopf (1972). Its inclusion does not affect the issues discussed here.

3. A concise history of the "classical" assumption can be found in Hufbauer and Adler (1968, pp. 1-7).

4. I am unaware of any comparable studies of industrialized countries other than Caves and Reuber (1970), which is discussed in the following sections.

5. In other words, both specifications yield the same result, the coefficient of $F$ when the dependent variable is $S$ equaling one minus the coefficient when the regressor is $I$ (Chenery and Syrquin, 1975).

6. Newlyn (1973, p. 808) extends this reasoning to all capital inflows, arguing that the representation of consumption out of extra-revenue sources (i.e., current account deficit, properly defined) as a dissaving is entirely justified in accounting terms (because it eventually involves a dissaving at time of repayment). It does not, however, reflect clearly the behavioral relationship between the capital inflow and the use of domestic resources (currently available). Newlyn's point is well taken if the issue is whether foreign capital results in more total savings ($-1$) than otherwise; however, when the issue of dependency is at stake, the crucial question is who finances investment, not only whether or not it is higher than otherwise.

7. Over (1975) demonstrates that if one drops the assumption that $F$ is exogenous, assuming instead that it is functionally related to the investment-income ratio, then the simultaneous estimation of the $S/Y$ function will invariably yield results that turn Griffin's conclusion on its head; a negative value of the regression coefficient estimated by ordinary-least-squares regression implies a positive value estimated in a two-stage least-squares procedure. Over's results in themselves do not inspire any more confidence than Griffin's, however, since they involve the same conceptual and data limitations.

8. Helleiner (1974, p. 25), reporting on a World Bank project, writes: "Preliminary results of a detailed study of 1400 firms in Israel, Columbia, The Philippines and Malaysia indicate that in industries in which capital-labor substitution is evident, the multinational firms used their capital more intensively than local firms so as more than to offset higher capital-in-place labor ratios." Similar evidence has been reported by B. I. Cohen (1973), R. H. Mason (1973), and J. Riedel (1975a).

9. According to U.S. Department of Commerce estimates, reinvested earnings of U.S. MNC affiliates in developed countries and LDCs in 1972 amounted to U.S. $3,692 million and U.S. $795 million, respectively; whereas net capital outflows to these two country groups in the same year amounted to only U.S. $1,989 million and U.S. $1,132 million.

# COMMENT

## JOHN H. DUNNING*

My first comment on Professor Riedel's paper is that it treats its subject matter in a very narrow way. While the author accepts the Dos Santos conception of economic dependence, he largely confines his attention to the contribution of foreign investment to national savings and capital formation in host countries—the latter which he also treats as a surrogate for entrepreneurial opportunities. Moreover, and the author acknowledges this, for most of the paper no distinction is made between the different forms of foreign investment—not between the total capital expenditure of the affiliates of MNCs in host countries and that part of it which is externally financed.

Technically, I have little quarrel with Professor Riedel's presentation, although, as will become clear as my comments proceed, I differ with him on points of interpretation and details. What I would primarily like to do is to approach the subject under discussion from a somewhat broader perspective, viewing the MNC first as a *provider* of resources to host countries and second as a *controller* of the way in which these, and complementary domestic resources, are used. But, first, a further word about the nature of economic dependence and how far it affects and is affected by the activities of MNCs.

*University of Reading, England

A country ceases to be economically independent as soon as it engages in commercial transactions outside its national boundaries. International trade in goods or factor services suggests that at least some decisions over the way in which the resources of any one participating country are used are made by institutions or individuals located in other countries, or by supranational organizations. Such involvement introduces an element of openness and dependence to national economies, and brings with it certain costs and benefits the balance of which will depend *inter alia,* first, on the extent and the form of the involvement; second, on the terms on which it takes place; and, third, on whether or not the dependence is mutual or symmetrical. Taking the dictionary definition of interdependence as 'dependence on each other,'' all nations are, of necessity, interdependent with each other, as, over time, imports and exports must necessarily balance. By contrast, particular *forms* of trade or trade with particular countries may be asymmetrical; most less developed countries (LDCs) are substantial importers of capital or technology; while many industrialized countries are largely dependent on the LDCs for some foods or raw materials. Some countries may balance their trade with each other; others may be substantial net exporters or importers of goods or services.

It is not easy to identify the boundaries between economic *dependence* and *interdependence,* and, even less, the specific effects of each. Dependence does, however, suggest an asymmetry in the economic relationship between any two countries in the sense that *(a)* if the relationship should cease, one nation—the more dependent nation—would be affected more than the other—the less dependent nation—and (b) that while the relationship persists, the more dependent nation is more controlled in its resource allocation by the less dependent nation than *vice versa.*

At a macro-level, economic dependence might be measured by such magnitudes as the proportion of GNP accounted for by foreign trade in goods and services or by the proportion of resources, e.g., capital, labor, and technology, supplied or controlled by foreign institutions. It might take the form of reliance on foreign customers, i.e., *demand-oriented* dependence, or on foreign suppliers of resources, i.e., *supply-oriented* dependence. Where a country is part of a larger regional or industrial grouping, or is party to a regional or international agreement, its economic maneuverability—at least in certain directions—may also be reduced. At a micro-level, the focus is on the role of nonresident institutions, individuals, or governments on the resource availability and usage of host countries. In the current context, the issue is the impact of MNCs, either individually or as a group, on the supply of human and nonhuman capital to the foreign countries in which they operate and the way in which indigenous resources managed by them are deployed. The extent and form of such dependence may affect not only the *level, stability,* and *growth* of output of host countries, but the structure of their resource allocation and their capacity to manage their own economic affairs. Moreover, and this is especially relevant to Professor Riedel's question as to whether the MNC is a symptom of dependence or a cause of it, the interaction between the MNC and the international economic order of which it is part, and how this, in turn, affects the economic relationships between nations, is a legitimate subject for investigation.

In line with the approach of Riedel's paper, I shall confine my attention to the effect of investment by foreign-owned firms on host countries. I shall ignore the effect of domestically based MNCs on the ability of home countries to acquire and use resources (though incidentally, as the new Brookings Institution study [Bergsten, Horst, and Moran, 1977] on U.S. investment abroad shows, this "reverse" dependence may be no less important). I choose to discuss investment by *foreign-owned* or/ *-controlled firms* (irrespective of how it is financed) rather than *foreign direct investment* (FDI) *per se,* because one of the key features of foreign direct investment is the *de jure* control it buys over resource allocation. Portfolio investment transfers resources between countries and also the right to control the use of these resources; like trade, it is an arms-length transaction between independent parties. Initially, as with any debt transaction, it creates dependence of the borrowing on the lending country; it also implies that the borrowing country has to arrange its affairs so the debt is serviced and eventually repaid.

As Professor Riedel points out, foreign borrowing may have various effects on domestic savings, investment, and entrepreneurship in the host country according to which, over time, it may become more or less economically dependent on the lending country. *Inter alia,* this will depend upon whether the foreign funds supplant or complement domestic resources, how the income eventually created is spent, the policy responses of host governments, the nature of the balance-of-payments constraints, and how these are affected by foreign borrowing. Empirically, it would seem that up to the take-off stage in development at least, foreign capital inflows are likely to increase the dependence of recipient countries (in the sense that they raise the foreign debt-GNP ratio); but that after take-off, as shown by the experience of advanced countries, the rise in GNP (and the consequent increase in domestic savings) may well be sufficient to offset any new inflows of portfolio capital.

With direct investment, the situation is very different. This is so for two reasons. First, capital supplied by MNCs is usually accompanied by other factor inputs, notably management, technology, and entrepreneurship, which effectively change the production function of the recipient country. Second, since direct investment implies no change in the ownership of the resources being transferred, the decisions on how they are used is retained by the investing enterprise. The *location* of their deployment may change; but that of their control does not—although, *de facto,* such control may sometimes be delegated to local management. This suggests, not only that the dependence generated by direct investment may be greater than when the resources transferred are bought separately and from different sources, but that the way control by the investing company is exerted may introduce an additional element of dependence—particularly when the affiliate is locked into a decision-making system over which it may have little influence. Such dependence may have both static and dynamic implications, not the least of which is that it can effect the whole structure of resource allocation in the host country.

The burden of these comments is, then, that the *form* of foreign participation by one country in another (in this case, foreign investment) may be as important in determining the type and consequences of the economic dependence generated as the *amount* of the involvement. Investment forms may be conceived as points on a continuum ranging from the supply of contractual (i.e., debt capital) through direct equity investment (accompanied to a greater or lesser degree by other resources, the allocation of which is only loosely controlled by the parent company) to a package of resources both provided and controlled by MNCs to serve their global interests. The dependence incurred by host countries from borrowing on the Eurodollar market is very different from that arising from an investment by ITT or IBM.

As Riedel points out toward the end of his paper, it is dangerous to generalize about the effects of FDI on the dependence of host countries; *inter alia,* this will vary according to the host country's industry and country characteristics (e.g., among the latter, size, stage of development, culture, and degree of sophistication in economic management spring easily to mind). Similarly the type of FDI—whether it is *import substitution* or *export generating* in intent—and the strategy of the investing company and its degree of multinationalism are relevant. As one moves along this continuum, the absolute or proportionate supply of foreign capital becomes less important as an indicator of dependency, and the other components of MNC involvement more important. Such indices as the contribution of MNCs to technology, management, skills, and the goals of host countries with respect to industrial strategy, income distribution, full employment, and so on may be better guides to the extent of MNC/host-country interaction; while a more behavioral approach, which seeks to identify particular control forms of MNCs, relates the dependency of host countries to the external decision making. Table 7.3 illustrates the kind of MNC/host-country dependence relationship by which industries or firms might be classified.

Table 7.3  Illustrative "Dependence" Host Country/MNC Relationship

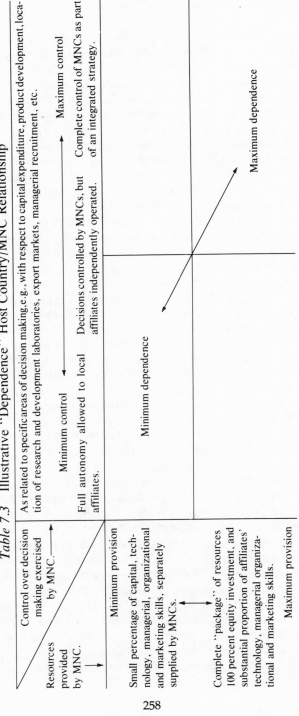

Control over decision making exercised by MNC. ——→

Resources provided by MNC. ↓

As related to specific areas of decision making, e.g., with respect to capital expenditure, product development, location of research and development laboratories, export markets, managerial recruitment, etc.

Minimum control ———————————————— Maximum control

Full autonomy allowed to local affiliates.

Decisions controlled by MNCs, but affiliates independently operated.

Complete control of MNCs as part of an integrated strategy.

Minimum provision

Small percentage of capital, technology, managerial, organizational and marketing skills, separately supplied by MNCs.

Complete "package" of resources 100 percent equity investment, and substantial proportion of affiliates' technology, managerial organizational and marketing skills.

Maximum provision

Minimum dependence

Maximum dependence

258

The problem of measuring the apparent dependence of host countries on foreign-based MNCs is difficult enough, the attribution of any dependence so identified is even more so. Professor Riedel touches on the "alternative position" several times in his paper. Put in statement and question form, the policymaker's dilemma is: "The presence of MNCs in our economy suggests that in certain sectors, areas of decision making, and time periods, our economic independence has been eroded. But if we take action to get rid of MNCs, will this necessarily reduce our dependence? Or, if we try to force the MNC to relinquish some of its control over decision making (*e.g.*, by gradual divestment of its equity interests, more local representation on the board of directors of the affiliate), or encourage it to behave in a way in which it does not want to behave (*e.g.*, to set up satellite R & D laboratories, or introduce more labor-intensive technologies) will this be at the expense of other benefits we gain from its presence?" And then, taking this argument a little further: "How far is our flexibility of action limited by the fact that the MNC is (a) more powerful or knowledgeable than we are and/or a better bargainer; and (b) that because MNCs have the ultimate option of investing elsewhere, we have to watch our step lest we "kill the goose that lays the golden egg!"

These are very large questions, some of which are touched on in other papers in this volume. In the present context, the issues are, first, whether and at what cost could the resources provided by MNCs have been better provided from indigenous sources (*i.e.*, what is the price of independence from any foriegn involvement?); second, if some form of foreign involvement is the only means, could the resources provided by equity investment have been better provided by alternative routes, *e.g.*, by licensing or other contractual agreement; and, third, if equity investment is the best form of equity involvement, what is the cost of minimizing control over the allocation of resources by the MNC? The issue is partly one of cost/benefit analysis and of evaluating the trade-offs between dependence and the other goals (where they are substitutes for each other); and partly of relating these to the efficiency of national and international policy instruments, so as to ensure that, whatever the desired state of dependence, the other benefits of direct investment are maximized. Sometimes, this may require harmonized international policy, either at a regional or industrial level or through agencies such as the OECD, U.N., etc. But here, to strengthen the hand of countries in their bargaining strategies with MNCs or to reduce the adverse effects of dependence, individual countries may be faced with the dilemma that to throw off the shackles of dependence in one direction, they have to take it up in another (Dunning & Gilman, 1976). Added to the questions "How much dependence?"; "What form of dependence?"; "In which areas is dependence most felt?"; and "What are the effects of MNC's dependence and other goals of host countries?";

one must also ask: "On whom does one wish to be dependent?" This is often a dilemma that faces countries, particularly small countries.

My comments thus far have been very general and I have raised more questions than I have given answers. Certainly I have not sought to produce an alternative to the models outlined by Professor Riedel, partly because I doubt whether any one model can capture the dependence component of the MNC/host-country relationship and partly because any model that is capable of econometric testing is almost bound to be too general to be helpful in identifying or explaining such dependence.

At the same time, I would have thought useful research could be done (and, to some extent, is being done) on the effect of MNCs on other aspects of dependence than those covered in the paper. For example, the impact of MNCs on the technological capacity of host DCs and LDCs is much under scrutiny at the moment. Arthur Lake and I are doing some work for the OECD on the role of MNCs in the pharmaceutical industry in various OECD countries. Do they inhibit or aid indigenous scientific and technological capacity? The answer suggests enormous variations between countries and companies. In a very general sense, MNCs would appear to have increased technological dependence in almost every host country outside Switzerland, the United States, and the U.K., as they account for a larger proportion of their capital formation than they did twenty years ago. Measured by their contribution to domestically located, R & D capacity (independent of form and ownership), they have probably lessened dependence on foreign-based R & D capacity; but measured by proportion of R & D accounted for by indigenous firms (except in one or two larger host countries such as the U.K.), they have increased it. Compared with what might have happened in the absence of MNCs in this sector, it is probable that, while some countries might have been more technologically independent, the size of their pharmaceutical industries would have been smaller and their efficiency less. In some of the smaller OECD countries, e.g., Ireland, it is doubtful whether there would have been any pharmaceutical industry at all (apart from simple dosage and packaging operations), since MNC activities have been set up to supply export markets.

Other studies on technology transfer by MNCs have concentrated more on types of technology transferred, or on the terms of transfer. A similar exercise could be done on the extent to which local entrepreneurship or technical and scientific skills have been advanced or retarded by MNCs. My reading of the literature suggests that MNCs have generally contributed to an increase in human capital in the countries in which they operate and, through their effects on industrial structure, have stimulated rather than inhibited local entrepreneurship. Evidence about the gradual indigenization of top management of affiliates of MNCs supports this; but this process is not always speedy enough for most countries. My substantive point, however, is that given the data, the effects of MNCs on various components of dependency can be measured both in the short and long run. In the short run, I agree with Professor Riedel that one normally expects the dependence to increase. In the long run, much depends on the character of the involvement, the policies of the host country, the size and markets of the host country and the potential capacity of the country, the nature of investment and the form of involvement one is considering. On this basis it should be possible to construct a matrix that could classify countries by degrees of dependence. Japan, for example, would work out as one of the least-dependent countries; the U.K. and West Germany and some of the larger LDCs like Mexico would come next; while those tending to be most dependent on MNCs would include countries in which their general significance is great or those in which key sectors are controlled by MNCs. One may also be able to observe countries going through phases of dependence and also look at different policies pursued by governments. In other words, research oriented toward identifying the determinants of dependence in all its various guises, the conditions under which this may be pronounced, and the effects of such dependence on national economic goals might be an alternative approach to that tackled in his paper.

One final point: Dependence on the MNC implies that the MNC possesses some kind of monopoly on resources that host countries need. But, in addition, MNCs may themselves control the extent to which such countries can obtain such resources from alternative sources. Again, this is a very different situation from the provision of resources by independent foreign institutions at arms-length prices where the decision over the use of the resources is left to indigenous firms. But if the decisions on use are taken by MNCs following a global strategy and operating in a protected economic environment, the final allocation may be very different. For example both U.S. and Swedish MNCs undertake more than 90 percent of their R & D in the home countries. This may mean that the resources controlled by such firms in host countries are such as to encourage dependence for innovations and other new knowledge on the parent company. The center-periphery debate has been well voiced by Hymer, Sunkel, and others,[1] and is now the center of the discussion on the new international economic order. Discounting the political rhetoric, I believe it deserves to be taken very seriously by scholars.

To what extent does the MNC, because of its control over the way in which resources are used, create or increase economic dependence of host on home countries? I think the evidence for this in vertically integrated industries in which MNCs are involved is fairly persuasive; it is, perhaps, less so for horizontally integrated industries (except in the most technologically intensive) and least of all for direct investment, which simply produces standardized products in different countries for sale in local markets. Note that we are hypothesizing that the effects of such dependence are always against the interests of the host countries. *Inter alia* this will rest on what these interests are and how they are ranked. Neither can any increase in dependence be automatically attributed to the multinationalism of MNCs; indeed, I suspect most of it reflects the fact that affiliates of MNCs are branch plants of enterprises with headquarters located elsewhere—enterprises that for one reason or another find it profitable to internalize their activities across national boundaries. In this respect, there is no basic difference between the dependence of certain regions in an economy dominated by branch plants of national firms whose headquarters are located elsewhere and those generated by the affiliates of foreign-based MNCs in the countries in which they operate.

## FOOTNOTE

1. For two recent summaries of this debate and the "dependence" literature, see Lall (1975) and Moran (1976).

# COMMENT

## WALTER A. CHUDSON*

James Riedel's critique of the empirical literature on the relationship between foreign capital inflow and domestic savings or investment (by Griffin et al.) is quite convincing. I confess that I had not been aware of much of the work cited by him. As I took the occasion to read some of it, I found myself increasingly skeptical over the crudeness of the regression analyses purporting to show a displacement of domestic savings by foreign capital inflow, particularly as regards the impact of MNC investments on either domestic savings or investment in developing countries. I also share Riedel's conclusion that the relationship between foreign investment and domestic investment opportunities defies generalization and can be reliably established only by considering prevailing circumstances of host countries and the nature of different types and forms of foreign investment.

From this position there are, as I see it, two directions in which one

*United Nations Centre on Transnational Corporations

may move. One is suggested at the end of Riedel's paper, where he offers a prescription for further econometric investigation. The other is in the direction of formulating policies that a developing host country may adopt to avert a possible negative impact reign direct investment on domestic savings and investment. Such a policy framework should be a part of the broader approach to maximizing the net social benefit of foreign direct investments to the host country.

## Econometric Analysis

The point of departure is the limitation stressed by Riedel: The excessive level of aggregation employed in the previous econometric studies. I can only affirm his criticism of the empirical studies; namely, that in their aggregation of foreign capital measured by the balance on current account they make an obviously unrealistic assumption for direct foreign investment (DFI), that *all* forms of "foreign capital" exhibit roughly the same behavioral relationship to domestic savings. More important is the implication that these studies defy interpretation in terms of meaningful policy guidelines for host countries. This applies also to the studies that analyze less aggregated capital flows: None has isolated as an independent variable direct foreign investment, let alone major subcategories such as direct investment in manufacturing, import-substitution, or export-expansion activities.

If the difficulty with the econometric analyses can be traced to the problem of aggregation (meaning that the entity "foreign capital inflow" comprises elements whose impact on domestic savings cannot by any stretch of the imagination be conceived of as being similar), the question arises what kind of regression model, if any, can be used to test the hypothesis of displacement of domestic savings by DFI, which consists largely of investments by multinational corporations (MNCs)? As Riedel observes, even though based on "somewhat disaggregated" flows, analyses by Areskoug, Papanek, and Gupta have not isolated DFI as the independent variable, so they do not provide a basis for demonstrating the effect of DFI on domestic savings.

But what methodology offers a better solution? He reasons that the nature and motivation of DFI and the internal conditions of developing host countries are such that "general propositions concerning the issue of preemption are all but impossible to establish, *a priori*".[1] If "general" is taken to mean analysis of DFI in the aggregate, this seems a valid observation. But now, whither? At first Riedel states that the problem must be analyzed by studying "country situations" and "investment types." Empirical studies, he says, which fail to account for even the broadest divergencies in country situations and investment types, are bound to be of little practical value.

Having shown that *net capital flows* across national boundaries account for a relatively small share of the total amount of foreign direct investment (a relevant though hardly new discovery), Riedel commends as a likely basis for empirical analysis an econometric model by Caves and Reuber on the effect of foreign investment on Canadian domestic investment. This model has the merit of avoiding balance of payments data as an indicator of DFI and uses a measure of "the total magnitude of foreign investment activity," including reinvested earnings and "foreign source" financing (host-country financing).

Riedel appeals for the collection of data on DFI and analysis of "the relationship" (displacement, stimulation, or supplementation) for a broad sample of countries as a research area of high priority. I drew the impression that the research he had in mind is of the Caves-Reuber regression type. If so, I am puzzled, in view of the limitations of this approach for developing countries, at least, and the acknowledged limitations on the availability of data.[2]

The main interest in empirical analysis of the type examined by Riedel is, I take it, to provide a basis for formulation of policies by a host country. The initial studies by Griffin and others were put forward, after all, to support doubts about the efficacy of foreign aid. Hirschman's impressionistic observations (in his 1969 article on divestment in Latin America) on the threat of displacement of domestic entrepreneurship (and implicitly of domestic savings) by DFI in Latin America were adduced to support his advocacy of a policy of divestment.

As I have said, it is my impression that Riedel, though advocating more empirical analysis, leaves us rather in the dark as to what the methodology of this analysis should be. Further, his analysis of the impact of direct foreign investment on supply conditions in the developing host country—and hence on costs of inputs to local firms and on prices—leads to a critique not of DFI as such but of DFI as a species of a larger category of possibly suboptimal investment allocations resulting from the prevalence of the wrong price and cost signals in the host country. This approach is part of the critique of excessive import-substituting investment induced by inappropriate restrictions on imports or other forms of national incentives or disincentives. In Riedel's words: "There is little question that import-substituting DFI, in making relatively heavy demands on the scarcest factors of production in developing countries, has acted to frustrate local investment by driving up production costs." To be precise, one should presumably say that production costs have been driven above opportunity costs or appropriate shadow prices of inputs. In any case, I think it is important to put this matter in the broad context of "excessive" import-substitution, whether by DFI or domestic investment, even though by definition the impact on the volume (rather than the quality) of domestic investment arises only in the case of foreign direct investment. In other words, if misallocation of resources by domestic investment decisions is bad, similar misallocation by DFI is all the worse for the national income of the host country, over and above its possible preemptive effect on domestic investment.

Despite Riedel's apparent commendation of more empirical work of the econometric type, it is notable that he concludes with the statement that "discussions of the relationship between foreign and domestic investment have rarely attempted to distinguish the characteristics of host countries and the nature of foreign investment. . . ." This is reinforced by another statement that "empirical studies of the relationship [between foreign and domestic investment] that fail to account for even the broadest divergencies in country situations and investment types are bound to be of little *practical* value." There are hints here and there in the paper of further development of this line of thought, but they are subordinated to the seductive lure of econometric analysis based on, hopefully, more and better data. One such hint appears in a footnote stating that the case of foreign investment in natural resources projects is excluded from the discussion, which is focused on manufacturing. I am not quite clear as to the logic of this exclusion, although I do indeed agree that different types of investment have generally different domestic impacts. Probably it is based on the notion that mining investment has fewer domestic linkages in the host country and therefore less impact on the cost and revenue structure. In any case, one should stress the fairly obvious point that mining investments today generally call for extremely large capital outlays (say, over $500 million in a copper project). It seems unrealistic, therefore, to think of a developing host country mobilizing domestic savings of this magnitude. Hence, the displacement of domestic savings of this magnitude by foreign investment seems far-fetched. In mining, the major portion of the foreign capital is, in any case, bound to be loan capital. The issue of displacement, if there is one, could only refer in all likelihood to displacement of domestic equity by foreign equity. It is probably no accident that in the Andean Pact, Article 24, mining is excluded from the fade-out provisions.

Turning to DFI in manufacturing, Riedel argues that export-oriented projects (while getting a low score on contribution to domestic linkages and including presumably mining projects) cause less distortion of domestic cost parmeters than sheltered import-substituting projects—a view that, as I have said, echoes the now conventional criticism (by Little, Scott, and Scitovsky) of "inappropriate" import-substitution, whether by DFI or domestic investment.

*Policy Formulation by Host Countries*

Where does all this leave the policymakers in developing host countries who are seeking guidance for their policies toward DFI? One must concede something, I think, to the merits of a theory of "infant entrepreneurship" in developing countries as an analogue to the "infant industry" argument. It is worth noting that the suppression of small-scale local entrepreneurs by excessive large-scale import-substituting projects is equally bad, or almost so, whether the suppression is by domestic or by foreign enterprises. A good example of this situation may be found in Kenya as described in the recent World Bank Report, *Kenya: Into the Second Decade* (1975).

The suppression of the infant entrepreneur by foreign investments is seemingly illustrated by the Kenya case. Investment in Kenya "involving foreign capital" is estimated at close to 60 percent of total manufacturing investment. According to the judgment of the World Bank's recent mission (1975), the domination of the formal (nontraditional) sector by foreign enterprises may have turned many enterprising Kenyans into managers, not entrepreneurs. If, as the Bank alleges, the greatest deficiency in Kenya is entrepreneurship, there is a possibly serious restraint here on the development of indigenous businessmen. The Bank's conclusion is that some deliberate restriction on foreign enterprise might be justified *even at the expense of some growth,* if it could lead to faster development of independent Kenyan entrepreneurship. The report calls for a policy of coexistence through adoption of "suitable policy instruments" (unspecified) and for positive policies to encourage linkages between foreign enterprise and small-scale African enterprise. This seems to be a good example of a pragmatic approach to a policy at the country level.

In formulating such a policy of "coexistence," account should also be taken of possible backward or forward linkages between DFI and domestic enterprises. And then, of course, there may be externalities of DFI that have some influence, positive or negative, on domestic entrepreneurial opportunities and hence on domestic investment.

Can one conclude a discussion of this subject without considering the pros and cons of joint ventures and of divestment? I doubt whether it is porticularly useful to dwell on the joint venture question here. If the domestic capital invested in a joint venture would otherwise not be saved and invested locally, the joint venture may be credited with stimulating local investment. On the other hand, the joint venture may absorb local managerial talent that might have been developed into more valuable entrepreneurial ability. No wonder Streeten and Lall found no way of quantifying these things.

One way to ask this question is: how can one test the Hirschman (1969, p. 6) hypothesis, namely, that DFI plays a "stunting role" at a stage of development at which local capabilities—entrepreneurial, managerial, technological, and savings—have grown (possibly with the stimulus of DFI) to a point where they are capable of fulfilling the function of the continuing inflow of DFI, presumably at lower cost (including various externalities)? Hirschman relies on a seat-of-the-pants judgment of historical evolution in certain Latin American countries (the larger ones, though he said "most of Latin America"). He referred to but did not specify "a considerable body of evidence, brought forth less by design than by accidents, such as wars, depressions, nationalist expropriations, and international sanctions."

Of course, we have examples of nationalization and expropriation that were technologically successful if not otherwise beneficial to the host country. The Suez Canal is one such case. But the hypothesis that Riedel proposes to test is a systematic relationship. One can think of reasons in specific cases for displacement, supplementation, or stimulation. And one can build more complex models including assumptions about linkages and externalities (both positive and negative). The historical record complicates the use of regression analysis (either time series or cross-country) by such major changes in host-government policy as the adopting of policies on compulsory joint ventures and nationalization. Even a detailed history of take-overs is inconclusive unless we know how the proceeds from the takeover were used.

Further, in the context of the development process, we are not talking merely of the impact on savings, but on the other factors (some of which may be correlated with domestic savings), notably entrepreneurship and managerial skills. It thus seems doubtful whether a model like that of Caves-Reuber can embrace these complexities in a way that provides a practical guide to host-government policy.

But how far can a host government get by using a project-by-project or sector-by-sector analysis based on some measurements of opportunity cost of the requisite inputs, including technology? In measuring the (opportunity) cost of domestic capital, presumably the authorities have somehow to take account of the proposition that domestic savings are partly dependent on the availability of investment opportunities. It seems to me that the best line of policy is for an evaluation, project-by-project, of the trade-offs between possibly reduced costs from unpackaging DFI (through licensing, joint ventures, management contracts), and the inability to obtain the technologies (including management) desired. In making such appraisal, an "informed" judgment of the effect of a given policy on the stimulation of infant entrepreneurs and, one may say, of infant savers seems unaviodable.

The relationship between foreign and local entrepreneurship is complex, not only because DFI can, at the same time, involve promotion of technologically less complex local industry and domination or displacement of more complex sectors by DFI, but also because the frontier between the two classes is a moving one. In Brazil, for example, a rough division of entrepreneurial functions has evolved according to technological and managerial complexity into three sectors: A predominantly local one using accessible technology, a sector of predominantly state enterprises, and a sector in which foreign enterprises dominate, using the most complex technologies and producing differentiated products with global management. What may appear as "dependencia" to some observers is considered by others as a pragmatic trade-off.

# FOOTNOTES

1. It may be recorded that Streeten-Lall in their massive UNCTAD study (1973) of the balance-of-payment and income effects of DFI were forced to analyze the impact of "local replacement" by admittedly simple assumptions of "most likely local replacement" without any attempt at truly empirical analysis. They note that "we do not know if there is such a thing as a 'typical local firm' with characteristics different from a 'typical foreign firm.'" They note that certain differences are indentifiable—ease of access to and cost of technology, knowledge of international markets, access to finance and perhaps the quality of management, but even these "are impossible to quantify" (UNCTAD, 1973, p. 23).

2. The model to be tested is the following. Domestic capital formation is "explained" by regression analysis in the absence of DFI. DFI is then entered as an explanatory variable in the model; if it is found to make a statistically significant contribution to the explanatory power of the model (improves the correlation more than the model which lacks DFI as an explanatory variable), this signifies that the hypothesis that DFI is strictly supplementary (neutral) is rejected. Then we check regression coefficients; if positive, we then infer DFI stimulates local investment; if negative, it is inferred to supplant (displace) domestic investment.

# 8. INTERNATIONAL MARKETS FOR EXHAUSTIBLE RESOURCES, LESS DEVELOPED COUNTRIES, AND MULTINATIONAL CORPORATIONS*

Carlos F. Díaz Alejandro, YALE UNIVERSITY

Both economic theory and history teach that the topic of international markets for exhaustible resources is a difficult and troubled one. This essay will survey the relevant literature, elaborating on the difficulties and troubles. Positive analysis will lead us to predict more of the same in the future. But perhaps a better understanding of the issues could lead to modest normative suggestions regarding ways of improving the workings of such markets.

Trade in exhaustible minerals, even when carried out by nationals of the same country, is different than trade in corn or screws. The first inevitably involves intertemporal calculations, while the latter do not.

Research in International Business and Finance, Vol. 1, pp. 269–311.
Copyright © 1979 by JAI Press, Inc.
All rights of reproduction in any form reserved.
ISBN 0-89232-031-1

When such trade is carried out internationally, further complications arise. The world is such that mineral deposits are typically neither evenly spread among countries nor of even quality, thus generating Ricardian rents. Uncertainty often surrounds the future of technical change in products using minerals as inputs, as well as the technology used in mines. Discovery of new mines has often been dramatic and discontinuous. Property titles to the new mines can be blurry. The exploitation of mines or deposits, as well as the distribution and processing of their output, usually requires large masses of capital relative to other inputs and a tight organization. The development of new mines or deposits usually takes a good deal of planning time. Exhaustible resources seem like special gifts from the gods, in the sense that they appear to be at a given time unique substances very difficult to substitute in consumption or production. Yet their uniqueness can be wiped out overnight by technical change.

Where markets are so plagued with both uncertainty and the need for large capital commitments, it is not surprising to find large organizations that try to control and regulate trade and investment in exhaustible resources. Since many governments have perceived that such resources are vital to "national security," it follows that those large organizations, even when theoretically private, have had special links with home and host governments.

Little wonder, then, that throughout history trade in minerals has been associated with a violence and conflict surprising even to a melancholy mid-ocean auctioneer. The regions now under the sovereignty of less-developed countries (LDCs) have held and still hold a good share of the world's store of economically valuable exhaustible resources; it could be argued that remaining deposits and ore bodies in LDCs are of higher grade than those in industrialized countries, as the latter have been worked and prospected more intensively. But from the days of the Spanish search for American gold, at least, through those of Belgian mines in the Congo, the people inhabiting those regions have had reason to wonder about the net benefits to them of such endowments, and of international trade in their outputs.

The first half of this paper will survey analytical points arising from several branches of economics, such as capital theory, international trade, and industrial organization. It will also deal, somewhat amateurishly, with bits of history and politics. The second half will review policy proposals ranging from grand designs for a new world order for trade and investment in exhaustible resources, to more modest suggestions in areas such as taxation and contracts. At the end of the paper the reader will be reminded of some of the areas neglected in this survey essay.

# THE PURE ECONOMICS OF EXHAUSTIBLE RESOURCES

A positive side effect of OPEC's success has been a rebirth of interest in the pure economics of natural resources. Some of the best brains in the profession have flocked to analyze issues largely dormant since the days of Hotelling's (1931) classic article. While the area has become a playground of high-powered theorists, the basic economic results of their work provide insights into the less formal issues of interest to us (see Kay and Mirrlees, 1975).

A fixed and known stock of an exhaustible resource in the ground may be regarded as a capital asset among the other assets an owner or country may have. The representative owner will have to decide whether to exploit the resource or to leave it underground. If the marginal costs of exploitation and the present and future prices of the resource are known to the owner, assumed to be a price taker, the decision for him will be straightforward. Stock equilibrium for resource owners will be realized when they expect the price of the resource, *net of costs,* to increase at a rate equal to that of the ruling interest rate. Only under these conditions will the resources in the ground, assumed to be homogeneous, yield a rate of return to their owners equal to those of other assets. Efficiency requires that all forms of investment have the same yields; in other words, Venezuela should "sow petroleum" into new factories and schools only while the rate of return of those produced assets is higher than the appreciation of oil in her ground. If the equilibrium condition does not hold, owners will be dissatisfied with the structure of their portfolios, and will wish to have more or less assets in the ground.

Under these assumptions, the equilibrium time profile for the net price will have an upward tilt. Consumers of the resource will pay the net price plus extraction unit costs. When current consumption is small relative to total stocks of the resource, the net price, or *pure rent* component in the final price, will be small. In that case, the economics of that good approaches that of renewable resources. Salt, limestone, and other minerals used in cement production may be given as examples. But for many exhaustible resources it can be expected that eventually the scarcity rent will begin to dominate the movement in the market price. The transition, in fact, may be abrupt, and expectations regarding future prices may be revised discontinuously. Notice that full equilibrium requires not only the portfolio conditions discussed above, but also a balance in the flows demanded and supplied for each time period, at the equilibrium price. The flow market that has to clear is not just one market, but the sequence of markets for the resource from now until the date of exhaustion.

Those who glibly take for granted the efficiency of existing world markets for exhaustible resources may wish to consider Robert Solow's evaluation of how likely is the efficient equilibrium described above to be observed in practice:

> But there clearly is not a full set of futures markets; natural-resource markets work with a combination of myopic flow transactions and rather more farsighted asset transactions. It is legitimate to ask whether observed resource prices are to be interpreted as approximations to equilibrium prices, or whether the equilibrium is so unstable that momentary prices are not only a bad indicator of equilibrium relationships, but also a bad guide to resource allocation. That turns out not to be an easy question to answer. Flow considerations and stock considerations work in opposite directions. The flow markets by themselves could easily be unstable; but the asset markets provide a corrective force (Solow, 1974, p. 6).

A whole set of additional difficulties hides behind previous references to interest rates, rates of return, and such, which were presumed to be equal, and given, and "right." In short, no difference was postulated between private and social rates of discount. Yet what may be a sensible discount rate for Anaconda or Exxon need not be the correct rate that should be used, say, by Chilean or United States government officials planning social policy. The former should take into account such things as taxes on capital returns, expropriation risks, etc., while the latter should not usually consider them. Some would go further, denying that private time preferences should form the bases for intertemporal decisions, and that the utilities of future generations should be given the same weight as those of present generations. At any rate, the choice of a rate of social time preference is crucial, involving a decision about intergenerational distribution. To quote Robert M. Solow again:

> The pure theory of exhaustible resources is trying to tell us that, if exhaustible resources really matter, then the balance between present and future is more delicate than we are accustomed to think; and then the choice of a discount rate can be pretty important and one ought not to be too casual about it (Solow, 1974, p. 10).

The Hotelling microeconomic model clearly makes a large number of simplifying assumptions, which explains why historical experience does not easily fit with its predictions (e.g., relative copper prices are lower today than 100 years ago).[1] Resources labeled exhaustible may better be referred to as nonrenewable. Nevertheless, the simplest natural resource models already highlight that even if we limit the analysis to competitive markets within one country, to homogeneous deposits, and little uncertainty, doubts arise regarding the stability and efficiency in those markets. Yet more complexities lie ahead.

## The International Dimension

Within a country, some regions will have an excess supply of minerals and fuels (e.g., Montana and Texas), while others will have an excess demand for them (e.g., New England). Both types of regions will, however, live under laws, customs, and habits that are not too dissimilar, so that depletion allowances, taxes, discount rates, and subsoil property rights are roughly common. Rules for the settlement of disputes, antitrust laws, etc., will be comparable. Within the United States, contracts made in one state must be honored in others, while trade restrictions between states are prohibited. Under these circumstances, markets have a reasonable chance to perform their functions, even if subject to the difficulties discussed earlier. In spite of this, the clash of divergent regional economic interests regarding natural resources will find an echo, and often more than that, in the political arena of Congress or Parliament, and the Texas Railroad Commission will consider necessary the sending of "a message to Washington" by ordering oil production cutbacks.[2]

Compared with most national markets, which are buttressed by laws and established customs, international markets are a jungle. For auction (Okun, 1975) or spot markets this may be relatively unimportant, but for markets involving long horizons the trouble is more serious. It was seen in the previous section that the theory of exhaustible resources underlines the importance of the long view.

Suppose one has countries with high discount rates and countries with low discount rates. Now assume that some countries are net users of exhaustible resources and others are net producers. If the number of both types of countries were large and the resources were more or less evenly spread among all countries, perhaps international markets could be organized so that every net consuming country can get what it wants from a willing net producer country without any discussion of freedom of access to supplies or political pressures.

But now suppose there is only a handful of net producers, and they happen to be firm believers in conservation, having a very low discount rate, perhaps for religious reasons. Net consumers of that exhaustible resource will be tempted to politicize this international market and will philosophize regarding the right of a handful of countries to control world supplies. The net producers, in turn, will philosophize on the right of a handful of countries to account for high shares of world consumption. The point was put forcefully, and in a rather extreme form, by R. G. Hawtrey as far back as 1930:

> Mankind has become dependent on the systematic use of the material resources of the world, and cannot afford to allow those resources to be withheld from use through the shortcomings of communities which rule over them. This applies not only to primitive

communities, but to any sovereign authorities which obstruct development (Hawtrey, 1930, pp. 139–140).

The positive guiding principle should be not justice but expediency, and expediency here means aiming at the maximum of material welfare, without restriction to any particular section, group or nation (*Ibid.*, p. 146).

The legitimacy of ownership of natural resources has other troubling dimensions. *Within* countries, laws may regard the subsoil as common property of the whole nation, not subject to private ownership. This can lead to the establishment of national monopolies for the exploitation of natural resources, whose presence in international trade and investment creates fresh difficulties for those hoping to establish clear rules of the game for international markets. It can also lead to the granting of very long-term leases whose original terms are made obsolete by changing circumstances. One may also note that in the United States, federal law restricts foreign participation in U.S. enterprises associated with the development of federally owned mineral resources.

A good share of the earth, such as the oceans and the poles, has no clear property titles, and its nonrenewable resources are open for exploitation to all capable of doing so. This free access generates technological external diseconomies and gross economic inefficiencies. It also sets the stage for dangerous political frictions among overlapping claimants.

*Further Annoying Complications of the Real World*

Of all factors of production, exhaustible natural resources are among the least evenly spread among nations, the least homogeneous, and the least mobile. Trade theorists familiar with "labor" and "capital" find this messy third input tricky to handle but difficult to ignore, particularly after Leontieff's paradox. All natural resources may be lumped together into an ill-defined Ricardian "atmosphere," influencing labor productivity while shattering the assumption of identical production functions. Linear homogeneity in labor and capital, of course, has to be revised. Location theorists may be called for help. And so on.

But trade theorists like those headaches. Perhaps more relevant to our preoccupations are the enormous costs involved in obtaining information about new deposits of resources, matched by the huge rewards awaiting those who find them. Throughout history, the hope of a fabulous bonanza has been a powerfully motivating force going far beyond narrow economic behavior. The hope for a bonanza, together with the hope for a major invention, triggers efforts qualitatively different from those of the representative entrepreneur who shaves costs in the struggle for a normal rate of return.

The search for both new deposits and inventions has become increasingly systematized; large organizations with massive exploration or research budgets have on the whole replaced the maverick inventor or prospector. Yet it remains difficult to pin down the chances of substantive technological breakthroughs or the discovery of important new mineral sources to a clearly defined probability distribution. Historically, at least, the search for new deposits does not appear to have been a matter of obtaining a bit more information by spending a little more. The information break between before and after discovery has often been sharp, a matter that, as will be seen below, also sets up cycles of bargaining strength between searchers and owners of resources.

Discovery of large new deposits may not much influence total world output of that commodity, particularly in the short run, but it is likely to have a dramatic impact on its price, if an open market exists for it, or on the plans of the organizations involved in the trade of that resource, if such organizations have replaced open markets. Output of existing mines will dominate observed quantities, while breakthroughs in information will be registered more in open market prices and/or investment plans.

The fact that often a handful of deposits are far superior to others (the Potosi' silver mines, the Saudi Arabian oil pool, the South African gold mines, etc.) is to some observers a more important characteristic in explaining the economic history of mineral trade than the exhaustible nature of those commodities. Advantage of one deposit over others can arise from location rather than mineral quality. The *Ricardian model* of differential rents, originally applied to an ever renewable resource (land), would be more relevant than a *Hotelling model* with exhaustible homogeneous deposits. Differential rents for minerals, of course, could be expected to be larger than for land, but otherwise (so the argument goes) little would be lost by dropping the exhaustible characteristic of the resources.

As noted earlier, when current consumption is small relative to total stocks of an exhaustible resource, its final price will only have a small component of what may be called *Hotelling rent*. It could, nevertheless, for deposits of high quality or choice location, include a high share of *Ricardian rent*. The average mix of rents will be different for different exhaustible natural resources; the analyst should take both of them into account.

Besides the uncertainty about reserves, the related uncertainty regarding future technologies will hamper the smooth operation of markets. The uncertainty can be, first of all, about techniques for searching for new deposits. New technologies can also appear for working known mines, influencing unit costs. Industries using resources as inputs can change their unit input requirements thanks to technical change; or changes in tastes or the introduction of new final goods (*e.g.,* the automobile) may drastically change the structure of the derived demand for resource inputs previously regarded as critical; witness the history of Chilean nitrates and Peruvian guano.

Economic life, of course, is full of all types of uncertainty. The argument is that in the field of exhaustible natural resources such uncertainty seems to be especially great. Economic activities also require capital and a certain minimum scale of operations to make sense. Both the search for new deposits and their exploitation appear to be, once again, especially capital intensive, where capital includes both physical and human capital as well as social overhead capital. Note that many mines are located in remote places. Such capital intensity plus organization requirements in production, transportation, and marketing combine to generate indivisibilities in the production and distribution of many exhaustible natural resources. As a result, for substantial output ranges marginal costs are considerably below average costs, even if the former are rising. Viewed in a more Austrian fashion, new mining projects also have long gestation periods, and many things can happen between the time it is decided to go ahead with the development of a new mine and the time output actually begins to flow out of it.

Some observers claim that both the capital and time intensity of new projects, as well as their lumpiness, have become even more marked in recent years. This could be attributable partly to a more intensive working of the Ricardian margin, which also raises intramaginal rents, but also to the realization that a resource previously regarded as free, i.e., clean environment, is after all yet another exhaustible natural resource. Although exhaustible and not subject to rising private marinal costs, clean environment has shared with ocean resources the feature of nonappropriability; in the absence of clear social rules there has been a tendency to use it inefficiently and excessively. But the new social rules to avoid using up clean environment too fast in the process of, say, mining copper, involve larger expenditures of capital. These rules could vary from country to country, either because of different social tastes for clean environment, or because of different endowments of clean environment in the various countries. It is perhaps unnecessary to elaborate on how different national rules on environmental protection, as well as on how imperfections in capital markets could increase the difficulties for open and competitive international markets for exhaustible resources that require ever-increasing and lumpy doses of capital for their socially acceptable exploitation.

Before turning to the examination of how real world nations and institutions have handled these textbook nightmares, a further complication, which perhaps should have been placed first in the list, may be added. Whether rightly or wrongly, many socieities have regarded some exhaustible natural resources as "critical," "essential" or "vital" to their welfare. Advanced industrial economies, for example, have so regarded oil. Nations whose economies are heavily dependent on the production of one or two of those resources have, for different reasons, similar fixations. It is a fair guess that markets are unlikely to operate in textbook fashion for commodities regarded as "lifeblood" and such.

# ENTER MULTINATION CORPORATIONS

A Martian reader of Arrow (1975) and Solow (1975) could expect that the complexities discussed so far would be handled by an intricate network of futures, insurance, and contingency markets, and would rush to *The Wall Street Journal* to delight in how November, 1982 copper quotations would mesh with insurance rates against the contingency of earthquakes in Chilean mines. But he would be lucky to find a handful of futures quotations, and for fairly close dates at that, for exhaustible resources (he would find more futures quotations for other raw materials). He may get some hints from stock market quotations for shares of companies owning mineral deposits. But the number of these are few, and declining.

Why the lack of futures prices? The immediate answer is that a dominant share of international (and national) commerce in exhaustible natural resources is carried out within large, vertically integrated firms, which substitute corporate planning for open competitive markets, either of the auction type or those involving long-term but arms-length contracts. Part of the explanation for such a substitution has to do with the relatively poor performance of open markets in the presence of the uncertainties and complexities discussed earlier. For commodities with high fixed and low variable costs, and where information is imperfect, badly diffused, or asymmetrically located, it is reasonable to expect a nonmarket institution to replace the market. Furthermore, incentives for vertical integration become large when uncertainty regarding the supply price of the upstream good pressures the informational needs of downstream firms (Spence, 1975; Arrow, 1975). Conditions in the trade of oil, bauxite, nickel, and copper appear to meet amply these requirements for the emergence of nonmarket institutions. Notice that once these institutions have become going concerns, they in turn undermine the possibility of open markets. Even if circumstances change, and auction markets or long-term contracts at arms-length become feasible alternatives, the previous existence of MNCs will hamper their emergence. Once they have come into existence, MNCs will routinely erect and protect barriers to entry, including hoarding mineral deposits, limiting technological diffusion, and establishing exclusive marketing networks.

The above rules out neither the existence of oligopolistic rivalry among MNCs engaged in international trade and investment, nor entry of new actors into the oligopolistic game. Patterns of rivalry and cooperation have changed over the years and have varied among resources; in copper and oil, for example, the degree of world market control by a handful of firms prior to World War II has been eroded during the postwar period, while the diamond cartel appears as strong as ever, and the nickel oligopoly remains robust. The standard scenario includes a few established firms (the "majors") controlling most known deposits and with a strong interest in preserving oligopolistic stability, for which purpose they raise barriers to entry. Lean and hungry potential entrants (the "independents") are their natural enemies. If the latter obtain access to rich new deposits, as Occidental did with Libyan oil during the 1960s, the majors can get into trouble.

New entrants into the exploitation of a given nonrenewable natural resource are often firms long established in another. The creation of totally new firms appears most likely in new types of activities, as with mining the seabed. The propensity of established natural resource firms to diversify and form consortia seems to be on the rise, partly to diversify risks and maintain oligopolistic orders, and partly to deter host countries from obtaining competitive bids from independent firms or to raise the costs to those countries of potential disagreements with foreign firms. Antitrust legislation in some industrialized countries checks somewhat this tendency toward collusion, but mainly insofar as it damages their own consumers. Collusion of national firms when dealing with foreigners, in fact, is often encouraged by that legislation.

Is this all there is to it? Why, in particular, have most MNCs engaged in the commerce of exhaustible natural resources come until recently from a handful of countries? It could be argued that nationals of those countries, which historically have been dominant both economically and politically, have a comparative advantage in dealing with the uncertainty and informational requirements of the commerce in exhaustible resources, or indeed in all international activities characterized by such requirements. This may be so, but only if such "comparative advantage" is broadly defined to include contacts with their home governments, and the symbiotic relationship that historically has characterized the dealings of MNCs with the governments of the United Kingdom and the United States, in particular.

The argument is neither that home governments are simply the tools of MNCs, nor that MNCs are the submissive instruments of hegemonic powers, but to stress that in an area plagued with uncertainty, and where information is highly prized, the pressures toward considerable interaction between MNCs and home governments have historically been very great. This mutually supportive relationship has been clearest perhaps in the case of oil, especially in the years around the First World War, and the decade and a half following the outbreak of the Second World War.

> Quite simply, parent governments have generally been willing to leave the industry's running to more-or-less private companies, but, being aware of the strategic importance of oil from the 1910s at least, have been willing to step in to support them whenever necessary . . . Occasionally when a major ran afoul of a producing government, the parental authorities have provided diplomatic support, though this has generally been in an overt form, and has not always been marked by total enthusiasm (particularly in later years) (Turner, 1976, p. 7).

It could be argued that the politician's concern with stable, secure, and cheap access for his country to exhaustible natural resources has been tinged with irrationality throughout history, from the Pharaohs to Tojo. Markets, after all, could have done the job and without being dominated or replaced by MNCs. We shall explore this possibility toward the end of this paper. But it is well to remember that not so long ago raw materials were regarded as the basis of military power, the cause of war, and the occasion for economic struggle. The Atlantic Charter gave prominent place to access to raw materials; earlier Herbert Hoover had given great weight to his fight as Secretary of Commerce against what he regarded as European cartelization of some raw materials. More recently, a sophisticated observer has flatly stated: "From an American perspective, military intervention might be most readily occasioned by our fears of resource scarcity" (Chace, 1976).

The case of Japan, after its defeat in World War II, is of particular interest when considering what is sometimes referred to as the three basic types of security: military, food, and energy. Japanese officials continue to worry that the growth of their country will be increasingly constrained by lack of available supplies of natural resource imports, and about the vulnerability of an economy so dependent on imported energy and natural resources. Such considerations heavily influence Japanese foreign policy: in the delicate balancing of links with China, which may become an important oil exporter, and the U.S.S.R., whose Siberia offers an even more attractive source of potential supplies; in foreign aid programs, frankly designed to please exporters of raw materials and their friends; and in the allocation of direct foreign investment, which increasingly goes into processing industries in resource-rich countries (Okita, 1974). Although now lacking in substantial military power of its own, it is not surprising that

Japanese officials prefer to handle their resource diplomacy to a large extent via Japanese firms, rather than foreign-owned MNCs. Japanese firms have accommodated themselves more readily to new modalities for obtaining natural resources, such as joint ventures with host country organizations and long-term contracts, than have the classic MNCs from the victorious nations of World War II.

The Japanese are remarkably candid regarding their resource diplomacy, and the linkages between their aid, trade, and direct foreign investment policies, on one hand, and their anxiety to secure access to LDC fuels and mineral resources, on the other. But much the same thing is likely to go on in France, Germany, and other industrialized countries.

It would be difficult to argue that the manner in which international trade and production of exhaustible natural resources has been carried out over, say, the last one hundred years was dependent on purely technological and economic data, independent of the political realities within and among countries. As those political realities change, even if no changes occur in other data, the actors involved in the production and trade of resources will also be modified, and their pattern of interaction will be different from the past. National rivalries present a barrier to MNCs in their efforts to control and internalize markets; for example, the Italian state oil corporation pioneered in the destruction of the hegemony of the "seven sisters." Under other circumstances, governmental actions can encourage the dominance of a handful of firms, as noted for pre-Word War II oil, and as may be happening with U.S. firms for undersea mining. And political decisions are thrusting forward names such as PETRO-BRAS (the Brazilian state oil company) and CODELCO (the Chilean state copper company) onto the financial pages of the world.

## ENTER THE LDCs

How does one explain the secular upward trend in Venezuela's share of oil revenues obtained from her soil, or the rise in the Chilean or Zambian shares in copper revenues? Has such a rise been at the expense of excess profits of MNCs exploiting the resource, or at the expense of consumers of the resource; or has it simply been the working of the invisible hand?

A first hypothesis could be that as both Hotelling and Ricardian rents have increased through time, they have naturally accrued to the owners of the scarce resources, i.e., the LDCs. LDC shares sixty years ago were low, so the argument would run, simply because pure rents at that time were negligible, competitive prices being made up almost wholly by real costs, including a normal rate of return to capital. This story does not ring ture; bits of evidence indicate that profits in many mining ventures and in oil were above the normal level, although it is far from clear whether the super-profits came from the appropriation by MNCs of Hotelling or Ricardian rents, or from their oligopolistic prices, or perhaps from unusual efficiency. Kennecott, for example, has been reported to have been making 20 to 40 percent per year on its investment in El Teniente, in Chile, during the late 1920s.[3]

"Increase in bargaining power" is the magic phrase that appears to answer best the first question raised in this section. But exactly what factors account for the rise in such power is a more debatable issue. To bargain effectively, the LDCs first needed sovereignty, a status not obtained until after the Second World War in many parts of the third world. Secondly, their policymakers needed a minimum of freedom from physical coercion, represented by foreign gunboats and such. Diffusion of world military power, and competition among the handful of superpowers, provided the necessary (even if limited) room for maneuver. Thirdly, and related to the previous point, the expansion during the last thirty years in the number of foreign firms of different nationalities that are buyers of raw materials and suppliers of capital and technology increased LDC options. Fourthly, LDC policymakers required the will to get a bigger share, and not just for themselves personally. Domestic political pressures in this direction increased as third world populations gained in political awareness. Last but not least, the creation of local expertise and knowledge regarding the relevant industry, its customers, and competitors, made credible the threat of having the host country run the mines and deposits by themselves. This process still has far to go; it is striking how few Chileans know the intricacies of world marketing in copper, how few Venezuelans are familiar with the Middle East oil industry, etc.

But the third world, and countries such as Australia and Canada, have come a long way since the days when Lázaro Cárdenas nationalized Mexican oil in 1937, while the not too unsympathetic Franklin D. Roosevelt was President of the United States. In retrospect, the amount of potential LDC revenues lost because of a lack of bargaining power are likely to be very large. I have elsewhere suggested the following mental experiment: What would have been the LDC share in the rents produced by their natural resources (say in 1900, or 1920, or 1950) had those countries granted permission to exploit those natural resources only on the basis of competitive bidding open to buyers from all over the world? The difference between the revenues obtained and those that could have been obtained is likely to have been substantial, and may be blamed basically on the use of political and oligopsonistic power by the major users of natural resources.

Yet, also in retrospect, it could be argued that the characteristics of mineral industries made the rise of LDC bargaining power almost inevitable. The concentration of mines or deposits, in contrast with the diffusion in the production of most tropical crops, made taxable surplus highly visible even to a "soft state," and, eventually, also quite vulnerable to the exchequer. Fed by revenues from mines, LDC governments could expand and improve their expertise. There has always been the danger that a sudden expansion of national revenues could lead to a rentier mentality with disastrous long-term developmental consequences; this is the fear of thoughtful Venezuelans who compare the situation in their country today with that of sixteenth-century Spain. But in spite of extravagance, under contemporary circumstances a good share of tax revenues will find its way to developmental expenditures that will further reinforce the nation's ability to bargain, while creating habits and expectations that place a floor on national claims on mineral activities. Those habits and expectations do limit the willingness of the host country to display bargaining power by shutting down mining operations, yet visible, concentrated, and vulnerable installations provide a continuous temptation to do so if the LDC feels sufficiently aggrieved.

Net resources subject to negotiation between MNCs and LDCs may be of two kinds: the Hotelling or Ricardian pure rents that would arise even under conditions of perfect competition, and the excess profits generated by departures from perfect competition in the sale of the resources. Until recently, one took for granted that LDCs were gradually increasing their share of pure rents, a process that need not affect prices paid by consumers. Since 1973, there has been a growing number of analysts suggesting that LDCs will bargain also for an increasing share of what may be called oligopolistic excess profits, and that they will also try to increase the level of such profits, naturally at the expense of consumers. In the struggle over pure rents, LDCs would match wits with MNCs, while consumers remain more or less indifferent spectators. The lure of oligopolistic excess profits would mute the LDC-MNC clash, as both would be allied against the consumer.[4]

It should be noted that oligopolistic excess profits need not be reflected in above-average book rates of return for MNCs, even in the absence of LDC pressures. Often such surplus is dissipated in buying security of supplies or sales, or in buying political power, tranquility, and comfort for the bureaucracies running the organization. Funds may be spent casting dollar ballots for favorite politicians, or in lavish advertisements showing how the company loves fish and fowl in the environment, or simply padding payrolls. The power and prestige attached to controlling such "costs" will lure LDC bargainers as much as declared excess profits.

The game has indeed become complicated. But one somewhat paradoxical trend should be stressed: Even as some observers in industrialized countries warn of LDC "cartelization" of resource markets, basing themselves mainly on the OPEC experience,[5] LDC actions have unleashed in several of those markets pressures pushing toward greater competition. The point is simply that the number of independent actors in those markets has increased with the proliferation of national companies in charge of at least the production of minerals. The national companies are not (as yet) as vertically integrated as the MNCs they replace. This means, *inter alia*, that users of natural resources see their range of choice expanded, while past special relationships between upstream and downstream firms become shaken. This may be a temporary phase in world markets, but while it lasts it creates an opportunity for open competitive world markets in minerals that did not exist while those markets were internalized by MNCs. It is peculiar that many worrying about LDC "cartelization" of bauxite showed little concern about how the bauxite and aluminum markets worked before LDC actions, and say little about the long-run effects of, say, Jamaican actions over the degree of competition in aluminum products.

## A NEW ORDER IN INTERNATIONAL MARKETS FOR EXHAUSTIBLE NATURAL RESOURCES?

Since 1973 a number of fresh and not-so-fresh proposals have been advanced for restructuring world trade and investment in exhaustible natural resources, ranging from those designed to stabilize the prices for those products, to more ambitious ones, such as the International Resources Bank idea, presented by U.S. Secretary of State Henry Kissinger to a surprised UNCTAD conference at Nairobi in May, 1976. But before examining possible scenarios for the new order, it will be desirable to examine some features of the old that have been only hinted at in earlier pages.

A central feature of the old order was that, for fuel and several minerals, MNCs, for all their oligopolistic rivalries, ran effective commodity stabilization schemes, at least for substantial segments of the market. During most of the post-World War II period, particularly during 1953–1971, world dollar prices for oil, iron ore, bauxite, nickel, molybdenum, and magnesium were relatively stable in nominal terms. This was done by a combination of (*a*) buffer stocks strategically held at several places within vertically integrated MNCs, (*b*) control over supplies with elastic production responses, and (*c*) information and marketing networks that could be used to allocate or ration available supplies among different types of customers, ranged from most preferred (often other departments of the MNC itself) to least preferred. In some products, such as copper, part of the market was under this kind of regime, while the remainder could be regarded as closer to an "auction market," centering around the London Metal Exchange, and operating under arms-length rules. Even as some copper users enjoyed special "customer relations" with producers, guaranteeing stable prices and a favored place in the queue for supplies, others faced considerable price instability for their raw materials, probably aggravated by the segmented nature of world copper markets.

Under the commodity stabilization regimes of the MNCs, investment planning, including the search for new deposits and new technologies, relied more on a long view generated by their intelligence networks than on the fluctuations of spot or future markets for minerals as registered in open markets. This, of course, made a great deal of sense as, for example, the fluctuations of copper prices on the London Metal Exchange (or of those for zinc, lead, or tin) are likely to be inefficient predictors of the situation in those markets five years hence. The central intelligence of MNCs, in short, can improve on segmented and marginal markets. Compared with nineteenth-century bonanza stories, they can also rationalize the worldwide search for new deposits; indeed, this has to be an integral part of their attempt to keep world markets orderly.

The MNC commodity stabilization regimes showed their clearest features during wartime, when MNC/parent-government cooperation naturally became quite open and when parent governments would insist on their role as *the* preferred customer. Thus, during the Korean War, the MNC rationing machinery, supervised by the U.S government, was used to dampen price increases in copper, to the unhappiness of copper-producing countries.

The rise in the bargaining power of the LDCs where mineral and fuel deposits are located are threatening the commodity stabilization regimes of the MNCs, and the hierarchies implicit in them for customers and governments. Already during the Vietnam War, for example, Chile extracted concessional loans from the United States as a condition for going along with arrangements that, during the Korean War, were simply imposed by the United States. As noted earlier, the greater number of key actors in world markets for exhaustible resources seems to promise greater competition and more choices for actual and potential consumers, including as potential actors and consumers the socialist countries of Eastern Europe, Asia, and the Caribbean. But there is little to assure us that this new competition will lead to reasonably efficient and stable world markets, or to politically acceptable ones. It is not so much that many of the new actors are state enterprises whose actions are likely to be at least as politically motivated as those of the classic MNCs. Nor is it that LDC pressures lead MNCs to dampen their oligopolistic rivalries, promoting corporate consortia and financial interpenetration within and across types of exhaustible natural resources, although some of this seems to be occuring. National rivalries among industrialized countries, at any rate, are likely to put a ceiling on such a process of concentration. The basic problem is that clear rules for these world markets do not exist on matters such as access to supplies, access to national markets, settlement of disputes, etc. Where some sort of authority is not present to impose "accountability conditions to guard against conscious fraud or unintentional overcommitment by individual economic agents" at a reasonable cost, one should expect "trade in any but short-term and easily monitored and enforced contracts to be severly limited" (Clower and Leijonhufvoud, 1975, p. 185).

Immediately after the Second World War, the Havana Charter for the International Trade Organization (ITO) provided a useful first approach toward such a framework, including both rules for state enterprises and what may be called Keynes-ITO commodity stabilization agreements. By the early 1950s hopes for United States ratification of the Havana Charter were dead, while world trade in exhaustible natural resources was once again dominated by central intelligence units in the form of MNCs from a handful of countries. Institutions arising from war and postwar planning, in fact, tended to support and consolidate such a regime; recall how the International Bank for Reconstruction and Development would refuse lending to state-owned LDC enterprises in oil on the grounds that private capital was available for those activities, naturally from MNCs.

So one possibility for the near future is that, with the MNC commodity stabilization regime in decline and no alternative regime in place, world markets for exhaustible resources will become more competitive in some sense, but also more unstable and unpredictable. Under these circumstances, prices observed in markets will be poor guides for fresh investments. Eventually the world market will once again become fragmented, as users of raw materials seeking predictability in prices and in the flow of supplies will seek special "consumer relationships" with producers. This might occur in geographical patterns of the "spheres of influence" type.

An alternative scenario would feature the emergence of a *modus vivendi* between LDC national enterprises, which could include "paper organizations," and the MNCs. This collusion between LDCs and MNCs to share in oligopoly profits is what some observers see as a key feature of OPEC, and what some see as desirable in the copper case.[6] The stability of this new partnership will depend on other changes in world markets, particularly those where management, technology, and capital can be hired separately, as well as the will of LDCs to expand their capacity to combine all of these inputs. But it would give a new lease on life to MNCs engaged in the trade of exhaustible natural resources.

It is the confused outlook for world trade and investment in exhaustible natural resources that explains the inclusion of ten rather terse paragraphs, proposing an International Resources Bank (IRB), in the 1976 Nairobi speech of Dr. Kissinger. The "many advantages and new concepts" of this proposal, according to its proponents, are the following:

—The IRB would be a kind of "honest broker" between host countries and foreign investors, encouraging both equity and project development.

—Its participation would reduce noncommercial risks, promoting investment.

—Deals would feature production-sharing, apparently not unlike the coproduction schemes of socialist countries.

—Projects could be financed by issuing bonds secured by a specific commodity, and they could be retired by delivery of a specific commodity. The IRB could guarantee these financial instruments against noncommerical risks. It is argued that the bonds would be a fruitful new international instrument for forward purchases of commodities, while providing added assurance for access to both markets and supplies.

—The IRB would encourage the progressive acquisition of technology by the host country.

The IRB would not invest its own equity in projects, although it could act as an agent in selling bonds issued by the project entity. The primary function of the IRB would be to guarantee project investment finance against noncommerical risk. Regardless of host-country equity participation in the project, the host government would have to participate in the contract for the IRB to join the mining project. It is not expected that the IRB would become involved in further stages of processing such as milling and fabricating. Proponents of the IRB emphasize that ore bodies being worked in LDCs are often much higher grade than those being developed in the industrialized world. Furthermore, the domain of industrialized countries has been prospected and explored much more intensively than that of the LDCs.

Perhaps the most interesting feature of the IRB proposal is its implicit criticism of past and actual arrangements for world trade and investment in exhaustible natural resources. (The proposal excludes agriculture; it is concerned mainly with minerals, although it could also play a role in the energy field.) Its tone is far from that of not-so-distant past U.S. official statements regarding the wonders of laissez-faire in international markets. It admits gross imperfections in commodity, capital, and technology markets, and *de facto* recognizes the crisis in the postwar MNC commodity stabilization regimes. Coming from an official of a capital-exporting and raw material-importing country, the proposal naturally arouses suspicions that would not surprise readers of either Kemp or Jones, who know how capital inflows can lead to immiserizing declines in host country terms of trade, or the history of pre-1914 British overseas investments. But the proposal opens fresh ways of looking at world markets for resources and candidly admits that wide differences exist between the quality of mineral deposits in industrialized countries and in LDCs, implicitly accepting LDC claims to at least Ricardian rents. Indeed, it is a somewhat back-handed tribute to those in the LDCs who have called for a new international economic order, without whose persistent claims proposals such as that for the IRB would have never come to pass.

It is unlikely that a new world order for trade and investment will spring full grown from anyone's brow, nor that anything as thorough as the Havana Charter will be forthcoming in the near future. The search for a new order is likely to be a complicated process, made up of several strands. We now turn to examining some of these strands.

### Contracts

In spot auction markets, contracts between parties can be fairly precise, but are usually superfluous, unless lags between agreement and delivery are long. In customer markets, it is difficult to pin down the substance of the relationship between the parties in a legal document, particularly when the parties are from different countries. The legal-economic history of contractual arrangements between MNCs and LDCs has also been plagued by emotional rhetoric, often forthcoming from private and public lawyers from industrialized countries, proclaiming the importance of "international law" against what is seen as LDC inability to respect contractual obligations. From recent years, incidentally, one can recall impassioned defenses of the "rule of law" against alleged LDC encroachments on the rights of MNCs from individuals later involved in legal problems of their own, having to do with the Watergate matter, as well as from MNCs later shown to have engaged themselves in rather peculiar practices. In LDCs, weak governments have sometimes not dared to release the full text of contracts with MNCs, for fear of public opinion outbursts.

A more analytical approach to the history and realities of LDC-MNC contracts, however, has already begun, in spite of the difficulty of having access to the relevant documentation (Smith and Wells, 1976; Moran, 1974). This approach recognizes, first of all, that in the past many concession agreements have contained provisions that no sovereign government could realistically be expected to tolerate for a substantial period, forming part of the sad history of unequal treaties imposed on LDCs by hegemonic powers. Concessions in perpetuity or for 99 years, control by MNCs of vast land areas, etc., would be included in what now can be regarded as unrealistic contract clauses in most LDCs, even if they still can be found in some industrialized countries.

The new approach also recognizes that concessions disputes between

LDCs and MNCs are inevitable. They may arise from different interpretations of complex provisions in a contract, or from changing circumstances that make explicit but out-of-date contractual provisions grossly unrealistic. Even for the case of OPEC-MNC dealings during the 1970s, which are often given as an example of LDC inability to keep atreements, Edith Penrose has noted:

> I think the evidence indicates that, although power had shifted, most of the governments wanted in good faith to reach agreement with the companies; they made concessions to do so and did not lightly abandon the agreements reached. But the fall in the value of the United States dollar, in terms of which prices had been set, combined with unexpectedly high rates of international inflation and unexpectedly rapid rises in the market prices of oil in 1972 and 1973, created circumstances that undermined the basis of the agreements by vitiating the expectations that were held by *both* companies and governments at the time when they were made. Renegotiation became essential if the agreements were reasonably to serve the mutual interests of the parties (Penrose, 1975, pp. 53–54).

As noted by Raymond Vernon in his pioneering work, there are inexorable cycles in the bargaining strength of MNCs and LDCs. When an MNC first goes into an LDC to look for a deposit, its bargaining power will be at a peak; unless the LDC government is quite sure that there *are* deposits of reasonable quality within its territory, it will have little leverage even if there are many MNCs as potential investors. Concessions at this point will be generous. Even when the MNC favored with a concession finds a deposit, its bargaining power will remain high, as the proper technology as well as transportation and marketing arrangements have as yet to be established. Asymmetrical access to information as between MNC and the host government will still be a fact of life; the latter, for example, is likely to have only a vague notion of what unit costs of operation are. Only when the operation is a going concern and a success will the bargaining power tilt in favor of the host country. In retrospect, early concessions will appear as excessively generous, if not to the government that negotiated them, then to the opposition eager to find an issue tying its political enemies to the seldom popular MNCs. It is in the nature of things that MNCs will press their early advantage, while the host country will press their advantage later on. It is not obvious that there is much to be gained either by MNC restraint early in the process, nor by LDC government restraint later on, from their respective viewpoints.

Lamentations and exhortations are unlikely to change the dynamics of this cycle, which is based on a sharp break from a situation of great uncertainty, asymmetries, and little MNC commitment, to a situation of much more information and symmetry as well as large MNC investments *in situ*. Recognition that conditions underlying most agreements are likely to change suggests the desirability of institutionalizing contract changes, as argued by Smith and Wells (1976). This could be done by including in the contract clauses called-for automatic, non-negotiable adjustment of certain terms (such as progressive reduction of concession area, or phase-in of host-country ownership), or by including clauses providing for the future renegotiation of selected terms. This mechanism could work better than arbitration provisions, which have a dubious record regarding either equity or effectiveness, and which in many parts of the third world are regarded as unacceptable impositions on national sovereignty, unless they involve local courts and local law.

The notion of contracts as a kind of framework for an ongoing relationship is unlikely to avoid many disputes, but could generate, as put by Smith and Wells, brief periods of harmony between points of negotiations for which it may be well worth striving. Anything more ambitious in this area must await the evolution of firmer and more equitable bases for true international law, to be distinguished from what in the past was unilaterally determined under that rubric by hegemonic powers.

There is a growing literature on the tactics of bargaining over new and old contracts, which include advice on who should be present in the bargaining room, whose secretaries should type drafts, etc. Much of this literature draws from the collective bargaining experience between trade unions and their employers. Rather than go into it, it may be best to focus on key economic issues over which the bargaining struggle takes place. One last remark before going into those issues: Both the literature and the practice of bargaining point out the uses of "wild men" to extract concessions from the other side. Often best results can be achieved for the side with "wild men" if they are *not* particularly well informed and have unrealistic expectations about the value of what they have to offer.[7] This, of course, does not help in the search for a quiet life and smooth international relations. Perhaps less troublesome for a peaceful international polity is the increasing willingness and ability of LDCs to exchange information among themselves regarding contracts with MNCs.

## Taxes

For many direct foreign investments, taxes represent the major benefit for host countries. In the area of exhaustible natural resources, which typically generate modest employment and linkages, taxes can be the only significant benefit. "Taxes" will be defined broadly in this section, to cover, for example, the tax-equivalent value of output-sharing arrangements.

The object of *taxation policy,* viewed from the side of the host government, should be simple: It is to capture all of the Hotelling and Ricardian rents, while letting the investor make the rate of return necessary to induce him to come in. Under competitive conditions in a world of certainty, such a policy would be easy to implement. Mining rights could be auctioned off, or excess profit taxes could cream off rents, or other schemes could achieve the desired objective. The prevalence of large, unique projects in mining suggests that case-by-case taxation, which squeezes all rents for the host government, would be an administratively feasible possibility. But uncertainty and conditions far from competitive complicate matters. On the one hand, besides Hotelling and Ricardian rents, there might be oligopoly excess profits to share. But uncertainty makes rents and profits difficult to predict, and raises bankruptcy fears for the investors. Accounting problems also arise, exacerbated by the lack of open competitive markets yielding arms-length quotations against which intracompany pricing can be checked. The pricing of the services provided by the social overhead capital of the host country can also raise accounting headaches.

Host countries with weak administrative machineries and eager to obtain tax revenues with some degree of certainty have historically relied on royalties levied as so many dollars (or whatever) per metric ton of mineral extracted or exported. Any beginning student of price theory could show why this crude output or export tax is inefficient, but its simplicity and ease of administration are appealing. Output will fluctuate less than profits, so the government will also thrust a greater share of risks onto the investor with this tax.

The next step in taxation is likely to be the introduction of some sort of profit tax, either written especially for mines, or as part of a general profits tax in the host country. It may or may not be accompanied by excess profits taxes, designed to increase the government cut at times of bonanza. It will be difficult to fine-tune such taxes so that all rents plus excess profits, no more and no less, are siphoned off by the host government. Unit costs will be uncertain to the MNC, particularly at the start of operations in a new mine, while the supply price of international capital for that specific industry will be only fuzzily known to the host governments. Both MNC and host government will share many doubts about the future of world markets. The problems surrounding intracompany pricing will create constant friction between the parties. At times the taxes will appear too high, and will be charged with repelling foreign investors; at other times companies will be seen as making a killing, which perhaps they share with foreign governments and customers. At neither time are publicly available data likely to settle the issue (many years later perhaps they will, but only some scholars will care then).

These difficulties with profit and rent taxation have led to new arrangements, such as those pioneered outside the socialist countries by

Indonesia and Peru in oil, involving service contracts that share output instead of profits. In the Peruvian case, the aim of the state corporation, PETROPERU, was to emphasize Peruvian sovereignty over the resources while seeking simplicity. The key is a fifty-fifty split of the oil at the well-head. As noted by Shane Hunt (1975), this assures the host country that in no case will the implicit profit tax fall below 50 percent, but it also implies that the tax rate can be much lower if oil prices rise significantly, or the companies that signed the contract (Occidental in this case) hit spectacular deposits. But the risk is shifted to foreigners, with PETROPERU committing itself to no capital outlay, while pushing Occidental to develop the assigned area rapidly. Hunt concludes: "Output sharing contracts probably obtain foreign capital and technology in as antiseptic a manner as possible. Their only danger is that they shift the risk all too well" (Hunt, 1975, p. 337).

A host country without pressing fiscal needs, confident of its administrative machinery and its ability to control phony intracompany pricing, may try what has been labeled a "Resource Rent Tax" (Garnaut and Ross, 1975). Assuming a supply price of capital for an activity, the value of the cash flow each year could be calculated for the project, accumulating negative balances (likely to occur during the early years) at a rate equal to the assumed capital supply price. Positive values would then be taxed at one of various escalating rates. To keep the MNC interested in minimizing costs, those rates would never reach 100 percent. Advocates of this tax argue that by reducing the risk of loss to the investors, who effectively will enjoy a "tax holiday" whose duration will be inversely related to the actual profitability of the project, it will allow host governments to raise expected tax yields without discouraging capital inflows.

A somewhat related tax has been put into practice in Papua, New Guinea, for a project involving Bougainville Copper Limited, which is subjected to a 33.3 percent company tax on earnings up to a 15 percent agreed return on capital, to which a marginal tax rate of 70 percent on additional earnings is added. However, the calculations are done on a year-to-year basis, with no provision for carrying forward any shortfall of profits below the 15 percent return on agreed capital, to count against possible future excess profits, as in the Resource Rent Tax proposal.[8]

During 1974, Jamaica imposed additional taxes on its bauxite industry, this time on output, but on output expressed in value terms (Gillis and McLure, 1975; Hughes, 1975). As an arms-length price for bauxite is not available, the tax was geared to the price of aluminum ingot. A minimum level of production, somewhat over 90 percent of capacity, is also assumed for tax purposes. If production falls below the stipulated level, the scheme is, in fact, a lump sum tax. With this action, Jamaica has certainly increased its share of the pure rents generated by its bauxite industry, which for Caribbean producers include a significant amount generated by their proximity to the major market. It is more debatable whether it has captured 100 percent of those rents, and whether it has eaten into the oligopolistic super-profits of the far-from-competitive aluminum producers. It would take remarkable economics to argue that consumers of aluminum have so far been the major losers from the Jamaican actions.

Auctioning exploitation rights was mentioned earlier as a theoretical device to assure host countries of all rents from mineral deposits. Why is this not done more often? Simply because when one goes to look at a specific project the potential number of interested parties narrows down sharply. This, in turn, is caused by lack of complete information regarding what is being auctioned off, by both government and companies. Firms are unlikely to explore without assurance that they will be able to exploit successful discoveries, so in practice some exploitation rights must be given to firms that will engage in prospecting. In other cases, complementarities in production act to further narrow down available candidates. The Peruvian government sought potential entrants from Europe, Japan, and the U.S.S.R. into the development of its Cuajone deposit.

> Few companies possess familiarity with the technology of open-pit copper mining. Fewer still have access to the enormous amount of capital required. Moreover, the potential difficulties of sharing transport, refinery, and export facilities with Southern Peru in its adjacent Toquepala deposit essentially ruled out the entry of a new company. The choice available became clear: it was Southern Peru or nothing" (Hunt, 1975, pp. 326–327).

In the case of oil, contemporary circumstances make the auctioning option more feasible. A relatively wide diffusion of oil drilling technology plus relatively easy marketability of oil contribute to this result.

Perhaps the simplest way for a host government to make sure that it is capturing all rents from mineral exploitation is to run the mines itself. What needs explaining is why many radical third world countries have stopped short of this solution to the taxation problem. One answer is that the generation of rents cannot be taken for granted, i.e., the efficient operation of mines may require skills not yet available in host countries. In some cases, secretaries as well as engineers may be in short supply. To this, one should add that the alternative of nationalization plus selective hiring in world markets by the LDC government of the inputs missing locally has advanced only slowly, partly because of the weaknesses in world markets for some of those inputs, particularly technological ones, and partly because of the difficulty of efficiently combining those disparate inputs. But as LDC national companies gain experience and broaden the demand for specialized services, this situation is likely to change, making the nationalization solution increasingly attractive.

In some cases, LDC reluctance to nationalize may come not from lack of technological self-confidence, but from a desire to maintain the oligopolistic structures built up by MNCs in the past, and to increasingly share in oligopolistic super-profits. If one assumes that in the past *parent* governments directly shared in those super-profits only by taxing the meagre declared "downstream" earnings of their MNCs, the taxation problem now becomes more complicated, as emphasized by C. Fred Bergsten (1975). The zero-sum-game features of the situation point to sharp conflict, or "investment wars," unless clear international rules are agreed upon.

## National Control, Training, and Linkages

Less tangible but no less important than the struggle for a higher share of mining rents and profits is the LDC search for greater national control over their mining industries, which often generate high percentages of their Gross National Products and even higher shares of foreign exchange earnings. The rationale for such a desire is well known and is increasingly accepted. Here it will be sufficient to stress the point that even total nationalization will not insure national control (defined in any common-sense fashion) over the mining activity unless formal ownership is accompanied by detailed knowledge of its operation both at the production and the marketing ends. Knowledgeable "hired hands" can get away with much without even ensuring efficiency if the owners lack mastery of technical and economic details. This applies, *a fortiori,* in joint ventures where nationals sit on the board of directors with foreigners. At the very least, special technical committees staffed by experts independent of the foreign partner should be used under those circumstances to advise national members of the board of directors.

It may also be noted that in spite of some torrid industrial-country rhetoric, in actual practice compensation has been paid in the majority of nationalizations, usually based on book value, which has increasingly been accepted as the standard for settlements. Often governments have paid foreign investors for the shares purchased out of future dividends. Programmed changes in ownership became fashionable in the early 1970s, although as noted by Smith and Wells (1976, Ch. 5), the concept appeared in much earlier agreements in the form of host-country options to buy shares at a later date. These authors speculate that future arrangements may build in put-options (options to sell at a specified price) by foreign investors if and when domestic ownership reaches a certain percentage of equity.

The training effects of gradual nationalizations can be strengthened by provisions calling on the partner MNC to set up minimum employment quotas for nationals, in different employment categories, as well as by fellowships for the study abroad of young people of the host country. One can conjecture that there is some tax payment that would be equivalent to the additional burdens placed on the MNC by such training requirements. Simplicity would call for consolidating bargaining over taxes alone, but both host countries and MNCs seem to prefer to spread their interaction over a broader area, including the enlisting of MNCs to help LDC efforts to diversify into industrial resources.

Besides the aspiration of control over mineral resources, LDCs in which the mines are located have for many years been eager to expand some backward and forward linkages of those operations with their national economies. Linkages have been limited partly for purely economic and technical reasons: Inputs required by the mines are frequently sophisticated manufactured goods, while the further processing and refining of ores may be best located near large customers. But distortions in the world economy have also deprived LDCs of a larger share of manufacturing activities servicing mines or processing their output. Perhaps the easiest one to recognize is that involving escalating tariffs in industrialized countries that yield substantial effective protection to their processing activities. More subtle distortions would include the packaged sale of inputs by branches of the same MNC exploiting the mine or by related foreign firms. Here one can find "customer relationships" that may make sense from the viewpoint of the MNC, but not necessarily from that of the host country. Locating processing plants away from the LDC providing the raw material may also be part of MNC strategy to reduce risks and increase its relative bargaining power. Placing the refinery in such an LDC could mean giving up the flexibility the MNC obtains by having more than one source of supply for its downstream operations. Costs to LDCs of a breakdown of its links to MNCs are raised: To this day Cuban efforts to expand nickel production are hampered by inaccessibility to the Port Nickel refinery, originally built in Louisiana by the Freeport Sulphur Company to process the difficult Cuban lateritic nickel-baring ores (Moran, 1976b).

Maximizing all linkages from mining operations remains, however, a dubious economic strategy for LDCs. In some cases, LDC resources may best be employed in activities totally unrelated to the mines. Indeed, traditiona attacks on enclaves within LDCs have been muted by recognition that some undesirable spillovers from activities run in cooperation with foreign capital can be minimized precisely by enclaves. Demonstration effects in luxury consumption, in wage claims, and in politics may best be held in check when the mining operation is tucked away in some remote part of the LDC, and its interaction with the national economy only goes through a few well-controlled channels. Remoteness from population centers is a clear advantage when the mines and refineries pollute or disfigure their surroundings.

Both world efficiency and equity could gain by greater LDC processing and marketing of minerals, and by their providing a greater share of the inputs to the mines. Forward and backward integration may, under some circumstances, be a necessary ingredient in LDC efforts to expand their bargaining power in world markets. An increasing share of LDC minerals and fuels is likely to be marketed directly by LDC organizations, cutting out the foreign middleman. But one worries that LDC enthusiasm for pushing some of these activities could generate inefficiencies. Processing can be very capital intensive, as well as skill intensive, and may not be the best investment LDCs can make. An oil-exporting country, in other words, may do better than investing in a fancy petrochemical complex.

## NEGLECTED ISSUES AND SOME CONCLUSIONS

A listing of issues neglected in this paper may be useful. The focus on LDCs kept us from inquiring about mineral policies of small industrialized countries, such as Australia, Canada, Ireland and Norway, as well as those of socialist countries. Their experiences in dealing with MNCs, the Soviet ventures in Siberia, etc., may yield insights not forthcoming from an exclusive focus on LDCs.[9] The topic of cooperation between LDCs and socialist countries in mineral technology is also intriguing. While socialist countries have called on MNCs for technological inputs in some areas, they may nevertheless be alternative sources of technology in others. The U.S.S.R. may not be able to help Cuba much in the development of lateritic nickel-bearing ores, but its contribution may be more important in the exploitation of the Masqalah phosphate deposits in Morocco. Intra-LDC cooperation may also grow, as national enterprises gain in experience. It remains to be seen whether the relations between, say Petrobras and Iraq, will be more harmonious than those between Iraq and older MNCs.

The paper analyzed LDC pressure for capturing greater shares of mineral rents and profits, but it has said nothing as to how those gains will be allocated within each LDC. A variety of outcomes is not only easy to imagine, but likley. One could speculate about the link between bargaining zeal and the manner of distributing internally the fruits of bargaining. Several LDCs groups could be isolated: The ruling group, the mine workers, the state bureaucracy, the poorest fifty percent of the population. How increasing national control over natural resources touches each of them will differ between Algeria and Saudi Arabia, between Iran and Cuba.

Many LDCs are poorly endowed with fuel and mineral resources. Tests of strength among industrialized countries, mineral-rich LDCs and MNCs will have important repercussions for those poorly endowed LDCs, a matter that has received little analytical (in contrast with propagandistic) attention.

The consequences of MNCs and minerals for the distribution of economic and political power within *developed* countries is another neglected topic. The growing debate within the United States regarding the desirability of breaking up oil MNCs indicates the importance of the issue. Industrialized country policies regarding strategic stockpiles of fuels and minerals, and how such stockpiles have influenced markets, have not been analyzed.

Mining the "commons" of mankind, such as the sea bottoms and Antarctica, has been mentioned as a clear case where international markets, as presently arranged, would yield inefficient results, also unlikely to be equitable. How to remedy the lack of clear property titles, the role of MNCs, and how to distribute the growing scarcity rents generated by the "commons" have been left for others to explore. One may notice, however, that potential remedies include taxes, which can improve efficiency in resource exploitation while generating resources that could be channelled to reduce poverty. This is one of those rare situations where both efficiency and equity could be served by taxes.

The controversy over the limits to long-term growth that may arise from finite stocks of natural resources has been ignored in this paper. It is well known that either optimistic or pessimistic models can be built by choosing suitable assumptions regarding technological progress, factor substitution, or population growth. The choice of assumptions depends much on one's animal spirits (Nordhaus, 1976, pp. 266ff).

This paper has laid great stress on the technical and political difficulties hampering the smooth functioning of international trade and investment in minerals. The skeptical reader may suggest that many of the points made to support this view apply equally well to all international markets. It may, in fact, be difficult to demonstrate statistically that international markets for oil, uranium, and gold have historically been less perfect than those for coffee and machine tools. Peering into the future, one can at least argue that policymakers are likely to continue perceiving international markets for most exhaustible natural resources as more imperfect than others. The United States proposal for an International Resources Bank, for example, stresses that world investment is being inefficiently allocated, with too little going to exploit LDC mineral deposits, because of fears of noncommerical risks. LDCs engaged in mineral production, on the other hand, are hardly satisfied with world markets as they are. Grumbling and agitation of this sort on both sides does not seem as great for other markets.

Movement toward more efficient and equitable international markets in this area is unlikely to be possible in isolation from movements in that direction in other international markets. Reasonably efficient world markets for technology and capital, for example, could do much to improve markets for exhaustible natural resources. It is a virtue of demands for a "New International Economic Order" that they emphasize the need to look at world markets in their totality, something not done since the days of the debate over the International Trade Organization.

Elsewhere, I have argued the case for international economic relations that are stand-offish, decomposable, and reversible, for a world of nation states that desire to maintain their autonomy and yet benefit from the international division of labor (Díaz Alejandro, 1975, pp. 213–241). Reasonably open and competitive markets working under clear and internationally agreed rules of the game are still the best bet for achieving movement toward such goals. Those markets have not existed in the past for minerals, and are unlikely to emerge spontaneously, or persist when they do. It was seen earlier that high doses of "customer relationships" are likely to characterize markets in minerals, making trade and investment in minerals less stand-offish and reversible than in cotton or steel. But one could imagine international rules promoting movement in the desired direction, particularly regarding closer vigilance of MNCs engaged in restraint-of-trade practices, establishing Keynes-ITO commodity stabilization agreements in selected areas, and encouraging long-term arms-length contracts of the type negotiated between Australia and Japan. With a minimum of trust between the parties, such contracts can provide a viable alternative to vertical integration, and yield both relative security of supply and sales. Fuels and minerals are fairly homogeneous and unchanging commodities not plagued by product differentiation, repair needs, etc., factors which make clear contracts problematical for many manufactured goods, such as machinery.

Changes in the structure of world trade and investment in nonrenewable resources will remain traumatic and complicated. Those whose comfortable positions are threatened by those changes, particularly MNCs, will no doubt warn about the danger of killing the goose that lays the golden eggs. This goose has cried wolf many times before, yet is alive and robust, thanks partly to its remarkable adaptive capacity. Adaptation will also be necessary for those who prefer to buy their fuels and minerals just from MNCs that speak their language. But the cultural adjustments required to be comfortable relying directly on Africans, Asians, and Latin Americans for one's fuel and minerals should not be so difficult. After all, there will not be many cheap alternatives to it in the future.

# FOOTNOTES

*Earlier versions of this paper benefited from comments and criticisms from James H. Cobbe, Benjamin I. Cohen, Richard N. Cooper, Charles P. Kindleberger, Assar Lindbeck, William D. Nordhaus, and Vahid Nowshirvani. Thanks are also due to Gail Ross for editing and typing.

1. More generally, the evidence for the United States during 1870/1900 to 1957 shows that unit costs of minerals have fallen relative to manufacturing and agricultural unit costs, as well as absolutely. See Barnett and Morse (1963, pp. 8–9). These authors optimistically conclude: "Thus, the increasing scarcity of particular resources fosters discovery or development of alternative resources, not only equal in economic quality but often superior to those replaced" (p. 10). In one of their few references to LDCs in the book, the authors note less optimistically for LDCs: "During the past generation or two, technological advances and economic policies in the industrial countries may have worked against the interest of the less industrialized countries more often than in their favor . . . [T]he tendency of technological advance to make natural resources more homogeneous . . . reduces the actual or potential value of high quality natural resources that once were essential for industry. Since the unexploited reserves of rich mineral resources are located mainly in the less industrialized countries, these countries are harmed, not helped, by such technological developments" (pp. 259–260).

2. See the story "Texas Sets December Oil Output at 99%; Cut is Bid to Send Washington a Message," *The Wall Street Journal* (Friday, November 19, 1976, p. 12).

3. See Theodore H. Moran (1974, p. 22). It has been asserted that "Virtually everywhere in the Third World concessions as they were written twenty years ago were giveaways" (Hunt, 1975, pp. 346–347).

4. There is another case, of at least theoretical interest, for LDC-MNC joint maximization. Suppose an LDC has many small mines each with rising marginal costs for the same mineral. Each mine is owned by a different, price-taking producer. Suppose further that a single MNC buys the mineral from the mine owners. Joint maximization by the MNC and the mine owners will be more profitable than the arms-length (monopsonistic) solution. The argument has been developed by Richard N. Cooper (1972). See also Chapter 2 in Raymond F. Mikesell (1971).

5. "Certainly, resource owners have become increasingly monopolistic over time, the most notable example now being the oil cartel OPEC, but, with cartels and oligopolies being formed in rock phosphates, bauxite and copper, the trend is a general one" (Editorial introduction in Pearce, 1975, p. 17).

6. On oil, see Adelman (1972, 1973); on copper, see Moran (1974).

7. I owe this point, among others, to James H. Cobbe, who is writing his Ph.D. thesis at Yale University on investments in natural resources.

8. See M. L. O. Faber (1974). Interest payments also continue to be allowed as a cost. Adjustments are allowed for abnormal inflation, exchange rate fluctuations, and new tax regulations. I am grateful to James H. Cobbe for explanations on the Bougainville arrangement.

9. Helen Hughes (1975, p. 817) has argued that there is no link between a country's level of development and its policies.

# COMMENT

## RAYMOND F. MIKESELL*

Professor Díaz Alejandro has written a stimulating and objective paper on a subject all too often obscured by political slogans and a recitation of historical injustices. I get a little weary of reading policy papers on the benefits and costs of modern direct investment in the LDCs in which the author has based his empirical evidence on the atrocities of King Leopold's enterprises in the Belgian Congo at the end of the last century. The basic problems of finding, extracting, and distributing the exhaustible resources of the Third World in the future can only be advanced by an understanding of the current economic and political situation.

Professor Díaz Alejandro's paper actually deals with three related subjects, namely: the economics of extractive resources, the past and future world markets for these resources, and the contractual relations between MNCs and LDCs for their development. I shall comment briefly on all three of these important topics.

First of all, I am not impressed with the relevance of either the Hotelling or the Ricardian models for an understanding of the exhaustible resource industries. In the absence of long-run monopoly power, I doubt whether the net price of any important resource may be expected to rise at a rate equal to the rate of interest appropriate to a resource investment or to the marginal productivity of reproducible capital. Developing countries are not well advised to delay development of their resources for a generation or so, except of course those resources whose development would not yield the current rate of return on the reproducible capital required to develop them. Private foreign investors in developing countries no longer have the choice of holding ore bodies for future development, since their right to hold them idle is seriously limited by most exploration contracts currently being negotiated. I might say in passing that I think this is often a mistake, since foreign companies are deterred from any exploration other than that which is expected to yield an ore body economically capable of being mined within a short period of time. They cannot invest in knowledge that is potentially productive at some future time.

As regards the Ricardian rent model, I would not deny the existence of differential rents. Rents or at least quasi-rents arise whenever a successful investment has been made. However, most mining ventures in the modern world do not resemble the story of the lucky finder of a rich lode who lives in luxury off the rents the rest of his life. It is more often the story of

*University of Oregon

a well-organized exploration program with each investigation initially
constituting a several hundred-to-one shot and each decision to carry the
investigation to the next stage, where the probabilities for a successful
investment are, say, ten-to-one and requiring hundreds of thousands or
millions of dollars, based on a fairly sophisticated estimation of probabilities derived from geological knowledge and experience. It is true that
luck helps, and I have heard it said that some exploration managers would
rather have a lucky geologist than a well-trained one, but the exploration
budgets of successful mining firms are not allocated as if their geologists
were playing a zero-sum crap game. By and large, modern exploration
involves a rational decision-making process and a long-run expected rate
of return.

Many, if not most, of the great mines today were not simply the products of mother nature that a lucky miner happened to stumble upon. Díaz
Alejandro refers to Kennecott's El Teniente mine in Chile. This mine,
12,000 feet in the Andes, had been worked by the Spanish explorers, who
were forced to abandon it because the snow, the wind, and the avalanches
proved too much for them. The modern El Teniente mine was a product of
American engineering and metallurgy, and of a risky $25 million invest-
ment in 1910 dollars over a ten-year period, before it was a success. Much
the same thing can be said about Chile's Chuquicamata mine, the largest
mine in the world, where mining on a small scale had gone on for many
decades before it was developed by U.S. capital in 1913; and no dividends
were paid until 1923. Without modern engineering and metallurgy for
extracting low-grade porphyry deposits, these mines would be worth
nothing. Much the same scenario can be painted for Toquepala and Cerro
de Pasco in Peru, and for many other great mines around the world.

I am saying that in modern mining the returns are mainly a reward for
risky investments in exploration and development and for skills and management without which the rocks in the mountains and the deserts containing perhaps a fraction of 1 percent mineralization would have little or
no value. This is not to deny the existence of rents, but to say that the
rents arise from the entire structure that constitutes a mine as a product of
man's ingenuity and toil.

Orris Herfindahl in his well-known book, *Copper Costs and Prices*
(1959, Ch. 8), advanced the hypothesis that the long-run price of copper
tends to equal the price that is sufficient to induce continued investment at
all stages of production from exploration to refining. Without going into
the details of his hypothesis, Herfindahl found that it held up fairly well
empirically over the period 1885 to 1956, and my own studies indicate that
it has held up fairly well since 1956. There may be a few bonanzas to be
found in the major minerals, and we all hope that there will be another
great oil field discovered that will rival that under the Arabian peninsula

and not too far from the continental United States. But when that happens, I suspect that as in the case of the Alaskan oil fields, the revenues, less the costs of discovery, production, transportation, and environmental controls plus royalties and taxes, will about equal a reasonable internal rate of return on the investment.

Turning now to the question of world markets for minerals, I agree that they have not been a model of either competition or of benign stabilization. However, I am not convinced that the transfer of market power from MNCs to LDCs either individually or collectively, or to a collusive conspiracy involving MNCs and LDCs would produce better results. What do we want from the world market structure for exhaustible resources? The producing governments want the highest possible prices without moving into the elastic portion of the long-run demand curve, but this is not what the world's consumers want. Although I agree with Solow (1974, p. 13) that governments or international organizations might provide better information for long-run investment decisions and that the establishment of longer-term futures markets would help, I have no enthusiasm for international commodity agreements. First, there is no basis for agreement on objectives: The LDC exporting countries do not want price stabilization—they want maximum export earnings. Second, I have no confidence in the ability of an international commodity cartel control mechanism to achieve its objectives, whatever they are. Imperfect competition is better than none, and despite temporary market rigging in the past, the mineral industry has not done too badly in expanding productive capacity to meet world requirements, and for most minerals at prices that have not been too far out of line with long-run costs. Petroleum is another story, but the OPEC monopoly may have conserved the world's oil supplies for another generation and stimulated the development of alternative energy sources. Speaking of the intergenerational problem, Professor Díaz Alejandro mentioned the possibility of employing an artificially low rate of discount in order to preserve exhaustible resources for future generations. I would disagree with this approach. Like Solow (1974, p. 11), I have considerable faith in the elasticity of substitution between exhaustible and reproducible goods, and I am not interested in making sacrifices for a future generation that is likely to be richer than my own. We may all be thankful for the sacrifices of poorer generations in the past that have made possible today's relative opulence, but many are inclined to ask, "What has the future generation done for us lately?"

I now come to the complex question of the future role of foreign direct investment in the development of exhaustible resources in the LDCs where the richest ore bodies for many minerals are to be found. This is a serious problem, because in my experience with mining companies, I find increasing reluctance to undertake exploration and development, given today's investment climate. I do not share Professor Díaz Alejandro's concern over the ability of the LDCs to capture the rents from mineral deposits. Not only do I think he has overstated the importance of the rents from the mineral lands, but the LDCs have sought to capture too much of the returns necessary to induce foreign investment in their extraction. We have just seen the abandonment by foreign private enterprise of what is potentially the richest large copper mine in the world, namely, Tenke-Fungurume in Zaire, following an expenditure of over $200 million. Southern Peru Copper Corporation will be fortunate if it is able to meet the service payments on over a half billion dollars in debt incurred on its Cuajone mine, and it will probably be many years before the owners receive any dividends on their $200 million equity investment. All of the alleged advantages from national ownership in terms of national employment, training, linkages, and processing are being achieved more efficiently under private ownership than they are likely to be under nationalization. Nor do I see any gain in breaking up the foreign investment package and buying the pieces at bargain world prices. The most important pieces—managerial experience embodied in a reputable international mining firm and the commitment of equity capital by the firm, the returns on which are dependent on the productivity of the enterprise—cannot be bought. It is true that some LDC governments can run a mining industry for a time after it has been established by an experienced international mining firm, but virtually none has been able to establish a new mining industry or to expand an existing one significantly without equity participation by foreign private enterprise. This, of course, may change in time, but the cost of waiting will be great.

Debt capital can be hired and the debt-equity ratio in the mining industry has been rising rapidly as large-scale mines now require hundreds of millions of dollars—perhaps billions in the future—to finance. I welcome Dr. Díaz Alejandro's endorsement of Secretary Kissinger's International Resources Bank both as a source of financing and as an "honest broker" between host countries and the foreign investor. But if Dr. Kissinger's proposal is, as Professor Díaz Alejandro suggests, a tribute to the LDCs's call for a new international economic order—which I frankly doubt—why has it been so coldly received by the Third World? To my mind the most important problem facing the LDCs with respect to their exhaustible resources, and for that matter for the world's consumers of those resources, is not how to squeeze out a little more of the rents by nationalization or otherwise, but now to attract international mining firms to explore for and develop these resources. Why strive for a larger piece of a smaller pie?

What kinds of contracts will assure a competitive return on high-risk capital without fear that the contract will be nullified on the grounds that

Third World governments have a sovereign right, and perhaps a social duty, to renounce their covenants whenever they believe such action is in the interest of public welfare? Professor Díaz Alejandro has made some interesting suggestions on which I will comment briefly.

The approach of limiting the life of mineral development contracts to twenty years or so is well taken, but this has already become a rather standard feature of such contracts. However, efforts to limit them to a period of less than twenty years after the initiation of production is likely to be uninteresting to prospective investors.

Recognizing that disputes between the host government and the foreign investor are inevitable does not help much if it means that the host government has a unilateral right to demand changes in contracts whenever there is a change in world conditions or a shift in bargaining power between the government and the investor. I do agree that flexibility in dealing with well-defined contingencies should be built into the contracts, and that disputes over the interpretation of contracts should be submitted to impartial arbitration. However, I do not believe that a provision for periodic renegotiation of the contract, say, every five years, constitutes a solution, since host governments will be under political pressure to win concessions from the foreign investor during each renegotiation period. The areas subject to renegotiation, and the conditions giving rise to renegotiation, should be carefully delineated and should provide for redress for both parties.

Above all, the opportunity of the investor to earn an agreed minimum internal rate of return on his investment should be protected. I am glad that Professor Díaz Alejandro mentioned the Garnaut-Ross "Resource Rent Tax" formula in his paper, because I think it is the most attractive approach to the tax problem that I have seen and embodies in a technical formula what I myself have been advocating for a number of years. If nothing else, the embodiment of this principle in contracts would educate host-government officials to the fact that a relatively high accounting rate of return after five to ten years of zero earnings does not mean a high internal rate of return on discounted-cash-flow.

I think we need more imaginative contracts between governments and investors in the resource field and this is an area to which advisors to both governments and MNCs can make a significant contribution. However, no contractual arrangement is worth much unless there is a commitment to honor it. Governments that take the position that they have a sovereign right to renounce contacts, whenever they believe it is to their advantage to do so, are in fact giving up an important aspect of sovereignty— namely, the ability to negotiate contracts that depend for their validity on faith in the integrity of the government.

# COMMENT

## DONALD L. GUERTIN*

Professor Díaz Alejandro has prepared an extremely interesting paper treating a number of important questions in the area of international markets for exhaustible resources. He has also raised a number of significant points on the relationships between less-developed countries and multinational corporations. My comment will focus on a limited number of these points and will emphasize two subjects raised in the paper:

—The competitive nature of the raw materials industry, on which I will draw heavily on information about the oil industry.

—Future relations between MNCs and less-developed countries, again drawing on the experience of the oil industry. I will stress the need to look at these relationships in the context of the supply/demand forecast for the raw materials of interest.

Turning first to the competitive nature of raw materials industries, I will provide some information that demonstrates that they have been competitive. While treating primarily the oil industry, some information on other raw materials industries will be provided.

I believe that after studying Professor Díaz Alejandro's paper, a reader would conclude that international markets for exhaustible resources have not been competitive in the past, and that MNCs have substituted their corporate planning activities for open markets. The paper does recognize that there has been competition among MNCs and also notes stability in prices in a number of key commodities. However, there is a clear impression that markets have not been functioning effectively. These markets have, in fact, been competitive, as I will demonstrate below.

The reader might also conclude that profits have been very high for MNCs involved in this area. The paper notes that some bits of evidence indicate that profits in many mining ventures and in oil were above the normal level. In addition, the paper states that " . . . one took for granted that LDCs were gradually increasing their pure rents, a process which need not affect prices paid by consumers." Industry profits have actually been reasonable, as I will demonstrate.

Lastly, upon reading the paper, it might be felt that there will be an extremely limited role for MNCs in the future because of new contractual mechanisms and other new approaches such as the International Resources Bank. I believe that there will continue to be a significant but changing role for MNCs in the resource area.

*Exxon Corporation

*Competition in the Resource Area*

Professor Neil Jacoby (1975) has done an extensive study demonstrating the competitive nature of one major resource industry—the multinational oil industry. In looking at the competition question, Jacoby reviews the structure of the industry by function and also a standard of effective competition " . . . by which the degree of competition in an industry is judged by the actual effect on consumers as measured by the price and quality of services." In the period from 1953 to 1972, Jacoby reports significant changes in the position of the major oil companies in international activities in terms of ownership of crude oil reserves, production and sales. The seven largest companies owned 92 percent of reserves in 1953 but only 67 percent in 1972. Similar changes occurred in percent of production (87 percent to 71 percent) and product marketing (72 percent to 54 percent). In the same period, 350 different firms entered the foreign oil industry. They included fifteen large U.S. companies (e.g., Amerada Hess, Arco), twenty medium-sized U.S. companies, ten other large U.S. companies in the natural gas, chemical, and steel industries, and forty foreign companies (twenty-five private and fifteen government-owned). After reviewing such structural changes, Jacoby applies four criteria to measure effective competition:

—The behavior of crude oil price.
—The behavior of prices for refined products.
—The pace of technological change and innovation in the industry.
—The return on investment and the annual volume of investments in the industry.

He states, "The reopening of the Suez Canal in 1957 marked a radical shift from a sellers' market to a buyers' market in the foreign oil industry." He also believes that, after 1962, crude oil prices were determined on a day-to-day basis by the refining value in major refining countries. He provides extensive documentation, using data from both Europe and Japan. He notes, for example, that the Saudi Arabian crude oil prices delivered in Japan on a weight basis were $3.42 barrels in 1958, declined to a low of $1.96 barrels in 1966, and increased to $2.34 in 1972. He provides similar data for refined product prices. He then notes the extensive R & D efforts undertaken in the industry to develop new technology and increase efficiency, observing that this would not be done if competition were limited. In 1972, for example, the group of petroleum companies analyzed by the Chase Manhattan Bank spent $462 million on R & D.

Perhaps the most significant information on competitive behavior is reflected in the earnings rates on investments in foreign industries. Extensive data are available on U.S. direct foreign investment, not only in the petroleum industry, but also other industries. In the case of petroleum, rates of return on foreign investment were about 40 percent in 1955, but from 1960–1970 ranged between 11 and 15 percent. We all recognize that rates of return increased to almost 20 percent in 1974. They were, however, below 15 percent in 1975. Up to the mid-1950s, petroleum consumption was expanding more rapidly than supply and profits were very strong. Significant investments followed to meet demand. As output increased, excess productive capacity appeared and prices and profits fell, resulting in a decrease in investments in the mid-1960s. These relations between prices and return on investment on the industry's foreign investments are an excellent example of the results of effective competition. While primarily discussing multinational oil, the Jacoby book also includes rates of return on U.S. direct investments abroad in the mining and smelting industries. These rates, over the period 1955–1970, fell in the range of 7.7 to 17 percent. In 1972 they were down to 6.2 percent. In both cases, these rates of return on investment are certainly in line with those of manufacturing and with returns necessary to encourage future investment. The lower end of range would certainly not encourage future investment.

*Prices to Consumers*

Having treated the question of profit levels, let me turn to the point of whether or not consumers will pay increased prices or whether LDCs can capture a larger share of the economic rent currently accruing to the companies. The data I have just reviewed demonstrate that increases in prices must, in the long run, be absorbed by consumers. The petroleum industry has not only made heavy investments in the past, but will have heavy investment patterns in the future. Estimates indicate $40 to $50 billion per year is required over the next fifteen years to meet energy financing needs. To meet both these investment needs and provide dividends for shareholders, therefore, requires adequate rates of return. On the issue of the ability of the oil industry to absorb increased prices without changes in final prices to consumers, it should be noted that while profits on Middle Eastern oil were 80 cents per barrel in 1960, they were running at a level of 25 cents per barrel in 1975. This is about ½ cent a gallon. In 1960, host-government take was about 80 cents per barrel. In 1975, the host-government take was 11 dollars a barrel. Any major shifting of economic rent must thus be from the consumer to the supplying countries, not from the companies to the latter.

I now turn to the future relationships between MNCs in the oil industry and host-country governments and discuss some of the concepts introduced by Professor Díaz Alejandro, including changes in formulations of contracts, and concepts such as the International Resources Bank. Before doing this for any particular raw material, it is necessary to have a perspective on the international supply/demand outlook for it, as this establishes the basis for these future relationships.

*Impact of Supply/Demand Outlook*

In the case of energy, Exxon has prepared a world supply/demand outlook. The purpose in developing these estimates is to identify broad ranges of feasibility and potential limitations in the future energy balance. There are obviously major uncertainties, and the confidence that can be placed on any single numerical projection diminishes rapidly as it is extended into time.

The world now uses the energy equivalent of almost 90 million barrels of oil a day. About 55 percent of this energy is supplied by oil. In looking out to 1990, when our forecast indicates world energy requirements at about 160 million barrels a day, we foresee that oil will still supply about 50 percent of energy requirements. As you know, while there is much discussion about the development of nuclear power and solar power, and increasing utilization of coal and hydro-power, we do not see these other energy sources changing the relative position of oil in the energy forecast. Even with concerted efforts, we estimate that the area of synthetics (tar sand, shale, etc.) could at the most provide 1 percent of world energy by 1990.

Given this forecast for continuing dependence on oil, and taking into account the very strong reserve position of OPEC and more specifically the Middle East, we can see a continuing dependency on Middle East oil to meet world needs. In the forecast noted, for example, of a total 78 million barrels per day forecast for 1990, 47 million barrels per day will come from OPEC. While there have been some important discoveries— the North Sea, Alaska, etc.—the overall rate of discovery of new oil has actually fallen in the past few years, indicating again a continuing dependence on Middle East oil.

Multinational corporations in the oil industry have to develop their future relations with producing countries in the context of this outlook. These relationships have changed significantly in the past few years. In the case of Venezuela, the industry did develop a *modus vivendi* that provides for a role for the MNC. Indications are that a similar pattern will emerge in Saudi Arabia.

The future relations between host governments and MNCs in other resource areas are similarly dependent on supply/demand outlooks for each resource. In some cases, world reserves are generally not as concentrated in developing countries as is the case in oil. In addition, there may be opportunities for recycling and substitutions for some metals.

*Contracts*

It is essential to keep in mind the need for predictability in the flow of supplies and pricing in any discussion of raw materials. Both the industrialized world and less-developed countries importing various raw materials are very conscious of the serious economic problems created by significant unpredictability in raw materials markets. While recognizing, therefore, the concerns of exporting countries, it is essential to maintain a balanced perspective in this area.

In discussing the future of MNCs, Díaz Alejandro stresses contracts with host countries and discusses a number of problems, including: the duration of the contract, the handling of disputes, renegotiating provisions, and institutionalizing contract changes, for example, fade-out formulas. He states that "brief periods of harmony between points of negotiations may be well worth striving for." The oil industry has had a great deal of experience with contracts and has demonstrated that it is possible to work with host governments to develop mutually satisfactory contractual relationships. But some basic principles must be kept in mind. Both parties, MNCs and LDCs, have much to gain from predictability in future relationships and a clear understanding of rights and responsibilities. With respect to duration, while there is general agreement that 99-year contracts are not feasible, it is possible to go to the other extreme of overly frequent renegotiation, based on changing economic circumstances or governments. This can create a climate in which additional investment is discouraged, and may then be detrimental to both parties.

While recognizing that there will be contract disputes, it is desirable to have agreement on arbitration mechanisms and not assume that renegotiations must always occur. There is undoubtedly a benefit to being able to handle some disagreements short of complete renegotiation.

Díaz Alejandro also raises the question of institutionalizing contract changes, for example, through fade-out formulas. This approach would cause a rapid pay-out period on an investment, thereby altering the beneficial long-term perspective of foreign investors. If a host country takes this approach, it should carefully consider potential economic benefits of a fade-out approach versus the economic benefits of a longer-term relationship with a foreign investor. A fade-out formula may appear attractive in the short term, but there can be many complications in providing satisfactory ways for a host country to replace the sources of capital, technology, and managerial support over a long period of time. There are many examples in host countries of the benefits of a long-term relationship with MNCs in such activities as the training and development of nationals, assistance in development of support industries, and assistance in developing infrastructure for local communities.

*New Approaches to Encouraging Investment*

Another subject addressed in the paper is the growing concern about the provision of adequate investment funds to develop raw materials in countries where the perceived investment climate has deteriorated. Díaz Alejandro discusses in particular the concept of the International Resource Bank presented by the U.S. at the UNCTAD meeting in Nairobi. I believe that he overstates the case, when he writes:

> Perhaps the most interesting feature of the IRB proposal is its implicit criticism of past and actual arrangements for world trade and investment in exhaustible natural resources . . . It admits gross imperfections in commodity, capital and technology markets, and *de facto* recognizes the crisis in the postwar MNC commodity stabilization regimes.

While attempting to respond to LDC concerns, the U.S. initiative does not admit gross imperfections. The proposal, for example, would be for a few billion dollars to guarantee bonds to assist development of resources in some LDCs against noncommercial risk. Overall world foreign direct investments in LDCs amounted to about $70 billion in 1975 (about $30 billion of which was estimated to be in the petroleum and mining areas), and while the proposal is significant, it does not in my view pose a completely new direction for international investment in the raw materials area. In addition, the recent OECD Declaration on International Investment and Multinational Enterprise reaffirms the interest of OECD governments in international investment and the contributions of MNCs. To quote from the Declaration:

> The Declaration and Decision . . . aim at improving the international investment climate through joint undertakings by the governments of Member countries which should strengthen confidence between multinational enterprises and States; aim further at encouraging the positive contributions of multinational enterprises—and minimize or resolve difficulties that may result from their activities, through internationally-agreed guidelines, intergovernmental consultations and review mechanisms.

A proposal to address some concerns of the LDCs should not be taken as an admission of gross past imperfections.

Other schemes for encouraging investment in countries having poor investment climates have been tried in the past. Efforts to form an International Investment Insurance Agency to provide political risk insurance have not succeeded. The International Finance Corporation, affiliated with the World Bank, is private-investment oriented, but its small capitalization rules out a significant role in natural resource development. OPIC and its counterparts in fourteen other countries insure private investors against political risk. They provide, however, limited coverage as to both countries and amounts.

These and other approaches must be judged on the basis of whether or not they actually add to net investment over the level of investment that would occur without them, as well as other factors such as their impact on current negotiations between private investors and host governments. The IRB and related concepts will undoubtedly receive continuing attention in future intergovernmental discussions, but as noted by Díaz Alejandro, "a new world order for trade and investment will 'not' spring full grown from anyone's brow."

*Future Role for Multinational Corporations*

In looking to the future within the frameworks now being developed by intergovernmental activities and more particularly the actions of individual governments, it seems that MNCs will continue to play a key role. This is supported by developments in Venezuela and Saudi Arabia. The MNC in the raw materials area has a number of advantages:

—It can conduct long-term planning activities, with emphasis on economic and commercial viability. Governments have to place greater emphasis on political considerations.

—The MNC is in a better position to take the high economic risk inherent in the major investments that must be undertaken in the raw materials area. The role of government insurance schemes is one that undoubtedly will receive further attention in the coming years because of the high political risk inherent in some countries.

—The MNC has the ability to continue meeting world needs for energy or other raw materials while political relations between countries may be strained. This was illustrated by the performance of the oil industry during the oil embargo period of 1974.

—The natural resource industry has demonstrated that it is able to combine capital, technology, and managerial capabilities on a continuing basis to meet world needs. It is undoubtedly possible on a spot or short-term basis for many organizations to pull together capital, technology, and managerial capabilities. Doing this on a long-term basis is quite another matter.

On a related point, the paper suggests that it would be desirable if there were a free market in capital and technology. Actually, it is possible to obtain capital if you have a sound credit rating, and further in a number of resource industries, for example, petroleum, a great deal of technology is available off the shelf. The selection, application, and management of this technology *on a continuing basis* are the real issues, and represent the benefits and continuing need for MNCs in the resources field to the LDCs and to consumers.

# BIBLIOGRAPHY

Adelman, M. A. (1972–1973) "Oil Companies as OPEC Tax Collectors." *Foreign Policy* (Winter).

Adler, M. (1974) "The Cost of Capital and Valuation of a Two Country Firm." *Journal of Finance* (March).

———, and Dumas, B. J. (1975) "The Long-term Financial Decisions of the Multinational Corporation." In E. Elton and M. Gruber, eds., *International Capital Markets*. Amsterdam: North Holland.

AFL-CIO (1976) *The AFL-CIO Platform Proposals Presented to the Democratic and Republican Conventions*. Washington, D.C.

———(1974) "The Changing World of Multinationals." *The American Federationist* (September).

Agmon, T., and Lessard, D. R. (1976) "The Multinational Firms as Vehicle for International Diversification: Implications for Capital Importing Countries." *Revista Brasileira de Mercados de Capitais* (December).

———, forthcoming (a) "Investor Recognition of Corporate International Diversification." *Journal of Finance*.

———, forthcoming (b) "Financial Factors and the International Expansion of Small Country Firms." M.I.T. volume, C. P. Kindleberger and T. A. Agmon, eds.

Aitchison, J., and Brown, J. A. C. (1957) *The Lognormal Distribution*. Cambridge: Harvard University Press.

313

Aliber, R. Z. (1970) "A Theory of Direct Foreign Investment." In C. P. Kindleberger, ed., *The International Corporation*. Cambridge: MIT Press.

Angle, F. W. (1975) "The Conduct of Labor Relations in General Motors' Overseas Operations." In D. Kujawa, ed., *International Labor and the Multinational Enterprise*. New York: Praeger.

Ansoff, H. I. (1965) *Corporate Strategy*, New York: McGraw-Hill.

Areskoug, K. (1969) *External Borrowing: Its Role in Economic Development*. New York: Praeger.

———(1973) "Foreign Capital Utilization and Economic Policies in Developing Countries." *Review of Economics and Statistics* (May).

———(1976) "Foreign Direct Investment and Capital Formation in Developing Countries." *Economic Development and Cultural Change* (April).

Armand, L., and Darancourt, M. (1970) *The European Challenge*, New York; Atheneum.

Arpan, J. S. (1971) *International Intracorporate Pricing: Non-American Systems and Views*. New York: Praeger.

Arrow, K. J. (1962) "Economic Welfare and the Allocation of Resources to Invention." *The Rate and Direction of Inventive Activity: Economic and Social Factors*. National Bureau of Economic Research. New York: Princeton University Press.

———(1975) "Vertical Integration and Communication." *The Bell Journal of Economics* (Spring).

Baer, W. (1974) "Technology, Employment and Development: Some Empirical Findings." *World Development* (February).

Bain, J. S. (1959) *Industrial Organization*. New York: John Wiley.

Balasubramanyam, V. N. (1973) *International Transfer of Technology to India*. New York: Praeger.

Balla, A. S. (1976) "Technology and Employment: Some Conclusions. " *International Labor Review* (March-April).

Baranson, J. (1969) *Industrial Technologies for Developing Economies*. New York: Praeger.

———(1970) "Technology Transfer Through the International Firm." *American Economic Review* (May).

———(1971) "International Transfer of Automotive Technology to Developing Countries." *UNITAR Research Reports*, No. 8. New York.

Barnet, R. J., and Muller, R. E. (1974) *Global Reach: The Power of the Multinational Corporations*. New York: Simon and Schuster.

Barnett, H. J., and Morse, C. (1963) *Scarcity and Growth: The Economics of Natural Resource Availability*. Baltimore: Johns Hopkins Press.

Bartels, C. P. A. (1975) "The Effects of Foreign Capital Inflow on Domestic Savings in Developing Countries: A Critical Survey." *Zeitschrift Für Nationalökonomie*, 35.

Basche, J. R. (1975) *Experience with Foreign Production Work Forces*. New York: Conference Board.

Behrman, J. N. (1970) *National Interests and the Multinational Enterprise*. Englewood, N.J.: Prentice-Hall.

———, and Schmid, W. E. (1959) "New Work on Foreign Licensing." *Patent, Trademark and Copyright Journal of Research and Education*, Vol. 3, Washington, D.C.

———, and Wallender, H. III (1976) *Transfer of Manufacturing Technology Within Multinational Enterprises*. Cambridge: Ballinger.

Belford, J. A. (1970) "The Supranational Corporation and Labor Relations." In A. Kannin, ed., *Western European Labor and the American Corporation*. Washington, D. C,: The Bureau of National Affairs, Inc.

Bendiner, B. (1974) "Multinationals and Transnational Bargaining: A Union View." *Conference on Industrial Relations Problems Raised by Multinationals in Advanced Industrial Societies*, November 10-13. East Lansing: Michigan State University.

Bergsten, C. F., Horst, T., and Moran, T. H. (forthcoming) *American Multinationals and American Interests*. Washington, D. C.: Brookings Institution.

Bhagwati, J. N., and Grinols, E. (1975) "Foreign Capital, Dependence, Destabilization and Feasibility of Transition to Socialism." *Journal of Development Economics* (June).

Blam, Y., and Hawkins, R. G. (1975) "Forms of Foreign Investment and the External Trade of Developing Countries: A Cross Section Study." Unpublished working paper.

Boon, G. K. (1964) *Economic Choice of Human and Physical Factors in Production*. Amsterdam: North Holland.

Borts, G. H. (1974) "Long-Run Capital Movements" *Economic Analysis and the Multinational Enterprise*, London: Allen and Unwin.

Bos, H. C., and Secchi, C. (1974) "A Macro-economic Model for Estimating Some Quantitative Effects of Private Foreign Investment in Less Developed Countries." *Planning, Income Distribution, Private Foreign Investment*. Paris: OECD.

Brash, D. T. (1966) *American Investment in Australian Industry*. Cambridge: Harvard University Press.

———(1970) "Austrialia as Host to the International Corporation." In C. P. Kindleberger, ed., *The International Corporation*. Cambridge: MIT Press.

Brooks, H. (1972) "What's Happening to the U.S. Lead in Technology?" *Harvard Business Review* (May-June).

Buckley, P., and Dunning, J. H. (1974) "The Industrial Structure of U.S. Direct Investment in the U.K." *University of Reading Discussion Paper in International Investment and Business*, No. 12.

*Business Week* (1970) "Special Report," April 20.

———(1975) "Multinationals: Bargaining on an International Scale," October 27.

Camp, H. H., and Mann, C. J. (1975) "The Mexican Law Regulating the Transfer of Technology: Summary of Experience to Date." *Columbia Journal of World Business* (Summer).

Caves, R. E. (1971a) "International Corporations: The Industrial Economics of Foreign Investment." *Economica* (February).

———(1971b) "Industrial Economics of Foreign Investment: The Case of the International Corporation." *Journal of World Trade Law* (May/June).

———(1974a) "Industrial Organisation." J. Dunning (ed.), *Economic Analysis and the Multinational Enterprise*. London: Allen and Unwin.

———(1974b) "International Trade, International Investment and Imperfect Markets." *Princeton Special Paper*. Princeton: Princeton University Press.

———(1974c) "Multinational Firms, Competition and Productivity in Host Country Markets," *Economica* (May).

———, and Reuber, G. L. (1971) *Capital Transfers and Economic Policy: Canada 1951–1962*. Cambridge: Harvard University Press.

Centre for Multinational Studies (1974) *The Group of Eminent Persons' Report on the Impact of Multinational Corporations on the Development Process and on International Relations: A Critical Analysis*. Washington, D. C., August 9.

Chase, J. (1976) "American Intervention." *The New York Times*, September 13.

Chamberlain, N. W., and Cullen, D. E. (1971) *The Labor Sector*. New York: McGraw-Hill.

Chenery, H. B., and Strout, A. M. (1966) "Foreign Assistance and Economic Development." *American Economic Review* (September).

———, and Syrquin, M. (1975) *Patterns of Development 1950–1970*. London: Oxford University Press.

Chudnovsky, D. (1975) "Empresas Multinacionales y Tecnologia en la Industria Argentina." *Comercio Exterior* (April).

Chudson, W. A. (1971) "The International Transfer of Commercial Technology to Developing Countries." *UNITAR Research Reports*, No. 13, New York.

Cilingiroglu, A. (1975) *Transfer of Technology for Pharmaceutical Chemicals*. Paris: OECD.

Clower, R., and Leijonhufvoud (1975) "The Coordination of Economic Activities: A Keynesian Perspective." *American Economic Review* (May).

Cobbe, J. H. "Investments in Natural Resources." Ongoing Ph.D. thesis at Yale University.

Cohen, B. I. (1973). "Comparative Behaviour of Foreign and Domestic Export Firms in a Developing Economy." *Review of Economics and Statistics* (May).

———(1975) *Multinational Firms and Asian Exports*. New Haven: Yale University Press.

———, Katz, J., and Beck, W. T. (1975) "Innovation and Foreign Investment Behaviour of the U.S. Pharmaceutical Industry." *NBER Working Paper*, No. 101 (August).

Cohen, B. J. (1973) *The Question of Imperialism: The Political Economy of Dominance and Dependence*. New York: Basic Books.

Cooper, C. (1971) *The Channels and Mechanisms for the Transfer of Technology from Developed to Developing Countries*. New York: UNCTAD.

Cooper, R. N. (1972) "Nationalism vs. Vertical Integration in Extractive Industries," mimeo. (May).

Copithorne, L. W. (1971) "International Corporate Transfer Prices and Government Policy." *Canadian Journal of Economics* (August).

Copp, R. (1973) "The Labor Affairs Function in a Multinational Firm." *Labor Law Journal* (August).

Corden, W. M. (1974) "The Theory of International Trade." In J. H. Dunning, ed., *Economic Analysis and the Multinational Enterprise*. London: Allen and Unwin.

Courtney, W. H., and Leipziger, D. M. (1974) *Multinational Corporations in LDCs: The Choice of Technology*. Washington, D.C., AID.

Cox, R. W. (1976) "Labor and The Multinationals." *Foreign Affairs* (January).

DasGupta, A. B. (1976) "Growth of Technology in Petroleum Exploration." *Eastern Economist*, March 12.

De la Torre, J. R. (1972) "Marketing Factors in Manufactured Exports from Developing Countries." In L. Wells, ed., *The Product Life Cycle in International Trade*. Boston: Harvard Business School.

———, Stobaugh, R. B., and Telesio, P. (1973) "Multinational Enterprises and Change in the Skill Composition of U.S. Employment." In D. Kujawa, ed., *American Labor and the Multinational Corporation*. New York: Praeger.

Dewald, W. G. (1975) "Do Imports and Exports Affect the Number of Jobs." *Bulletin of Business Research* (June), Ohio State University, Center for Business and Economic Research.

Díaz Alejandro, C. (1970) "Direct Foreign Investment in Latin America." In C. P. Kindleberger, ed., *The International Corporation*. Cambridge: MIT Press.

———(1975) "North-South Relations: The Economic Component." *International Organization* 29, No. 1 (Winter).

Dos Santos, T. (1970) "The Structure of Dependence." *American Economic Review* (May).

Driscoll, R. E., and Wallender, H. W. (1974) *Technology Transfer and Development: An Historical and Geographic Perspective*. New York, Fund for Multinational Management Education.

Dronkers, P. L. (1975) "A Multinational Organization and Industrial Relations: The Phillip's Case." In D. Kujawa, ed., *International Labor and the Multinational Enterprise*. New York: Praeger.

Duerr, M. A. (1970) *R & D in the Multinational Company*. New York: Conference Board.

Dunlop, J. T. (1958) *Industrial Relations Systems*. New York: Henry Holt.

Dunning, J. H. (1958) *American Investment in British Manufacturing Industry*. London: Allen and Unwin.

———(1969) "U.S. Subsidiaries and their U.K. Competitors." *Business Ratios* (Autumn).

———(1970) *Studies in International Investment*. London: Allen and Unwin.

———(1973a) "The Determinants of International Production." *Oxford Economic Papers* (January).

———(1973b) "Multinational Enterprises and Domestic Capital Formation." *The Manchester School of Economics* (September).

———(1974) "Multinational Enterprises, Market Structure, Economic Power and Industrial Policy." *Journal of World Trade Law* (November/December).

———, and Stever, M. (1969) "The Effects of United States Direct Investment in Britain on British Technology." *Moorgate and Wall Street* (Autumn).

Eastman, H. C., and Stykolt, S. (1967) *The Tariff and Competition in Canada*. Toronto: Macmillan.

English, H. E. (1964) *Industrial Structure in Canada's International Competitiveness*. Montreal: Canadian Trade Committee.

Eshag, E. (1971) "Foreign Capital, Domestic Savings and Economic Development." *Bulletin of Oxford University, Institute of Economics and Statistics* (May).

Faber, M. L. O. (1974) "Bougainville Re-negotiated—An Analysis of the New Fiscal Terms." *Mining Magazine,* (December).

Field, M. (1974) "State Taxation of Interstate Commerce: Its Relevance to the International Taxation of Corporate Income," mimeo., Washington, D. C.

Finan, W. (1975) "The International Transfer of Semiconductor Technology Through U.S.-Based Firms." *NBER Working Paper 118* (December).

*Financial Times* (1973), October 23.

Frankena, M. (1972) "Restrictions on Exports by Foreign Investors: The Case of India." *Journal of World Trade Law* (November/December).

Franko, L. G. (1973) "The Growth, Organization, Structure and Allocative Efficiency of European Multinational Enterprise." In G. Bertin, ed., *The Growth of the Large Multinational Corporation*. Rennes, France: University of Rennes.

———(1974) "The Origins of Multinational Manufacturing by Continental European Firms." *Business History Review* (Autumn).

Freeman, C. (1971) "Comment on Keith Pavitt: The Multinational Enterprise and the Transfer of Technology." In J. H. Dunning, ed., *The Multinational Enterprise*. London: Allen and Unwin.

Freeman, C. (1974) *The Economics of Industrial Innovation*. Manchester: The University Press.

Frerk, P. (1974) "Review of Transnational Activities in Automotive Worker Unions and Volkswagen Experience." *Annual Meeting of the American Society for Personnel Administration,* Minneapolis, Minnesota, June 18.

Frowein, F. (1964) "Den Deutche Lizenzvenkehn mit dem Ausland." *Gewerolichen Rechtsshutz, Und Urheberrecht, Auslands-und Internationalen Teil*. Weinheim/Bergstrasse.

Fulgate, W. L. (1971) "The International Aspects of the U.S. Anti-trust Laws." In J. B. Heath, ed., *International Conference on Monopolies and Mergers*. London: H.M.S.O.

Garnaut, R., and Ross, A. C. (1975) "Uncertainty, Risk Aversion and the Taxing of Natural Resource Projects." *The Economic Journal* (June).

Gerardi, G. (1976) "Transfer Pricing and Profit Shifting: An Empirical Analysis." Doctoral Dissertation, American University.

Gillis, M., and McLure, C. E., Jr. (1975) "Incidence of World Taxes on Natural Resources with Special Reference to Bauxite." *The American Economic Review* (May).

Globerman, S. (1973a) "Technological Diffusion in the Canadian Tool and Die Industry." Toronto, York University.

———— (1973b) "Technological Diffusion in the Canadian Paper Industry." Toronto, York University.

Goldfinger, N. (1973) "An American Trade Union View of International Trade and Investment." In D. Kujawa, ed., *American Labor and the Multinational Corporation*. New York: Praeger.

Governeur, J. (1971) *Productivity and Factor Proportions in Less Developed Countries*. Oxford: Oxford University Press.

Government of Canada (1972) *Foreign Investment in Canada*. The Gray Report, Ottawa, Queen's Printer.

Gray, H. P. (1972) *Economics of Business Investment Abroad*. New York: Crane, Russak.

Grayet, R. M. (1973) "Other Aspects of Multinational Companies." *Annals of Public and Cooperative Economy* (June).

Griffin, K. (1969) *Underdevelopment in Spanish America*. London: Allen and Unwin.

———— (1970) "Foreign Capital, Domestic Savings and Economic Development." *Bulletin of Oxford University, Institute of Economics and Statistics* (May).

———— (1971) "The Role of Foreign Capital." In K. Griffin, ed., *Financing Development in Latin America*. London: Macmillan.

————, and Enos, J. L. (1970) "Foreign Assistance: Objective and Consequences." *Economic Development and Cultural Change* (April).

Griffin, K., Newlyn, W. T., and Papanek, G. F. (1973) "The Effect of Aid and Other Resource Transfers on Savings and Growth in Less Developed Countries: An Interchange." *Economic Journal* (September).

Grinols, E., and Bhagwati, J. N. (1976). "Foreign Capital, Savings and Dependence." *Review of Economics and Statistics* (November).

Grubel, H. G. (1968) "Internationally Diversified Portfolios." *American Economic Review* (December).

Gruber, W. D., and Vernon, R. (1970) "The Technology Factor in a World Trade Matrix." In R. Vernon, ed., *The Technology Factor in International Trade*. New York: Columbia University Press.

————, Mehta, D., and Vernon, R. (1967) "The R & D Factor in International Trade and International Investment of United States Industries." *Journal of Political Economy* (February).

Gupta, K. L. (1971) "Dependency Rates and Savings Rates." *American Economic Review* (June).

———— (1975) "Foreign Capital Inflows, Dependency Burden, and Savings Rates in Developing Countries: A Simultaneous Equation Model." *Kyklos,* Fasc. 3.

Hahn, Y. K. (1974) "The Effect of Foreign Resources on Domestic Savings." *South African Journal of Economics* (March).

Hall, G. R., and Johnson, R. E. (1970) "Transfers of United States Aerospace Technology to Japan." In R. Vernon, ed., *The Technology Factor in International Trade*. New York: Columbia University Press.

Hammer, R. M., Marrione, M. S., and Ryan, E. (1972) "Concepts and Techniques in Determining the Reasonableness of Intercompany Pricing between United States Corporations and Their Overseas Subsidiaries." In Henry Sellin, ed., *New York University Thirtieth Annual Institute on Federal Taxation*. New York: Matthew Bender.

Haq, M. W. (1975) "A New Framework for International Resource Transfers." *Insight* (October).

Haverman, H. A. (1969) Lizenzuen-gabe und Normung als Sonderprobleme technologischen Anpassung. *Kühel-Stiftung, Technologische Anpassung Fachgesprach* (April).

Hawkins, R. G. (1972) "Job Displacement and the Multinational Firm: A Methodological Review." *Center for Multinational Studies, Occasional Paper No. 3* (June).

—— (1975) "The Impact of MNCs on Host Countries: The Arena for Continuing Conflict." Unpublished.

—— (1976) "Jobs, Skills and U.S. Multinationals." *New York University Graduate School of Business Administration Working Paper No. 76-07* (February).

Hawtrey, R. G. (1930) *Economic Aspects of Sovereignty.* London, New York, Toronto: Longmans, Green.

Helleiner, G. K. (1973) "Manufactured Exports from Less Developed Countries and Multinational Firms." *The Economic Journal* (March).

—— (1975) "The Role of Multinational Corporations in the Less Developed Countries' Trade in Technology." *World Development* (April).

Hellman, R. (1970) *The Challenge to U.S. Dominance of International Corporation.* New York: Dunellen.

Herfindahl, O. C. (1959) *Copper Costs and Prices: 1870–1957.* Baltimore: John Hopkins Press for Resources for the Future, Inc.

Hershfield, D. C. (1975) *The Multinational Union Faces the Multinational Company.* New York: Conference Board.

Hirschman, A. O. (1958) *The Strategy of Economic Development.* New Haven: Yale University Press.

Hogan, W. P. (1962) "The Impact of the Foreign Sector on Industrial Structure." Paper to Australia-New Zealand-A.A.S.

—— (1966) "British Manufacturing Subsidiaries in Australia and Export Franchises." *Australian Economic Papers,* No. 22 (July).

—— (1968) "Capacity Creation and Utilization in Pakistan Manufacturing Industry." *Australian Economic Papers* (June).

Hopper, K. (1969) "The Nature of American Management." *Moorgate and Wall Street* (Autumn).

Hotelling, H. (1931) "The Economics of Exhaustible Resources." *Journal of Political Economy* (April).

Houthakker, H. S. (1965) "On Some Determinants of Savings in Developed and Underdeveloped Countries." In E. A. G. Robinson, ed., *Problems in Economic Development.* London: Macmillan.

Hufbauer, G. (1975a) "The Multinational Corporation and Direct Investment." In P. B. Kenen, ed., *International Trade and Finance.* New York: Oxford.

—— (1975b) "The Taxation of Export Profits." *National Tax Journal* 28 (March).

——, and Adler, F. M. (1968) *Overseas Manufacturing Investment and the Balance of Payments.* U.S. Treasury, Washington, D. C.: U.S. G.P.O.

Hughes, H. (1975) "Economic Rents, the Distribution of Gains from Mineral Exploitation, and Mineral Development Policy." *World Development* (November/December).

Hulin-Cuypers, G (1973) "Aspects of Multinational Companies." *Annals of Public and Cooperative Economy* (June).

Hunt, S. (1975) "Direct Foreign Investment in Peru: New Rules for an Old Game." In A. F. Lowenthal, ed., *The Peruvian Experiment: Continuity and Change Under Military Rule.* Princeton: Princeton University Press.

Hymer, S. H. (1960) *The International Operations of National Firms: A Study of Direct Foreign Investment.* Ph.D. Dissertation, M.I.T. Cambridge: MIT Press (1976).

―――― (1970) "The Efficiency (Contradictions) of Multinational Corporations." *American Economic Review* (May).

Iacuelli, D., Kirvy, J. C., Samuelson, W. F., Stobaugh, R. B., and Warren, T. R. (1973) *The Effect on the U.S. Economy of Eliminating the Deferral of U.S. Income Tax on Foreign Earnings*. Cambridge: Management Analysis Center.

International Labor Office (1973) *Multinational Enterprises and Social Policy*. Geneva.

―――― (1975) *Multinationals in Western Europe: The Industrial Relations Experience*. Geneva.

―――― (1976a) *The Impact of Multinational Enterprises on Employment and Training*. Geneva.

―――― (1976b) *Wages and Working Conditions in Multinational Enterprises*. Geneva.

International Metalworkers' Federation (IMF) (1966) *Report: First International Conference: World Auto Councils*, Detroit, May 31–June 6. Geneva, I.M.F.

――――(1968) *Regional Reports: 1. The State of the West European Automobile Industry* (February). Geneva, I.M.F.

―――― (1971) *Survey of Collective Bargaining Agreements in the Automobile Industry in North America, Europe and Australasia*. Geneva, I.M.F.

―――― (1974) *Proceedings of the Twenty-Third Congress*, Stockholm, July 2–6, Geneva, I.M.F.

*International Organization* (1975) "North-South Relations: The Economic Component" (Winter).

Iverson, C. (1936) *Some Aspects of the Theory of International Capital Movements*. Oxford: Oxford University Press.

Jacquemin, A. P. (1974) "Application to Foreign Firms of European Rules on Competition." *Antitrust Bulletin* (Spring).

Jager, E. R. (1975) "U.S. Labor and Multinationals." In D. Kujawa, ed., *International Labor and the Multinational Enterprise*. New York: Praeger.

Jedel, M. J., and Staumm, J. H. (1973) "The Battle over Jobs: An Appraisal of Recent Publications on the Employment Effects of U.S. Multinational Corporations." In D. Kujawa, ed., *American Labor and the Multinational Corporation*. New York: Praeger.

――――, and Kujawa, D. (1976) "Management and Employment Practices of Foreign Direct Investors in the United States." *Foreign Direct Investment in the United States: Report to the Congress*, Vol. 5, U.S. Department of Commerce, Washington, D. C.

Jéquier, N., ed. (1976) *Appropriate Technology: Problems and Promises*. Paris: Development Center, OECD.

Johns, B. L. (1967) "Private Overseas Investment in Australia: Profitability and Motivation." *Economic Record* (June).

Johnson, H. G. (1970a) "The Efficiency and Welfare Implications of the International Corporation." In C. P. Kindleberger, ed., *The International Corporation*. Cambridge: MIT Press.

―――― (1970b) "Multinational Corporations and International Oligopoly: The Non-American Challenge." In C. P. Kindleberger, ed., *The International Corporation*. Cambridge: MIT Press.

Johnson, P. S. (1970) "Firm Size and Technological Change." *Moorgate and Wall Street* (Spring).

Kaplinsky, R. (1976) "Accumulation and the Transfer of Technology: Issues of Conflict and Mechanisms for the Exercise of Control." *World Development* (March).

Kapoor, A. (1974) "U.S.-Japanese Investment in the Pacific Basin: The Intensifying Battle." *New York University Graduate School of Business Administration Working Paper* (November).

Kassalow, E. M. (1975) "The International Metalworkers' Federation and the Latin American and Asian Automotive Industries." In D. Kujawa, ed., *International Labor and the Multinational Enterprise*. New York: Praeger.

—— (1976) "MNCs and their Impact on Industrial Relations." *International Conference on Trends in Industrial and Labor Relations,* Montreal (May).

Kay, J. A., and Mirrlees, J. A. (1975) "The Desirability of Natural Resource Depletion." In D. W. Pearce and J. Rose, eds., *The Economics of Natural Resource Depletion*. London: Macmillan.

Keesing, B. (1967) "The Impact of Research and Development on United States Trade." *Journal of Political Economy* (February).

Kenen, P. B., and Lawrence, R., eds. (1968) *The Open Economy: Essays on International Trade and Finance*. New York: Columbia University Press.

Kennedy, C., and Thirlwall, A. P. (1971) "Foreign Capital, Domestic Savings and Economic Development: Comment." *Bulletin of Oxford University, Institute of Economics and Statistics* (May).

Kindleberger, C. P. (1969) *American Business Abroad: Six Lectures on Direct Investment*. New Haven: Yale University Press.

King, T. (1971) "Private Savings." In K. Griffin, ed., *Financing Development in Latin America*. London: Macmillan.

Knickerbocker, F. T. (1973) *Oligopolistic Reaction and Multinational Enterprise*. Harvard University, Graduate School of Business Administration.

——(1976) "Market Structure and Market Power Consequences of Foreign Direct Investment by Multinational Corporations." *Center for Multinational Studies, Occasional Paper,* No.8.

Kopits, G. F. (1972) "Dividend Remittance Behaviour Within the International Firm: A Cross-Country Analysis." *Review of Economics and Statistics* (August).

——(1976a) *Taxation and Multinational Firm Behaviour: A Critical Survey*. Unpublished IMF Working Paper (March).

——(1976b) "Intrafirm Royalties Crossing Frontiers and Transfer Pricing Behaviour." *The Economic Journal* (December).

Krishnamurit, R. (1973) "Some Effects of the Multinational Corporations." *Intreeconomics,* No. 12.

Kujawa, D. (1971) *International Labor Relations Management in the Automobile Industry*. New York: Praeger.

—— (1972) "Foreign Sourcing Decisions and the Duty to Bargain under the NLRA." *Law and Policy in International Business,* No. 3.

——, ed. (1973) *American Labor and the Multinational Corporation*. New York: Praeger.

—— (1974) "Book Review: Implications of Multinational Firms for World Trade and Investment and for U.S. Trade and Labor." *Law and Policy in International Business,* No. 2.

—— (1975a) "Transnational Industrial Relations and the Multinational Enterprise." *Journal of Business Administration,* No. 1.

—— "Transnational Industrial Relations: A Collective Bargaining Prospect?" In D. Kujawa, ed., *International Labor and the Multinational Enterprise*. New York: Praeger.

Lal, D. (1975) *Appraising Foreign Investment in Developing Countries*. London: Heinemann.

Lall, S. (1973) "Transfer Pricing by Multinational Manufacturing Firms." *Oxford Bulletin of Economics and Statistics* (August).

Lake, A. W. (1976a) "Transnational Activity and Market Entry in the Semiconductor Industry." *NBER Working Paper 126* (March).

—— (1976b) "Foreign Competition and the U.K. Pharmaceutical Industry." *NBER Proposed Working Paper* (March).

Leff, N. H. (1969a) "Investment in the LDCs: The Next Wave." *Columbia Journal of World Business*.

—— (1969b) "Dependency Rates and Savings Rates." *American Economic Review* (December).

Lessard, D. (1976) "World, Country and Industry Relationships in Equity Returns: Implications for Risk Reduction Through International Diversification." *Financial Analysts Journal* (January/February).

Levinson, C. (1973) *International Trade Unionism*. London: Allen and Unwin.

Lipsey, R., and Weiss, M. (1975) "Exports and Foreign Investment in the Pharmaceutical Industry." *NBER Working Paper 87* (May).

Little, I. M. D., Scitovsky, T., and Scott, M. (1970) *Industry and Trade in Some Developing Countries: A Comparative Study*. London: Oxford University Press.

Lovell, E. B. (1969) *Appraising Foreign Licensing Performance*. New York: Conference Board.

Macaluso, D., and Hawkins, R. G. (1977) "The Avoidance of Restrictive Monetary Policy in Host Countries by Multinational Firms." *Journal of Money, Credit, and Banking* (November).

Magee, S. P. (1976) *International Trade and Distortions in Factor Markets*. New York: Marcel Dekker.

—— (1977a) "Information and the Multinational Corporation: An Appropriability Theory of Direct Foreign Investment." In J. N. Bragwati, ed., *Proceedings of Conference on the New International Economic Order*. Cambridge: MIT Press.

—— (1977b) "Multinational Corporations, the Industry Technology Cycle and the Transfer of Technology to Developing Countries." *Journal of World Trade Law*.

Mansfield, E. (1963) "Intra Firm Rates of Diffusion of an Innovation." *Review of Economics and Statistics* (August).

—— (1968) *Industrial Research and Technical Innovation*, London: Longmans.

Mantel, I. M. (1975) "Sources and Uses of Funds for a Sample of Majority Owned Foreign Affiliates of U.S. Companies, 1966–72." *Survey of Current Business* (July).

Marshall, H. D., and Marshall, N. J. (1971) *Collective Bargaining*. New York: Random House.

Mason, R. H. (1971) "The Transfer of Technology and Factor Proportions Problem: The Phillipines and Mexico." *UNITAR Research Report* No. 10. New York.

—— (1973a) "The Multinational Firm and the Cost of Technology to Developing Countries." *California Management Review*, No. 4.

—— (1973b) "Some Observations on the Choice of Technology by Multinational Firms in Developing Countries." *Review of Economics and Statistics* (August).

Mast, H. (1972) "Schwierige Wege zur Lösung des Technologie Transferno." *Blichdurct die Wirtschaft*. (November 20).

—— (1975) "Lizenz politik schädlich für Entwichlungsländen." *Manager Magazine* (June).

McDougall, G. D. (1960) "The Benefits and Costs of Private Investment from Abroad: A Theoretical Approach." *Economic Record* (March).

McLure, E., Jr. (1974) "State Income Taxation of Multi State Corporations." Mimeo., Texas.

Menck, K. W. (1973) "The Concept of Appropriate Technology," *Intereconomics*. (November 1).

—— (1975) "Problems of a Code of Conduct." *Intereconomics* (October).

Mikesell, R. F., ed. (1971) *Foreign Investment in the Petroleum and Minerals Industries*. Baltimore: Johns Hopkins Press.

——, and Zinser, J. E. (1973) "The Nature of the Savings Function in Developing Countries: A Survey of the Theoretical and Empirical Literature." *Journal of Economic Literature* (March).

Miller, M. H. (1977) "Debt and Taxes." *Journal of Finance* (May).

Miller, R. R., and Weigel, D. R. (1972) "The Motivation for Foreign Direct Investment." *Journal of International Business Studies* (Fall).

Modigliani, F., and Miller, M. H. (1958) "The Cost of Capital, Corporation Finance, and the Theory of Investment." *American Economic Review* (June).

—— (1961) "Dividend Policy, Growth and the Valuation of Shares." *Journal of Business* (October).

—— (1963) "Corporate Income Taxes and the Cost of Capial—A Correction." *American Economic Review* (June).

Moran, T H. (1974) *Multinational Corporations and the Politics of Dependence: Copper in Chile*. Princeton: Princeton University Press.

—— (1976a) "Multinational Corporations and Dependency: A Dialogue for Dependentistas and Non-Dependentistas." Unpublished mimeo, SAIS, Johns Hopkins University (June).

—— (1976b) "The International Political Economy of Cuban Nickel Development." Mimeo., SAIS, Johns Hopkins University.

Morawetz, D. (1974) "Employment Implications of Industrialization in Developing Countries: A Survey." *Economic Journal* (September).

—— (1975) "Import Substitution, Employment and Foreign Exchange in Columbia: No Cheers for Petrochemicals." In C. P. Timmer, ed., *The Choice of Technology in Developing Countries*. Center for International Affairs, Harvard University.

Morgenstern, O. (1975) "Does GNP Measure Growth and Welfare?" In J. Backman, ed., *Social Responsibility and Accountability*. New York: New York University Press.

Morley, S. A., and Smith, G. W. (1977) "The Choice of Technology: Multinational Firms in Brazil." *Economic Development and Cultural Change* (January).

—— (forthcoming) "Limited Search and the Technology Choices of Multinational Firms in Brazil." *Quarterly Journal of Economics*.

Moxon, R. W. (1974) "Offshore Production in the Less-Developed Countries—A Case Study of Multinationality in the Electronics Industry." *The Bulletin*. Institute of Finance of New York University, Graduate School of Business Administration (July).

Muller, M. (1976) "Drug Companies and the Third World." *New Scientist* (April 29).

Musgrave, P. (1972) "International Tax Base Division and the Multinational Corporation." *Public Finance* 27, No. 4.

—— (1975) "Direct Investment Abroad and the Multinationals: Effects on the United States Economy. *A Report prepared for the Subcommittee on Multinational Corporations of the Committee on Foreign Relations, U. S. Senate*. Washington, D. C., U.S. Government Printing Office.

Myers, S. C. (1974) "Interactions of Corporation Financing and Investment Decisions— Implications for Capital Budgeting." *Journal of Finance* (March).

National Labor Relations Board (1962) *Town and Country Manufacturing Company* 136 N.L.R.B. 1022.

—— (1965) *G. E. Company,* 150 N.L.R.B. 192.

—— (1971) *A Layman's Guide to Basic Law under the National Labor Relations Act*, Office of the General Counsel.

Nelson, P. (1970) "Information and Consumer Behaviour." *Journal of Political Economy* (March/April).

Ness, W. L. (1973) U.S. Income Tax Deferral and the Dividend Remittance Policy of Multinational Corporations. *New York University Graduate School of Business Administration Working Paper* No. 73-675 (November).
—— (1975) "U.S. Corporate Income Taxation and the Dividend Remittance Policy of Multinational Corporations." *Journal of International Business Studies* (Spring).
—— (1976) "Financial Advantages of Multinational Firms." *Eastern Regional Meetings of the Academy of International Business.*
*New York Times* (1975) "A Multinational vs. United Nations." November 2.
—— (1976) "Unions: Setback Abroad." February 1.
Nordhaus, W. D. (1976) "Energy and Economic Growth." In J. C. Hurewitz, ed., *Oil, The Arab-Israel Dispute, and the Industrial World; Horizons of Crisis.* Boulder, Colorado: Westview Press.
Northrup, H. W., and Rowan, R. L. (1974) "Multinational Collective Bargaining: The Factual Record in Chemicals, Glass and Rubber Tires." *Columbia Journal of World Business* (Spring and Summer).
O.E.C.D. (1968) *Gaps in Technology Between Member Countries.* Paris.
—— (1969) *Gaps in Technology Between Member Countries: Various Reports.* Paris.
—— (1974a) *Choice and Adaptation of Technology in Developing Countries, An Overview of Major Policy Issues.* Paris.
—— (1974b) *Interim Report of the Industry Committee on International Enterprises.* Paris.
—— (1974c) *Mergers and Competition Policy.* Paris.
—— (1976) *International Investment and Multinational Enterprises.* Paris.
Ohlin, B. (1933) *Inter-regional and International Trade.* Cambridge: Harvard University Press.
Okita, S. (1974) "Natural Resource Dependency and Japanese Foreign Policy." *Foreign Affairs* (July).
Okun, A. (1975) "Inflation: Its Mechanisms and Welfare Costs." *Brookings Papers on Economic Activity,* No. 2.
Oldham, C. H. G., and Freeman, C. (1969) "The Technological Balance of Payments." *Development Digest.* Washington, D. C. (January).
Olson, M. (1971) *The Logic of Collective Action.* Cambridge: Harvard University Press.
Over, A. M., Jr. (1975) "An Example of the Simultaneous-Equation Problem: A Note on Foreign Assistance: Objectives and Consequences." *Economic Development and Cultural Change* (July).
Ozawa, T. (1971) "Transfer of Technology from Japan to Developing Countries." *UNITAR Research Reports,* No. 7, New York.
—— (1972) "Japan's Technology Now Challenges the West." *Columbia Journal of World Business* (March/April).
Pack, H. (1974) "Employment and Productivity in Kenyan Manufacturing." *Yale University Economic Growth Center Discussion Paper No. 196* (February).
Papanek, G. F. (1972) "The Effect of Aid and Other Resource Transfers on Savings and Growth in Less Developed Countries." *Economic Journal (September).*
—— (1973) "Aid, Foreign Private Investment, Savings, and Growth in Less Developed Countries." *Journal of Political Economy* (January/February).
Parry, T. G. (1972) "Some Aspects of Asset Creation by the International Firm." *Journal of Business Policy* (Autumn).
—— (1973) "The International Firm and National Economic Policy." *Economic Journal* (December).
—— (1974a) "Size of Plant, Capacity Utilization and Economic Efficiency: Foreign Investment in the Australian Chemical Industry." *Economic Record* (June).

—— (1974b) "Technology and the Size of the Multinational Corporation Subsidiary: Evidence from the Australian Manufacturing Sector." *Journal of Industrial Economics* (December).

—— (1974c) "The Role of R & D in the International Trade and Investment of U.K. Manufacturing Industry." *Journal of Economic Studies* (November).

—— (1974d) "Australia's Foreign Investment Policies: In Search of an Objective." *Journal of World Trade Law* (September/October).

Patel, S. J. (1974) "The Technological Dependence of Developing Countries." *The Journal of Modern African Studies* (March).

Pavitt, K. (1971) "The Multinational Enterprise and the Transfer of Technology." In J. H. Dunning, ed., *The Multinational Enterprise*. London: Allen and Unwin.

Payne, M. (1969) "The American Challenge on a Chip." *Electronics* (January 20).

Pearce, D. W., ed. (with the assistance of J. Rose) (1975) *The Economics of Natural Resource Depletion*. London: Macmillan.

Penrose, E. (1968) *The Large International Firm in Developing Countries*. London: Allen and Unwin.

—— (1973) "International Patenting and the Less-Developed Countries." *Economic Journal* (September)

—— (1975) "The Development of Crisis." *Daedalus* 104 (Fall).

Pickett, J., Forsyth, D. J. C., and McBain, N. S. (1974) "The Choice of Technology, Economic Efficiency and Employment in Developing Countries." *World Development* (March).

Plasschaent, S. (1971) "Emerging Patterns of Financial Management in Multinational Companies." *Economisch und Sociaal Injdschrift* (December). Antwerp: St. Ignatius University.

Polk, J., Meister, I., and Veit, L. (1966) *U.S. Production Abroad and the Balance of Payments*. New York: Conference Board.

Pomper, C. (1976) *International Investment Planning: An Integrated Approach*. New York: North Holland.

Prachowny, M. F. J. (1972) "Direct Investment and the Balance of Payments of the United States: A Portfolio Approach." In F. Machlup et al., eds., *International Mobility and Movement of Capital*. New York: Columbia University Press.

Ragazzi, A. (1973) "Theories of the Determinants of Direct Foreign Investment." *IMF Staff Papers* (July).

Rahman, M. A. (1968) "Foreign Capital and Domestic Savings: A Test of Haavelmo's Hypothesis with Cross-Country Data." *Review of Economics and Statistics* (February).

Reuber, G. L. (1973) *Private Foreign Investment in Development*. London: Clarendon Press.

Rhadu, G. M. (1973) "Some Aspects of Direct Foreign Private Investment in Pakistan." *Pakistan Development Review* (Spring).

Rhomberg, R. R. (1967) "Private Capital Movements and Exchange Rates in Developing Countries." In J. H. Adler, ed., *Capital Movements and Economic Development*. London: Macmillan.

Richardson, J. R. (1971) "On Going Abroad, the Firm's Initial Foreign Investment Decision." *Quarterly Review of Economics and Business* (Winter).

Riedel, J. (1975a) "The Nature and Determinants of Export-Oriented Direct Foreign Investment in a Developing Country: A Case Study of Taiwan." *Weltwirtschaftliches Archiv* (September).

——(1975b) "Factor Proportions, Linkages and the Open Developing Economy." *Review of Economics and Statistics* (November).

Robbins, S. M., and Stobaugh, R. B. (1973) *Money in the Multinational Enterprise: A Study in Financial Policy*. New York: Basic Books.

Roberts, B. C. (1973) "Multinational Collective Bargaining: A European Prospect?" *British Journal of Industrial Relations* (March).

Robinson, R. D. (1973) *International Business Management: A Guide to Decision Making*. New York: Holt, Rinehart and Winston.

Rosenbluth, G. (1970) "The Relation between Foreign Control and Concentration in Canadian Industry." *Canadian Journal of Economics* (February).

Rosenstein-Rodan, P. N. (1961) "International Aid for Underdeveloped Countries." *Review of Economics and Statistics* (May).

Rostow, W. W. (1956) "The Take-Off into Self-Sustained Growth." *Economic Journal* (March).

Rowan, R. L., and Northrup, H. R. (1975) "Multinational Bargaining in Metals and Electrical Industries: Approaches and Prospects." *Journal of Industrial Relations* (Australia) (March).

Rugman, A. R. (1975) "Motives for Foreign Investment: The Market Imperfections and Risk Diversification Hypothesis." *Journal of World Trade Law* (September/October).

Rutenberg, D. P. (1970) "Maneuvering Liquid Assets in Multinational Companies: Formulation and Deterministic Solution Procedures." *Management Science* (June).

Safarian, A. E. (1966) *Foreign Ownership of Canadian Industry*. Toronto: McGraw-Hill.

—— (1973) "Perspectives on Foreign Direct Investment from the Viewpoint of a Capital Receiving Country." *Journal of Finance* (May).

Saldern, S. von (1973) "Internationalen Vergleich den Direktinvestitionen Wichtigen Industrieländen." *H.W.W.A. Report No. 15*. Hamburg.

Samuelson, H. S. (1973) "A Study of the Transfer of Technology Via MNC's—Problems and Design." (Stencil) *Industriens Utredvinginstitut* (November).

Sato, M., and Bird, R. M. (1975) "International Aspects of the Taxation of Corporations and Shareholders." *IMF Staff Papers* (July).

Scherer, F. (1970) *Industrial Market Structure and Economic Performance*. Chicago: Rand-McNally.

Scitovsky, T. (1976) *The Jobless Economy*. Oxford: Oxford University Press.

Servan-Schreiber, J. J. (1968) *The American Challenge*. New York: Atheneum.

Shulman, J. (1967) "When the Price Is Wrong by Design." *Columbia Journal of World Business* (May/June).

Singer, H. W. (1974) "Transfer of Technology in LDCs." *Intereconomics* (January).

Smith, D. N., and Wells, L. T., Jr. (1976) *Negotiating Third World Mineral Agreements; Promises as Prologue*. Cambridge: Ballinger.

Smith, R. (1974) "Private Power and National Sovereignty: Some Comments on the Multinational Corporation." *Journal of Economic Issues* (June).

Solnik, B. H. (1974) "Why Not Diversify Internationally?" *Financial Analysts Journal* (July).

Solow, R. M. (1974) "The Economics of Resources or the Resources of Economics." *American Economic Review* (May).

Sorenson, R. Z., and Wiechmann, V. E. (1975) "How Multinationals View Marketing Standardization." *Harvard Business Review* (May–June).

Spence, A. M. (1975) "The Economics of Internal Organization: An Introduction." *The Bell Journal of Economics* (Spring).

Steur, M. D. (1971) "Competition and the Multinational Firm: The United Kingdom Case." In J. B. Health, London, ed., *International Conference on Monopolies, Mergers and Restrictive Practices*. H.M.S.O.

—— (1974) "Policy Options for the U.K." *Intereconomics* (March).

————, et al. (1973) *The Impact of Foreign Direct Investment in the U.K.* London: Department of Trade and Industry.

Stevens, G. V. G. (1972) "Capital Mobility and the International Firm." In F. Machlup et al., eds., *International Mobility and Movement of Capital.* New York: Columbia University Press.

———— (1974) "The Determinants of Investment." In J. H. Dunning, ed., *Economic Analysis and the Multinational Enterprise.* London: Allen and Unwin.

Stewart, F. (1974) "Technology and Employment in LDCs." *World Development* (March).

———— (1973) "Trade and Technology." In P. Streeten, ed., *Trade Strategies for Development.* New York: John Wiley.

Stillman, D. (1976) "UAW Demands Major Contract Gains." *Solidarity* (July-August).

Stobaugh, R. B. (1970a) "Utilising Technical Know-How in Foreign Investment and Licensing Programme." *Proceedings of the 1970 Annual Meeting of the Chemical Marketing Research Association.* Houston (February).

———— (1970b) "The Product Life Cycle and World Trade Patterns." *Proceedings of the Third International Conference of the European Chemical Marketing Research Association.* Amsterdam (June). Reprinted by Marketing Science Institute as a *Working Paper* (November).

———— (1971a) "The Neotechnology Account of International Trade: The Case of Petrochemicals." *Journal of International Business Studies* (Autumn). Also in L. T. Wells, ed., (1972) *The Product Life Cycle and International Trade.* Boston: Harvard Business School Division of Research.

———— (1971b) "The International Transfer of Technology in the Establishment of the Petrochemical Industry in Developing Countries." *UNITAR Research Report,* No. 12.

———— (1971c) "A study of Economic Conditions in the United States Tariff Commission Investigations No. TEA-1-21." *Hearings Before the United States Tariff Commission,* October 6. Washington, D. C.

———— (1972) "U.S. Multinational Enterprises and the U.S. Economy." The Multinational Corporation: Studies on U.S. Foreign Investment, Part II, Vol. I, U. S. Department of Commerce. Washington, D. C.: Superintendent of Documents.

———— (1973a) "A Proposal to Facilitate International Trade in Management and Technology." *New York University Multinational Corporation Series Working Paper.*

———— (1973b) "Summary and Assessment of Research Findings on U.S. International Transactions Involving Technology Transfers." *Colloquim on International Technology Transfers.* National Science Foundation (November).

———— (1975a) "International Technology Transfer and Multinational Enterprises in Basic Materials Industries." *Report for the National Materials Advisory Board of the National Academy of Sciences.* Washington, D. C.: National Research Council.

———— (1976) *Nine Investments Abroad and Their Impact at Home.* Boston: Harvard Business School, Division of Research.

————, Telesio, P., and de la Torre, J. (1973c) "Multinational Enterprises and Change in the Skill Composition of U. S. Employment." In D. Kujawa, ed., *American Labor and the Multinational Corporation.* New York: Praeger.

————, and Townsend, P. L. (1975b) "Price Forecasting and Strategic Planning: The Case of Petrochemicals." *Journal of Marketing Research* (February).

Stopford, J. M. (1968) *Growth and Organizational Change in the Multinational Firm.* Doctoral Précis, Harvard Graduate School of Business Administration (June).

———— (1973) *External Influence on Strategy and Style: The Case of British Based Multinational Firms.* NATO Symposium, Brussels (March).

———— (1974) "The Origins of British-Based Multinational Manufacturing Enterprises." *Business History Review* (Autumn).

————, and Wells, L. T., Jr. (1972) *Managing the Multinational Enterprise*. New York: Basic Books.

Strassman, W. P. (1968) *Technological Change and Economic Development: The Manufacturing Experience of Mexico and Puerto Rico*. Ithaca, N.Y.: Cornell University Press.

Streeten, P. (1971) "Costs and Benefits of Multinational Enterprises in Less-Developed Countries." In J. H. Dunning, ed., *The Multinational Enterprise*. New York: Praeger.

———— (1974) "Theory of Development Policy." In J. H. Dunning, ed., *Economic Analysis and the Multinational Enterprise*. London: Allen and Unwin.

Sutter, R. (1974) "Technology Transfer into LDCs." *Intereconomics* (December).

Telesio, P. (1977) *Foreign Licensing Policy in Multinational Enterprises*. Unpublished D.B.A. Thesis. Harvard Business School.

Tell, H. (1976) *Offshore Production by American Multinational Corporations: A Substitute for Manufacturing Activities in the United States*. Unpublished Ph.D. Dissertation, New York University.

Teplin, M. F. (1973) "U.S. International Transactions in Royalties and Fees: Their Relationship to the Transfer of Technology." *Survey of Current Business* (December).

Thomas, J. W. (1975) "The Choice of Technology for Irrigation Tubewells in East Pakistan: Analysis of a Development Policy Decision." In C. P. Timmer et al., eds., *The Choice of Technology in Developing Countries*. Center for International Affairs, Harvard University.

Tilton, J. E. (1971) *International Diffusion of Technology: The Case of Simiconductors*. Washington, D. C.: Brookings Institution.

Timmer, C. P. (1975) "The Choice of Technique in Indonesia." In C. P. Timmer et al., eds. *The Choice of Technology in Developing Countries*. Center for International Affairs, Harvard University.

Toulmin, S. (1968) "Innovation and the Problem of Utilization." In W. Marquis and W. Gruber, eds., *Factors in the Transfer of Technology*. Cambridge: MIT Press.

Tsurumi, Y., and Tsurumi, H. (1973) *A Bayesian Estimation of Macro and Micro CES Production Functions*. Meeting of the Econometric Society, New York, December 27–30.

Turner, L. (1976) *The Oil Majors in World Politics*. Mimeo, Royal Institute of International Affairs.

United Auto Workers (1966) "Declaration at Detroit: 3 June 1966."

———— (1970) "Survey of Latin American Auto Contracts." (February)

———— (1974) "Woodcock Calls for New Laws on World Firms, Multinational Bargaining." (November 11)

United Nations (1973) *Multinational Corporations in World Development*. New York.

UNCTAD (1972a) *Guidelines for Study of the Transfer of Technology to Developing Countries*. New York.

———— (1972b) *Restrictive Business Practices*. New York.

———— (1972c) *Report by the UNCTAD Secretariat*, TD/106. Santiago.

———— (1973) *The Flow of Financial Resources: Private Foreign Investment; Methodology Used*. Geneva, 29 May.

———— (1974a) *Major Issues Arising From the Transfer of Technology to Developing Countries*. New York.

———— (1974b) *The Role of the Patent System in the Transfer of Technology to Developing Countries*. New York.

U.S. Dept. of Economic and Social Affairs (1972) *Transfer of Operative Technology at the Enterprise Level*. St./ECA 151. New York.

UNIDO (1973) *Guidelines for the Acquisition of Foreign Technology in Developing Countries*. New York.

U.S. Congress (1959) *The National Labor Relations Act and the Labor-Management Relations Act, 1947, as Amended by the Labor-Management Reporting and Disclosure Act of 1959*. Pub. L. 101, 80th Cong.

———— (1974) *Trade Act of 1974*. Pub. L. 93-618, 93rd Cong.

U.S. Congress, House (1970) "Statement of Hon. George P. Shultz." *Tariff and Trade Proposals*. Committee on Ways and Means, Part 2, 91st Cong., 2d sess.

U.S. Congress, Senate (1971) Senator Vance Hartke introducing "The Foreign Trade and Investment Act of 1972." S. Res. 2592, 92d Cong., 1st sess. September 28, *Congressional Record*, CXVII, No. 142.

U.S. Department of Commerce (1972) *Policy Aspects of Foreign Investment by U.S. Multinational Corporations* (January).

U.S. Tariff Commission (USTC) (1972) *Competitiveness of U.S. Industries*. TC Publication 473, Washington, April.

———— (1973) *Implications of Multinational Firms for World Trade and Investment and for U.S. Trade and Labor: Report to the Committee on Finance of the U.S. Senate and its Subcommittee on International Trade*, 93d Cong., 1st sess.

Vaitsos, C. V. (1970) "Transfer of Resources and Preservation of Monopoly Rents." *Economic Development Report* No. 168. Harvard University, Center for International Affairs.

———— (1974a) *Intercountry Income Distribution and Transnational Enterprises*. Oxford: Clarendon Press.

———— (1974b) "Welfare Considerations and the Multinational Firm." In J. H. Dunning, ed., *Economic Analysis and the Multinational Enterprise*. London: Allen and Unwin.

Vernon, R. (1966) "International Investment and International Trade in the Product Cycle." *Quarterly Journal of Economics*. (May).

———— (1971a) *Sovereignty at Bay: The Multinational Spread of U.S. Enterprises*. New York: Basic Books.

———— (1971b) "A Skeptic Looks at the Balance of Payments." *Foreign Policy* (Winter).

———— (1972a) Restrictive Business Practices: The Operations of Multinational United States Enterprises in Developing Countries. United Nations.

———— (1972b) "United States Enterprise in the Less Developed Countries: Evaluation of Cost and Benefit." In G. Ranis, ed., *The Gap Between Rich and Poor Nations*. London: Macmillan.

———— (1974a) "Competition Policy Toward Multinational Corporations." *American Economic Review* (May).

———— (1974b) "The Location of Economic Activity." In J. H. Dunning, ed. *Economic Analysis and the Multinational Enterprise*. London: Allen and Unwin.

———— (1976) "Multinational Enterprise in Developing Countries: Issues in Dependency and Interdependence." In D. E. Apter and L. Goodman, eds., *The Multinational Corporation as an Instrument of Development–Political Considerations*. New Haven: Yale University Press.

*Wall Street Journal*, Eastern Edition (1970) "Chrysler UK Says Labor Woes Could Put Firm Out of Business." November 30.

———— (1971) "Ford Says Profit Hurt by Strikes in Britain, Blasts Industry Again." March 16.

———— (1972) "Increasingly Workers Give Up Some Benefits So as Not to Lose Jobs." November 26.

———— (1976a) "Mansfield Tire, Union Set Pact; Ohio Plant To Continue Operating." October 12.

———— (1976b) "Texas Sets December Oil Output at 99%; Cut is Bid to Send Washington a Message." November 19.

330                                                                      BIBLIOGRAPHY

—————— (1976c) "Rise in Foreign Controls on U.S. Concerns that Operate Abroad Said to be
   Problem." November 19.
Watkins Report (1968) *Foreign Ownership and the Structure of Canadian Industry*. Report
   of the Task Force on the Structure of Canadian Industry. Government of Canada.
Weisskopf, T. E. (1972) "The Impact of Foreign Capital Inflow on Domestic Savings in
   Underdeveloped Countries." *Journal of International Economics* (February).
Wells, L. T., Jr. (1973) "Economic Man and Engineering Man: Choice of Technology in
   Low-Wage Country." *Public Policy* (Summer). Reprinted in SEADAG Paper No. 73-1
   and *The Choice of Technology in Developing Countries: Some Cautionary Tales*. Cam-
   bridge: Harvard Center for International Affairs.
—————— (1974a) "Don't Overautomate Your Foreign Plant." *Harvard Business Review*
   (January/February).
—————— (1974b) "International Trade: The Product Life Cycle Approach." *Ritsumeikan
   Business Review* (July).
——————, and Chudson,W. A. (1974) *The Acquisition of Proprietary Technology from Multi-
   national Enterprises by Developing Countries*. Department of Economic and Social
   Affairs, United Nations, New York.
Wertheimer, H. W. (1971) "The International Firm and International Aspects of Policies on
   Mergers." In J. B. Heath, London, ed., *International Conference on Monopolies,
   Mergers and RTP's*. Cambridge: H.M.S.O.
Weston, J. F. (1973) *Are MNC's Using Market Power to Overprice?* National Conference on
   Multinational Corporations, Washington, D. C.
Wieberdinck, A. (1973) "Das Philips-Zentrum für Entrwicklung und Enprobung mittlerer
   Technologien in Utrecht." In J. Baranson, V. Hones, K. W. Menck, M. R. Schams,
   and A. Wiebendinck, selected contributions, *Technologie Transfer, Ausgewählte Beit-
   räge*. HWWA—Report No. 20, Hamburg.
Wilkins, M. (1974) "The Role of Private Business in the International Diffusion of Technol-
   ogy." *Journal of Economic History* (March).
Wing, A. F. E. (1976) "UNCTAD and the Transfer of Technology." *Journal of World Trade
   Law* (May/June).
Wionczek, M. S. (1973) "Changing Attitudes in the Developing World." *Intereconomics*
   (January).
Wolf, A. (1972) "USA-Stanksten Lizenzgeben den Welt." *UDI-Nachrichten*. Düsseldorf,
   No. 32, August 9.
—————— (1973) "Trends in the International License Trade." *Intereconomics* (May).
——————, and Werth, C. (1972) *Den Internationale Technisch Industrielle Lizenzaustrausch*.
   Düsseldorf.
Woodcock, L. (1974) "Labor and Multinationals." Conference on Industrial Relations Prob-
   lems Raised by Multinationals in Advanced Industrial Societies. Michigan State Uni-
   versity, East Lansing, Michigan, November 10–13.
Wortzel, L. H. (1971) "The International Transfer of Technology in the Establishment of the
   Pharmaceutical Industry in Developing Countries." *UNITAR Research Report*, No.
   14.
Yeoman, W. A. (1968) *Selection of Production Processes for the Manufacturing Sub-
   sidiaries of U.S.-Based Multinational Corporations*. Unpublished doctoral thesis, Harvard Business School.
Yoshino, M. Y. (1974) "The Multinational Spread of Japanese Manufacturing Enterprises."
   *Business History Review* (Autumn).

# RESEARCH IN FINANCE

Series Editor: Haim Levy, School of Business, The Hebrew University

Volume 1.    1979    Cloth    350 pages (Tent.)    Institutions: $25.00
ISBN NUMBER 0-89232-043-5                          Individuals: $12.50

The aim of this series is to include only those research papers which explore new frontiers of knowledge. The contributions will represent original research by both the established scholars as well as younger researchers presenting substantive material furthering knowledge in the field.

CONTENTS: **Consumption and Saving in Economic Development,** Jean Crockett and Irwin Friend, The Wharton School, University of Pennsylvania. **An Inter-Industry Approach to Econometric Cost of Capital Estimation,** David W. Glenn and Robert H. Litzenberger, Graduate School of Business, Stanford University. **The Effect of Increasing Uncertainty of Inflation of Consumers Behavior With and Without Indexation,** David Levhart and Nissan Liviatan, The Hebrew University. **Goodwill: Financial Statement and Valuation,** Yoram C. Peles, School of Business Administration, The Hebrew University. **Test of Capital Asset Pricing Hypotheses,** Barr Rosenberg and Viriag Marathe, School of Business Administration, University of California—Berkeley. **Spot, Forward and Future,** Jerome L. Stein, Department of Economics, Brown University.

A 10 percent discount will be granted on all institutional standing orders placed directly with the publisher. Standing orders will be filled automatically upon publication and will continue until cancelled. Please indicate which volume Standing Order is to begin with.

 **JAI PRESS INC.**

P.O. Box 1285
165 West Putnam Avenue
Greenwich, Connecticut 06830

(203) 661-7602    Cable Address: JAIPUBL.

# OTHER ANNUAL SERIES OF INTEREST FROM JAI PRESS INC.

*Consulting Editor for Economics:* Paul Uselding, University of Illinois

**ADVANCES IN APPLIED MICRO-ECONOMICS**
Series Editor: V. Kerry Smith, Resources for the Future,
Washington, D.C.

**ADVANCES IN ECONOMETRICS**
Series Editors: R. L. Basmann, Texas A & M University, and George F.
Rhodes, Colorado State University

**ADVANCES IN ECONOMIC THEORY**
Series Editor: David Levhari, The Hebrew University

**ADVANCES IN THE ECONOMICS OF ENERGY AND RESOURCES**
Series Editor: Robert S. Pindyck, Sloan School of Management,
Massachusetts Institute of Technology

**APPLICATIONS OF MANAGEMENT SCIENCE**
Series Editor: Randall L. Schultz, Krannert Graduate School of
Management, Purdue University

**RESEARCH IN AGRICULTURAL ECONOMICS**
Series Editor: Earl O. Heady, Director, The Center for Agricultural and
Rural Development, Iowa State University

**RESEARCH IN CORPORATE SOCIAL PERFORMANCE AND POLICY**
Series Editor: Lee E. Preston, School of Management and Center for
Policy Studies, State University of New York, Buffalo

**RESEARCH IN ECONOMIC ANTHROPOLOGY**
Series Editor: George Dalton, Northwestern University

**RESEARCH IN ECONOMIC HISTORY**
Series Editor: Paul Uselding, University of Illinois

**RESEARCH IN EXPERIMENTAL ECONOMICS**
Series Editor: Vernon L. Smith, College of Business and Public
Administration, University of Arizona

**RESEARCH IN FINANCE**
Series Editor: Haim Levy, School of Business, The Hebrew University

**RESEARCH IN HEALTH ECONOMICS**
Series Editor: Richard M. Scheffler, University of North Carolina,
Chapel Hill and the Institute of Medicine, National Academy of
Sciences

**RESEARCH IN HUMAN CAPITAL AND DEVELOPMENT**
Series Editor: Ismail Sirageldin, The Johns Hopkins University

**RESEARCH IN INTERNATIONAL BUSINESS AND FINANCE**
Series Editor: Robert G. Hawkins, Graduate School of Business
  Administration, New York University

**RESEARCH IN LABOR ECONOMICS**
Series Editor: Ronald G. Ehrenberg, School of Industrial and Labor
  Relations, Cornell University

**RESEARCH IN LAW AND ECONOMICS**
Series Editor: Richard O. Zerbe, Jr., SMT Program, University of
  Washington

**RESEARCH IN MARKETING**
Series Editor: Jagdish N. Sheth, University of Illinois

**RESEARCH IN ORGANIZATIONAL BEHAVIOR**
Series Editors: Barry M. Staw, Graduate School of Management,
  Northwestern University, and Larry L. Cummings, Graduate School of
  Business, University of Wisconsin

**RESEARCH IN PHILOSOPHY AND TECHNOLOGY**
Series Editor: Paul T. Durbin, Center for the Culture of Biomedicine and
  Science, University of Delaware

**RESEARCH IN POLITICAL ECONOMY**
Series Editor: Paul Zarembka, State University of New York, Buffalo

**RESEARCH IN POPULATION ECONOMICS**
Series Editors: Julian L. Simon, University of Illinois, and Julie DaVanzo,
  The Rand Corporation

**RESEARCH IN PUBLIC POLICY AND MANAGEMENT**
Series Editors: Colin C. Blaydon, Institute of Policy Studies and Public
  Affairs, Duke University, and Steven Gilford, Chicago

*ALL VOLUMES IN THESE ANNUAL SERIES ARE AVAILABLE*
*AT INSTITUTIONAL AND INDIVIDUAL SUBSCRIPTION RATES.*
*PLEASE WRITE FOR DETAILED BROCHURES ON EACH SERIES*

---

A 10 percent discount will be granted on all institutional standing orders placed directly
with the publisher. Standing orders will be filled automatically upon publication and will
continue until cancelled. Please indicate which volume Standing Order is to begin with.

---

 **JAI PRESS INC.**
P.O. Box 1285
165 West Putnam Avenue
Greenwich, Connecticut 06830

(203) 661-7602    Cable Address: JAIPUBL.

# CONTEMPORARY STUDIES IN ECONOMIC AND FINANCIAL ANALYSIS

*An International Series of Monographs*

# RESEARCH IN CORPORATE SOCIAL PERFORMANCE AND POLICY
## An Annual Compilation of Research
### Series Editor: Lee E. Preston, School of Management and Center for Policy Studies, State University of New York, Buffalo

Volume 1    Published 1978    Cloth    306 pages  Institutions: $25.00
ISBN NUMBER: 0-89232-069-9                       Individuals: $12.50

CONTENTS: **Introduction,** Lee E. Preston. **Corporate Social Performance and Policy: A Synthetic Framework for Research and Analysis,** Lee E. Preston, State University of New York, Buffalo. **An Analytical Framework for Making Cross-cultural Comparisons of Business Responses to Social Pressures: The Case of the United States and Japan,** S. Prakash Sethi, University of Texas, Austin. **Research on Patterns of Corporate Response to Social Change,** James E. Post, Boston University. **Organizational Goals and Control Systems: Internal and External Considerations,** Kenneth J. Arrow, Harvard University. **The Corporate Response Process,** Raymond A. Bauer, Harvard University. **Auditing Corporate Social Performance: The Anatomy of a Social Research Project,** William C. Frederick, University of Pittsburgh, **Managerial Motivation and Ideology,** Joseph W. McGuire, University of California, Irvine. **Empirical Studies of Corporate Social Performance and Policy: A Survey of Problems and Results,** Ramon J. Aldag, University of Wisconsin, and Kathryn M. Bartol, Syracuse University. **Social Policy as Business Policy,** George A. Steiner and John F. Steiner, University of California, Los Angeles. **Government Regulation: Process and Substantive Impacts,** Robert Chatov, State University of New York, Buffalo. **Managerial Theory vs. Class Theory of Corporate Capitalism,** Maurice Zeitlin, University of California, Los Angeles. **Appendices A, B, C.**

A 10 percent discount will be granted on all institutional standing orders placed directly with the publisher. Standing orders will be filled automatically upon publication and will continue until cancelled. Please indicate which volume Standing Order is to begin with.

 JAI PRESS INC.
P.O. Box 1285
165 West Putnam Avenue
Greenwich, Connecticut 06830

(203) 661-7602    Cable Address: JAIPUBL.

## DATE DUE

| | | | |
|---|---|---|---|
| | | | |
| | | | |
| | | | |
| | | | |
| | | | |
| | | | |
| | | | |
| | | | |
| | | | |
| | | | |
| | | | |
| | | | |
| | | | |
| | | | |
| | | | |
| | | | |
| | | | |
| | | | |
| | | | |
| | | | |

GAYLORD | | | PRINTED IN U.S.A.